Praise for *Robert*

P9-DNB-155

3 9082 08134 0500

"Well-researched and elegantly written. At last the many readers of Robert Frost have a biography so engaging, informed, and sympathetic that they can follow this great American artist's journey down the road less travelled, the lonely road of genius." —Dana Gioia, *Book of the Month*, BBC Radio 3

"A fine new biography. Parini has made a valuable addition to our understanding of this great and very complicated poet." —*The National Review*

"Rarely has Frost's story been told this dexterously, or with a better understanding of the relation of Frost's personality crises to his accomplishment as a poet." —*Publishers Weekly*

"A sensitive life of Frost that highlights the poet's struggle to find light and stability in an existence filled with darkness and chaos. Parini's life magnificently details how Frost, through fortitude and lifelong dedication to craft, sought to heed his own advice to be whole again beyond confusion." —*Kirkus Reviews*

"Parini gracefully intermingles superb close readings with sensitive accounts of Frost's many personal losses and artistic accomplishments." —*Booklist*

"Parini's book is the best record we have of this man, possibly America's most enduring poet, and it will make you want to read Frost himself—the real job of literary biography." —*Men's Journal*

"Parini expertly guides the reader through Frost's life and explains his poetry in a way that is understandable to all, not just literary scholars. Those interested in the life of a great American literary figure, as well as his body of work, will find this very readable biography enormously satisfying." —*New York Post*

"A rich and balanced biography. At last Frost has found in Jay Parini a biographer prepared to read the poems and the life with care and wisdom. He gives us Robert Frost, the poet, in all his rich contradictions." —*Sydney Morning Herald*

"Parini serves Frost well as a comrade-in-arms: He, too, is a distinguished poet. Metaphor by metaphor, he tracks his subject into the snowy woods of Frost's imagination, and the visions there are lovely, dark and deep." —*The Philadelphia Inquirer*

"What sets Parini off from other Frost biographers is his fine critical judgment of Frost's poetry. His crowning accomplishment is bringing home to us the true glory of Frost. A biographer can do no more." —*Newark Star-Ledger*

"Parini has his Frost to give us, his narrative to shape, and in broad outline the shape is convincing, even satisfying. Parini is also an accomplished and insightful reader, and many of his treatments of individual poems are cogent and revealing." —*The Boston Globe*

"A narrative that gracefully and clearly takes the reader through Frost's private and public career, while offering insights into the poetry and its making that are both tactful and persuasive." —John Boland, *Irish Times*

ROBERT FROST

ROBERT FROST

A Life

JAY PARINI

An Owl Book

Henry Holt and Company

New York

Henry Holt and Company, LLC
Publishers since 1866
115 West 18th Street
New York, New York 10011

Henry Holt® is a registered trademark
of Henry Holt and Company, LLC.

Library of Congress Cataloging-in-Publication Data
Parini, Jay.
Robert Frost: a life / Jay Parini.
p. cm.
Includes bibliographical references and index.
ISBN 0-8050-6341-2
1. Frost, Robert, 1874–1963—Biography.
2. Poets, American—20th century—Biography.
I. Title.
PS3511.R94Z868   1999   98-26690
811'.52—dc21   CIP
[b]

Henry Holt books are available for special promotions and
premiums. For details contact: Director, Special Markets.

First published in hardcover in 1999 by
Henry Holt and Company

First Owl Books Edition 2000

Designed by Michelle McMillian

Frontispiece courtesy of the Jones Library
and the estate of Robert Frost

Printed in the United States of America

1   3   5   7   9   10   8   6   4   2

For Devon, now and always

CONTENTS

PREFACE

Robert Frost has been my favorite poet ever since the ninth grade, when I was handed a copy of his *Selected Poems*. Reading "Dust of Snow" and "Stopping by Woods on a Snowy Evening," I experienced the physical and intellectual thrill of poetry for the first time. When I went to teach at Dartmouth College in 1975, the idea of writing a life of Frost first struck me. The opportunities at hand were certainly enticing. The archives at Dartmouth (where Frost had been a student in 1892) were full of tempting documents: manuscripts and drafts of poems, journals kept throughout Frost's career, hundreds of letters written or received by the poet—a considerable portion of them never published. There were also countless tapes of readings and lectures, transcripts of public addresses, and miscellaneous accounts of Frost by others. I plunged immediately into this material.

There were many people who had known Frost in the immediate vicinity, such as Edward Connery Lathem, Richard Eberhart, Thomas Vance, Alexander Laing, Harold Bond, and John Sloan Dickey. I made a point of talking to as many of them about Frost as I could, and took notes for what I first planned as an article about Frost at

Dartmouth. In fact, the chapters on Frost's tenure at Dartmouth as Ticknor fellow, in the forties, were largely written at this time, as was the part about his undergraduate days in Hanover. During this period I also met Robert Francis, a poet who had known Frost in Amherst for many years, and interviewed him on the subject of Frost. It was Francis who suggested to me that a full-scale life of Frost would be a good project, although I put this idea on a back burner.

In 1982 I joined the faculty at Middlebury College—yet another of Frost's haunts. He lived for a part of each year on a farm in Ripton (near Middlebury) from 1939 until his death in 1963, and was closely associated with the Bread Loaf Writers' Conference, a summer program at Middlebury College. Not surprisingly, the Middlebury College Library was also rich in Frost documents. I resumed work on Frost at this time, and among those I interviewed were Reginald L. Cook, a longtime professor at Middlebury who had known Frost well; Victor Reichert, a rabbi and close friend of the poet's; and Robert Penn Warren, who summered in Vermont and had known Frost for many years. These three redirected my thinking in important ways, and they are quoted throughout this volume.

Although I published several pieces about Frost in the eighties, this book lay in scattered chapters until the mid-nineties, when I resumed work on it full-time. I revisited the Dartmouth archives, reading through the two thousand pages of biographical notes left by Lawrance Thompson after his death, and made a careful study of his notebooks, which proved an invaluable resource. (The original set of Lawrance Thompson's notes are in the University of Virginia Library.) I also revisited Frost collections elsewhere, at Amherst College, the University of Virginia, and Plymouth State College. In particular, I want to thank Philip Cronenwett of the Dartmouth College Library and John Lancaster of the Amherst College Library for their help and support in the making of this book.

I was given extraordinary guidance in my research by Lesley Lee Francis, the poet's granddaughter, and by Peter Gilbert, his executor. Edward Connery Lathem, Hyde Cox, Philip Booth, Peter J. Stanlis, Jack W. C. Hagstrom, William H. Pritchard, James M. Cox, William

Cook, Donald E. Pease, F. D. Reeve, Alastair Reid, Peter Davison, Richard Wilbur, Robert Pack, Ed Ingebretsen, William Meredith, John Elder, Robert Hill, Donald G. Sheehy, Gore Vidal, and many others (who are acknowledged in the Notes and Sources) aided and abetted my work. I am deeply grateful to them all. In particular, Lathem, Stanlis, and Sheehy were kind enough to read a manuscript version of this book; they offered countless suggestions for revision, and I remain deeply grateful to them for their generosity and direction. I must also thank my editors, Allen Peacock and Victoria Hipps, for their assistance and advice.

With a few notable exceptions, the facts of Robert Frost's life were not in question. A procession of biographers, especially Lawrance Thompson and R. H. Winnick, have gone before me, and I remain in their debt. (In "Frost and His Biographers," an afterword to this study, I examine in detail the line of previous biographical writing on Frost.) What was left for me was assimilation, arrangement, and emphasis: the work of constructing from the myriad details of Frost's life a coherent story. My narrative presents Frost as a major poet who struggled throughout his long life with depression, anxiety, self-doubt, and confusion. His family life was not often happy, and he experienced some extremely bad luck with his children. On the other hand, he was a man of immense fortitude, an attentive father, and an artist of the first order who understood what he must do to create a body of work of lasting significance, to "lodge a few poems where they can't be gotten rid of easily," as he often said.

Robert Frost did what was necessary, for him, to achieve what he did, at times risking the welfare of others, even his own. Each major poem was, in the complex circumstances of his life, a feat of rescued sanity as well as "a momentary stay against confusion," as he memorably put it. Each class brilliantly taught, each vivid public reading, each child comforted or cared for, each tender moment with his wife was accomplished by steadiness of vision and hard spiritual work. I hope that much becomes clear in the following pages.

This biographical study offers a comprehensive reading of the poet's life and work. I have tried to understand how Frost got from day to day and from poem to poem, tracing his rich, always developing, intellectual and artistic life over many decades. My intention was not to supplant or overtake previous biographers and critics but merely to add a significant layer. I can say without fear of exaggeration that this life of Frost was a labor of love. It is one of the few books I have ever finished with deep reluctance.

ROBERT FROST

I   ONCE BY THE PACIFIC

1874–1885

Europe might sink and the wave of her sinking sweep
And spend itself on our shore and we would not weep
Our cities would not even turn in their sleep.
Our faces are not that way or should not be
Our future is in the West on the other Sea.

—FROST, UNPUBLISHED FRAGMENT, 1892

I know San Francisco like my own face," Robert Frost once told an audience in that city, late in his life. "It's where I came from, the first place I really knew. You always know where you come from, don't you?"[1]

Because Frost is so intimately associated with rural New England, one tends to forget that the first landscape printed on his imagination was both urban and Californian. That he came to appreciate, and to see in the imaginative way a poet must see, the imagery of Vermont and New Hampshire has something to do with the anomaly of coming late to it. "It's as though he were dropped into the countryside north of Boston from outer space, and remained perpetually stunned by what he saw," Robert Penn Warren observed. "I don't think you can overemphasize that aspect of Frost. A native takes, or may take, a place for granted; if you have to earn your citizenship, your locality, it requires a special focus."[2]

Frost certainly had that intensity of focus. The lush valleys and rocky mountains of northern New England, with their dry stone walls meandering through dense second-growth forests, their cellar holes and abandoned barns, acquire an almost hallucinatory clarity in his poems. He was a poet who took nothing for granted, who could cast his thoughts upon the objects around him, as Emerson—always a central figure in Frost's imagination—urged poets to do.

And yet the urban surroundings of Frost's earliest years affected him permanently. "My father was a great walker," Frost said, recalling that he had hiked the streets of San Francisco countless times during the first decade of his life. "I used to trail him everywhere, in the way a boy does." And it was quite a city, as Rudyard Kipling noted on a brief visit there in the 1880s: "San Francisco is a mad city," he wrote, "inhabited for the most part by perfectly insane people. . . . Recklessness is in the air. I can't explain where it comes from, but there it is. The roaring winds off the Pacific make you drunk to begin with. The aggressive luxury on all sides helps out the intoxication, and you spin forever 'down the ringing grooves of change,' as long as the money lasts."[3]

Robert Frost was born on March 26, 1874, in a small apartment on Washington Street—one of many similar, second-rate dwellings that the Frost family would occupy during their anxious decade in California. According to family legend, the poet's brash, talented father, William Prescott Frost, Jr., warned the doctor who delivered his son that he would shoot him if anything went wrong. This was no idle threat. Will Frost was well known among his colleagues on the *Daily Evening Bulletin* (and, later, on the *Daily Evening Post*) as a slightly mad easterner who packed a Colt pistol in emulation of the westerners around him. The pioneer mentality, with its wildness and bravura, suited him just fine.

Frost would occasionally accompany his father to the ramshackle offices of the *Post*. His father, who eventually became city editor, then business manager, of the paper, worked at a large oak desk piled high with books and papers. Bullets rolled around in the center drawer, where he kept his pistol during the day. There was a jar on the desk filled with pickled bull's testicles—a suggestion to all comers that Will Frost was not someone they should treat lightly. Loose tobacco, for chewing, was kept in a tin in a lower left-hand drawer, and a brass spittoon was located behind the editor's chair. A small engraving of Robert E. Lee was propped on the desk, as if to symbolize Will Frost's independent nature. Indeed, he had been an aggressively free spirit throughout his life—a character trait that he passed on to his son. His own father, who managed a mill in Lawrence, Massachusetts, had tried his best to discipline the boy, but it never took. During the Civil War, Will ran away to fight under General Lee, his hero (and after whom he named his son), although he got only as far as Philadelphia before the police found him and packed him home to his angry parents.

Will's father had hoped his son might get into West Point, thinking that a military setting would be appropriate for a young man of Will's tendencies, but the boy was not admitted. He did, however, get into Harvard, and he found the freedom of college life exhilarating. In those days, education took second place to play on most campuses, and Will Frost played hard; he gambled, drank heavily, and visited brothels in Boston, while still managing to do well enough in his studies to graduate with honors in 1872. His goal was to enter politics after a period in journalism, and in preparation he had spent his senior year working part-time for the Boston *Saturday Evening Gazette*. The idea of trying his hand at more literary work also attracted him, though his lack of self-discipline would foil him here, as elsewhere.

The puritanical mores of New England appalled him, and his relationship with his parents was, at best, strained. He hoped to move to the West Coast in due course, following in the adventurous footsteps of Mark Twain, Bret Harte, and Ambrose Bierce—each of whom had recently found San Francisco a good place for a young man with literary ambitions. But Will needed money for the transcontinental journey, so he took a job as principal of Lewistown Academy, a private school in Lewistown, Pennsylvania, with the intention of quitting after one year.

He was temperamentally ill-suited for such a job, but he tried to give it his best. Only twenty-two, with lank dark hair, sideburns, and a flowing mustache, he was described by the school yearbook as "dashing and energetic." That fall term he met a young teacher (the only other teacher at this small school) who agreed to give him lessons in stenography—a skill he rightly guessed would come in handy when he turned his hand to journalism. Six years his senior, this teacher was Belle (Isabelle) Moodie, a pretty, ethereal woman born in Leith, near Edinburgh, on the North Sea; indeed, throughout her life she retained the slight rustle of a Scottish accent.

Her father, Thomas Moodie, was drowned at sea when she was eight; her mother, Mary, shipped Belle off at the age of eleven to a wealthy uncle and aunt in Ohio—not a peculiar thing to have done in those days, when the New World beckoned to so many immigrants. Still, the rumor that Belle had been the child of an illegitimate relationship would persist in the Frost family.

At first, certain obvious differences between Isabelle and Will got in the way of their courtship. She was by nature a religious person, attracted to the mystical sides of Christianity, whereas Will was a rationalist with little taste for revealed religion. He was impetuous, reckless, and willful; she was demure, hesitant, and cautious. Nevertheless, the young couple found themselves growing close: to a degree, both were mavericks, and they shared an interest in literature and ideas. In a note to her written in February, he put his feelings on paper:

> It is now five months since I shook hands with you on your arrival here. To say that I liked you at the very outset of our acquaintance would be superfluous,—for who could do otherwise? Yes, I liked you. That was all. I have always thought that that was the only feeling I could have towards any woman. And I little dreamed that this sentiment,—if sentiment it can be called,—was to be supplanted by a passion whose hold upon me, oh! how dear a hold! has now for some time been stronger than any other tie that connects me with the world, and which makes my heart beat faster, faster, faster, as I write these lines.[4]

Belle had already turned down a proposal from a Presbyterian clergyman some years before, feeling herself unworthy of him (perhaps because of the nature of her parents' relationship). She told Will firmly that she would never marry him, nor anyone else. Her life would be dedicated to teaching, which was not unusual for young women in the nineteenth century. But Will's persistence impressed her, and in January she accepted his offer of marriage; the ceremony itself took place only two months later, on March 18, 1873. In early June, when the school year ended, they both said farewell to Lewistown Academy forever.

They traveled together by coach and train to Columbus, Ohio, where they stayed with Belle's uncle and aunt, who seemed quite pleased with Belle's choice of a Harvard man. The plan was for her to remain there, with her family, while he made his way to San Francisco. It was a scouting mission of sorts. He would look over the terrain, find an apartment, and try to secure an acceptable post on a newspaper.

Will arrived in Oakland in midsummer, then took the ferry across San Francisco Bay to his new home. He found a room in a boarding-house, and immediately wrote six sample editorials, which he sent around to the most important papers in the city, including the *Bulletin* and the *Chronicle*. All six were accepted, much to his surprise and delight, and he was promised a regular position with the *Bulletin*. He wrote back proudly to his wife, telling her to come at once, as there seemed to be endless opportunities here for them both. "Home is now to me the sweetest thing in life," he wrote, with a lyric panache typical of his letters, "and home is anywhere in the wide world where you are."[5]

Given Will Frost's romantic mind-set, San Francisco was just the place for him. The famous Gold Rush was long over, but a boom in silver mining that had lured millions of treasure hunters across the continent was at its peak in the 1870s. Eighty or more ships arrived each day, freighters and passenger vessels alike, bringing upwards of sixty thousand immigrants each year to San Francisco, many of them from China. It was a city on the boil, with vastly contradictory and potentially conflicting elements pouring into it daily. "The excitement of the place appealed to my father," said Frost. "He was part of it. There was gold dust in his eyes, you might say."

Indeed, Frost would register some of the atmosphere of that city by the sea in "A Peck of Gold," which opens:

> *Dust always blowing about the town,*
> *Except when sea fog laid it down,*

> *And I was one of the children told*
> *Some of the blowing dust was gold.*

Frost, like so many other children in San Francisco of that time, had been told that gold "was what they would eat, presumably instead of the plebeian dust mentioned to ordinary children in ordinary places."[6]

Will Frost followed rigorously the original game plan of his career, setting out purposefully to befriend many of the best-known politicos of his day. He campaigned for Samuel Tilden, the unsuccessful presidential candidate, in 1876. Four years later he was picked as a delegate to the national Democratic convention in Cincinnati, where Winfield Scott Hancock (a hero of the Union during the Civil War) was chosen to run against James A. Garfield, and one of Frost's keener memories was of seeing his father, in frock coat and top hat, depart for the East from the train station in Oakland. In 1882, Will tried without luck to win the Democratic candidacy for Congress in his district—one in a string of defeats that seems to have worn him down.

Will Frost moved from the *Bulletin* to the *Daily Evening Post* in 1875, drawn to the latter by its crusading editor, Henry George, whose ideas on Christian socialism had proved attractive to a wide range of intellectuals around the world, including George Bernard Shaw and Leo Tolstoy, both of whom corresponded with him. George developed the concept of a single tax in *Progress and Poverty* (1879), arguing that free enterprise did not mean private monopolies were morally justified. In this vein, Will's editorials called repeatedly for "a democracy uncorrupt and sensitive to the people's needs."

Unfortunately, Will also came under the influence of Christopher "Boss" Buckley, often referred to in the press as the "Blind White Devil." Buckley—a prototype for the bloated political tyrant who dominates his party by bribing some people and bashing others—found in the young newspaperman a gullible and eager lackey. Robert Frost later remarked, with disdain, that his father had let himself become "the willing slave of the blind boss, rushing to do his every bidding without question" in the hopes of being "named to some important post" that never materialized.[7]

Perhaps the finest moment of Will Frost's life came when he chaired the Democratic committee for San Francisco in 1884, when Grover Cleveland, the governor of New York, won the presidency; young Robert—called Robbie by his parents—recalled "being carried through the streets" afterward "atop a fire engine, by torchlight." Inspired by this success, Will put himself forward again, this time for the post of city tax collector; he lost, resoundingly, and was so humiliated and angry that he went on a drunken binge lasting most of the week.

Will and Belle were, by this time, seriously at odds with each other. The original contrast of temperaments that had made them seem an unlikely couple had only grown more severe. He had begun to drink heavily the year after his son was born, finding any excuse to join his friends at the Bohemian Club, where writers and journalists, actors and musicians gathered, especially on the weekends, to drink whiskey and exchange lewd jokes. Belle increasingly took solace in the Swedenborgian Church, named after the eighteenth-century mystic Emanuel Swedenborg, whose elaborate system of beliefs had appealed to the likes of Emerson (who wrote about Swedenborg in *Representative Men*) and Henry James, Sr., the father of William, Alice, and Henry James. Her mentor in the Swedenborgian faith was the charismatic Reverend John Doughty, a black-bearded mystic who had been raised in Worcester, Massachusetts, and had graduated from Harvard.

Robert Frost was always a bit uncomfortable with his mother's religious predilections, and would occasionally refer to her "incipient insanity," tracing many of his own mental crises and those of his children back to this source. Nevertheless, he later said, "I looked on at my mother's devoutness and thought it was beautiful."[8] Indeed, one finds more than a trace of mysticism in his work. "Frost liked to play down his own religious sense of things," said Rabbi Victor Reichert, a good friend during the poet's last decades, "but it was there. And he always said he learned about those things from his mother, who could see right through the material world as if it didn't exist."[9]

Doubtless Belle Frost was driven deeper into her religion as a means of escape from a life that was not going in the direction she had hoped. "She was unhappy," her son recalled, "and couldn't find a way around it."

Will Frost, in the meanwhile, lost interest in trying to mend the relationship, which tumbled quickly from bad to worse. It seems little wonder that so many of Frost's early poems, especially the dramatic monologues of *North of Boston*, were crammed with grueling portraits of husbands and wives at odds, unable to communicate their feelings, unable to find common ground.

One harsh interlude in the Frost marriage occurred in the summer of 1876. Belle was pregnant with her second child, and she could no longer abide the level of emotional abuse that, in her view, had been inflicted on her—mostly a result of Will's drinking. Without her husband's consent, she set off for the East to visit her in-laws, in Massachusetts. The elder Frosts were not happy to see her, but they took her in, and Jeanie Florence Frost was born there, on June 25, 1876, just before midnight, with Will's mother and an aunt in attendance.

The birth went well, but relations between Belle and her husband's family grew increasingly strained; they could not understand why a pregnant woman would set off so cavalierly on such a lengthy journey, and without her husband. Not wishing to have to justify herself, Belle left as soon as she could for Greenfield, where an old friend, Sarah Newton, was spending the summer with her parents on the family farm. Belle had met Sarah in Ohio, and they had remained close friends through correspondence. Belle was welcomed warmly by the Newtons, a devoutly religious family who immediately took to this forlorn young woman with a baby girl and a two-year-old son in tow.

The relationship between Belle and Will slowly began to heal as they corresponded throughout the summer. She knew that his health was poor, and it upset her when she learned that he had entered a six-day footrace—motivated by a desire to beat Dan O'Leary, a legendary local runner. Will lost the race, and his letters darkly hinted that his health was waning. Belle's sympathy was thus drawn. In September, she started back to San Francisco, breaking her journey in Ohio, where she stayed with her aunt and uncle, who adored the children and felt sorry for Belle's obvious marital stress.

One of the more curious facts of this visit was Belle's reacquaintance with an old high school friend, Blanche Rankin, who suddenly decided to accompany Belle and the children to San Francisco. The idea was that Blanche would live temporarily with the Frosts while looking for a teaching job. This "temporary" situation would last for several years, and Blanche became "Aunt Blanche" to the children and a companion to Belle, whom she later described as "a queer woman."

When Belle finally arrived back home, her worst fears were realized. She found Will in a hospital, where doctors were treating him for what looked terrifyingly like consumption, one of the dread diseases of the age. Already a thin man, he had lost a good deal of weight in her absence, and now appeared gaunt and jaundiced; he was also coughing blood—the telltale sign of consumption. Horrified, Belle withdrew even more willfully into her religion, trying occasionally to win over her seriously ill and often depressed husband, without success.

He, on the other hand, refused to admit the seriousness of his illness, which he repeatedly brushed off, resorting to his favorite remedy: whiskey. What little money he managed to save from his salary of thirty-five dollars a week was foolishly invested in silver mining shares, and he boasted he would take his family to Hawaii for "the cure" as soon as his ship came in. But it never did. Indeed, the family circumstances only grew steadily worse.

The Frosts moved from hotel to hotel, from apartment to apartment, as Will's fortunes shifted. During relatively good periods, they would lodge at the Abbotsford House, a fairly posh hotel on the corner of Broadway and Larkin Street. "Those rooms at the Abbotsford stay with me," Frost later said, recalling the heavy velour curtains, the pressed-tin ceilings, Oriental rugs, and brass railings. But these good times were few and far between, and the Frosts had to be content with drab, sparsely furnished apartments.

The Frost children were well looked after by their mother and Aunt Blanche, both experienced teachers who put a premium on a disciplined, traditional education. When Robbie was five, arrangements were made for him to attend a private kindergarten in the home of a Russian woman, Madame Zitska, even though he had to go halfway across the city of San Francisco by horse-drawn omnibus to get there. The experience was not a success, and the boy was often unable to go because of nervous cramping in his stomach. *

*He entered his first public school in 1880, when the Frosts were once again living in the Abbotsford. The school was only a short distance away, across the busy street, which came as a relief to Frost after the journey to Madame Zitska's place. Unfortunately, the stomach pains returned, preventing him from attending first grade, and his mother decided to school him at home for the rest of the year. She found that Robbie had no talent for arithmetic or reading, but he loved to write. She rewarded him one day with a new copybook, which he treasured. She would supply him with a text, and he would copy it meticulously into his book; if he made a mistake, his rage would be so extreme that he would tear out the page and crumple it up. *

Frost entered the second grade without a hitch, excelling in geography and writing. His mother and Aunt Blanche hovered over him, making sure that he did not lose his focus. They were indulgent and kindly, much in contrast to Will Frost, who could be difficult, a fierce disciplinarian whose progressively worsening illness made life hard for everyone. Fortunately for the children, Will Frost was busy with his work, trying hard to earn enough money to support the family and himself in the manner he thought appropriate, while having to deal simultaneously with bouts of spitting up blood and his own urge to drink heavily.

*Frost could recall many scenes of violence, such as the time he and a friend were building a ship from wood fragments gathered from a nearby lot. Will Frost came home drunk in the late afternoon, saw sticks and glue lying all over the living room carpet, and flew into a rage; he stepped on the half-built ship and hit young Robbie several times with the back of his hand while Belle stood anxiously in the doorway, unable to restrain him. She knew enough to wait until he was sober. *

Belle tried her best to make life pleasant for Robbie and Jeanie, taking them for long walks on weekends, climbing Telegraph Hill, Russian Hill, and Nob Hill to show them the views from the top. The grand mansions on Nob Hill made a lasting impression on the young boy. They would sometimes trek to the waterfront to see the massive schooners loading or unloading, and to watch the flocks of cormorants and gulls feeding on scraps dropped overboard. They would go for long drives in horse-drawn carriages, sometimes crossing the peninsula for lunch or dinner at the Cliff House restaurant below Lands End, where they would follow the winding paths along the cliffs to see the ocean blast and shatter against Seal Rocks, a well-known landmark. On warm Sundays in spring, they often went to the botanical displays at Woodward's Gardens in the old mission district—the setting for "At Woodward's Gardens," which Frost published in 1936. As a boy, Frost was most impressed by the aquatic merry-go-round at the gardens.

On weekends, they would venture into the California countryside. Memories of these excursions stayed with Frost in later years, and some were folded into late poems, such as the beautiful and underrated "Auspex," from *In the Clearing*, which opens:

> *Once in a California Sierra*
> *I was swooped down upon when I was small,*
> *And measured, but not taken after all,*
> *By a great eagle bird in all its terror.*

The Frost family would regularly attend the picnics put on at Cliff House by the Caledonian Club, to which Belle, an enthusiastic Scot, belonged. Robbie and Jeanie would wander down to the sea to watch seals on the rocks. Fiddlers played traditional Celtic music on the beach, and there were footraces for the children and folk dancing for the adults. Will Frost, being a runner himself, encouraged his son in the races, buying him a special pair of running shoes on one occasion; he was pleased when the boy proved a talented sprinter.

Will prided himself on his ability to walk twenty miles at a clip or swim long distances in icy waters. It was therefore agonizing for him, and his family, to witness the steady onslaught of tuberculosis. His weight continued to drop, and he often lay in bed on the weekends or evenings without energy. Living in a perpetual state of denial, he insisted on doing things his body could not withstand. Some evenings after work, for example, he would take Robbie to a favorite swimming spot near the harbor. The boy was left on shore to guard his father's clothes, towel, and whiskey bottle while he swam a half mile through cold, choppy waters to a bell buoy. He would climb up the buoy and wave defiantly to his son before leaping back in the water to swim ashore. "When his father swam out into San Francisco Bay, and he was left alone on the beach, he was in a terrible state of agitation until his father returned," recalled Peter J. Stanlis, with whom Frost reminisced about his early days.[10]

Frost's mind often returned, in later years, to the Pacific coastline of his childhood. He especially remembered walking along that rocky beach near the Cliff House with his father at dusk as the surf boomed in the broken rocks. In a famous poem, "Once by the Pacific," he recalled this scene, noting: "The shore was lucky in being backed by cliff, / The cliff in being backed by continent." With a bleakness that seemed to attend his memories of these early years, he concluded:

> It looked as if a night of dark intent
> Was coming, and not only a night, an age.
> Someone had better be prepared for rage.
> There would be more than ocean-water broken
> Before God's last Put out the Light was spoken.

The rage discovered in the natural world, with its threat of a dangerous storm, was not unlike the rage often found in Will Frost, who might well erupt before the household lamps were finally extinguished on any given night. Not surprisingly, one finds threats of rage quite often in Frost's poetry, and an underlying awareness that any moment of stasis, however idyllic, can easily be shattered.

Belle Frost, meanwhile, did her best to protect the children from the vicissitudes of her husband's mental state, as well as from his physical decline. She also tried to counter Will's skepticism, which at times erupted into tirades against organized religion. Belle was convinced that she had the gift of second sight, and could therefore see into the future. Her bedtime stories teemed with fairies and spirits, and she taught Robbie and Jeanie to respect the spirit-world as much as the world visible to the naked eye. An odd mix of skepticism and faith (often tinged with a streak of Calvinism, with its emphasis on God's arbitrary preselection of certain souls for heaven) became typical of Frost, and is present in poems such as "The Fear of God," which begins:

> If you should rise from Nowhere up to Somewhere,
> From being No one up to being Someone,
> Be sure to keep repeating to yourself
> You owe it to an arbitrary god
> Whose mercy to you rather than to others
> Won't bear too critical examination.

Around the time of his seventh birthday, Frost himself began to hear voices and experience a touch of clairvoyance. His mother found this unsurprising, and comforted him with stories of other gifted people who could see and hear things that "ordinary" people could not. "To the end of his life," said one friend, "Robert believed he could hear voices, real voices. His poems came to him like voices from nowhere. He liked to be alone just to listen, to communicate with the spirit-world."[11]

Frost later described his formal religious progression as "Presbyterian, Unitarian, Swedenborgian, Nothing."[12] Having moved around so many churches in childhood, he deliberately stayed away from most churches in later life; nevertheless, his correspondence, conversation, and poems are saturated with religious feeling, with questing after God, with evocations of doubt, with meditations on time and eternity. Indeed, one of the last letters Frost ever wrote moved straight to the heart of the matter: "Why will the quidnuncs always be hoping for a salvation man will never have from anyone but God? I was just saying today how Christ posed Himself the whole problem and died for it. How can we be just in a world that needs mercy and merciful in a world that needs justice?"[13]

Belle loved to read to her children, and she favored stories by

George MacDonald, whose mystical Christianity appealed to her. *At the Back of the North Wind* (1871) was a particular favorite of Robbie's, who saw himself in the story's central character, a boy named Diamond, whose real and imagined adventures ultimately collapse into each other. Belle would read aloud from many of the standard, popular works for children: *Tom Brown's School Days*, by Thomas Hughes, and *The Last of the Mohicans*, by James Fenimore Cooper. Because of her sentimental connection to Scotland, she took special care to introduce Robbie and Jeanie to Scotland's heroes, such as Sir William Wallace and Robert the Bruce. She loved the poems of Robert Burns and could recite many of them by heart. Another book of Scottish interest that she introduced to her children was *The Scottish Chiefs* (1810), a work of popular history by Jane Porter. She would also read stories of her own composition, one of which—*The Land of Crystal, or, Christmas Days with the Fairies*—was published in 1884.

ıı Frost disliked and did not attend elementary school beyond the third grade, but even sixty years later he could recall the names of his first principal and teachers.[14] "When I was a child in San Francisco," he later told Louis Untermeyer, "I played sick to get out of going to school."[15] Again, a pattern was put in place early in his life that would play out in distinct ways later on. Organized education, as he later said, was "never my taste." He would attend college sporadically, dropping out of Dartmouth and Harvard before getting a degree, and he would never fit comfortably into any academic setting, even though he held various distinguished posts at Michigan, Harvard, Amherst, Dartmouth, and elsewhere. "He was always a round peg in a square hole at these colleges," said a former colleague. "He didn't teach in any conventional way. He didn't do anything in a conventional way."[16] *ıı*

Belle Frost and Aunt Blanche tutored Robbie and Jeanie in the mornings, and they were free to roam about the streets in the afternoon. The last address of the Frosts in San Francisco was 1404 Leavenworth Street, near Washington, where Robbie had been born. The apartment was tiny and cramped, but there was a small garden at the back with a shed that Robbie converted into a chicken coop—the first sign of his interest in animals and farming. When not working with his chickens, Robbie liked to set off alone on foot, often hiking to Nob Hill, where the new millionaires—men such as Charles Crocker, Leland Stanford, Mark Hopkins, and D. D. Colton—were building huge Victorian houses as monuments to their own egos, crafting them from the best imported materials, including English brick and marble from Italy. James Clair Flood, a brash Irishman whom Will Frost had met several times and often talked about, constructed a handmade brass fence around his entire property, giving it an air of glittering menace. (One can easily imagine Will Frost standing at the gates of this mansion like John Dickens with his impressionable son, Charles, saying, "One day you will grow up to live in a house like that one.")

Young Robbie's rebellious side gradually came forward, and he fell in with a local gang that roamed the streets around Leavenworth, Washington, and Clay; the gang was led by a tall, muscular boy of fourteen called Seth Balsa. Robbie soon "learned to live by his fists," he said. His mother was quite naturally appalled by her son's activities, most of which he kept from her (including the petty thievery that was part of any gang's reason for existence), but his father took this roguish play as a sign of the boy's inherent toughness and character. A brawler himself, he did not want to raise a son afraid to stand his own ground. Indeed, this fighting instinct never deserted Robert Frost, and "many of his friends in later life considered his eagerness to take on all comers a defining characteristic."17

Life should have been good for Robbie and his family. His father was earning a considerable amount of money for those days, over $2,000 a year by 1884. But his penchant for speculation, gambling, and hard drinking inevitably took a heavy toll on the family finances. When Will Frost decided to run for the fairly lucrative public office of San Francisco city tax collector, he brashly resigned from his job as city editor of the *Post* in June 1884, throwing the family finances into a turmoil. The possibility that he might actually lose the election seems never to have occurred to him. But lose it he did, that September, and he was forced to scrounge around for another newspaper job.

The *Daily Report* hired him, more out of pity than interest, but he never felt well enough to perform his duties. Tuberculosis had by now ravaged his lungs, and his children would occasionally see him spit blood into a handkerchief, then nervously cram the evidence into his pocket. Some days he was so weak he never left the apartment, and Belle would cover for him and tell Robbie and Jeanie that their father had a case of the flu. Eventually he resorted to desperate remedies; once, for example, he took young Robbie with him to a slaughter-house, where he drank cup after cup of fresh blood from the slit throat of a steer—a popular folk remedy.

Will Frost began coughing blood profusely in late spring of 1885, and it became obvious to his wife and children alike that the end was close. He remained calm throughout the final ordeal. Aware that he was leaving his family in precarious circumstances because he had not managed to meet the monthly payments on a life-insurance policy worth $20,000, he wrote his parents in Massachusetts asking them to look after Belle and the children. "You must do what you can for them," he said. He signaled the hopelessness of his situation by claiming to have "lost control" of his bowels.

It was lucky for everyone that death came swiftly. Will Frost actually managed to work at the newspaper office the day before he died, at age thirty-four, on May 5. Despite this sense of putting things in order, he left almost no money for his family. After funeral expenses were paid, Belle had only eight dollars in the bank—hardly enough to get through a week, let alone get the family back to Massachusetts, where Will had requested that his remains be sent for burial. Fortunately, his parents sent enough to cover traveling expenses for Belle, the children, and the body of their son.

Despite her reluctance to put herself into the debt and control of her husband's family, Belle saw clearly that there was no alternative for her and her young children. Once again, Will Frost's controlling hand was felt, even from the grave.

It would be hard to overestimate the impact these first eleven years in California had on the development of Robert Frost. One's early experience is, of course, essential in the formation of character. Frost absorbed from his father a great deal, including a feral drive to make something of himself, to exercise influence, to feel the world bending to his will. Frost's lifelong love of competitive sports, and his passion to excel and win in whatever he did, were also a legacy from his father. But Frost also learned the price of failure from Will Frost, and how easily one's ambitions may be thwarted, by others and oneself. In later years, Frost himself would swing between the poles of brash self-confidence ("I expect to do something to the present state of literature in America")[18] and deep self-doubt ("I have been bad and a bad artist").[19] In this oscillation, he closely resembled his father in disposition.

Will Frost's skeptical view of religion would affect his son, too. Frost would never attach himself to any specific dogma; but from Belle, his mother, he acquired a religious sensibility, a gift for spirituality. His poems, in fact, would live on that perilous fault line between skepticism and faith. At times these contrarieties would merge in moments of complicated, synthetic vision, as in "All Revelation," which concludes:

> *Eyes seeking the response of eyes*
> *Bring out the stars, bring out the flowers,*
> *Thus concentrating earth and skies*
> *So none need be afraid of size.*
> *All revelation has been ours.*

With the death of Will Frost, a vivid chapter closed for Belle, Robbie, and Jeanie. They traveled, with the coffin, across the Bay to Oakland, where they boarded the train for the long, sad journey east. Aunt Blanche (who had moved to the Napa Valley a year before, much to Belle's distress) accompanied them to the station, in tears. Frost later told Peter J. Stanlis that the journey from San Francisco to Massachusetts was "the *longest, loneliest* train ride he ever took."[20] It would be many years before Robert Frost, as an adult, would return to the city of his childhood, which he called "the first place in my memory, a place I still go back to in my dreams."

2   HOME IS WHERE THEY
HAVE TO TAKE YOU IN
1886–1892

Once we have learned to read, the rest can be trusted to add itself unto us. —FROST, "POETRY AND SCHOOL"

It is hard to imagine what that long journey eastward must have felt like for Belle Frost. Penniless, having to cast herself on the pity of her in-laws, whom she reflexively disliked, she must have summoned every ounce of internal strength to present herself at the front door of their austere, three-story clapboard house at 370 Haverhill Street in Lawrence, Massachusetts, on the Merrimack River, twenty-five miles north of Boston.

A second funeral service was held for Will Frost, whose coffin was buried at the Bellevue Cemetery. The elder Frosts, and their community, offered a chilly welcome to this bereft, impoverished family. Frost later recalled: "At first I disliked the Yankees. They were cold. They seemed narrow to me. I could not get used to them."[1] In particular, Grandfather Frost, with his flowing white beard and small, wire-rimmed glasses—an important man in this working-class community, and a dominant figure in this small mill town—seemed austere. Grandmother Frost, an intense, nervous woman, was scarcely any warmer. Belle Frost's openness of manner, her liberal idea of child rearing, and her Swedenborgian serenity did not settle well with the elder Frosts, who may also have blamed her on some unspoken level for the early death of their beloved Willie.

The Frosts did, however, provide a temporary home for their son's beleaguered family. Belle at once began looking for a job in teaching, although the market in elementary school education was saturated, and her qualifications were not exceptional. She had considerable teaching experience, in Ohio and at Lewistown, but she had no college degree or teaching certificate. After six painful months of searching, she landed a meager post as the fifth-grade teacher at an elementary school in Salem, ten miles from Lawrence, just over the New Hampshire border, with a salary of four hundred dollars a year. Desperate to move away from the elder Frosts, Belle found a two-room apartment for herself and the children near Salem.

There is a photograph of Belle Frost taken outside her school surrounded by almost three dozen children.[2] She is tall, angular, and slightly hunched, with a broad forehead and dark, penetrating eyes that stare ahead with determination. Her graying hair is bunched at the back, with a lock straying over her face. She wears rimless glasses and looks more like a grandmother than a middle-aged mother. Young Robbie is standing beside her, serious and handsome, and Jeanie is nearby: her hair tumbles to her shoulders, and she has a slightly defiant look on her face.

It was not an easy life, especially for Belle, who apparently had difficulty controlling her classes and found few friends in the Salem area. Her best attention was lavished on Robbie and Jeanie, to whom she often read poetry in the evenings. " 'That Robbie can do anything,' my mother would say," the poet recalled in later years. "I'd sometimes complain or run off to go swimming, but on the whole I guess I liked to try myself out in a job—helping a man load a wagon, pile firewood, rake or hoe. It was all odd jobs in those days. I liked working with characters, listening to them, their stories, the way they had to tell a story—the country was full of characters."[3]

Some of Frost's happier times during this period were spent in Amherst, New Hampshire, on the farm of his Aunt Sarah (his father's sister), who had married a man called Ben Messer, always called

"Uncle Messer" by the children. He was an outgoing, robust man who appreciated the unhappy circumstances of these children. Frost recalled "joining the Messers for blueberry and raspberry picking" in the summers. The Messer farm offered a welcome escape from the tiny apartment in Salem, and it provided Frost with his first taste of rural imagery: the dirt roads shadowed by huge elms, the luxuriant pasture-land surrounded by stone walls, grazing herds of cows, horse-drawn ploughs, beautifully weathered barns, and farm machinery. There were stands of maple trees for sugaring, and woodlots full of beech and pine. Frost tried his hand, for the first time, at swinging birches. "It was almost sacrilegious," he told an audience once, "climbing a birch tree till it bent, till it gave and swooped to the ground. But that's what boys did in those days."[4]

Frost liked going to school in Salem, and having his mother as teacher. He won the respect of his classmates because of his talent for hurling a baseball; in the school yard on weekends and after school, he developed a fastball, which he called a "jump ball," a curve, and a drop ball. His first career goal, as of 1886, was to pitch in the major leagues. "He loved to talk about baseball," said a friend, "and knew the players going back half a century—even minor ones."[5] He played into late middle age, often dazzling his colleagues and students at the Bread Loaf Writers' Conference with his pitching ability and determination. "He played to win," recalled Reginald L. Cook, a professor of American literature at Middlebury College and the director of the Bread Loaf Graduate School of English. "In fact, if he didn't win, there was a price to pay. Winning was the point, he would say."[6]

The Frosts moved from apartment to apartment in Salem, eventually landing in the sympathetic company of Mr. and Mrs. Loren E. Bailey, who were immigrants from Scotland. They occupied a mid-nineteenth-century farmhouse on a windy knoll, with a wide porch and clapboard siding. Behind the house were a barn and a large chicken coop, where Bailey kept several dozen chickens, much to Frost's delight. Because he had, in San Francisco, dabbled in raising chickens, the prospect of helping Bailey was attractive. There was also a small cobbler shop attached to the barn, and Bailey had hired several workers to staff his small business. Frost was encouraged to work there on weekends and after school; indeed, he'd already had some experience in shoemaking in Salem, and he liked working with his hands. The job consisted of nailing shanks, three nails to each side of the shoe; the boy could earn as much as a dollar and a half a day, an important supplement to the family income.

It was clear to Belle Frost by now that her son had a gift for learning. He excelled in all subjects at school and begged his mother to read to him in the evening from various favorite books, such as Walter Scott's *Tales of a Grandfather*. This was supplemented by readings from traditional ballads, mostly Scottish, and from Percy's *Reliques*— perhaps the most widely used anthology of all time, next to Palgrave's *Golden Treasury*. Belle also read aloud from Ossian, Poe, Wordsworth, Longfellow, and Bryant, among other poets. Frost learned Bryant's classic "To a Waterfowl" by heart, and would recite it to himself while working beside Mr. Bailey in the shoemaking shop. But Emerson was his favorite, and would become a crucial influence on his thought.

Life continued to be difficult for Belle Frost, in part because she could not easily control a roomful of children. Her inward nature, compounded by a refusal to act in authoritarian ways, often produced chaos in the classroom. On several occasions parents grew impatient with her. At one point, a school board meeting was called to see whether or not she must be fired. She wasn't, mostly because an influential friend on the school board admired her. But the writing was on the wall. Belle soon took a job in the nearby town of Methuen, Massachusetts, hoping she could put the trouble in the Salem school behind her.

Although they lived in Methuen, Frost and his sister, Jeanie, traveled each day to the neighboring town of Lawrence to attend high school at their father's alma mater. It was the fall of 1888, and both Frosts had passed the entrance exams with flying colors (Jeanie had done even better than Robbie). One had to choose one of two basic programs: the classical or the general, also known as the Latin and the English tracks. It went without saying that Frost would opt for the first: it was the course that Will Frost had followed, and it was designed to prepare a student for college work.

In keeping with the revival of classical learning that was part of the Victorian age, Frost's teachers prescribed a heavy dose of Greek and Roman history, with classical languages at the center of the curriculum. "I read Virgil, Homer, Horace, and the rest—all before I even went to college," Frost later said. "I don't think the teacher understood how much poetry was in those pages." He took himself seriously as a scholar, rising to the top of his class of thirty-two students, where he remained until his graduation. (His grades for 1888–89 included a 96 in Latin—something of a record for that era, when few students ever crossed the line into the 90s.)

During the summer of 1889, he devoted himself in the evenings and on weekends to reading books not found in the classical course at Lawrence: Cooper's *The Deerslayer* and *The Last of the Mohicans*, Mary Hartwell Catherwood's *The Romance of Dollard*, and Prescott's *History of the Conquest of Mexico*. Weekdays were spent working on the farm with Mr. Bailey. Robbie was assigned the task of haying, and he learned to use a pitchfork properly for the first time. He was also taught to use a grindstone, and to build a stone wall.

Frost remained something of a loner well into his sophomore year, when he met Carl Burell, a young man in his mid-twenties who had returned to school to complete his education after a decade of supporting himself by doing odd jobs in Vermont and New Hampshire. Burell had a strong interest in books, and he made regular forays into the public library in Lawrence. He had taken a room with Frost's great-uncle, Elihu Colcord, and Frost would often visit him there after school. Burell was keenly interested in the science of botany, and he succeeded in winning his younger friend's attention with books that offered detailed drawings of local flora—an interest that would have a crucial impact on Frost's later work. Burell also introduced him to many of the great American humorists: Mark Twain, Artemus Ward, Josh Billings, Petroleum V. Nasby, John Phoenix, Orpheus C. Kerr. (It is worth noting that Frost, whose father had died when he was still a boy, was strongly attracted to someone older than himself, a figure of authority who was not, like his grandfather, remote and frightening.)

The debate over evolution was in the air, and Burell was reading closely the writings on this subject by men like Thomas Huxley and Herbert Spencer. About this time Frost inherited a copy of *Our Place Among Infinities*, by Richard A. Proctor. Though its primary subject is the evolution of the universe, it also takes up the related issues of theology and cosmology—subjects that would continue to fascinate Frost to the end of his life. It was in Proctor that he first came across the "argument from design," which became a subject in "Design," one of his most ferocious, and original, poems—although his reading of Darwin was perhaps more important here, since Darwin's principle of natural selection deeply altered the argument.[7] The impression this book made on Frost was such that he continued to refer to it decades later; indeed, in 1935 his wife, Elinor, wrote to a friend: "One of the books longest in his possession came to him from a friend of his father's in San Francisco, who died in the early eighties—Proctor's *Our Place Among the* [sic] *Infinities*. He read it several times about 1890 and got a telescope through the Youth's Companion. He has been astronomical ever since."[8]

Carl Burell was also a budding writer, contributing verse and prose pieces to the *High School Bulletin*. Frost read this work and decided he might well try his hand at some poetry. He had just finished reading Prescott's *Conquest of Mexico*, and this inspired a ballad. "The lines came into my head walking home from school," he recalled. The quatrains were written down quickly, at the kitchen table in his grandmother's house. The poem was called "La Noche Triste," referring to a horrible night when the Spaniards retreated in disarray across the causeway over Lake Tezcuco from the island city of Tenochtitlán. It was published in the *Bulletin* in April 1890, in the poet's second year at Lawrence High School—quite an accomplishment for a sophomore. This was followed a month later by a second poem, "Song of the Wave," evoking images of the sea below Cliff House in San Francisco—a dry run for "Once by the Pacific," one of his memorable later poems.

Meanwhile, the family had moved into a small apartment in a poor section of Lawrence. By the summer of 1890, their finances were so wretched that Belle Frost moved the three of them to Maine, where all were employed by a hotel in Ocean Park, twenty miles south of Portland. Belle and Jeanie worked as chambermaids, while Frost fetched groceries and mail, carried suitcases, painted woodwork, and mowed lawns. The only recreation, for Frost, occurred on the tennis courts in the evenings, when he was often called on to make up a fourth in doubles with the guests.

Belle Frost returned to a job as teacher in the Merrill District School in Methuen that fall, while her children eagerly began their third year at Lawrence High School. The previous spring, Frost had been admitted to the Debating Society, having been sponsored by Carl Burell and the boy who edited the *Bulletin*, Ernest Jewell. One of the subjects that most attracted Frost was a debate framed as: "Resolved, that Bryant was a greater poet than Whittier." Carl spoke first, in the affirmative, followed by Frost, who was apparently eloquent on the subject. A second debate concerned "a bill for removing the Indians from Indian Territory to more fertile districts and ceding said districts to the tribes forever; and for giving them some compensation for the losses already suffered."

Frost hurled himself into his studies, aware that in the spring of his junior year he would have to take some preliminary entrance exams at Harvard, where he assumed he would go after graduation. His interest in Latin, in particular, grew intense under the strict but inspired tutelage of a young teacher, Miss Newell, who recognized in Frost a pupil of special promise. He spent hours at home, in the evenings, translating passages from Cicero, Tacitus, Virgil, and Ovid. He later recalled "translating, and performing in class, passages from the Roman playwrights, too—Plautus in particular."[9]

Frost entered his senior year on top of the world. He was elected chief editor of the *High School Bulletin*, and most of his teachers and fellow students considered him the leading scholar in the Class of 1892, although Elinor Miriam White was hard on his heels as top student. "I didn't know I was head of the class of 1892," Frost later recalled. "In the third year it became a school issue and I was in distress. There was a rivalry between the Greek and Latin teachers, and Elinor bobbed up in the last year as a rival."[10]

Elinor was a brilliant girl, and Frost had been noting her presence for some time. She was enrolled in the general course, and so he did not commonly meet her in class, although he had often seen her in the school yard or in the halls. Her father had been a Universalist minister in Lawrence, but had abandoned his calling. She was a year and a half older than Frost, and had missed a good deal of school owing to a mysterious disease called "slow fever"—a sickness that entailed fevers and periods of acute exhaustion. Their friendship did not really begin in earnest until the winter of their senior year, when their rivalry for class valedictorian was at its height—although Frost feigned absolute indifference to the situation. (He later claimed that he told the principal just to give the honor to Elinor, but that the principal refused and called it a tie.)

Frost sat the Harvard entrance exams in October 1891, as expected, finishing seventh in English literature, a subject he had never studied formally in school. That visit to Cambridge prompted a poem in tripping anapests, which began:

> As I went down through the common,
>   It was bright with the light of day,
> For the wind and rain had swept the leaves
>   And the shadow of summer away.
> The walks were all fresh-blacked with rain
>   As I went briskly down:—
> I felt my own quick step begin
>   The pace of the winter town.

Already, Frost has begun to apply the rhythms of a natural speaking voice to a traditional meter, casting off all worries about regularity. "I felt my own quick step begin," for example, calls attention to itself by the even spread of the stresses from foot to foot. The imagery, too, shows promise: "The walks were all fresh-blacked with rain."

That same fall, in addition to editing the *Bulletin* and breezing toward first place in the classical course, Frost played on the varsity football team. His interest in baseball had always been strong, but football was another matter. A colleague on the school paper wrote in salute of Frost's talents: "No one would think the man who played football on the right end was the same person who sits with spectacles astride his nose in the Chief Editor's Chair. Keep up the good work, Bobby."[11]

It would have been especially nice if Jeanie had managed to keep up with her brother, but this was not the case. She had always been a nervous girl, but her condition worsened in her junior year. She moved back and forth between periods of extreme insomnia, when she would keep Frost and her mother awake into the wee hours of the morning, and stretches of bleak depression, when she could hardly manage to leave her bedroom. At times, her temper flared, and she seemed frighteningly out of control. Often, she sulked and refused to socialize with her classmates. Belle Frost noted in a letter to a friend that Jeanie was "beyond reaching"; her situation made her incapable of steady academic work by her senior year. She did not, as her mother had hoped she might, apply to any colleges; indeed, after a bout of typhoid fever in December of her final year in school, she dropped out permanently. Belle called her "my poor fragile girl," and fretted about her eventual prospects.

Frost himself was quite troubled by Jeanie's condition. He was also acutely conscious of his own tendency toward anxiety and depression, and worried about skidding down the same slope. Perhaps in reaction, he applied himself to his activities, academic and otherwise, with increased strength, even fury. A pattern of behavior was established wherein Frost, to compensate for his depressive bent, would hurl himself into frentic activity—a pattern that stayed with him to the end.

His term as chief editor ended in January 1892, under complex circumstances. Jeanie had been hospitalized in December 1891, and Frost (apparently unwell himself) stayed away from school during her illness. Before leaving, however, he instructed his staff at the *Bulletin* to assemble enough material for future issues. When he came back to school, in January, he discovered that no December issue had been published and that the vaults were empty of copy. He was furious, and first thought of resigning, then decided to write enough himself to complete an issue. "I got mad," he said, "and I went down to the printer's office, and in the little cubby hole down there I wrote the whole number. I wrote a story; I wrote an essay; I wrote editorials; I wrote a poem . . . and I wrote a fictitious report of the debating society. And then I wrote a fictitious article on exchange magazines. I wrote the whole thing myself right there, delivered it to the printer's devil, and resigned!"[12]

He was, however, later invited to serve temporarily as acting editor, and he took the occasion to contribute to the *Bulletin* several fascinating, precocious editorials. He had by now clearly severed most ties with his mother's religious views, and his reading of Darwin, Huxley, and Proctor was beginning to bear fruit. He divided the world three ways in one of these pieces, into "unquestioning followers" of religious custom, "enemies," and "rethinkers." He now put Carl Burell, secretly, in that class of "enemies"—those who simply reject an idea because it seems conventional. He put himself into the "rethinker" category, identifying with those who "follow custom—not without question, but where it does not conflict with the broader habits of life gained by wanderers among ideas."[13]

These "dangerous" notions brought Frost into conflict with his mother, as might be expected. They apparently quarrelled frequently about his seeming "atheism," although Frost consistently defended himself against this charge. He was not an atheist, he maintained, though he did subscribe to many of the views put forward by people who were. At one point he referred to himself, with a touch of self-flattery, as a "freethinker," and his mother objected: "Oh, please don't use that word. It has such a dreadful history."[14]

Frost determined to go his own way, or to *seem* to go his own way, as in "The Road Not Taken," his most famous poem, which he ends with a wry self-critical note that he will be telling people "with a sigh" that he "took the road less traveled by." In fact, Frost was a rugged traditionalist, a man highly conscious of the forms, and one who found his freedom within the limits of those forms. Part of his great originality lay with this discovering of freedom within form, a way of extending a given tradition in a direction that seemed to redefine it.

Frost's interest in English poetry, per se, acquired new dimensions in the spring of his senior year as he began, haltingly, to court Elinor White. They often met, after school, in the Lawrence Public Library, a small but stately building surrounded by elms. Elinor had focused her studies on English poetry, and she was able to introduce Frost to poets like Sir Philip Sidney, Edmund Spenser, John Clare, and Edward Young. In turn, Frost presented her with books by two of his favorite contemporary poets, Edward Rowland Sill, whose work he had come across in the *Century Magazine*, and Emily Dickinson, whose poetry had recently been published (posthumously) for the first time. Dickinson would become a major influence on Frost's own verse.

The principal of Lawrence High School, Nathaniel Goodwin, divided the final valedictory honors between Frost and Elinor. Thus far, their courtship had been slow, even desultory; now, as they shared with each other their separate graduation speeches, it struck them simultaneously that their interests and temperaments were surprisingly similar. Both adored poetry; furthermore, both felt, to some degree, like outcasts in Lawrence. Elinor's own family circumstances were no less troubled and troubling than Frost's: her father's financial situation had recently gone from bad to worse, and he was barely holding the family together with occasional carpentry jobs; her parents fought constantly, about money and—more seriously—about Elinor's neurotic sister, who (much like Jeanie) had recently dropped out of school for emotional reasons.

Elinor's valedictory speech was entitled "Conversation as a Force in Life," an intriguing subject, given her attachment to a man who prized conversation—his own, in particular—over almost anything. Frost delivered a somewhat obscure, grandiloquent speech called "A Monument to After-Thought Unveiled," where he intoned, "Not in the strife of action, is the leader made, nor in the face of crisis, but when all is over, when the mind is swift with keen regret, in the long after-thought. The after-thought of one action is the forethought of the next."

In essence, Frost was elaborating on a theme made extremely popular in the nineteenth century by thinkers like Thomas Carlyle, who celebrated in extravagant terms the rise of the individual. "It is when alone," Frost continued, "in converse with their own thoughts so much that they live their own conventionalities, forgetful of the world's, that they [the great leaders] form those habits called the heroism of genius, and lead the progress of the race."

The graduation took place on a muggy afternoon, a Thursday, at the end of June in the upstairs auditorium of City Hall, a sturdy granite building on the town common. The stage was lavishly decorated with cut flowers and potted plants. Thirty-two seniors graduated that day, and Frost was the last of thirteen speakers. He was so overcome by anxiety by the time his turn came that he nearly bolted from the building. He did, however, manage to deliver the address, and was called back onto center stage by the superintendent of schools, who awarded him the Hood Prize, "for excellence in academic work and general deportment."

On the following morning, one of the local newspapers commented on Frost's speech, suggesting that it "combined in a rare degree poetic thought, a fine range of imagination, and devotion to a high ideal, and evinced intellectual compass much beyond the usual school essay."[15] Elinor was also given high marks for her "thoughtful and praiseworthy piece of work."

The emotional high point of the summer was nevertheless deeply private. By the end of June, Frost's feelings for Elinor had become intense, and they were reciprocated. One afternoon, walking in the fields just beyond the edge of town, they secretly pledged to marry. Frost wanted Elinor to marry him at once, arguing that if he went to Harvard, she could go to the Harvard Annex (as Radcliffe College was then called), but this flew in the face of her parents' recent decision to send her to St. Lawrence University, in Canton, New York. Elinor firmly, patiently, fended him off. He was, after all, only eighteen (and she was nearly twenty). There would, she argued, be plenty of time for marriage when their circumstances were different.

Frost had never really doubted that he would go to Harvard, but in the spring of his senior year at Lawrence he stumbled on his grandparents' objections. Harvard, they argued, was "a drinking place." They remembered only too vividly what had happened there to their son. Belle Frost agreed with her in-laws, arguing that it was full of freethinkers— just the sort of people who might lead her impressionable son in the wrong direction. A teacher whom Frost admired had graduated from Dartmouth College, in Hanover, New Hampshire, and he now suggested that Frost follow in his footsteps. Neither Belle nor the elder Frosts knew much about Dartmouth, but they decided to take up this suggestion.

Frost applied to Dartmouth and was offered a scholarship that covered most of the tuition costs. Room and board was to be paid by Frost's grandparents, although he was able to contribute twenty dollars, having worked through the summer after graduation as a clerical assistant at the Everett Mill in Lawrence. In later years, Frost recalled with some consternation the arrangement that he had with his grandfather: "Since he paid me five dollars a week for my keep, it was only natural, from his viewpoint, that he should desire a return on his investment, usury. He had the New England shrewdness which demanded a dollar back with interest. Now, in as much as I got my room for $30 a year, meals proportionately reasonable, the five dollars was plenty for ordinary needs. What made it bad was the fact that he insisted on an itemized account for every penny spent, where it went, and what it was for. I rebelled and wanted to tell him to go to hell. But I didn't. I held. It wasn't that I objected to being dependent on him. That sort of thing has never bothered me. . . . It was just that I hated to keep an account of every little dab I spent."[16]

❧ To the end of his life, Frost was casual with money and refused to worry about small amounts. His early memory of accounting to his grandparents for every penny would, in the middle of the 1930s, yield a little aphoristic poem, "The Hardship of Accounting."

> Never ask of money spent
> Where the spender thinks it went.
> Nobody was ever meant
> To remember or invent
> What he did with every cent.

Perhaps *because* he was so casual with money, and never knew how much was coming in or going out, Frost spent a good deal of time fretting in later years about his income, and often had the feeling that there was never quite enough, that he must concoct a plan to get more.

The summer of 1892 had been an idyllic one for Frost. The job at the mill was light (or decidedly undemanding), and he was able to spend most evenings and weekends with Elinor. His grandfather had a small rowboat, and he would take her on short voyages up the Merrimack River, stopping at the Lawrence dam, where secluded areas for picnics could easily be found. These outings were, however, often spoiled by Frost's efforts at lovemaking—a subject he later approached in "The Subverted Flower," which Elinor would not let him publish during her lifetime. In this tense, compulsively rhythmical narrative, a teenage boy and girl contend with strong, almost overwhelming impulses:

> She drew back; he was calm:
> "It is this that had the power."
> And he lashed his open palm
> With the tender-headed flower.
> He smiled for her to smile,
> But she was either blind
> Or willfully unkind.
> He eyed her for a while
> For a woman and a puzzle.
> He flicked and flung the flower,
> And another sort of smile
> Caught up like fingertips
> The corners of his lips
> And cracked his ragged muzzle.

The girl, like Elinor, kept resisting him, afraid of "The demon of pursuit / That slumbers in a brute." The couple is finally caught, as it were, in flagrante, by the girl's mother, who "wiped the foam" from her daughter's chin, then "drew her backward home." The cumulative effect of the poem is withering, with its three-beat insistent rhythm and heavily enjambed lines, which spill forward compulsively, checked only by the rhymes, which build to a strong crescendo in the poem's closing triplet.

Frost reluctantly saw Elinor off to St. Lawrence, then journeyed by train into New Hampshire. Hanover, then as now, was difficult to get to; one took a train to White River Junction, Vermont, then switched for a commuter train to the Lewiston Station, in Norwich; from there, one hiked to the nearby Connecticut River (which divides New Hampshire from Vermont) and crossed at the Ledyard Bridge. It was then a steep climb up Wheelock Street to the Hanover green, where Dartmouth Hall stood magnificently on a slight hillock, its wooden facade painted white. The town itself was famous for its tall elms, which continued to shade the village until the late 1970s, when Dutch elm disease killed most of these long-necked, elegant trees.

High on the plain of Hanover, one had a sense of being thrillingly isolated. *Vox clamantis in deserto* was the Dartmouth motto—a voice crying in the wilderness, and it was indeed a wilderness of sorts, even academically. Frost had been expecting more. He moved into a small room in Wentworth Hall, one of only four freshmen in that dormitory this semester, and soon found himself the object of hazing. It was part of the Dartmouth tradition that sophomores made life as difficult as possible for freshmen during their first term by playing all manner of practical jokes on them. Frost was by no means a stick-in-the-mud, and he enjoyed the horseplay that went along with hazing, but he also considered it childish. He would often retreat to the library, where he buried himself in Homer for a course he was taking from George D. Lord, an assistant professor whose learning he admired.

He was also taking a course in Latin prose, focused on Livy's history of Rome and taught by a shy young instructor, Charles H. Gould, whom Frost did not especially like. (Gould's introversion was such that the class ran him rather than the other way around.) His only other course was in mathematics—a subject that interested him in principle, although his professor, Thomas W. D. Worthen, was keener on maintaining discipline than teaching his subject.

Frost found it difficult to study, given the students' focus on what amounted to war games between freshmen and sophomores. A game much like "capture the flag" dominated the campus one weekend; the object of the exercise was for freshmen to try to steal the sophomore pennant. With his natural agility and strength, as well as his experience as a high school football player, Frost excelled in this exercise. On one memorable occasion he was himself among the small band of freshmen who grabbed the pennant and ran away with it.

Frost did not take to fraternity life, which was central at Dartmouth. "I was invited into a fraternity—Theta Delta Chi—and joined up," he recalled. "One of my 'rich' classmates paid my initiation fee. But somehow I was no fraternity brother." His room in Wentworth was famously untidy: "The rooms in Wentworth were heated by coal stoves, and I never emptied my ashes—just let them pile up on the floor till they reached the door. My mother had to send up my high school friend, Carl Burell, to dig me out." His closest friend among the Dartmouth undergraduates was Preston Shirley—a "frail boy and always a sufferer from ailments, he was the life of the place in many ways." They would talk for hours about "religion, politics, and history."[17]

Always a great walker, Frost took to going by himself (or with Preston Shirley) on hikes along the Connecticut River, usually heading north toward Lyme. He would occasionally take a carriage along a dirt road up to Etna, where he could find a mountain trail. Sometimes he went into the woods alone at night, a habit that deeply puzzled his fraternity brothers, who sent a delegation to his room in Wentworth one day to ask what on earth he did on those walks in the woods. "I gnaw bark," he told them.

In the college bookstore, he bought a copy of Palgrave's *Golden Treasury*, and he began his first systematic study of English poetry. In the library, he encountered a copy of a magazine called the *Independent*, which, on November 17, ran on its front page a poem called "Seaward" by the Dartmouth poet Richard Hovey.[18] Frost later said, "This was the first time I realized you could publish a poem in a national journal." It was natural for him, when, a year later, he finally had a poem he thought worth publishing on this scale, called "My Butterfly," to send it to that magazine.

Frost's literary activity at Dartmouth was limited, as he later remembered:

> It is strange that there is so little to say for my literary life at Dartmouth. I was writing a good deal there. I have ways of knowing that I was as much preoccupied with poetry then as now. "My Butterfly" in *A Boy's Will* [his first book] belongs to those days, though it was not published in *The Independent* until a year or two later. So also "Now Close the Windows" in the same book. I still like as well as anything I ever wrote the eight lines in ["My Butterfly"] which begin: "The grey grass is scarce dappled with the snow." But beyond a poem or two of my own, I have no distinctly literary recollections of the period that are not chiefly interesting for their unaccountability. I remember a line of Shelley's ("Where music and moonlight and feeling are one") quoted by Prof. C. F. Richardson in a swift talk on reading, a poem on Lake Memphremagog by Smollet in the Lit Course, and an elegy on the death of T. W. Parsons by Hovey in *The Independent*. I doubt if Hovey's poem was one of his best. I have not seen it from that day to this, but I will swear that it talks of "horns of elfland faintly blowing." So the memory of the past resolves itself into a few bright starpoints set in darkness. (The sense of the present is diffused like daylight.) Nothing of mine ever appeared in Dartmouth publications.[19]

Most of the writing Frost did at Dartmouth actually consisted of long, confessional letters to Elinor at St. Lawrence University, where it seemed to him that she was settling in too comfortably. He had hoped that the distance between them would create misery, and that this would spill over into her letters. Now her apparent satisfaction with college life fueled his anxieties and frustrations, and soon he found himself utterly disinclined to study Homer or Plato or Livy. Examinations loomed as the Thanksgiving recess drew to a close, and—much to his mother's displeasure—he decided to withdraw from school.

⁴The situation at home was such that he had a good rationale. Belle had been having a difficult time with her class in Methuen—"discipline problems," she called them. Frost determined to help her by taking over the class and whipping the students into shape. "I was glad to seize the excuse (to myself) that my mother needed me in her school," he said, "to take care of some big, brutal boys she could not manage."[19]

Preston Shirley helped him carry his trunk down two flights of stairs at Wentworth, and Frost unceremoniously fled from Dartmouth. "I wasn't suited for the place," he later said. He was by nature an autodidact, which meant he intensely disliked being told what to read and when to read it. He preferred to go his own way, despite what his family or friends might think or say. "We go to college," he said, "to be given one more chance to learn to read in case we haven't learned in High School. Once we have learned to read, the rest can be trusted to add itself unto us."[20]

3   MASKS OF GLOOM

1893–1895

This inflexible ambition trains us best.
—FROST TO WILLIAM HAYES WARD,
MARCH 28, 1894

Having left Dartmouth prematurely, Frost found himself uncomfortably adrift, prone to fall into one of those depressive states that would for the rest of his life periodically overwhelm him. Although Belle assured him it was not necessary, she was in genuine trouble with her class of rowdy seventh and eighth graders, many of whom took advantage of her emotional fragility, and Frost insisted on taking over her classroom. Already his strong-willed nature was beginning to show through.

That he was persuasive, as well as determined, is evident from the fact that he managed to convince the Methuen school board to take the unusual step of letting him substitute for his mother that spring. (She, meanwhile, was given a class of younger, more pliant, children to look after.) Frost bought a rattan cane from a local hardware store and immediately set about taming this unruly classroom. Although he was forced to resort to a kind of violence that would nowadays land a teacher in jail, he succeeded in winning the attention, if not the affection, of his pupils. A report circulated at the Methuen annual town meeting in March 1893 put the matter succinctly: "The Second Grammar school, left vacant by the appointment of Mrs. B. M. Frost as teacher of the second primary, has been assigned to Mr. Robert L. Frost, a student in Dartmouth College. Mr. Frost, although young, bears an unusual record for scholarship and maturity of character and has shown marked success in the management and instruction of a difficult school."

The school year came to an end with some relief for everyone concerned. Frost knew by now that teaching children was not for him, although he had no idea how else he might earn a living. He boldly proclaimed to Elinor, still at St. Lawrence, that he intended to write poetry, but he understood that poets rarely earned a living from their craft. "People thought I was lazy," he later admitted. But this seemed not to bother him. He planned to "pursue his own headstrong folly without interference."[1]

With Elinor away, Frost hovered around her family. Her sister Ada began to suffer from acute anxiety attacks, and the family was unsure of how to deal with this crisis. She sat in the White family home in Lawrence with the shades of her bedroom windows tightly drawn, complaining about the noise outside. She ate almost nothing and was, through the locked door of her bedroom, often heard sobbing. When she begged to be taken to the country that summer for peace of mind, Mrs. White found a place for the family on Canobie Lake in Salem, New Hampshire. She asked Rob to come along as general caretaker, largely because her husband refused to accompany them.

Elinor was summoned home from St. Lawrence before the term was finished, on the theory that her presence would help calm Ada. Frost was delighted to have her back, and in mid-April the four of them moved into a large house called the Saunders Place, a four-bedroom dwelling with a stone fireplace, green shingles, and a broad plank porch that overlooked the lake. A short while later, they were unexpectedly joined by Leona, the eldest of the White sisters, who was heavily pregnant and in flight from her abusive husband, a farmer called Nathaniel Harvey, who lived in Epping, New Hampshire. Thus was Frost surrounded by the female members of the White clan, who relied on him for everything from counsel to elbow grease.

The courtship between Elinor and Rob continued, fueled by

propinquity. He insisted that their "secret marriage" be made public, but she refused. It was not a "real" marriage, she said. If this were so, he suggested, they should get married in the usual public fashion, with a proper wedding. Elinor resisted, saying that he should think first about how he proposed to support her and a family. She urged him to consider returning to Dartmouth in the fall, but he insisted that this was out of the question. The main thing he had learned at Dartmouth was that education did not necessarily happen in a classroom, he told her. He would educate himself, in his own way and his own time.

By the end of the summer, Leona had gone back to Nathaniel Harvey, who had come to the lake begging forgiveness, and Ada seemed much better. Mrs. White insisted, quite rightly, that Elinor return to St. Lawrence, where she had proved herself a gifted student. Frost was left alone in the house by the lake. The solitude and his emotional situation were conducive to writing. In late August 1893, he wrote "Bereft," although it was not published until 1927:

> *Where had I heard this wind before*
> *Change like this to a deeper roar?*
> *What would it take my standing there for,*
> *Holding open a restive door,*
> *Looking down hill to a frothy shore?*

In a mood of wonderfully youthful paranoia, which is carried through the poem, the poet-narrator believes that "Something sinister in the tone" of the wind suggests that his "secret must be known." The poem concludes with a cumulative force typical of Frost at his best:

> *Word I was in the house alone*
> *Somehow must have gotten abroad,*
> *Word I was in my life alone,*
> *Word I had no one left but God.*

The poem shows Frost beginning to find a distinct voice well before his twentieth birthday. It also reveals the delicate, precarious state of his late-adolescent consciousness: he felt that he was alone, and that only God offered any comfort or company. With youthful narcissism, he imagined the whole of nature responding to his frenzied emotional state: the wind, the leaves that whirled against him, "got up in a coil and hissed, / Blindly struck at my knee and missed."

// Frost did not need a concrete reason for anxiety and depression, but it was useful to pin these states on something. He had a reason for being upset in late August, when he got a telegram telling him that his grandmother had unexpectedly died in her sleep. Although they had never been close, the elder Mrs. Frost had urged her husband to support Rob financially at Dartmouth, and she had appreciated her grandson's artistic leanings. Her hope was that her grandson would be able to accomplish things her son had not. Frost intuited her support and concern, and her death hit him surprisingly hard.[2] //

He returned to Lawrence in September, moving back into his mother and sister's shabby, four-room apartment at 96 Tremont Street. He had no plans for the future; indeed, the extent of his dislocation is suggested by his answering an ad in a Boston newspaper for someone to "manage" a Shakespearean actor. Fired with enthusiasm, he went immediately by train into Boston to meet the actor, who was many years his senior. Pretending to have experience as a theatrical manager, he crossed the Charles River into Cambridge to enlist the help of William James Rolfe, a venerable scholar of English Renaissance literature at Harvard; he also called for assistance on Richard Clapp, a well-known theater critic for the *Boston Evening Transcript*. Having rented a hall in Boston for a showcase performance, he somehow managed to talk both men into attending. The actor, unfortunately, proved stilted and dull, as both Clapp and Professor Rolfe explained to Frost on their way out. Frost agreed, and decided to cut his losses. His career as impresario quickly ended.

Desperate for cash, he found a job at the Arlington Woolen Mill as a light trimmer in the dynamo room. His job was to replace the carbon in the arc lamps, as needed; this meant climbing tall ladders and balancing in precarious positions. When the work was slow, he would hide on the roof, where he'd read Shakespeare, often in the company of an old high school friend, Edward Gilbert. Decades later, he wrote to Gilbert: "I don't suppose we think those days in the mill ever hurt or hindered us a mite. I often speak of them not to say brag of them when I want to set up as an authority on what kind of people work with their hands, what they earn, or used to earn, what becomes of them." He could recall vividly "the bulb throwing and the talks over in your quiet dynamo room" as well as "the carbon dust and the ladders we slid on one leg ahead of us along the well-oiled floors." Frost learned a lot, he said, but never how to "stand over going machinery on the top step of a step-ladder with nothing to hold on to or brace a shin against and unsling an arc lamp from the ceiling for repairs."[3]

In the evenings, he devoted himself to his poetry, and it was during the fall of that year, at home, that "My Butterfly" was composed, based on a fragment he had written four years earlier and inspired by a time at Dartmouth when he found some butterfly wings amid some dead leaves. Frost later called it his "first real poem." "I wrote it all in one go in the kitchen of our house on Tremont Street," he said.[4] "I locked the door and all the time I was working, Jeanie my sister tried to batter it down and get in."

This story obviously made a sharp impression, since Frost repeated it often. There was clearly a sense of having to protect himself from the onslaught of the family—as well as the psychological pressure represented by Jeanie, whose mental state (bordering on schizophrenia) was deeply threatening. He was already aware of those dark tendencies within himself, and he was doing whatever he could to ward them off. Poetry quickly became, for him, "a momentary stay against confusion." Nevertheless, he had to battle for those momentary stays, and they would never come easy.

As he wrote "My Butterfly," he had a profound sense that "something was happening. It was like cutting along a nerve." He later famously observed that a poem should "ride on its own melting," and this poem did. The second stanza, in particular, felt like his first breakthrough into a voice of his own (even though he was still a long way from discovering the style of the more mature work, the essential Frostian note):

> The gray grass is scarce dappled with the snow;
> Its two banks have not shut upon the river;
> But it is long ago—
> It seems forever—
> Since first I saw thee glance,
> With all thy dazzling other ones,
> In airy dalliance,
> Precipitate in love,
> Tossed, tangled, whirled and whirled above,
> Like a limp rose-wreath in a fairy dance.

Frost was elated when the poem was accepted by William Hayes Ward, editor of the *Independent*, a respectable national journal. His correspondence with Ward suggests the unusual degree of self-confidence building up in the young poet. When questioned about his education, he replied: "If you mean what might be called the legitimate education I have received when you speak of 'training' and 'line of study,' I hope that the quality of my poem would seem to account for far more of this than I have really had. I am only graduated of a public high school. Besides this, a while ago, I was at Dartmouth College for a few months until recalled by necessity. But this inflexible ambition trains us best, and to love poetry is to study it. Specifically speaking, the few rules I know in this art are my own afterthoughts, or else directly formulated from the masterpieces I reread."[5] The gravity and expressive force of a major poet are already audible here, especially when he declares that "inflexible ambition trains us best." A kind of all-consuming *artistic* ambition was, indeed, Frost's own, and part of his genius. He had set his eyes firmly on the path of poetry, and nothing would distract him.

Ward's sister, Susan Hayes Ward, was the managing editor of the journal, and she and Frost began to correspond about the technical aspects of poetry. In these letters, one sees that Frost had certainly

been thinking seriously about literary matters. He explained that he
had been reading extensively:

> When I am well I read a great deal and like a nearsighted person
> follow the text closely. I read novels in the hope of strengthen-
> ing my executive faculties. . . . Thomas Hardy has taught me the
> good use of a few words and, referring still to me, "struck the
> simple solemn." And as opposed to this man, Scott and Steven-
> son inspire me, by their prose, with the thought that we Scotch-
> men are bound to be romanticists—poets. Then as for poems my
> favorites are and have been these: Keats' "Hyperion," Shelley's
> "Prometheus," Tennyson's "Morte D'Arthur," and Browning's
> "Saul"—all of them about the giants. Besides these I am fond of
> the whole collection of Palgrave's.[6]

He goes on to say that he is studying Greek, with the hopes of
being able to read Homer comfortably one day. All of this suggests that
Frost had set himself a program of advancement and was not just
dreaming. He knew that "to love poetry is to study it," and he had no
fear of concentrated work. "My Butterfly" is not one of Frost's best
poems, but the clarity and emotional focus that are the source of his
originality suffuse its lines. This was recognized at once by one of
Frost's earliest readers, the novelist Maurice Thompson, who was sent
the poem for comment by Dr. Ward; he noted that "it has some secret
of genius between the lines, an appeal to sympathy lying deep in one's
sources of tenderness; and moreover its art is singular and biting, even
where the faulty places are almost obtruded. My wife read it aloud to
me the other evening when my eyes ached after too hard a day's work;
and it made me ashamed I could feel discouraged when I thought of
the probable disappointment in store for young Frost all his life long."[7]

This "probable disappointment" was, of course, bedded in the profession of poetry itself, in what T. S. Eliot in "East Coker" characterized as this "raid on the inarticulate / With shabby equipment always
deteriorating / In the general mess of imprecision of feeling." There
may also have been an intuition of the young poet's idealism, which

was bound to be thwarted as he attempted to make his way in a world that cares nothing for poetry.

The job at the mill did not last. One day he arrived late, having overslept, and found the doors locked. "You can't do this to me!" he shouted through the iron grill, to the glowering foreman.[8] The situation was especially traumatic because Belle Frost had recently been relieved of all teaching duties; the Methuen school board had concluded that she was just too unstable to remain in her post. So Frost was now responsible for keeping the family afloat, by whatever means he could invent.

He tried briefly to follow in his father's footsteps, writing occasional pieces for the Lawrence *Daily American* and the weekly *Sentinel*. Initially, he found the prospect of newspaper work appealing, though he later claimed that it involved "too much prying into other people's lives." He abandoned the profession almost before starting it. Soon he paid a call on Clinton Leroy Silver, the head of the Salem, New Hampshire, school board. Several elementary schools lacked teachers, and he was willing to try his hand again at a job he had previously considered disagreeable. Silver found the young man impressive and hired Frost on the spot, at a salary of twenty-four dollars a month; he began teaching in South Salem two days later. This salary equaled what he got at the Arlington Mill, but the hours were far shorter. Moreover, the work of teaching children between the ages of six and twelve was a clear improvement upon his previous teaching situation, where he'd been forced to discipline a pack of unruly adolescents.

Meanwhile, ripples widened from "My Butterfly," that little stone tossed into the public pond. The Wards seemed delighted by their discovery, and they put Frost in touch with various people, including a Congregationalist minister in Lawrence, the Reverend William E. Wolcott, who responded warmly to the poem and wanted to help the young poet. Frost already knew Wolcott slightly, and he was flattered when this respected member of the community offered to serve as his literary adviser. Frost gave him a sheaf of poems, but Wolcott found nothing in the collection equal to "My Butterfly." He suggested that Frost try for a more elevated note; his poetry was too close to the speaking voice, he said. Frost listened impatiently. The speaking voice was all he had, and—although none of this was yet articulated—he hoped to write poetry that would adhere to the bones of human speech. Indeed, this was the precise moment when Frost first began to understand the connection between poetry and ordinary speech. It was, indeed, a "moment of epiphany," as Peter J. Stanlis says. "The discovery that he was after 'poetry that talked' was like a religious revelation to him."[9] Frost himself later observed to Louis Mertins, "Perhaps when that preacher friend of Ward's looked me up shortly after my first poem appeared in the *Independent* and talked to me about it, something providential was happening to me. I'm sure the old gentleman didn't have the slightest idea he was having any effect on a very stubborn youngster who thought he knew what he knew. But something he said actually changed the whole course of my writing. It all became purposeful."[10]

Despite advice from others, Frost was curiously, almost defiantly, unwilling to accept help from external quarters; he wanted to go it alone, to depend only on himself. He even rejected an offer by his grandfather: the elder Frost offered to support him so that he could write full-time for a year, on the condition that if he did not succeed, he must give up trying to be a poet. Frost argued that he would need twenty years to become a recognized poet, and this proved uncannily accurate. *A Boy's Will*, his first collection of poems, would not appear until 1913.

Advice poured in from Susan Hayes Ward as well, beginning a relationship that would last for over twenty years. She insisted that he read Sidney Lanier's *The Science of English Verse*, which put forward notions of musicality in poetry that cut against Frost's grain. The prevailing aesthetic on both sides of the Atlantic favored mellifluous rhythms and a kind of verbal prettiness, as seen in poets like Tennyson, Swinburne, and Dowson in England and Longfellow in America. Miss Ward followed up her letter by sending a copy of Lanier's *Collected Poems*, with a preface by her brother. Frost gritted his teeth and replied warmly, thanking her. But this was not his kind of poetry.

Frost had to restrain his irritability, which he acknowledged (to

Miss Ward) as a character flaw. But this testiness was increased by his feeling that Elinor was enjoying the company of other young men at St. Lawrence University. He feared the competition, and he wanted Elinor there, beside him, sharing his dreams, becoming a part of his intimate world. He went so far as to try to persuade Mrs. White to bring her daughter home, dropping hints that she might not be associating with the best sort of company while away. He warned Elinor herself about the dangers of her situation, and sent her a fiery poem, never collected in a volume:

> The day will come when you will cease to know,
>   The heart will cease to tell you; sadder yet,
> Tho' you say o'er and o'er what once you knew,
>   You will forget, you will forget.
>
> There is no memory for what is true,
>   The heart once silent. Well may you regret,
> Cry out upon it, that you have known all
>   But to forget, but to forget.
>
> Blame no one but yourself for this, lost soul!
>   I fear it would be so that day we met
> Long since, and you were changed. And I said then,
>   She will forget, she will forget.[11]

Elinor found the poem more than a little histrionic, protesting that she was no "lost soul." She made matters worse by mentioning in the same letter the names of various male friends, which sent Frost into a panic. When she returned to Lawrence for the summer, he tried everything he could think of to convince her to marry him at once, but to no avail. She maintained, coolly, that if he managed to establish himself—even in a minimal way—she would marry him after graduation. Frost, for his part, could not hear what she was saying and interpreted her remarks as another rebuff. He was convinced now that she was in love with someone else.

Elinor returned to St. Lawrence, much to Frost's dismay, in the fall of 1894. Deciding that he must do something dramatic to win back her affections, he had printed in an edition of two copies a small volume that contained "My Butterfly" and four other poems; the slim volume was made of handmade paper and bound in rich, brown pebble leather. *Twilight* was stamped in gold on the cover. One copy was his, the other hers. At a time when he could ill afford the train fare, he delivered her volume by hand, arriving unannounced on the campus one evening. When she seemed not to understand the symbolic import of this gesture, he grew wild with despair. His state of mind at the time is clarified by the fact that on the way home he destroyed his own precious copy.[12]

Frost now believed that Elinor had shifted her allegiance to a student at St. Lawrence called Lorenzo Case; furthermore, he imagined that his engagement to Elinor was completely broken. (He carried this conviction into later life, although—according to Elinor—it was without substance.) Back in Lawrence, he received a letter from Elinor that seemed calculated to brush him off. In a fury, he packed a small bag and left home without even a note to his mother.

It was early November, and already the leaves had blown from most of the trees lining the streets in Lawrence; a cold wind from Canada made this one of the chilliest falls in recent history. But Frost sought a place that would mirror his bleak mood exactly, in name as well as character. What came immediately to mind was the Dismal Swamp, which runs along the Virginia–North Carolina border for twenty miles. It had been regarded by poets from Longfellow to Thomas Moore as a place where those who have lost hope run away from the world. Frost could easily see himself as Moore's young lover "who lost his mind upon the death of the girl he loved, and who, suddenly disappearing from his friends, was never afterwards heard of."[13] Frost took the most direct route possible, heading by train from Lawrence to Boston and New York, where he boarded a steamer to Norfolk, Virginia, and began asking around for directions to the Dismal Swamp.

The swamp was, indeed, a frightening place, full of bogs and quicksand. Lake Drummond, near its center, was a black eye in the forest, full of stumps and reeds. A canal pushed through the muck, and it was used by loggers to carry timber (cypress and juniper) out of the woods, although by the 1890s only engine-driven boats could manage its reedy waters. Briars and honeysuckle, cross vine and other thick-growing plants made the surrounding woods a jungle; water moccasins and rattlesnakes lay concealed underfoot. It was no place for the casual walker—especially one dressed, like Frost, in ordinary street clothes, with a light wool overcoat and city shoes.

Frost pressed on, mostly by foot, toward the village of Deep Creek, then set off blindly into the swamp itself. It is interesting that so many of Frost's best later poems—"The Wood-Pile" among them—return to the scene of a lone walker in a swamp or dense forest, which rapidly takes on symbolic aspects. Indeed, if Frost can be said to have an archetypal poem, it is one in which the poet sets off, forlorn or despairing, into the wilderness, where he will either lose his soul or find that gnostic spark of revelation. The pattern of setting out into the unknown, of casting free from the bonds of society and family, is there in everything from "The Sound of the Trees" and "Birches" to "Directive." As in "Traces," a late, uncollected poem, the forest is regarded as a place where barely controllable emotions are subject to the crucible of wilderness experience:

> These woods have been loved in and wept in.
> It is not supposed to be known
> That of two that came loving together
> But one came weeping alone.

Frost had come "weeping alone" in the Dismal Swamp, walking ten miles through tangled briars into the interior as dark settled. "I often think how hard that would have been for Robert," recalled a friend, years later. "He was always terrified of the dark. I would have to go into the house before him at night, to turn on all the lights. It was a thing left over from boyhood."[14] But something stronger than simple fear was pulling Frost forward; he was desperate. The prospect of losing Elinor to another man was more than he could bear, and he preferred oblivion to the anguish of living day by day without her. This mood inhabits the startling first stanza of "Into My Own," with which his first book of poems would open:

> One of my wishes is that those dark trees,
> So old and firm they scarcely show the breeze,
> Were not, as 'twere, the merest mask of gloom,
> But stretched away unto the edge of doom.

The real perils of his walk into the swamp are difficult to calculate, but Frost would certainly have to have been unlucky to die. Indeed, he did not really have the will to push himself to oblivion; when he encountered a group of rowdy duck hunters, he eagerly joined their party, accepting a lift on their boat back to Elizabeth City, North Carolina, and then across Albemarle Sound to Nags Head on the Outer Banks. He tried to hop a freight train home, but after a series of misadventures, he went looking for some relatives in Baltimore. Learning that they had moved to a nearby town, he headed there; when he failed to find them, he was given room and board in exchange for doing odd jobs for a grocer named Williams. A few days later, he was stricken by homesickness and wired his mother for the train fare; his symbolic journey came to an end rather flatly. If he had hoped to prove his independence, he had done just the opposite.

One of the fruits of this strange journey, however, was the poem "Reluctance," where frustrated hopes are mirrored in a dying landscape. It ends with one of Frost's most poignant stanzas:

> Ah, when to the heart of man
>   Was it ever less than treason
> To go with the drift of things,
>   To yield with a grace to reason,
> And bow and accept the end
>   Of a love or a season?

Frost was clearly not willing to "yield with a grace to reason," even though Elinor was not asking him to do this. Nobody overreacted to the young man's self-dramatizing act of disappearance, though all had been worried. And Frost was grateful for their restraint. He decided to approach his life again methodically, and to win Elinor's love by establishing himself in the community. The only job he could imagine for himself was that of journalist, so he began to cast about for a position, encouraged by his mother and grandfather.

A family friend, the Swedenborgian pastor John A. Hayes, introduced him to several newspaper editors in Boston, though nothing came of this. Frost himself approached the Lawrence *American* and was hired, much to his own amazement. "I am a reporter on a local newspaper!" he wrote breathlessly to Susan Ward. But the *American* proved an uncongenial workplace, and Frost returned to his previous post at the *Sentinel*—a job that lasted only until mid-March, when he resigned in frustration, convinced he did not have a gift for daily journalism. The need to write something on call made the act of writing seem too much like hard work; furthermore, he felt it would certainly ruin him as a poet. A poet, he would later say, needed "time when nothing was happening, or seemed to be happening."[15]

Elinor unexpectedly announced that she was coming home for a visit in the third week of March, and asked Frost to meet her at her family home on Spring Street. He nervously agreed. They met in the kitchen, alone, and had a tremendous row. Frost blew up, saying that she no longer believed in him, and that this failure of belief undermined his attempts to make something of himself. Elinor replied that if he insisted on talking this way he could take his ring back. Boldly, she held out her hand. Almost at once, he pulled the ring off her finger, flung it into the coal stove, and stormed out.

Not quite ready to repeat the Dismal Swamp episode, he dashed to Boston to visit his sister, who had recently been hospitalized for an operation. Eager to vent his fury in conversation, he prowled the Harvard campus in Cambridge, looking up two old friends from high school. When he came home, after three days, he found a Swedenborgian prayer meeting under way at his house, led by Pastor Hayes. His mother, noticing her son at the back of the room, passed him a letter that Elinor had hand-delivered to their door. In it, she apologized for the argument, urging him to return to Spring Street.

He did so, but the reconciliation was not perfect. Nevertheless, she had rescued the ring from the fire. There was no tearful embrace, no declaration of undying love. Frost wanted some sort of emotional catharsis, but Elinor held back. A pattern in their relationship was established that would frustrate them both for years to come. It was as if some invisible wall existed between them, and neither could get through it to the other side; but neither could do without the other. They both realized that their futures—for better or worse—were twined, although nothing was said explicitly about marriage.

Frost explained to Elinor that he did have a plan for making a living. His mother believed it would be possible to start a private school at the elementary school level in Lawrence. Dissatisfaction with local schools ran high, so there was clearly an opportunity at hand. Belle had already begun to move by taking on some private pupils, and Jeanie—as her health permitted—had proved eager to help; Belle was now convinced that if everyone (including Elinor) joined forces with her, they could get a school up and running.

That spring, Frost himself began tutoring students in Latin and mathematics; by the end of May, there was so much enthusiasm in Lawrence for the idea of a new school that twenty children had been signed up for the fall term. Frost wrote encouragingly to Elinor—now on the verge of graduation—that the project was going to happen; he held out the fantasy of them all working side by side in their own school.

Elinor liked the idea, and agreed to join in. Frost wanted her to come back immediately to Lawrence, but she had already made arrangements to spend the summer with her sister Leona, who had once again left her husband. A freelance portraitist, Leona had agreed to paint several children of a wealthy businessman who lived at Ossipee Mountain Park, near Lake Winnipesaukee, in New Hampshire. Elinor, herself gifted as an artist, would assist in any way she could—mostly by keeping the children who were not being painted occupied.

Frost could not bear the thought of spending the summer without Elinor, so he followed the White sisters, renting a room in the home of Henry Horne on Ossipee Mountain (now Mount Shaw) in Moultonboro. He spent much of his time tutoring two local boys who were about to enter the Phillips Exeter Academy in the fall. It was a fairly peaceful summer, after so much turmoil, and he loved having Elinor close by, although the vexed nature of their relationship did not change. He complained that she was spending too much time with her sister and ignoring him, and she argued that she had never invited him to Ossipee Mountain in the first place. He would occasionally pass her on a steep mountain path as he hiked into the local village, and they would stop briefly, stare at each other, then pass on. The strange mixture of intimacy and emotional distance that marked these meetings was caught, seventeen years later, in "Meeting and Passing," a haunting poem from *Mountain Interval*. The poem begins:

> *As I went down the hill along the wall*
> *There was a gate I had leaned at for the view*
> *And had just turned from when I first saw you*
> *As you came up the hill. We met. But all*
> *We did that day was mingle great and small*
> *Footprints in summer dust as if we drew*
> *The figure of our being less than two*
> *But more than one as yet. . . .*

At this point, the two lovers were certainly "less than two / But more than one as yet." Their ultimate union was still tentative—more prospect than reality. A distance still gathered between them, awkwardly, whenever they were alone. It was unsettling.

When Frost returned to Lawrence, he discovered that his mother was still unsure enough about the new school to want her son to try to make some money elsewhere. Elinor and she would teach the children, and Jeanie would assist in whatever way she could. Frost agreed, reluctantly, and signed up for another year at the Salem school where, the previous year, he had taught with considerable success. Once again, he would make twenty-four dollars a month—not a lot, but it would help cover the rent on several rooms in an office building in Lawrence that would house Belle's school.

The great problem for Elinor was that, despite inward reservations, she had put herself in a situation where *not* marrying Frost seemed impossible. After all, she had become partners with Belle. Frost fully expected her to marry him before Christmas. On the other hand, her father considered Frost incurably lazy, and therefore a disastrous prospect for his daughter. The young man had shown definite signs of instability: dropping out of Dartmouth, shifting among jobs, throwing temper tantrums. His moodiness was apparent to all who encountered him at this time.

Because of his reservations, Mr. White did not offer a church wedding and made clear that he would refuse even to attend any wedding between Elinor and Robert. But Elinor persisted, encouraged by her mother, and despite her father's absence, the ceremony took place on December 19, 1895, on an icy day just a week before Christmas. The twenty-one-year-old Frost at last married his high school sweetheart, then twenty-three, in one of the rooms of his mother's school. Pastor Hayes, the Swedenborgian, officiated. A high school friend recalled the occasion in a piece written for the Lawrence *Eagle-Tribune*: "I gazed at Robert, and couldn't understand how our happy-go-lucky playmate could change into this solemn young man who replied to the pastor in such serious tones. Congratulations, handshaking, kissing—bewildering! First wedding ever I attended, and I did not like it too well."[16]

The union was finally made, although the ambivalence of Elinor and the frustrations of Robert were never quite resolved. The fact remains, however, that Elinor encouraged and loved him, and served as a permanent muse until her death in 1939. The scenes of their courtship were branded on Frost's unconscious, and would recur frequently in dreams and poems—a perpetual source of inspiration and anxiety.

4 TRIALS BY EXISTENCE
1896–1900

We make ourselves a place apart
Behind light words that tease and flout,
But oh, the agitated heart
Till someone really find us out.

—FROST, FROM "REVELATION"

The honeymoon was postponed until summer, and Frost resumed his duties at the school in Salem shortly after the new year began; Elinor returned to Belle Frost's school. The newlyweds had no money for a place of their own, so they moved in with Belle, who had converted two rooms of the school into a makeshift apartment. These cramped surroundings made for a dire beginning to married life, and Frost soon discovered that he could barely cope.

The feeling that Frost had convinced Elinor to marry him under false pretenses soon arose, though nothing was said. "The whole point about marriage," Frost later remarked, "is learning how *not* to take hints when none were intended. It took me a while to figure this out."[1] The idea had been that the school would carry them all financially, but this seemed less and less likely as the year wore on. Belle Frost could not even meet the rent, and she would have been turned out had it not been for the generosity of her landlords, a couple of Irish brothers named Sweeney, who essentially deferred the payment of her monthly rent indefinitely.

Another spanner was thrown into the works in March, when Elinor discovered she was pregnant. At first, Frost was delighted; but he soon began to suffer sympathetic pains, believing that his own nausea and discomfort exceeded those of his wife. It was with great relief to everyone that, in June, Carl Burell found them an inexpensive cottage in Allenstown, New Hampshire, for the long-postponed honeymoon.

Burell worked in a box factory in Pembroke, near Concord, New Hampshire, but his main interest was botany. He kept an elaborate garden, growing flowers as well as a wide variety of vegetables. One of the unexpected and lasting consequences of Frost's honeymoon was that it sparked an interest in botany, an avocation that would last a lifetime. Indeed, few poets in the English language have been so specific in their knowledge of plants and flowers, or filled their poetry with so much flora and fauna. Burell would read passages from Linnaeus and Darwin to the Frosts, and give them long, entertaining lectures on the cycles of nature. Frost's reading that summer included *How to Know the Wild Flowers*, by Mrs. William Starr Dana, a volume rich in quotations from Emerson, Bryant, Whittier, Longfellow, and Wordsworth—all writers Frost knew and admired. This book also contained extracts from Thoreau's *Journal*, Frost's first introduction to this subtle masterwork of American nature writing. It was here he came upon Thoreau's comment that "a true account of the actual is the purest poetry," which in Frostian terms became "The fact is the sweetest dream that labor knows," a central line in "Mowing." Frost was just learning to become one (to quote Wordsworth) who finds

> *among least things*
> *An undersense of the greatest; sees the parts*
> *As parts, but with a feeling of the whole.*

Frost went for long walks in the woods and meadows around Allenstown, sometimes with Elinor for company but often not; at this stage of her pregnancy, it was difficult for her to take extended walks, especially when climbing was involved. Frost's guilt over going on these walks without her was caught in "Flower-Gathering," which opens:

I left you in the morning,
And in the morning glow
You walked a way beside me
To make me sad to go.

A hint of accusation is apparent here, as if Frost were chiding his wife for purposefully going a little way just to make him feel bad about continuing on by himself. The wife in the poem is somewhat reproachful when her husband appears with a bouquet; he is firm, however, in saying:

They are yours, and be the measure
Of their worth for you to treasure,
The measure of the little while
That I've been long away.

Frost was also compelled to spend a good deal of time away from Elinor at the sickbed of Carl Burell, who had been injured at the box factory that summer. This prompted some bad feelings, too, between the Frosts. A honeymoon is, after all, a time for union and solitude; Frost's need to be away from Elinor for sustained periods would take some getting used to on her part. But, overall, their summer was idyllic, as reflected in "The Quest of the Purple-Fringed," a poem that was not collected into a volume until *A Witness Tree* in 1942; the poem is about the poet's encounter with a cluster of gentians:

I felt the chill of the meadow underfoot,
But the sun overhead;
And snatches of verse and song of scenes like this
I sung or said.

I skirted the margin alders for miles and miles
In a sweeping line.
The day was the day by every flower that blooms,
But I saw no sign.

> Yet further I went to be before the scythe,
> For the grass was high;
> Till I saw the path where the slender fox had come
> And gone panting by.

At last, the poet comes upon "the far-sought flower," with its "purple spires." It is this satisfied quest which leads him to conclude that "the fall might come and whirl of leaves / For summer was done." The poem is full of nostalgia for the summer that has gone before, and there is a powerful sense of needing to lunge forward into the fall, into its organic dissolutions, without resentment or fear. The important thing one sees here is that Frost has developed the patience to wait upon the natural world, and to let its meaning come to him slowly, detail by detail. He was becoming a man like Thoreau, who could enjoy twelve hours "of congenial and familiar converse with the leopard frog."

Returning to Lawrence that fall, the Frosts moved into an apartment on the second floor of a house that Belle Frost had managed to rent on Haverhill Street, near the high school, overlooking the common. It was a tall, wood-frame house with large bay windows, and there was at last enough room for everyone. It was here, on September 25, 1896, that their first child, Elliott, was born. Elinor, who had become increasingly sullen during her pregnancy, suddenly perked up at the birth of the child, and her maternal pleasure in looking after him was gratifying to Frost.

One of the odder events this fall turned on an incident with a boarder, Herbert Parker, who had worked with Frost at the Arlington Mill. Frost considered Parker a friend, and persuaded his mother to rent Parker and his wife a room at the top of their house. All went smoothly until Mrs. Parker upset Elinor by entertaining a certain Mrs. Hindle, reputedly a prostitute. Frost approached Mrs. Parker to discuss the woman in question one day after lunch, and she pointedly called him a coward for bringing up this subject while Herbert was at work. All afternoon Frost seethed, and when Herbert appeared that night, Frost burst into the room and asked if, indeed, he considered Frost a coward. Quite reasonably, Herbert explained that he did consider it cowardly to approach Mrs. Parker while he was away.

A fistfight, initiated by Frost, ensued, and Parker—with a seriously blackened eye—went straight to the police. Frost was brought up before a judge, who listened to both sides of the story, then offered him a choice: a ten-dollar fine or thirty days in jail. Frost took the former, and was further humiliated when one of the local papers, the Lawrence *Daily American*, ran a blow-by-blow account of the fight and the subsequent court appearance on its front page. This was followed by another story, sarcastic in tone, in the *Weekly Journal*. Frost was humiliated in public in a way that he would never forget. In particular, his grandfather told him that the incident had disgraced the family.

"I was living in Amesbury [Massachusetts] one summer, reading Tacitus, when it came to me that maybe I should be studying the classics at Harvard," Frost later told a gathering at Bread Loaf.[2] It was a story he liked to repeat, encapsulating one of those emblematic moments that were part of his self-definition. The truth is, there was now nowhere for him to go but up. By the winter of 1896, he had seemingly hit bottom. It was impossible to make a decent living by teaching elementary school, and he could not afford to raise a family on his own. Boldly, he wrote to Dean LeBaron R. Briggs at Harvard, explaining his situation, and was told that he would have to take a final sequence of entry exams, in Greek, Latin, ancient history, English, French, and physical science (astronomy and physics). With Elinor's help, he managed in a remarkably short while to bring his French (which he had never formally studied) up to an acceptable level, and he passed everything quite easily. He was admitted for the fall term of 1897 as a special student. As before, his education was underwritten by his grandfather, who was so embarrassed by the incident with Herbert Parker that he was glad to get his grandson out of town.

There was no time for Frost to move his family to Cambridge, so he went ahead by himself, taking a room at 16 Rutland Street, just off Massachusetts Avenue; it was a brief walk from there to Harvard Yard. To supplement his grandfather's meager stipend, he found a tutoring job at the Shepard Evening School in North Cambridge; the appointment involved two hours of teaching, three nights per week. The hope was that Elinor and Elliott would follow in the winter term, perhaps with Mrs. White as well.

From the beginning, Frost got on awkwardly with his instructors. He had hoped to be able to skip ahead into advanced English composition, but the professor in charge of freshman writing, a supercilious man called John Hayes Gardner, ridiculed him for thinking that because he had published a few poems he qualified for anything more than basic freshman English. "So we're a writer, are we?" he asked. Frost did not protest, but he was furious. It seemed that wherever he turned, insult followed injury.

His instructor in English A was Alfred Sheffield, a twenty-six-year-old man whom students called "the bearded lady." He asked the students to compose a poem in class on the subject of autumn, and Frost quickly jotted down from memory one of his own verses:

> Now close the windows and hush all the fields:
>   If the trees must, let them silently toss;
> No bird is singing now, and if there is,
>   Be it my loss.
>
> It will be long ere the marshes resume,
>   It will be long ere the earliest bird:
> So close the windows and not hear the wind,
>   But see all wind-stirred.

The poem had been written in 1892, at Dartmouth, then tinkered with over the years; it eventually appeared in A Boy's Will. But Mr. Sheffield found it highly unsatisfactory, especially because it was not actually composed on the spot. Frost dared to show him another poem, "The Tuft of Flowers," and that was rebuffed as well. Quite rightly, Frost found this attitude toward his work intolerable. Yet he was in no position to resign from Harvard in a huff; he must get through the term, through the year; he must eventually earn his degree. If he were to support a family, there was no other choice.

He fared better in Latin and Greek, studying with Maurice W. Mather and Frank Cole Babbitt, two highly regarded teachers at Harvard. In Babbitt's Greek course he studied epic verse—and got straight A's; Theocritus and Greek pastoral verse would have to wait until the next year, but he did (under Mather) work his way carefully through the Latin pastoral poets. He also excelled in Latin versification, and this study formed the basis for much of his own thinking on the technical aspects of English prosody.

Midway through the academic year, Mrs. White arrived with Elinor and Elliott, and they all moved into a small apartment. Frost felt that everything was finally going to work out for him. The women cooked and cleaned the apartment, did the laundry, looked after his son, and generally made life easy for him to think and study. Money, however, was still dreadfully short, so it was to everyone's relief when, at the end of the spring term, he was awarded a two-hundred-dollar scholarship for excellence in his studies. This confirmation of his abilities could not have come at a better time.

That summer, financed by Frost's grandfather, the family retreated once again to Amesbury, renting the same house. Frost took long walks in the woods, read and wrote poetry, and worked to make further gains in Latin and Greek. He was also reading *The Will to Believe*, by William James, the brother of Henry, and hoped that he might take a course with James when he returned. Always sensitive to the underlying tone of whatever he read, Frost found in James a sympathetic spirit: a man racked by self-doubts and religious skepticism who nevertheless understood that one must have a degree of faith—in oneself and in the nature of the universe—to proceed at all. James was a depressive by nature, like Frost, and his massive intellectual formulations were the philosophical equivalent of Frost's "momentary stays" against confusion. (When Frost began teaching at the Pinkerton Academy, a decade later, he regularly assigned readings by James.)

The influence of James on Frost was profound, and continued long after his time at Harvard, as critics from Richard Poirier to Robert Faggen have shown. In particular, James's *Principles of Psychology* attracted Frost. As Daniel Wilson has noted, James's volume was not so much a survey of the state of psychology as a book that "expressed aptly the pluralism, even confusion, of an era slowly and painfully shedding its reliance on theology and philosophy as the touchstones of culture and yet not ready to declare its allegiance to science."[3]

Professor James, unfortunately, had been granted a leave of absence, due to illness, for the next academic year, so Frost was denied direct access to the man he so admired. He did, however, take a course in philosophy, where James's textbook introduction to psychology was central. In James, he found a fellow skeptic, and he admired the philosopher's approach to the concept of selfhood, which according to James exists as a kind of social fiction, many-faceted, thus allowing a single person to appear differently to different people. In the healthy person, this occurs as a natural separation of parts, harmonious and ultimately integrated on some higher level of consciousness; or, less healthily, it may become manifest as "a discordant splitting, as where one is afraid to let one set of his acquaintances know him as he is elsewhere."[4]

Like Frost, James was a believer in "will," in what Frost had earlier called "inflexible ambition." As Robert Faggen has ably shown, this notion was central to James and Frost, and derived largely from Darwin, whose "model of natural selection was adopted by James as a model for the process of encompassing all of the ideas of change, contingency, and fallibility that one finds in the evolutionary productions of nature."[5] The individualism of Emerson, which Frost had always found "inspiring but a little vague,"[6] was given a certain toughness and clarity by James, and Frost heartily approved. He also found appealing James's idea of heroic models—another version of Emerson's notion of "representative men." James argued that "just as our courage is so often a reflex of another's courage, so our faith is apt to be a faith in someone else's faith. We draw deeply from the heroic example."[7]

In his second year at Harvard Frost did manage to study under one of the great figures in the philosophy department, George Santayana, a Spanish-born aesthetician who also wrote poetry and fiction. Santayana was only eleven years Frost's senior, but his distinguished publishing record and patrician aura had quickly made him an important figure on the faculty. Santayana's personal philosophy, grounded in a careful study of Greek aesthetics, was skeptical in complex ways; he considered religion an expression of symbolic truth rather than literal truth, a point not lost on Frost, who had been quietly entertaining his own religious doubts for many years.

William James had been Santayana's teacher, and the pupil had understood his teacher's basic position on faith, that one can believe anything one wishes, as long as it remains useful and is "live enough to tempt."[8] In fact, Santayana's belief in religion as a form of poetry and poetry as the essence of any spiritual understanding of the world would have a shaping influence on Frost's important contemporary Wallace Stevens, who believed that the job of poetry was "to supply the satisfactions of belief" in a time when these satisfactions were no longer available through conventional religious forms. Frost always kept a wary distance between himself and Santayana, remaining canny if not coy when it came to his own religious views.[9] Indeed, he eventually fashioned a blend of skepticism and mysticism uniquely his own: sly, irreverent, pragmatic. But one can easily imagine that Frost modeled some aspects of his later persona on Santayana, whose classroom presentations at Harvard were marked by a certain wry detachment, a playful sense of humor, and an evasive wit.

Frost also studied with Josiah Royce, an important figure in American philosophy. Royce was, like James, a devotee of Darwin, and Frost would have learned a good deal about evolutionary theory from two lectures in particular that were offered the year Frost was there: "The Rise of the Doctrine of Evolution" and "Nature and Evolution: The Outer World and Its Paradox." Royce was preoccupied with reconciling idealism (or Platonism) with the realities of natural science, and he passed these concerns on to Frost, who continued to think and write about this issue for many decades. In poems like "The Demiurge's Laugh" and "Design," he reflects on this philosophical conflict, taking different positions at different stages of his development. Even toward the end of his life, he "often talked about James, Darwin, and the problem of faith in a world that seems to value scientific truth over religious or poetic truth."[10]

Meanwhile, Elinor had become pregnant during the summer, so it seemed best for Elinor and Elliott to remain with her parents in Lawrence. Frost was thus thrown back upon solitary living during his second year, moving into a boardinghouse on Oxford Street. Lonely, he often rejoined his family on holidays and, increasingly, for long weekends. When he was by himself in Cambridge, he tended to roam the campus in a desultory fashion, dropping in on courses he was not officially taking. Among the influential teachers he encountered were George Lyman Kittredge, who would make his name as one of Harvard's most distinguished teachers of English literature, and Nathaniel Southgate Shaler, who taught geology, a subject that would become an abundant source of metaphors for Frost in later years. He also studied the Greek pastoral poets under Professor Babbitt, a crucial experience for a poet who would revitalize, even reinvent, the pastoral tradition in American verse.

Frost did so well during his first semester that he was awarded a prize for excellence in classical studies. The feelings of academic failure that had clung to him since he left Dartmouth were washed away at Harvard. Nevertheless, he already knew that he was not going to stick it out. "They could not make a student of me here," he later told an assembly of Harvard students, "but they gave it their best." By March, he was suffering from what he called "nervous exhaustion," but this was simply another version of the depression that would haunt him periodically to the end. As usual, he would locate and substantiate his psychic distress in physical ailments, and he took to his bed for days on end, complaining of headaches, night sweats, and breathing problems. The fear of tuberculosis—quite natural, given his father's death—was always ready to hand, and he began to imagine the worst. "I had to leave Harvard because of my health," he later said. "My heart was bad, and my stomach." On top of this, Elinor's pregnancy was going poorly; she wrote constantly of back pain, nausea, and exhaustion. Only too eager for a good cause to do so, Frost decided to withdraw from Harvard.

This time, however, he would not turn tail and run without telling anyone. He went directly to the office of Dean Briggs and explained his predicament. Briggs volunteered a letter attesting to the young man's honorable departure: "I am glad to testify that your dismissal from College is honorable; that you have had excellent rank here, winning a Detur as a result of your first year's work; and that I am sorry for the loss of so good a student. I shall gladly have you refer to me for your College record."[11]

One can never really know what goes into the making of a poet, but surely Frost's encounter with Greek and Latin poetry at Harvard, and elsewhere, was significant. He told an interviewer that he "probably read more Latin and Greek than [Ezra] Pound," and this was no exaggeration. He explained, "When I came back to college after running away, I thought I could stand it if I stuck to Greek and Latin and philosophy. That's all I did in those years."[12] In fact, Frost felt so confident of his abilities as a classicist that he once thought of teaching a course on Latin versification at Harvard, and in 1916 he addressed a convention of classicists with a talk called "The Discipline of the Classics and the Writing of English"—a lecture that foreshadows one that T. S. Eliot would give decades later called "Education and the Classics."

Frost was actually more of a classicist by training than either Eliot or Pound, who tended to wear their erudition on their shirtsleeves. "From Pound down to Eliot," Frost wrote to his daughter Lesley, in the 1930s, "they have striven for distinction by a show of learning, Pound in Old French, Eliot in forty languages. They quote and you try to see if you can place the quotation. Pound really has great though inaccurate learning. Eliot has even greater."[13]

Though easily as learned as Eliot or Pound, Frost held a view of education that was very different from theirs, more egalitarian and less pompous. Especially in reading Eliot, one senses that education is a kind of class marker, a way of separating the intellectual sheep from the goats. Frost's goal, as an educator, was to teach what he called freedom: "The freedom I'd like to give is the freedom I'd like to have. It's the freedom of my material. You might define a schoolboy as one who could recite to you everything he read last night, in the order in which he read it. That's just the opposite of what I mean by a free person. The person who has the freedom of his material is the person who puts two and two together, and the two and two are anywhere out of space and time, and brought together. One little thing mentioned, perhaps, reminds him of something he couldn't have thought of for twenty years."[14]

By the time Frost left Harvard, he had read enough in the classics, and enough in the standard repertory of English and American poetry as well as world philosophy, that he was beginning to have the kind of associational freedom he treasured, the range and flexibility that would characterize his thought and animate his poetry. Frost enjoyed a rich intellectual life to the end, and read widely in a range of subjects from literature and philosophy to geology and astronomy. His grand-daughter Lesley Lee Francis, for example, recalled "his reading *The Tragic Sense of Life* by Unamuno, the Spanish philosopher, in a single night, and wanting urgently to discuss it the next day."[15] That was when he was well over the age of seventy.

Frost returned to Lawrence from Cambridge in April, believing that the separation from Elinor had unsettled him emotionally, and that once reunited with her he would feel better. As it happened, he felt immediately worse upon arrival, and took to his bed, even though Eli-nor was eight months pregnant. A local doctor whom he trusted stopped by one day to check on him and said forcefully that he must change his sedentary way of life, which only exacerbated his symp-toms; he recommended farming as a plausible occupation for someone with Frost's temperament. This was, in retrospect, the best piece of advice he ever got.

The idea of poultry farming had always appealed to him, ever since the days in San Francisco when he'd raised a few baby chicks in the backyard of the house on Leavenworth Street. Frost picked up on this notion at once and consulted Dr. Charlemagne C. Bricault, a veteri-narian who raised chickens in the countryside near Methuen. Dr. Bricault, though only seven years older than Frost, welcomed a pro-tégé; he agreed to sell the younger man enough incubator eggs to get a business going and helped him find a place near his own farm to rent: a small clapboard house and rickety barn on a knoll called Powder House Hill. From the front steps, one got a splendid view of the sur-rounding woods and meadows. It was owned by a fussy woman in late middle age, Miss Mary Mitchell, who lived in Methuen. Frost was introduced to her by Dr. Bricault, and she agreed to rent the place cheaply. The young man turned, as usual, to his grandfather for a loan. Farming was, Frost later said, "a practical way to earn a living, although I'd not yet shown a talent for practicality." The Frosts moved into their new home in June, shortly after the birth of their second child, Lesley, on April 28, 1899.

Though never especially handy in the past, Frost quickly adapted; he built incubators from raw lumber and took delivery of the eggs from Dr. Bricault. With two young children, a farm, and a renewed sense of energy, Frost thought the future looked surprisingly rosy. But trouble lay ahead. Belle Frost, who had been losing weight rapidly throughout the spring, was diagnosed with advanced cancer and given less than a year to live. She did not complain, however, and moved in with Rob and Elinor at Powder House Hill. It comforted her to see her son working so happily at farming, which appeared to suit him. She saw that Frost had taken eagerly to the ritual life of agriculture, with its appointed rounds and predictable rhythms.

The fall and winter were blessedly mild, and Frost was pleased as one batch of chickens was sold, and another begun. Frost's physical health, always closely connected to his mental health, took a robust turn for the better. Even his mother's cancer (which seemed to have gone temporarily into remission) did not get him down, especially since she was able to help with looking after Elliott and Lesley.

The tranquillity of the household was soon disturbed by an unexpected illness in Elliott, who began to experience severe digestive problems; his stomach was often cramped, and he ran terrifyingly high fevers at night. The local doctor who visited Belle every other week was now consulted about the boy. Digestive pills were prescribed, but these seemed not to help. Making matters worse, Mrs. White had recently converted to Christian Science, and she argued with her daughter that a doctor could not help the boy; they must all pray for God's help. Frost scoffed at this, but delayed taking action. In early July, when the boy began vomiting helplessly, Frost called in his own doctor, a well-known physician from Lawrence. "It's too late now," the doctor said, barely able to control his anger. "The child will be dead by morning." Elliott had apparently contracted a severe case of typhoid fever.

Elinor, stunned, stayed by the child all night, as did Frost. Elliott died at 4:00 A.M. on July 8, 1900, with his parents beside him. It was horrific for them both, although Frost blamed himself for not calling a good doctor sooner: it was "like murdering his own child," he said.[16] Elinor slipped helplessly into a deep depression, saying that if there was a God, he was malevolent. Her husband preferred to think that heaven was simply indifferent to human suffering, referring in "Stars"—a poem written near the time of Elliott's death—to "Those stars like some snow-white / Minerva's snow-white marble eyes / Without the gift of sight." His own gloss on this poem in the table of contents to A Boy's Will rephrases the point of these lines: "There is no oversight of human affairs." The goddess of wisdom, Minerva, is less than useless to the poet, who can find no consolation from above, who cannot believe in a rational or just universe.

Frost would often return in his finest lyric moments to the idea that God is not in heaven and all is not right with the world, as at the end of "Design," where he writes, "What but design of darkness to appall?— / If design govern in a thing so small," referring to a small aberration in the natural order that he has observed—a white spider with a dead white moth on a white (instead of blue) heal-all. If even this travesty signals a malevolent or nonexistent God, how much more evidence is to be found in the death of a helpless child?

The death of a child is, indeed, at the center of two of his greatest early poems: "Home Burial" and " 'Out, Out—'." The former, a long dramatic poem about a young couple on a farm who have lost a child, was written in England, and may have been triggered by his recollection of Elliott's death. The poem came to him in a blaze, having been smoldering for years: "I was not over two hours with 'Home Burial,' " he recalled to an interviewer, perhaps exaggerating slightly for effect. "It stands in print as it was in the first draft."[17] Frost's close friend Sidney Cox observed that the "poem was too close to home, bringing back memories of the death at three and a half of his firstborn child,

Elliott, at the Powder House Hill farm, some fifteen years before. 'Home Burial' (the very title has double meaning) evoked strongly the differing ways Frost and his wife, Elinor, responded to Elliott's death. He covered his pain with talking, she with silence."[18] (Frost himself always said the idea for this poem, in fact, came from a recollection of the death of Elinor's sister's child, perhaps hoping to dissuade naive readers from jumping quickly to biographical conclusions when reading his poems, which were never intended as a record of literal events.)

Certainly the experience of having lost a child made a permanent mark on Frost. Even half a century after Elliott's death, in the play *A Masque of Mercy* (1947), Frost in the guise of Jonah would say, "She's had some loss she can't accept from God," which suggests that he was still obsessed by the child's death on some level, or would at least find it a source of pain that could be converted into poetic language. "The poet rubs his finger on old wounds, makes them burn," he once told an audience at Bread Loaf.[19] Indeed, one can see him using his own burdens ingeniously, with poetry as a way of making sense of them; the pain must also be seen as a kind of magnet, drawing his poetic needle toward the true north of authentic feeling.

One must be careful when using poems, which are constructs of the imagination, as though they were mere transcriptions of a poet's experience; indeed, Frost's previous biographers have been particularly faulty in this regard. The most one can venture here is that the death of Elliott gave Frost a bitter firsthand experience of loss that would pick away at him, and be reconstituted in poem after poem, often coming out in ways a reader could never calculate. One can hardly assume that Elinor was like the wife in "Home Burial," deeply resentful of her husband's covert grieving and his attempts to relieve his grief through the act of burying the child himself. The husband in that rueful, endlessly subtle poem says: "Three foggy mornings and one rainy day / Will rot the best birch fence a man can build," thus exorcizing his own grief, or making sense of it, through metaphor. The wife, of course, interprets this line as sheer indifference instead of understanding it as another (more male, Frost seems to be suggesting) way of mourning:

"Think of it, talk like that at such a time!" As in so many of his dramatic poems, Frost dwells on points of miscommunication, the fathomless depths of isolation inherent in all acts of utterance, the gaps that cannot be bridged by words. "Poems are about what you don't mean as well as what you do mean," he would say at his readings. And his poems, too, are as often as not about what he didn't mean, about what language cannot signify, however hard it tries. In moments like this, one locates Frost's early modernism, and sees how a line opens from "Home Burial" to *Waiting for Godot*.

In " 'Out, Out—' " the narrator says of the grief-stricken family, who has just lost a boy in a buzz-saw accident: "And they, since they / Were not the one dead, turned to their affairs." However heartless these lines have sounded to some ears, Frost is making a point about a way of dealing with grief; by plunging back into the affairs of life, which demand attention (especially in the context of a poor farm at the turn of the century), the grieving family is able to work through grief. In this same way, the Frosts could not simply stop in their tracks after Elliott's passing. Lesley, for a start, was only fourteen months old when her brother died, and she was herself unwell, suffering from strange fevers and rashes. Furthermore, the chickens needed tending. There was also the health of Belle Frost, which had begun to deteriorate again. Having so much to deal with at once, Frost not surprisingly found his old symptoms returning: stomachaches, headaches, breathing problems. Although he was commonly afflicted with hay fever at this time of the year, he became convinced again that he was now in the early stages of tubercular disease.

On the advice of her doctor, Belle moved into the Alexander Sanatorium in nearby Penacook, New Hampshire, in mid-August. It was a crisp, no-nonsense sort of place, with about twenty-five beds; Belle knew several people there, and she was not unhappy to go. Frost was relieved, but Jeanie, who now lived in Boston, believed that her brother had turned out Belle because she had become a burden. This led to tensions between brother and sister that made Frost extremely unhappy.

Making matters worse, Miss Mitchell, the landlady of Powder

House Hill farm, stopped by one day to see if she could get any of the rent that was due (the Frosts were several months behind in payments) and was appalled by the sight of chickens wandering into every nook and cranny of the property. She also saw that the house was filthy, the dishes unwashed, the floors unswept. She decided she had had enough of the undisciplined Frosts, and she wrote a letter the next day telling them to get out by the end of the month.

Aware that her daughter and son-in-law were in desperate straits, Mrs. White began asking about for another place for them. A fellow Christian Scientist told her about a farm on thirty acres in Derry, a town of five thousand residents, in Rockingham County, just to the north of Salem and roughly twelve miles from Lawrence; it boasted a relatively new farmhouse, a barn, and an apple orchard. Better yet, the price was right: $1,700. Even in 1900, this was a good deal: the Derry town records show that few farms of this size sold for less than $2,000 between 1895 and 1910, while a good many sold for much more.

Elinor, making a wise move, went quietly to Frost's grandfather, who had thus far been reasonably impressed by his grandson's efforts at poultry farming. She asked for help in buying the Derry farm, and the elder Frost agreed to put up the money if the house could pass inspection by Frost's great-uncle, Elihu Colcord. The house, known locally as "the Magoon place" (to this day, most farms in northern New England are named after their previous owner), proved ideal; it was nestled snugly in rolling countryside, with hills and ridges for a view. One could easily get into Derry Village, two miles away, by horse and buggy. The house itself was white clapboard, with a gabled roof and newly painted green shutters. The apple orchard on the north side of the house was ripe for picking: Northern Spies, Gravensteins, Baldwins, and other varieties would soon be ready for market. Because the previous owner had been interested in fruit farming, there were also plenty of peach, pear, and quince trees.

From all sides of the house the view was appealing. Beyond a rolling hay field to the east, one saw a large woodlot, composed mostly of maple, oak, and beech. On the south side a stand of alders concealed a west-running brook fed by a pasture spring. A cranberry bog lay nearby. Patches of raspberries and blackberries grew beside the barn, where a sizable vegetable garden could also be found, its contents ready for harvest. There was plenty of space where one might build chicken coops on the north side, beyond the barn.

The house was substantial, though not large. Three bedrooms were found on the second floor; on the first were a small country parlor and another large room that doubled as a living and dining room. There was another bedroom on the lower floor, and access to an ell, which contained the kitchen, with its large iron woodstove, and the pantry, where the newly painted cabinets provided lots of storage space. Beyond the ell were a woodshed and, as usual, an outdoor privy.

Uncle Elihu shared the enthusiasm of the young couple, and he agreed that the price was remarkably good. Grandfather Frost was satisfied, too, though he insisted that Robert allow Carl Burell to come and help. (The elder Frost contacted Burell on his own to see if he might help Robert settle into farming, and Burell agreed on the condition that his eighty-four-year-old father come as well.) William Frost knew that his grandson was still a novice when it came to farming, and he wanted nothing to go wrong this time around. Frost was apparently annoyed that he was given so many conditions, but he could hardly show ingratitude in the face of so much generosity. There was also the fact that he liked Carl very much, and welcomed his company.

The move took place on the first day of October and was tersely recorded by the local *Derry News*: "R. Frost has moved upon the Magoon place which he recently bought. He has a flock of nearly 300 Wyandotte fowls." Thus began what is unquestionably the most important phase of Frost's long life, the period when he came into close contact for the first time with the material that would furnish him with a lifetime of imagery. He would learn to take metaphors where he found them, often in the rustic world around him. And he would find poetry in the speech of the outwardly unremarkable men and women who lived on the surrounding farms, many of whom he came into contact with as a working poultryman. "It all started in Derry," Frost later remarked, "the whole thing."

5 — A FARM IN DERRY
1901–1905

> *To a large extent the terrain of my poetry is the Derry landscape,*
> *the Derry farm. Poems growing out of this, though composite, were*
> *built on incidents and are therefore autobiographical. There was*
> *something about the experience at Derry which stayed in my mind,*
> *and was tapped for poetry in the years that came after.*
>
> —FROST TO LOUIS MERTINS

The years spent at the farm in Derry, roughly from the fall of 1900 until the house was sold in November 1911, might be thought of as a chrysalis in which the young poet could mature. By the time he emerged at the end of this decade of farming, writing, and teaching, he would be fully formed: a major modern poet who had found his voice. Many of his best poems were written in these years, too, forming the bulk of his first two volumes, *A Boy's Will* and *North of Boston*. In fact, later volumes—right up through *A Witness Tree* (1942)—would be seeded with poems (often in rough-draft form) composed during this fertile period. To the end of his life, he would draw on imagery and incidents from this time.

One of the unexpected boons of the Derry years was a small group of friends who would mean a great deal to him in retrospect. This aspect of life in Derry, Frost later admitted, in his poem "New Hampshire," had come as a surprise:

I hadn't an illusion in my handbag
About the people being better there
Than those I left behind. I thought they weren't.
I thought they couldn't be. And yet they were.
I'd sure had no such friends in Massachusetts
As Hall of Windham, Gay of Atkinson,
Bartlett of Raymond (now of Colorado),
Harris of Derry, and Lynch of Bethlehem.

But these friends did not come easily and quickly to the reclusive and shy Frost, who kept to himself and his family at first.

During these years both Frosts were working to overcome their immense grief over the loss of Elliott. That sort of pain never really goes away; it is simply dulled. But Frost, more than Elinor, was a survivor by nature, and inflexible ambition kept him going, as always. Even so, he did not attempt to publish any poetry during his first six years in Derry. Instead, he devoted himself, despite later rumors (generated by himself) to the contrary, to the daily rituals of farm life.

Carl Burell (and sometimes Carl's father) worked side by side with Frost, building hen coops, picking apples and pears, tending livestock. Burell's optimism and energy far outshone that of Frost, who soon came to resent this friend thrust upon him by his grandfather. Burell was a constant reminder that his grandfather did not fully trust his abilities. Nevertheless, the two worked well enough together, and Frost was grateful for the company. Elinor's silences, now as always, upset him; Burell, on the other hand, was talkative, more so than Frost. The two of them often simply took off into the woods for the day, on what Frost would call a "botanizing walk."

Frost's own accounts of farming life, in later years, would emphasize his laziness, as when he told Louis Mertins that his neighbors in Derry "would see me starting out to work at all hours of the morning—approaching noon, to be more explicit. I always liked to sit up all hours of the night planning some inarticulate crime, going out to work when the spirit moved me, something they shook their heads ominously at, with proper prejudice. They would talk among themselves about my lack of energy. I was a failure in their eyes from the start."[1] One must always take care when dealing with this sort of statement from Frost; like all poets, perhaps, he liked to mythologize himself, and had a vested interest in putting forward certain views of himself. The idea that he might have been a reasonably hardworking farmer in these years was not consistent with the persona he had been busily inventing for himself.

Dr. Bricault was still involved in Frost's venture, handling the marketing end of the poultry business for him with enthusiasm. Almost no farmers were making a good living in New Hampshire at the turn of the century, and Frost did not do badly, given that the soil was poor, the winters harsh, and the economy stagnant. His modest enterprise was subsistence farming, with eggs and apples supplying enough cash to meet the needs of his family. "I was a poor farmer in those days," Frost later said, "but rich, too. There was plenty of food, and time, too. Lots of time. I was time-rich."[2]

Belle Frost had been hit hard by the death of Elliott, too; she saw its effect on Elinor and Rob and was troubled by their lack of religious faith. Jeanie Frost was among the first visitors to the Derry farm, although she came mostly to scold her brother for failing to pay enough attention to Belle, who was clearly dying. Chastened, Frost went to see his mother at Penacook, driving there in the horse and buggy that he and Burell had just bought in Lawrence for twenty-five dollars—on a further loan from Frost's grandfather. He was shocked by her condition: she was thoroughly wasted by the cancer, and her voice was barely audible. Leaving Penacook, he knew he would probably never see her again. Indeed, Belle died shortly thereafter, and the funeral oration was given by her Swedenborgian friend John Hayes; she was, he said, "one to whom religion was a way of life." She was buried in Lawrence between the graves of her husband and Elliott.

That Frost was struggling to keep his chin above water is evident from "Despair," written at this time but never included by him in a volume because of its self-pitying stance. The poem turns oppressively self-accusatory at the end:

> I am like a dead diver in this place.
> I was alive here too one desperate space,

And near prayer in the one whom I invoked.
I tore the muscles from my limbs and choked.
My sudden struggle may have dragged down some
White lily from the air—and now the fishes come.[3]

Another early poem, probably written in the spring of 1900, was "Mowing," which Frost told Sidney Cox he considered the best poem in *A Boy's Will*.[4] He called it a "talk song," and it catches in uncanny ways the sound of the speaking voice, although there is nothing casual about it. Frost has made sure to lace the voice tightly to the frame of a sonnet format:

There was never a sound beside the wood but one,
And that was my long scythe whispering to the ground.
What was it it whispered? I knew not well myself;
Perhaps it was something about the heat of the sun,
Something, perhaps, about the lack of sound—
And that was why it whispered and did not speak.
It was no dream of the gift of idle hours,
Or easy gold at the hand of fay or elf:
Anything more than the truth would have seemed too weak
To the earnest love that laid the swale in rows,
Not without feeble-pointed spikes of flowers
(Pale orchises), and scared a bright green snake.
The fact is the sweetest dream that labor knows.
My long scythe whispered and left the hay to make.

The poem shows Frost in complete mastery of the sonnet form, and free enough to move away from any obvious, conventional patterns of rhyming. Rhythmically, the poem mimics the action of mowing, beginning with a double anapest in the first line, which quickly falls into a straightforward iambic foot. The second line might be called "sprung rhythm," to use Gerard Manley Hopkins's term for irregular meters. Essentially, Frost (like Hopkins) counts only the strong beats in the line:

And thát was my lóng scythe whíspering to the gróund.

This line, whose near twin had already been used in "The Tuft of Flowers" ("And hear his long scythe whispering to the ground"), is typical of Frost at his best: the rhythm comes perilously close to prose, but is lifted just enough so that it stays inside the boundary lines of verse. One can hear the poet talking here: the rough-hewn New England accent not tripping along or lunging from stress to stress but giving almost equal weight to each vowel sound. In later years, Frost would frequently refer to what he called "the sound of sense," as in a letter to John Bartlett from England in 1913: "The sound of sense. You get that. It is the abstract vitality of our speech. It is pure sound—pure form. One who concerns himself with it more than the subject is an artist." He claimed that "an ear and an appetite for these sounds of sense is the first qualification of a writer, be it of prose or verse. But if one is to be a poet he must learn to get cadences by skillfully breaking the sounds of sense with all their irregularity of accent across the regular beat of the metre."[5]

This is the essence of Frost's theory of poetry: the writer has to contend with the abstract possibility of the line. (In iambic pentameter, for instance, he deals with five feet in each line of verse, each foot comprising one unstressed and one stressed beat.) Every line of "Mowing," therefore, is written with a covert feeling for the abstract line: *dee-dum, dee-dum, dee-dum, dee-dum, dee-dum.* But spoken English does not comfortably or naturally fit a rigid line, or rarely does. Only one line—"(Pale orchises), and scared a bright green snake"—comes even close to lockstep iambic pentameter, and even there one has to pretend that "pale" and "green" are unstressed, which is clearly not the case. The poetry, in Frost as in most good poets, occurs in the difference between the abstract possibility of the line and its vernacular performance, where stresses fall as they do normally in human speech. Without that slight tug toward the formally perfect line, however remote, there would be no poetry. The form, indeed, makes the poetry possible.

"Mowing" is, like all of Frost's work, playful in the extreme. Frost would have been aware that "mowing" was also a traditional euphemism for lovemaking, thus giving a distantly erotic echo to the last phrase: "and left the hay to make." More to the point, he was writing about physical labor, one of the few poets in the language to make good poems out of real work. But this work is endlessly compromised by the poet's inner voice, which keeps wanting to create meaning out of what is inherently meaningless: the rhythmical sway of the scythe as it mows down the high grass. The poem is, as much as anything, about the impulse to impose meaning, this peculiar urge to talk about "fay or elf," when there is really nothing so fantastic at hand. Frost commented on this line years later, at Bread Loaf, saying that "poetry is not getting up fanciful things."[6]

In the same talk, he said that "a definition of poetry" was to be found in the line "The fact is the sweetest dream that labor knows." One interpretation of this line might be that the imagination of the actual is superior to "made up" things. William H. Pritchard, wisely, points us in the direction of Emerson to understand the last two lines of the poem.[7] Emerson, in *Nature* (1836), wrote:

> Undoubtedly we have no questions to ask which are unanswerable. We must trust the perfection of the creation so far as to believe that whatever curiosity the order of things has awakened in our minds, the order of things can satisfy. Every man's condition is a solution in hieroglyphic to those inquiries he would put. He acts it as life, before he apprehends it as truth.

The tone of the above passage is buoyantly Emersonian, not skeptically Frostian, but the last line might be seen as a gloss on "Mowing." One must inhabit the factuality of life, embrace it, then slowly come to understand its ideality, its loftier "truth." The "work of knowing" (as Richard Poirier puts it)[8] is, always, a mysterious process; one plunges in, gets to work, and slowly comes to understand some aspect of life. "Anything more than the truth would have seemed too weak / To the earnest love that laid the swale in rows": the imagination must not override or outdistance the truth (by which Frost refers to the reality of everyday experience) but come into its orbit, its ambience; the imagination of reality is the essential poetic act, not reality versus the imagination.

The poem is endlessly complex, as Katherine Kearns has suggested. It is "earnest love," she notes, that "laid the swale in rows," thus "biting off the spikes of orchises and scaring the bright green snake." She suggests that a love that "leaves the hay to make also lays bare the potential simultaneity of desire and of pain as the long scythe whispers to the ground," adding that "it cannot be entirely accidental that Frost chose the spiked orchis (órchis is the Greek word for 'testicle') to be sliced by the loving scythe or that, coupled as it is with the startled snake, the flower, so earnestly loved, becomes sexualized, in one moment uncovered and eradicated."[9]

The poem is appealing on so many levels. There is first the lovely sound of the poem, with its countless internal rhymes and half rhymes: note how the word "sound" in the first line, for example, is picked up as the end rhyme of the second line. There is the subtle alliteration: the "w" sound, for example, that goes from "wood" to "one" in the first line to "was" and "whispering" in the second line to "What was" and "whispered" in the third line—thus giving a remarkable sense of motion to the poem. Beyond this, there is the literal description of the act of mowing, rendered in concrete detail, simply, without the slightest affectation, as the poem gathers around a single, deep image: that of a man mowing. Finally, there are the metaphorical levels, the endlessly suggestive layers of meaning that make this a poem about writing, a poem about the process of knowing, a poem about the sexual act and what it means, and a poem about the elusive relations that exist between "fact" and "truth" and the role of the imagination in this interaction.

Frost was not writing poems openly now. He was farming openly, and did not want his neighbors—or even Carl Burell—to know about his poetry. Once in 1901 he did send out a small packet of new poems to Susan Hayes Ward ("The Quest of the Orchis" was sent out and accepted in January 1901). But there were no more packets of poetry for five years after this. Frost was buried deep in daily life and in wide reading, which included a careful rereading of *Walden*—urged upon him by Burell. This classic of American autobiography seemed to speak to him directly: "I went to the woods because I wished to live deliberately, to front only the essential facts of life, and see if I could not learn what it had to teach, and not, when I came to die, discover that I had not lived." This passage from Thoreau, which Frost often quoted in later years, must have echoed in his head. He was himself engaged upon a deliberate act of living, fronting the essential facts of his life.

In the summer of 1901, his first summer on the Derry farm, his grandfather died unexpectedly in his sleep. In his will, the good feelings he harbored toward his grandson were made explicit; Frost was left five hundred dollars per annum for ten years, then eight hundred per annum in subsequent years, assuming the trust set up for Frost and Jeanie held out. The farm would become entirely Frost's property in 1911, and until that time he would be able to live without paying rent. All promissory notes (Frost had borrowed endlessly from him, of course) were torn up. The young man was hardly set up for life, but he was now assured a certain minimal income. The fact is that few of his neighbors had an income of five hundred dollars each year; by comparison, the Frosts were well off.

Frost felt oddly liberated after the death of his grandfather and his mother. He was now genuinely on his own for the first time. While the pain of Elliott's death had not disappeared, and never would, Frost (and to a lesser extent Elinor) had come to terms with this loss. Lesley was well, and was giving great pleasure to her parents. The only remaining impediment to complete freedom was Carl Burell, who still hovered over Frost and seemed to disapprove of his late rising. Now that Frost had a separate income, the tensions between them became more acute. Burell was forced to supplement his own income by taking on projects for the local road commissioner: digging culverts, building wooden bridges, cutting brush. On several occasions, Frost implied that Burell was neglecting his work on the farm, and this led to even greater tension between them.

Burell's father had been desperately ill during the winter, and he died in March 1902. Burell left soon after, and the local paper recorded his departure warmly: "Mr. Carl Burell, who has lived for some time past on the Magoon place, has decided to leave there and will go to Suncook where he has made an engagement in the Osgood mills for Mr. Bailey. Mr. Burell has won the highest esteem and respect of the people here and we are sorry to have him leave the place."[10] That Frost and Burell parted on reasonably good terms is attested to by an invitation from Burell to "go botanizing" with him in Suncook only a short while later.

After the departure of Burell, Frost occasionally found himself frightened by night sounds in the house. He was suddenly alone, in charge, and felt the responsibility of his new situation gravely. It is likely that "Storm Fear," a particularly fine poem, was written about this time (though much revised nearly a decade later). The flexible line lengths and the oddly spaced rhymes contribute greatly to the poem's unusual sound effects:

> When the wind works against us in the dark,
> And pelts with snow
> The lower chamber window on the east,
> And whispers with a sort of stifled bark,
> The beast,
> "Come out! Come out!"—
> It costs no inward struggle not to go,
> Ah, no!
> I count our strength,
> Two and a child,
> Those of us not asleep subdued to mark
> How the cold creeps as the fire dies at length,—
> How drifts are piled,
> Dooryard and road ungraded,
> Till even the comforting barn grows far away,
> And my heart owns a doubt
> Whether 'tis in us to arise with day
> And save ourselves unaided.

The brilliance of that first line owes something to its alliterative progress: "When the wind works against us in the dark." As usual, the speaking voice is broken against the abstract possibilities of an iambic, five-foot line. But all expectations are reversed in the second, two-beat line, which swings with harsh enjambment into the simple, more conventionally iambic, third line. The poem personifies the weather itself, turning it into a beast: typically for Frost, the narrator is terrified of the elements, eager to retreat into the warmth of the hearth. This is a depressive's poem, to be sure: a poem, like so many of his poems, about the threat of exposure and fear of nature. The last three lines leave little doubt that the speaker wonders if, indeed, he can survive the onslaught of the storm or summon the will to continue. It may take some external aid (God, Carl Burell, luck) to save the "us" into which the poet-narrator has withdrawn: the "two and a child" that presumably refers to himself, Elinor, and Lesley.

As usual in Frost, the poem moves subtly beyond the physical circumstances of the poem, reaching toward a level that could be called metaphysical. The loneliness is more than simple isolation in a farmhouse during a snowstorm. There is real fear as one moves from "Two and a child" to "How the cold creeps as the fire dies at length"—a line which, by its metrical length and rhythmical extension, seems to exhaust the heat that might be needed for survival. By the end, it isn't that we fear that the family in the poem will not be dug out; rather, the fear rises to an existential level, as if the storm were some Miltonic Chaos threatening to absorb the fragile identity of the narrator. One senses that Frost and his family will need some deus ex machina to make it through the dreadful weather, which is "inner" as well as "outer."

Spring did eventually come, and Frost and his family survived. Elinor had become pregnant in September, and she delivered Frost another son, Carol, on May 22. The following October she was pregnant again, and the child was expected in June. Aware that Elinor was highly anxious about her situation, with young Lesley in tow and a new baby to look after, Frost decided to take the whole family to New York City in March 1903, a move that startled his neighbors, who were already suspicious of Frost. None of them, of course, could ever have afforded such an excursion, had they actually wanted to make it in the first place.

In New York, the Frosts rented for a month a small furnished apartment on Sixth Avenue, and they took Lesley to see the usual sights of the day: the aquarium at the Battery, the zoo in Central Park, the famous Hippodrome. But Frost had other things in mind, too: he wanted to make some literary contacts. While two editors politely entertained him in their offices, he was generally frustrated by his efforts. "The literary world didn't want to hear from me when I was a farmer in New Hampshire," he later said. "I had mud on my shoes. They could see the mud, and that didn't seem right to them for a poet."[11]

The family returned to Derry for the birth of Irma on June 27, 1903. With three small children to raise, Frost found himself immersed in the role of paterfamilias, and happily so. One can see from the journals kept by Lesley, and by reports from friends and family, that he felt quite comfortable in the role of farmer-father. "It's often overlooked that Frost was devoted to his young family, that he played with the children, educated them, thought about their development. He was present on the scene, daily. He took them for walks, put them to bed, sat at the dinner table with them. There was almost nothing else in his life in the Derry years, when the children were young and growing up," recalls his granddaughter.[12]

He also became extremely fond of his chickens, devoting himself to their care, taking pride in them—as in "A Blue Ribbon at Amesbury," where he celebrates the success of one particular bird at a contest he attended. That Frost's imagination was engaged in poultry farming is clear from the eleven brief sketches that he wrote for the *Eastern Poultryman* and *Farm-Poultry* (two trade journals) between 1903 and 1905. While none of the stories is particularly good, one can hear in them Frost trying on the idiomatic speech of local people—the speech that would become a staple of his poetry in the years to come.

"Life on the Derry farm was relaxed and varied," Lesley Lee Francis recalls, looking back through her mother's childhood diaries. "While there was little money for the extras we take for granted today, by contemporary standards the Frosts enjoyed a happy and healthy existence, one they certainly looked back on with nostalgia. Activities divided up the day: tending to the farm animals (chickens, a cow, and a horse), writing and 'playing school,' chasing the cow or a stray bull (or even a stray hunter), going into town to shop (and, on one occasion, to church) with mama or papa, or, in the evenings playing games (dominoes, a civil war game with dice, 'puss-in-the-corner,' bobbing for apples) and reading aloud. In one family scene, mama is raking up the yard, papa is cutting with the scythe, and Carol and Irma are sitting on the hay cart, while grandpa (Elinor's father) is preparing a bonfire. Irregular hours, exacerbated by Frost's and Elinor's differing biological clocks—Frost was a late riser, Elinor a morning person—and the at-home school arrangements, permitted a great deal of flexibility in the daily activities."

Life on the Derry farm was quite comfortable, in fact. "The Frosts did not go hungry," Francis continues. "We know, from the journals, that meals, prepared by one parent or the other, were haphazard, and not surprisingly were high in dairy products and poultry produced on the farm. They were supplemented by the abundance of nuts, berries, and fruits gathered by family members throughout the year."[13] Breakfasts were hearty: scrambled eggs, homemade bread, fresh cream over fruit from the farm, when fruit was in season. There was always lots of maple syrup, which was poured over pancakes and used to flavor breads. At dinner, usually served midday, they had plenty of meat, with fresh vegetables in summer and canned in winter.

Much has been made by previous biographers of Frost's ineffectualness as a farmer. It is true that he liked to sleep late, wasn't especially comfortable around livestock, and got sick quite often, thus having to neglect his chores. There seems to be little doubt that regular bouts of depression weighed him down, making it difficult for him to function well. In spite of this, he did keep a farm for a decade, and enjoyed it. Perhaps more important, he was smart enough to fit himself into a way of life that allowed for the flexibility a writer needs in daily life. "A writer has to cultivate leisure," Robert Penn Warren once said.

"People made much of Frost's so-called laziness. It was a necessary laziness. It was the way his mind, his imagination, worked; he needed all that time, the spaciousness, the ease of getting from day to day. Poems could root in those spaces. In his case, they did."[14]

The Frosts decided to educate their children at home, and since both parents were qualified teachers, the local school board gave them permission to do so. Each weekday, at ten, Elinor called the children into the parlor and sat them on the large blue sofa (which had once belonged to Belle) and began their first lesson of the day. Reading and writing were primary subjects, but elementary mathematics also had a place in the lesson plan. "Taught the alphabet on a typewriter," Lesley Frost said, "by the age of three [I] was writing, phonetically but legibly, on the machine. By five, I was writing longhand, also legibly, though highly misspelled. . . . My mother taught the organized subjects, reading (the phonetic method), writing (then known as penmanship), geography, spelling. My father took on botany and astronomy. They both went over our stories for criticism, though it was my mother who scanned them first for spelling and grammar. . . . Reading was most important."[15] The Frosts subscribed to the *Youth's Companion* and *St. Nicholas*—two popular magazines for children.

Lesley remembered that the children would follow their father into the woods, through the cranberry bog, or along a stream, listening to his tales of goblins and fairies, absorbing his detailed botanical expositions, taking in stories meant to inform them about historical figures and epochs. They were forced to memorize large chunks of English and American poetry, and to learn the names of every plant, weed, bush, tree, and animal that they encountered on their hikes.

When the children and Elinor were asleep, Frost sat at the kitchen table, often well past midnight, writing his poems. Not surprisingly, the atmosphere of the Derry farm permeates the products of those years. It was here, for example, that Frost wrote "Hyla Brook," one of his finer lyrics. Years later, he recalled to John Haines that the poem was about "the brook on my old farm. It always dried up in summer. The Hyla is a small frog that shouts like jingling bells in the marshes in the spring."[16]

> By June our brook's run out of song and speed.
> Sought for much after that, it will be found
> Either to have gone groping underground
> (And taken with it all the Hyla breed
> That shouted in the mist a month ago,
> Like ghost of sleigh-bells in a ghost of snow)—
> Or flourished and come up in jewel-weed,
> Weak foliage that is blown upon and bent
> Even against the way its waters went.
> Its bed is left a faded paper sheet
> Of dead leaves stuck together by the heat—
> A brook to none but who remember long.
> This as it will be seen is other far
> Than with brooks taken otherwhere in song.
> We love the things we love for what they are.

In many of Frost's better poems, one finds him musing on his art surreptitiously, keeping the focus elsewhere. "You don't want to say directly what you can say indirectly," he once remarked, echoing Emily Dickinson's injunction to "Tell the truth but tell it slant." In another poem, "Spring Pools," he muses on much the same theme: the things we love often seem to disappear on us, but they come up elsewhere. Typically, in "Hyla Brook" Frost begins with a fetching line and ends with a totalizing aphorism; also typically, it is not easy to connect the aphorism to what has apparently gone before. Why should we "love the things we love for what they are," especially when they have gone underground, have deserted us? There is something willful about this stream, which has "gone groping underground"—not a pretty image. It has ruined the lovely Hyla breed, too, both the frogs and their music.

The poem is, as much as anything, about the source of inspiration, and what one does when it has dried up—literalized here in the stream. The frogs represent song, or poetry: the voice that "shouted in the mist a month ago, / Like ghost of sleigh-bells in a ghost of snow." That last line, so unexpected and haunting, is Frost to a T: the sort of gorgeous linguistic turn that moves the language into a realm beyond normal discourse. This "otherness" in Frost is also apparent in the odd, penultimate lines that precede the final aphorism: "This as it will be seen is other far / Than with brooks taken otherwhere in song." What can this mean? There is, perhaps, an echo here of Tennyson's "The Brook," which Frost knew well. Tennyson wrote, "For men may come and men may go, / But I go on forever." The brook, as poetic inspiration, goes on forever, though hidden from view. One rarely, if ever, comes upon "other far" or "otherwhere"—colloquialisms that Frost has naturalized as poetic language. These lines seem to suggest that the disappearance of this brook, and its underground life, are quite different from the usual disappearing brook. The very oddness of the language ingeniously guarantees their untranslatability; one cannot even put these lines into standard English without losing something essential to their meaning.

The origins of this poem lay in the happy conjunction of Frost's firsthand observation of the frogs near his house in Derry and his reading of Darwin's *The Voyage of the Beagle*, which he numbered among his favorite books. In the relevant passage, Darwin writes:

> Nature, in these climes, chooses her vocalists from more humble performers than in Europe. A small frog, of the genus Hyla, sits on a blade of grass about an inch from the surface of the water, and sends forth a pleasing chirp: when several are together they sing in harmony on different notes.[17]

In Frost's own developing aesthetic, he "set the hyla against the haughtiness of 'European performers' and lauded these 'humble' singers performing in a difficult theater," suggests Robert Faggen.[18]

The foundation of Frost's later work was laid in those years in Derry, as his friend Hyde Cox noted. "He had read voraciously at Derry," Cox said, "the classics, English and European philosophy, history."[19] Frost also groped his way toward a poetics of speech, what he would later call "the sound of sense," the strange vitality that is caught in living speech. "When I first began to write poetry," he said, "before the illumination of what possibilities there are in the sound of sense came to me—I was writing largely, though not exclusively, after the patterns of the past." As a young poet, he began by imitating voices of the past. "The young poet is prone to echo all the pleasing sounds he has heard in his scattered reading. He is apt to look on the musical value of the lines, the metrical perfection, as all that matters. He has not listened for the voice within his mind, speaking the lines and giving them the value of sound."[20]

It was in Derry that he began to listen keenly to the people around him, many of them farm laborers, and to catch their way of talking, their "sound postures." One of these was John Hall, a local poultryman whose speech cadences and casual, country wit fascinated Frost, who also began to cultivate his own conversational style in these years. This style became the bedrock of his own original poetics—a point made recently by Peter J. Stanlis, who argues that Frost's mastery of conversation played a huge role in his developing style as a poet, providing a key aspect of his aesthetic theory and poetic practice.[21] The connection between poetry and conversation dawned on him, according to Frost, when he was talking one day with a friend of William Hayes Ward's. "I didn't know until then what it was I was after," he recalled. "I was after poetry that talked. If my poems were talking poems—if to read one of them you heard a voice—that would be to my liking!"[22]

While there were some harrowing moments in this period (1902–05), it was also a time of recovery and reconstitution for Frost. The farm work was relatively light, and aided by the annuity from his grandfather, Frost was able to pace himself—a crucial thing for anyone trying to become a poet. He knew few people in the village and had few commitments beyond his immediate family life.

Marjorie was born on March 29, 1905, swelling the brood again. Frost lavished attention on her, as he had on the others in their infancies. That he took parenting seriously, was a devoted and careful father, is not in question. He was also a natural teacher, and he loved introducing his children to the world. As early as 1905, Lesley wrote in her own journal: "papa and i took a long wake [walk]." Indeed, her father would write in a poem called "The Fear" that "Every child should have the memory / Of at least one long-after-bedtime walk." Frost associated walks with talks, as we see in "A Time to Talk." Lesley Lee Francis recalls: "The wildness and excitement my mother sensed in her father (his genius, she and I would surmise) came out in these long walks, sometimes with all the children, to gather checkerberries or play house or store in the grove, but more often with Lesley alone."[23]

Frost's lively sense of play made him an ideal father in many respects. Lesley said that when the snow fell, the children could be sure that he would eagerly rush them outside to ride a sled or build a snowman. In all seasons there were joyful things to do, and Frost made sure a high-spirited time was had by everyone. In springtime, for instance, the children were taken into the woods to find flowers to bring back to the house, roots and all, for transplanting. There were also bonfires, which Frost constructed with the enthusiasm of a ten-year-old pyromaniac. In Lesley's journal she describes one typical summer outing with her father: "We went over across the road in the little pasture. Papa and I went way out in Noise's land. We found two little ponds and a watering trough. One of the ponds was where we tried to get some cat-tails last year but they were too far in the water, and have seats in it and a fence around to keep people out. They have a cow path down to the pond and pretty. We found a [shotgun] shell, shot just a little while ago."

The record of family life as seen in Lesley's journal stands in ferocious contrast to some later portrayals of these years. Lawrance Thompson, who wasted no opportunity to present Frost as a monster, reports—supposedly quoting from Lesley, two months after her father's death, in 1963—that Elinor and Frost were fighting one night when she stumbled downstairs into the kitchen. Frost was holding a revolver, and he told Lesley to choose which parent she preferred, since one of them would be dead by morning. If indeed this is true, it suggests a side to Frost darker than most people would imagine. There is no doubt that on occasion he behaved horribly. But even as Thompson describes it, the scene with the gun is not entirely without a human side. "Her mother got up from the table, put her arms around Lesley, pushed her out of the kitchen, led her back to her bed, and sat beside her until the child had cried herself to sleep. In the morning she remembered all the facts and wondered if they had actually happened. Perhaps she had only dreamed them."[24] Perhaps, indeed. Lesley's daughter Lesley Lee Francis says: "In all the years my mother and I talked about her father, there was never any mention of this scene. And, indeed, she was prone to nightmares, especially in childhood. I don't doubt that tensions did arise in the family, and that Robert Frost was, at times, moody and difficult; but the idea that he would threaten Elinor with a gun is absurd, and the story runs against the whole tenor of the Derry years, which were quite idyllic, and recalled fondly by the children for decades after. My grandfather was devoted to his wife and children, and always protective. The story just doesn't ring true."[25] Lillian Frost, Carol's wife, also roundly dismissed Thompson's story in her letters, explaining in one that her husband "always said that Lesley was dreaming, that the incident with the gun never happened."[26] If the scene did actually occur, there was obviously no fear on Elinor's part that anybody was really going to get shot.

Nonetheless, there was a dark side to Frost—hardly anyone who knew him has ever denied as much; in fact, in "Desert Places" Frost himself would write: "I have it in me so much nearer home / To scare myself with my own desert places." But Frost was able to make use of these dark places, too, dipping into them—as in "Spring Pools"—"to bring dark foliage on."

The flowering of the Derry years included such poems as "Ghost House," "Love and a Question," "My November Guest," "Storm Fear," "A Prayer in Spring," "Going for Water," "The Trial by Existence," "October," "Pan with Us," "A Line-Storm Song," and many others— some of which would emerge, in revised form, decades later. Reading through A Boy's Will, one begins to assemble a visual and emotional portrait of those years of bucolic isolation, their range of imagery and metaphor. "Ghost House," for instance, is about an abandoned house (an image that would stay with Frost throughout the decades, as in "Directive"—a poem written in the mid-1940s). Written in 1901, it was inspired by an old cellar hole with a broken chimney standing in it—what remained of a nearby farmhouse after a fire had destroyed it in 1867. "Love and a Question" was inspired by the unexpected visit of a tramp to the Derry farm. Frost offered the man food, blankets, and a place by the woodstove to sleep. When the man was gone, he began to muse on the question of this man's claims on his and his wife's resources (which were minimal) and affections. Frost often linked poems in this book, and later ones, to specific incidents from the Derry years, "a time when my eyes and ears were open, very open," as he said.[27]

Frost's characteristic voice did not, as he himself noted, emerge at once. "You may go back to all those early poems of mine in *A Boy's Will*, and some that are left out of it. You will find me there using the traditional clichés."[28] The texture of "My Butterfly," "Waiting," "Flower-Gathering," "Rose Pogonias," "In a Vale," and other poems written before Derry differ markedly from those that show the influence of having actually lived on the farm and talked to the local people. "Storm Fear," for instance, exhibits a rugged syntax based on the rhythms of living speech. But it was not until *North of Boston* that one really began to see and hear the results of the Derry years, those after-echoes and effects that continued for decades, shaping Frost's vision, giving a grain to his voice.

6 THE ACHE OF MEMORY—
PINKERTON AND PLYMOUTH
1906–1911

Why bother to dispute what someone else has affirmed? If you wait a little, you will find something to affirm yourself and so won't be left out of the game or conversations. Wait for your chance for affirmation. —FROST, NOTEBOOK ENTRY, 1910

Frost was never good with money, especially at budgeting; he tended to dislike details of this kind, and he often did not know how much money was in his account. Even with his grandfather's generous legacy, he was having difficulty paying his bills in Derry. The poultry business was hardly remunerative, however much advice he acquired from Napoleon Guay, his friendly neighbor. They lived, as Elinor later recalled, "on lease, with a line of credit at most of the local merchants." In January 1906, when the annual check from his grandfather's estate arrived, Frost carried it eagerly to the bank in Derry Village. The teller studied the check carefully, lifted an eyebrow, then asked with undisguised contempt, "More of your hard-earned money, Mr. Frost?" Frost was humiliated.

At thirty-two, with four young children in tow and the prospect of mounting expenses, Frost began to look around for other ways to earn money, and Pinkerton Academy seemed an obvious place to begin. Founded in 1815 by Scottish Congregationalists, the school was only two miles north of the Frost farm. By chance, he had casually made the acquaintance of several members of the Pinkerton faculty since arriving in Derry half a decade before, so he was not starting out unknown. While visiting Lawrence one day in winter, he ran into William E. Wolcott, pastor of the First Congregational Church and a friend of William Hayes Ward's. It was an icy day, and they stood talking on Essex Street, with snow falling around them. Frost mentioned in passing that he had an eye on Pinkerton, and Wolcott brightened. He had, he explained, recently given a talk in the school chapel, and he knew well the local Congregationalist minister, Charles Merriam, who was a trustee of the school. He promised to see what he could do.

Wolcott wrote at once to Merriam: "I have been acquainted with Mr. Robert L. Frost for a number of years. I know of my personal knowledge that he is a man of scholarly interests and habits, and I have had testimony from former pupils that he was an efficient and inspiring teacher. I am glad to commend him cordially for any position for which he may apply."[1]

Frost, meanwhile, approached the local school board in Derry, hoping that his earlier experience would make him an attractive candidate. He also dropped in on Merriam at the Congregationalist church and found the man surprisingly receptive. Merriam suggested that Frost, as a way of getting acquainted with the local Congregationalist community, read a few poems to the upcoming annual banquet of the Men's League. Frost explained that he had never before read his work in public, and that he would be too frightened to do so. Merriam persisted, however, and Frost agreed to attend if Merriam himself read the single poem that he wished to have presented that evening.

A few days later he appeared at the church with "The Tuft of Flowers" in manuscript, a poem written a decade before. He may well have guessed that the poem's last, moralizing couplet would seem especially appropriate in this setting: "Men work together, I told him from the heart, / Whether they work together or apart." In any case, Merriam liked the poem, and he read it aloud while Frost cowered. The audience seemed to appreciate the poem, and several teachers from Pinkerton approached Frost to congratulate him. For the first time, Frost experienced what would in later years become everyday fare: the adulation of the crowd. One teacher suggested that a part-time position at Pinkerton was a good possibility.

Pinkerton commanded a small hill with a broad, northern view. It had been founded by two Scottish merchants; its catalog at the time made its purpose clear: "The school is a good, safe one for diligent people who have a definite purpose. . . . Others are not desired."[2] This stern tone was upheld by Pinkerton's longtime headmaster, the Reverend George Washington Bingham, a tall, white-bearded Congregationalist from Boston who had graduated from Dartmouth in 1843. His spirit of no-nonsense religiosity pervaded the school, and Pinkerton's faculty had been in his thrall for decades. Yet Bingham was close to retirement now, at seventy-five, and was relinquishing many of his duties—among them the supervision of English studies at the school. There was certainly room for a young teacher who could meet his high standards.

Frost was summoned to the school by Bingham and told, without fuss, that he had made a good impression on Merriam; Bingham offered him a job on the spot, proposing that he assume responsibilities for two sections of sophomore English. Frost would be expected to teach for two hours a day, five days a week, and would be paid ninety-five dollars for the spring term. He was asked to begin immediately, and Bingham explained that the position would be renewed in the fall term if all went reasonably well. Frost did not hesitate to accept.

He began teaching at Pinkerton in early March, walking the two miles from his farm to the village, then up the hill to Pinkerton's impressive redbrick structure, with its Romanesque arches lending atmosphere to the entrance as one entered beneath a clock tower. Because Frost's classes began late in the day, he was (to his relief) excused from morning chapel. He would usually leave the school as soon as classes finished.

Frost's pleasure in his new work, and his generally positive state of mind in the spring of 1906, is reflected in the poems he was writing at this time, such as "A Prayer in Spring," which opens:

Oh, give us pleasure in the flowers today;
And give us not to think so far away
As the uncertain harvest; keep us here
All simply in the springing of the year.

Oh, give us pleasure in the orchard white,
Like nothing else by day, like ghosts by night;
And make us happy in the happy bees,
The swarm dilating round the perfect trees.

The poem is rigidly conventional in form, its iambic pentameter almost numbingly regular, with rhyming couplets in quatrains sounding almost too pat; but one hears the Frostian note in that gorgeous sixth line: "Like nothing else by day, like ghosts by night." Frost often used the metaphor of ghostliness, especially when describing things witnessed in an altered or oddly lit condition, as when the orchard is observed by night. Yet one cannot easily swallow the poet's bid to "make us happy in the happy bees," which seems to bathe in a weak solution of Tennysonian rhetoric. The poem goes on for two more quatrains, without much else to attract our attention. But the mood is consistently cheerful in a conventional, unproblematic way that seems out of place in Frost.

Full-time teaching at Pinkerton began in the fall. His daily schedule represented, for him, an abrupt departure of routine from poultry farming, where a leisurely pace had been sought and found. Frost taught five English classes and was expected to tutor students in Latin, history, and geometry. He was extremely popular with his classes, and the Debating Club invited him to be its coach. The high point of each day was his meeting with the senior English class (thirteen girls and four boys), where he taught some of his favorite authors: John Bunyan, Thoreau, and the poets of Palgrave's *Golden Treasury*.

Frost adored teaching, in part because he found himself able to overcome his natural shyness in a context where the conventional expectations encouraged self-performance. On a more elemental level, his teaching schedule forced him to get out of bed, to shake off the melancholy that seemed otherwise to bear him down. One simply cannot be self-absorbed in front of students; one has to open up, to share one's thoughts. Fortunately for Frost, the students at Pinkerton were eager to learn, and he went out of his way to make his classes interesting, although he was not then, nor ever would be, a conventional teacher. He did, however, pay close attention to the writing he assigned, and would not tolerate grammatical mistakes.[3] Considerable emphasis was placed on memorization, and students left his classes with a hoard of poems by Wordsworth, Longfellow, Whittier, Browning, Tennyson, and Coleridge in their memories. Long passages from Shakespeare's plays would also be learned by heart, and the students, under Frost's direction, put on plays at frequent intervals. These included A *Midsummer Night's Dream*, Marlow's *Doctor Faustus*, Sheridan's *The Rivals*, and two plays by Yeats: *The Land of Heart's Desire* (1894) and *Cathleen ni Houlihan* (1902). The Yeats plays were considered daringly contemporary in 1906, and it was unusual for a young instructor to bring such complex, modern work into the school.

The image we get of Frost at Pinkerton is that of an idiosyncratic but attractive teacher. One student remembered that he usually entered the classroom "at a gallop." "His hair, cut at home, was blown in all directions by the wind," she recalled, "and if that weren't enough, he'd run his fingers through the tousled locks defying any accidental order. His clothes were rumpled and ill-fitting. There were no indications that he made any effort to 'spruce up' for the job. In class, unlike the ramrod-straight Miss Parsons who taught Greek or the stiff-collared Art Reynolds who taught history, Frost would slump down in his chair behind his desk, almost disappearing from sight except for his heavy-lidded eyes and bushy brows. In such a position Frost would 'talk,' or he might read aloud or let a discussion go its own length. Teachers didn't know how to 'take him,' and students, accustomed to 'prepared lessons,' were inclined to think they could take advantage of a teacher who was not strict in the way they knew."[4]

While Frost enjoyed the support of the principal and most of his students, he was plagued by several jealous colleagues who considered him an unqualified interloper who should not be meddling in education. One of these was Art Reynolds, mentioned above; a Harvard graduate, he lost no opportunity to commiserate with Frost about his lack of a college degree. This rivalry was fueled by the publication, in the *Independent*, of "The Trial by Existence" on October 11, 1906. Principal Bingham read the poem at chapel, with much deference to Frost, and congratulatory notes arrived at the school from both Charles Merriam and the secretary of the Board of Trustees, John Chase. Once again, Frost was invited to read a poem before the Men's League of the First Congregational Church, and he accepted on the condition that, as before, Merriam would read the poem. Especially for this occasion, Frost wrote "The Lost Faith," a long poem about his regret that the ideals for which the Union soldiers had fought in the Civil War had been forgotten. (It was never collected by Frost in any volume, although it appeared in the March 1, 1907, edition of the *Derry News*.) It is an embarrassingly conventional poem, with no signs of Frostian originality, but it served Frost well on this occasion—and further heightened the tension between himself and Reynolds.

Not all of Frost's students found his unconventionality appealing, and one of his detractors scratched on the chalkboard before class one day an insult, referring to Frost as a "hen-man." Frost examined the handwriting; it matched that of a student whom he already suspected of being hostile to him. After class that day, he told the boy abruptly that he was no longer welcome in his classroom. This led to frantic consultations between Frost and Principal Bingham, who understood Frost's outrage but worried that if the boy were not allowed into this class, he would have to be expelled. There was nowhere else for him to go. "Then he will have to leave Pinkerton," Frost said, without hesitation. The boy was thus expelled, and from this time on Frost was respected by colleagues and students alike. They understood that, in the end, Frost meant business, and that he would not be pushed around.

Frost worked extremely hard during his first full-time year of teaching, coaching the sophomore debating team, helping with sports, taking on tasks that most teachers at Pinkerton would not have accepted—all to show his mettle. But hard work turned to overwork, and Frost paid a huge penalty in the spring of 1907, when he came down with a severe case of pneumonia—so severe that his physician was terrified that it might be fatal. He was forced to stay home for two months, March and April, to recuperate, and this of course put a strain on Elinor, who was pregnant again, for the sixth time. She became quite ill herself and was forced to move into the home of a nurse in Derry Village, where she would stay until the child was born, on June 18.

The child, a daughter called Elinor Bettina, died soon after she was born, and Frost blamed himself for having put so much pressure on Elinor to look after him when he was ill. For her part, Elinor did not blame him. She understood that one cannot account for these terrible things. It had become clear to them both, however, that a major change in their circumstances was required—for the sanity of both. They decided to move into the village in the fall.

For six weeks in July and August, during the height of the hay-fever season, Frost took the family to the tiny village of Bethlehem in the White Mountains of New Hampshire, where he rented two bedrooms from a man called John Lynch, whose farm was perched on a steep slope with a thrilling westward view into Vermont. The family took their meals at a hotel nearby, owned by Michael Fitzgerald, an exuberant Irishman who made the Frosts feel extremely welcome. It was a healing time, and Frost grew stronger as he took long walks in the woods with the children and, late in the afternoons, played sandlot baseball with a group of local farmhands.

Evenings were spent on the porch of the Lynch house, where everyone gathered to play games and tell stories. Frost hurled himself into this activity, and his storytelling skills were honed on these occasions. He would keep the Lynches up until late at night, talking and recounting stories—many of them going back to his childhood in San Francisco. His talk, "full of hijinks and humbug," would "bubble and boil past midnight," Lynch would later recall: a pattern of late-night monologuing that remained a feature of his life till the end.

Susan Hayes Ward visited him during this time in Bethlehem, and Frost wrote to her in November with a fond recollection of his time there: "Our summer was one of the pleasantest we have had for years.

But it is almost hard for me to believe in the reality of it now. I have been that way from boyhood. The feeling of time and space is perennially strange to me. I used to lie awake at night imagining the places I had traversed in the day and doubting in simple wonderment that I who was here could possibly have been there and there. I can't look at my little slope of field here with leaves in the half dead grass, or at the bare trees the birds have left us with, and fully believe there were ever such things as the snug downhill churning room with the view over five ranges of mountains, our talks under the hanging lamp and over the fat blue book, the tea-inspired Mrs. Lynch, baseball, and the blue black [Mount] Lafayette. There is a pang there that makes poetry. I rather like to gloat over it."[5]

Frost plunged into teaching with renewed vigor at Pinkerton that fall, taking upon himself the task of curriculum revision, with an emphasis on writing and reading aloud. Although he continued to feel snubbed by several colleagues, there was no denying his effectiveness as a teacher. Henry Morrison, the state superintendent of public instruction, visited his class one day and was mightily impressed. He wrote a report that talked about this "class of boys and girls . . . listening open-mouthed to the teacher who was talking to them about an English classic . . . talking to them as he might talk to a group of friends around his own fireside." Morrison invited Frost to speak to a group of New Hampshire teachers on his teaching methods, and he agreed—with trepidation. Although he was by now a little more accustomed to public speaking, having honed his skills in the classroom, he was hesitant to speak before his peers. He managed to do it, however, focusing his talk on the need for teachers to develop their own minds before they thought about developing the minds of their students. He also said it was important that students be made to feel so dependent on books that without them, ever afterward, they would feel lonely. As for writing, he emphasized the need for putting things in memorable, concrete language.

He himself continued to find memorable language for his experiences. One such occasion came in the summer of 1909, when he and his family camped throughout the worst part of the hay-fever season on Lake Willoughby in northern Vermont. The little town by the lake was dominated by Mount Lafayette, which inspired his poem "The Mountain," among the most richly descriptive of Frost's early poems:

> The mountain held the town as in a shadow.
> I saw so much before I slept there once:
> I noticed that I missed stars in the west,
> Where its black body cut into the sky.
> Near me it seemed: I felt it like a wall
> Behind which I was sheltered from a wind.
> And yet between the town and it I found,
> When I walked forth at dawn to see new things,
> Were fields, a river, and beyond, more fields.

"I never invent for poetic expression," Frost said, "No poet really has to invent, only to record."[6] It was during this camping trip that he met a farmer's wife, one Mrs. Connolley, whose appalling circumstances and voice are firmly caught in "A Servant to Servants," although Frost later noted to Edward Lathem that the speaker in this poem was a composite figure created from three different women. Set on Lake Willoughby, presumably in 1909, this portrait of a lonely woman run ragged by her circumstances lies at the heart of *North of Boston*, and is one with the other fine narrative poems of that volume. It is a poem where Frost deals forthrightly with madness, which had touched his family closely and would continue to haunt him.

In the poem, the speaker describes her insane uncle, who lived at home with his family but within a special "house" within the house, a cage of hickory-wood bars. He apparently destroyed all of his own furniture, and lived like an animal in this cage, naked, carrying a suit of clothes on his arm. He "went mad quite young," though we never learn exactly what provoked the madness except that he was "crossed in love. . . . Anyway all he talked about was love." Another important figure in the poem is the speaker's mother, brought to this house where "She had to lie and hear love things made dreadful / By his shouts in the night." Now she, the speaker, has moved to a cabin "ten miles from anywhere," but on a lake that seems to mirror her continuing discontent. We learn, in passing, that she too had been thought insane, and was put into an asylum. Now she is forced to act as "a servant to servants," taking care of Len, her husband, and the endless parade of hired men who tramp through. It's a searing portrait of a mad, stunted, rueful housewife—one of a continuing series of portraits of rural women in distress. These women perpetually claw at their surroundings, hoping to subvert the male strictures (and structures) that bind them, or seem to push them toward insanity.

Slowly but unmistakably, Frost was acquiring a portfolio of poems of the first order, working at tight, small lyrics (often in traditional forms, such as the sonnet) as well as larger, narrative poems that employed a variety of local voices, male and female. He knew it could not be long before he would have enough good material for a collection, although he remained doubtful that a publisher would want to publish what he wrote. On some deep level, he could still not believe he was not just a "hen-man," as his derisive student at Pinkerton had suggested.

The Frosts returned to Derry in September and, having reluctantly decided to give up the farm, moved into Derry Village itself, where they rented the top floor of a large Victorian house owned by a young, unmarried lawyer, Lester Russell, who quickly became a good friend to the whole family. Indeed, Russell would often have dinner with the Frosts, and would take the older children (who were now placed in local schools) into the nearby woods for walks.

Principal Bingham had retired the previous spring, and the new principal was Ernest L. Silver, a graduate of Dartmouth (Class of 1899). He and Frost were nearly the same age, and had much in common—a love of poetry, an interest in sports, and a belief that good teaching was not necessarily conventional teaching. Ernest was the son of Charles L. Silver, who had twice hired Frost to teach in Salem, years before, so there were many threads to bind these men.

Another important friendship developed between Frost and one of his pupils, John Bartlett, whom he had already known for two years. Bartlett was now captain of the football team, president of his class, and editor of the school newspaper. He was Frost's prize pupil, and he became a lifelong friend. Much as Frost had done, he later married his high school sweetheart. (Frost took an active part in promoting this relationship, as he would often do in later years with young men whom he considered his protégés.)

In the fall of 1909 Frost published in the school magazine, the *Pinkerton Critic*, a poem called "A Late Walk." A version of it had been written in 1897, to Elinor; it is typical of the poems in *A Boy's Will*— vaguely romantic, adhering closely to the common measure of Puritan hymns, four beats alternating with three, and rhymed on the second and fourth lines only. Thematically conventional, the poem has a rather wistful tone; but that Frostian note, unmistakable, is present in the first lines:

> *When I go up through the mowing field,*
> *The headless aftermath,*
> *Smooth-laid like thatch with the heavy dew,*
> *Half closes the garden path.*

Here, Frost has taken his level of diction down, as he said, "even lower than Wordsworth." As ever, the vividness of the imagery—the dewy field "Smooth-laid like thatch"—is tied to its particularity, the sense of a poet writing about something that he has repeatedly observed himself.

Frost's career as a teacher blossomed that year, as he took a central role in putting on five plays—a selection designed to illustrate the dramatic conventions of different periods of English literature. John Bartlett, who played Mephistopheles in *Doctor Faustus*, later commented in a letter to Gorham Munson (the poet's first biographer) that Frost had "turned the school around" with these productions, drawing attention to himself as a teacher in such a manner that nobody could now doubt his seriousness and originality, or rival his energy.

Bartlett later wrote fondly of Frost as a teacher: "A few of the boys spent considerable time with Frost out of school hours. I remember a walk over the turnpike to Manchester in late afternoon, an hour spent in a bookstore, an oyster stew, and then a ride home on the electric railway. Our conversation on walks touched books only now and then. Frost had an interest in everything wholesome, and on a walk of two hours the conversation might include reminiscences of his early life, discussion of school affairs, including athletics, aspects of farm life in New Hampshire, some current news happening of importance, and nearly anything else. If, passing a farmhouse, the aroma of fried dough-nuts came out to us, Frost might propose we buy some. Down around the corner, we might encounter a fern he hadn't seen since last in the Lake Willoughby region. And if darkness overtook us, and it was a favorable time for observation, Rob would be sure to take at least five minutes to study the heavens and attempt to start our astronomical education. Rob always talked a good deal, and his companions did, too. There was always an abundance of conversation, and almost never argument. Rob never argued. He knew what he knew, and never had any interest in arguing about it."[7]

Frost's reputation as a teacher now attracted statewide attention, and he was invited to give two lectures on his classroom methods in the winter of 1910—in Meredith in January and, a month later, at the Farmington Institute, where he talked about the relationship between teaching literature and getting students to write well themselves, always a subject dear to him. For the first time, he was beginning to feel relatively at ease on a platform, and to gain some confidence in expressing his opinions in a public way. He had never, of course, been short of strong opinions, nor unwilling to express himself to those near him, but now the public manner was finally catching up with the pri-vate manner.

John Bartlett, in the meanwhile, went off to Middlebury College, in Vermont, where—much as his mentor had done at Dartmouth—he abandoned his academic career rather abruptly, leaving school in the middle of his freshman year. Frost, in a burst of sympathy, rushed to visit his young friend (who was back at home, on a farm in Raymond, not far from Derry), advising him not to worry about the future. He explained that college was not necessarily the best route to an educa-tion; indeed, his skepticism about the value of a college degree was intense. The bond between Bartlett and Frost was strengthened when it turned out that pulmonary problems had played a part in Bartlett's withdrawal.

Frost's career at Pinkerton ended, rather unexpectedly, in 1910. He was, he said, exhausted by the teaching load, "practically in a coma" from overwork. Adding to his troubles was the suicide of his landlord and friend, Lester Russell, who had been caught diverting funds from a trust he managed to pay off his own gambling debts. The poor fellow drank a bottle of arsenic, then died an agonizing death. The effect on the Frost family was considerable: Carol, in particular, was horribly shaken by the event, and would become obsessed with the idea of suicide—an obsession that worried his parents gravely.

A further disturbance came in July, when Ernest Silver resigned as principal at Pinkerton to take up a similar position at the New Hampshire State Normal School in Plymouth, a college for teachers. This dark cloud soon passed, however: Silver insisted that Frost come with him as a member of his faculty. There was, it so happened, no position available in English; the only openings were in psychology and the history of education. But Silver told Frost he could "teach anything he put his mind to." With some trepidation, Frost agreed to take on these two new assignments, insisting that he would not continue in this job beyond one year.

He had long planned to take a leave of absence from teaching—even quit altogether—when, by the terms of his grandfather's will, he was permitted to sell the farm in Derry. In 1911, he was at last free to put the property on the market. Unfortunately, he had neglected the farm since taking up the job at Pinkerton, and the place had begun to crumble. "The porch had brokens steps and many windows needed replacing," Elinor recalled. The garden was now "a terrible jungle." No buyers came forward, and Frost was forced to sell the mortgage back to a bank in Concord for twelve hundred dollars—considerably below market value. The mixed feelings that accompanied this sale are registered in a poem dating from that spring:

> Well-way and be it so,
> To the stranger let them go.
> Even cheerfully I yield

Pasture or chard, mowing-field,
Yea and wish him all the gain
I required of them in vain.
Yea, and I can yield him house,
Barn, and shed, with rat and mouse
To dispute possession of.
These I can unlearn to love.
Since I cannot help it? Good!
Only be it understood,
It shall be no trespassing
If I come again some spring
In the grey disguise of years,
Seeking ache of memory here.[8]

Plymouth, a county seat, sits in the foothills of the White Mountains, a small village that, then as now, overlooks a picturesque valley. The Pemigewasset River runs beside it, providing a source of waterpower for several small industries dating back to the late eighteenth century. Because of good railway connections to Boston and Montreal, Plymouth had attracted summer visitors for many decades: indeed, Nathaniel Hawthorne was a great admirer of this "fine, gemlike town in the mountains," as he called it, and spent his last days there.

Plymouth Normal School had originally been founded as Holmes Academy, in 1808. After more than five decades of service, enrollment fell off and the school languished for nearly a decade. It was reshaped in 1871 as an institution devoted to training women for the teaching profession. Just over a hundred students were enrolled there in 1911, when Frost arrived. The campus consisted of a single brick structure that housed both administrative and faculty offices as well as classrooms; this impressive edifice was surrounded by a dozen clapboard cottages, which were used as dormitories. Plymouth's moderately prosperous town center was not far away—a single main street bustling with horse-drawn carriages, a redbrick post office, a bank, a dry-goods store, a butcher and greengrocer, and various ancillary shops.

By now, Frost was feeling buoyed by his triumphs at Pinkerton, where he had made a name for himself as a teacher and a responsible citizen. His lectures at various teachers' conventions had been so well received throughout the state that he was at once accepted by his colleagues at the Normal School as a man who deserved a good deal of respect. The beginnings of the famous public manner were apparent in his self-presentation as a witty, playful, teasing performer in the classroom. "There was something earthy and imperfectly tamed about him," one student remembered. Another recalled his "original approach to teaching, with a sharp wit and headstrong manner that was so different from any of the other teachers." Others pointed to his "folksy" style—a self-consciously composed manner that he would perfect in later years. This involved speaking in a clipped style, with homespun imagery and examples, and a Yankee way of seeming to imply more than was actually said. One hears it on tapes of his readings in later years: the dropped endings of certain words, the broad accentuation of certain vowels, the sly, winking quips. In his speech as well as in his poetry, Frost began to favor strong, simple verbs; he used a rough-hewn, flinty language that seemed to reek of the northern New England soil. His clothing, too, was chosen to reinforce this emerging style; he favored unpressed jackets, gray, soft-collared shirts, and heavy boots of the kind farmers normally wore. His hair was now rarely combed.

The unruliness of his personal style was reflected in the content of his lectures as well as in his dress and manner. In his course on education, Frost went directly to such classics as Plato's *Republic* and Rousseau's *Émile*. He also insisted that the students read *How Gertrude Teaches Her Children* (1801), a controversial book by Johann Pestalozzi, a Swiss theorist of education and a school reformer. In the psychology course, Frost focused on William James, as might be expected. Students read his *Talks to Teachers on Psychology* and *Psychology: The Briefer Course*—the latter a favorite of Frost's since he'd encountered it at Harvard.

Frost never gave formal lectures, although a certain passage in a text might provoke a lengthy personal anecdote or commentary—he was growing increasingly fond of his own voice. Though he'd been hired to teach psychology and education, his interest in literature could not be contained, and he would often read aloud to the students from Palgrave's *Golden Treasury* or the stories of Mark Twain. Once he read the whole of *A Connecticut Yankee in King Arthur's Court*, over several days, to a class. Few requirements were placed on the students with regard to written work, although Frost could be demanding in class, forcing students to face their own prejudices directly. "Some of us were made quite uncomfortable by him," one student recalled, "but we admired him. He was very popular."

The Frosts had been invited to share a cottage with Ernest Silver, whose wife was an invalid and had not yet joined him in Plymouth. This arrangement led, perhaps inevitably, to problems between Silver and Frost. Elinor's casual housekeeping and her chaotic approach to meals did not sit well with Silver, a fastidious man with a penchant for order. There was also the matter of the Frost children, whom Silver considered undisciplined, even unruly. He blamed the parents for their behavior, and Frost resented this; he soon began to imagine that Silver had been secretly working against him for some time, even back at Pinkerton—an absurd proposition, given that Silver had gone out of his way to bring Frost to Plymouth in the first place.

It was lucky for Frost that Silver was a patient and diplomatic fellow. He managed to soothe his difficult friend and housemate, and Elinor (to her credit) made an extra effort to conform to Silver's not unreasonable wish for more order. The children went along with this change of routine, largely because they liked Plymouth much better than Derry Village. The Normal School ran a program for a limited number of children from Plymouth, and all four of the Frost offspring were now happily enrolled there; the children enjoyed having a spacious campus for roaming, lots of opportunities for sports, and the enthusiastic attention of many young teachers in training.

Frost himself liked the facilities, and he avidly took up the game of tennis at this time. One of his opponents on the court was a young teacher in the local high school, Sidney Cox, who was then twenty-two. Cox would later become one of Frost's closer friends, but—at least in the first month of their relationship—the going was rough. Cox was a young man of considerable seriousness, at times bordering on self-importance. "He was a gentle fellow," recalled one colleague at Dartmouth (where Cox later taught for many years), "but he had no sense of humor, especially when it came to himself. His feelings could be easily hurt."[9] Sensing an easy target, Frost could not help himself; he teased Cox mercilessly. At one point, Cox asked Ernest Silver if the reason Frost had not yet achieved more in his career was related to "a drinking problem"—a curious assumption, given that Frost drank very little. When Frost heard about this, he could not help but laugh. As he later recalled: "Sidney's seriousness piqued the mischief in me, and I set myself to take him. He came round all right, but it wasn't the last time he had to make allowances for me."[10]

This friendship soon became central to Frost's life at Plymouth, and he and Cox began taking long walks together in the surrounding woods and fields; in the evenings Cox often had dinner with the Frosts and then settled into an armchair in the parlor by a log fire for dramatic readings by Frost, who had recently discovered Synge's *Playboy of the Western World*, which he admired greatly, and Shaw's *Arms and the Man*. Frost also took pleasure in reciting the poetry of W. B. Yeats, from whom he learned a good deal about versification. (Frost and Yeats would meet, a couple of years later, in England. Indeed, in 1913 Frost wrote back home to Sidney Cox: "How slowly but surely Yeats has eclipsed Kipling. I have seen it all happen with my own eyes."[11])

The Yeatsian note in Frost is heard, most vividly, in early poems such as "Love and a Question," "In Hardwood Groves," and "October." The latter, with its taut, formal rhythms and almost Celtic wistfulness, is vividly Yeatsian, especially in the opening four lines:

> O hushed October morning mild,
> Thy leaves have ripened to the fall;
> Tomorrow's wind, if it be wild,
> Should waste them all.

Although written some years earlier, in Derry, it was revised in the fall of 1911 and accepted for publication by the *Youth's Companion* in the spring of 1912, during Frost's last term at Plymouth; the poem "was meant as a kind of prayer," Frost said.[12] Though imitative to a degree, it shows that Frost was wholly in command of this kind of rhetorical exercise, and there are throughout the poem touches that make it unmistakably Frostian, such as the whimsical suggestion to the personified season that it release its leaves at a very slow pace:

> *Release one leaf at break of day;*
> *At noon release another leaf;*
> *One from our trees, one far away.*

Frost was beginning to feel the full weight of his power—as a poet, and as a force in the world. He was reading widely now, not only in English poetry and drama, but in philosophy. Henri Bergson's *Creative Evolution*, for example, had just been released in translation, and Frost read it eagerly. Just how eagerly this book was being read and discussed by young intellectuals in 1911 is evident from the memoirs of Conrad Aiken, who was Frost's contemporary. Aiken met T. S. Eliot, a Harvard classmate, at a café in Paris that very autumn and their talk centered on Bergson's book.[13]

Bergson was skeptical of abstract intellect, which he regarded as destructive, favoring what he called "creative construction," a force in the human mind that parallels a vital force in nature, the defining element in what he called "creative evolution." Life, which he identified with that creative element, is always "striving, rising upward" toward some unnamed pinnacle, and battering against the material world, which—much like a building that the wind must evade—only diverts it, never ultimately blocks it. As a consequence of these views, Bergson praised the imaginative person, such as the poet or prophet, who could rise above the "sterile scientific pretensions of the age," advocating a "right relationship to the Source," by which he meant something like God. (George Bernard Shaw's play *Back to Methuselah* is an undiluted version of Bergsonian thinking.) In his efforts to naturalize supernaturalism, Bergson had great appeal to intellectuals of Frost's generation, who were trying to shake off religious (and artistic) orthodoxies of all kinds. Hardly a major writer in the early part of the century was not, to some degree, influenced by Bergson.

Bergson was a dualist, after Plato and Plotinus, who ultimately put his faith in the spiritual world, yet he firmly believed that the human mind must work "*in* nature, *through* nature," and not attempt "a flight from the material world." His dualism turned on a perceived difference between the natural world, which was "always pulling down," and the human mind, which was always "rising," thus running counter to nature. Frost liked the dynamics of this concept, perhaps because it affirmed his own individualistic and contrary spirit. In *Creative Evolution*, Bergson put forward the Lucretian idea of "life as a stream," noting that our consciousness is "continually drawn the opposite way." Indeed, the stream is a central metaphor in many of Frost's poems, including "Hyla Brook," "West-Running Brook," "The Mountain," and "The Generations of Men." Robert Faggen notes, "The Frostian stream has obscure origins and moves in unpredictable and unknowable directions."[14]

Frost was perpetually "expressing his own stubborn contrariness to dominant intellectual movements," as Richard Poirier has said. His lone-striking spirit worked stubbornly against whatever grain was presented, and he found a justification for this tendency of his in Bergson, who celebrated the élan vital, that creative spirit (or enlightened stubborness) expressed by the artist or seer as resistance to any "drift" or "stated plan." On the other hand, even Bergson represented a creed that Frost must necessarily oppose. More like Lucretius than Bergson, Frost was attracted to a wild, untamed nature that was ultimately incompatible with any human intention, any teleological twist. The ferocious, inhuman quality of nature is embodied, for example, by the "great buck" in "The Most of It," who appears out of the wilderness of the lake and stumbles with "horny tread," ignoring its human observer, alien and awesome.

Like his hero, William James, whose *Pragmatism* he taught at Plymouth in the spring of 1912, Frost wanted to believe in some higher power, what Bergson called the Source; he also wanted to ground his beliefs in the natural world, and to have room for his own innate skepticism. In the wake of Darwin, it was no longer possible to believe in the literal idea of creation; one had to adopt some form of evolutionary theory, to find a way of accommodating the needs of spirit to this convincing theory of human origins. James (who acknowledged Bergson as a major influence) suggested that a "new opinion counts as 'true' just in proportion as it gratifies the individual's desire to assimilate the novel in his experience to his beliefs in stock."[15]

The "argument from design," the classic rationale for the existence of a deity, had fascinated James. Thomas Aquinas had famously argued that God fashioned each detail in nature toward some particular end. If so, James suggested, then God was obviously malevolent. "To the grub under the bark the exquisite fitness of the woodpecker's organism to extract him would certainly argue a diabolical designer." James wanted design to be, by contrast, "a term of *promise* . . . a vague confidence in the future." Though James was desperately fudging here, trying to have his cake and eat it, too, the iconoclastic quality of his arguments appealed to his young disciple, Frost, who encoded his own thinking on the argument from design in a sonnet called "In White," later revised as "Design." The original went as follows:[16]

> *A dented spider like a snowdrop white*
> *on a white Heal-all, holding up a moth*
> *Like a white piece of lifeless satin cloth—*
> *Saw ever curious eye so strange a sight?*
> *Portent in little, assorted death and blight*
> *Like the ingredients of a witches' broth?*
> *The beady spider, the flower like a froth,*
> *and the moth carried like a paper kite.*
>
> *What had the flower to do with being white,*
> *The blue Brunella every child's delight?*
> *What brought the kindred spider to that height?*
> *(Make we no thesis of the miller's plight.)*
> *What but design of darkness and of night?*
> *Design, design! Do I use the word aright?*

Frost's small but deeply significant revisions turned this interesting but awkward draft into one of his most devasting poems. An odd line such as "The blue Brunella every child's delight," for instance, is vaguely hackneyed ("every child's delight" is precut language); Frost revised it: "The wayside blue and innocent heal-all"—a more complex and suggestive line by far. The last lines, which in the rough version are convoluted and indirect, are with a bold stroke converted into three of Frost's most vivid concluding lines. It's worth noting how Frost revised by going back into the syntax already present, extending it, then savagely and directly answering the question posed:

> *What brought the kindred spider to that height,*
> *Then steered the white moth thither in the night?*
> *What but design of darkness to appall?—*
> *If design govern in a thing so small.*

Frost was feeling his strength now, intellectually and artistically, and ready to confront the world head-on. One senses this in the fact that he went to New York City over Christmas in 1911 to visit William Hayes Ward. He wanted desperately to move beyond the narrow circles in New Hampshire where, at least, he had established himself as an educator of some consequence. By the spring of 1912, he had passed his thirty-eighth birthday, and yet he had still not fulfilled his dream of publishing a volume of poetry. His feelings of mortality were by now intense; after all, his father had lived only to the age of thirty-four. Given the fluctuations of his health, Frost imagined there was little time left. He must withdraw from the daily demands of teaching, become selfish, and find the time to devote himself wholly to the task at hand: the completion of a book of poems.

"He always said that a turning point came in 1912, at Plymouth. He had to make a decision: to be a poet or a teacher, primarily. There was no way to reconcile both careers at this time. The poems had to get his full attention, which is why he left teaching. He had written just enough poetry of the highest quality to make that apparent to him. He understood what had to be done."[17]

In spring of 1912, a small flurry of acceptances from magazines encouraged Frost, and he determined to push ahead boldly. He had enough money in hand from the sale of the Derry house and his grand-father's annuity to make a move that would involve considerable financial risk. Encouraged by John Bartlett, who was about to head off to Vancouver Island in British Columbia for a year, Frost decided to have his own adventure, to live, as he said, "a life that followed poetically." His first inclination was to join Bartlett and his wife, Margaret, in Canada, but Elinor favored England. She wanted, she said, "to live under thatch," and be as close to Stratford as she could. Frost wished to oblige her, and was himself attracted to England; the idea of living in the cradle of English lyric poetry was irresistible. They flipped a coin, and England—to the relief of both—won out over Canada. "It became increasingly clear," Lesley would later recall, that her parents "wanted a dramatic change of scene together with a time, away from the burdens of teaching, for getting more poetry written. . . . All that had been contemplated was fresh scenery, peace to write, the excitement of change."[18]

In a letter to Mrs. John Lynch of Bethlehem, New Hampshire, Elinor would write the following October: "Last summer we spent several weeks trying our very best to decide where we wanted to go, and gradually we came to feel that it would be pleasant to travel about the world a little. And finally we decided to come to England and find a little house in one of the suburbs of London, and two weeks from the day of our decision, we were on our way out of Boston Harbor."[19] There is a charming, somewhat naive, quality about the tone that Elinor adopted here; the Frosts were going to be innocents abroad, and they seemed almost to cultivate this innocence.

Ernest Silver was dismayed, but there was no dissuading Frost. He had enjoyed his year at Plymouth, and the students had been increasingly enthusiastic about his classroom performance, but Frost had found little time for his own creative work. Contemplating teaching, he looked ahead, uncomfortably, to many years of toil without sufficient time for his own writing. He gambled that if worst came to worst, he could always return to New England and high school teaching.

"We stored our furniture, and brought only bedclothes, two floor rugs, books and some pictures," Elinor told a friend.[20] By August 1912, the family was ready to go. Lesley, who had just turned thirteen, was eager, as were Carol, now ten, Irma, who was nine, and Marjorie, who was seven. Their steamship, the SS *Parisian*, was scheduled to leave for Glasgow on the evening of August 23, carrying a full list of passengers and a heavy cargo that included 211 barrels of apples and 46,665 bushels of wheat. Ernest Silver helped them pack, and he put Elinor and the children on the train for Boston, since Frost himself had gone ahead to make final arrangements for their passage. The ship's departure was delayed until the next morning, but the Frosts didn't mind. They were putting everything beyond them now. They were starting fresh.

7

A PLACE APART

1912–1913

No man can know what power he can call rightly his unless he presses a little. —FROST, NOTEBOOK ENTRY, 1913

England, with its vast literary resonances, was the ideal place for Frost to complete the task of bringing himself forward as a poet. Removed from the pressures of his own country, where ghosts of his past hovered discouragingly, he was able to shake free, to make those critical revisions that would loft his poems successfully into the heady atmosphere of early modernism, and to finish the difficult work of shaping his first two volumes.

Frost's English interlude lasted for just over two years, from September 1912 through February 1915—the tail end of England's glory days of empire. The genteel Edwardian Age, which began with the death of Queen Victoria in 1901 and lasted through Edward VII's death in 1910, had recently given way to the Georgian period, which began gently enough in 1910, when the devastation of the Great War lay only a few years down the road but still seemed unimaginable. One journalist looking ahead at the time could envision only "a prospect of great prosperity and endless peace."[1]

The trip over was described by Elinor to a friend back in New Hampshire: "We sailed from Boston to Glasgow, and enjoyed the ocean trip on the whole, though Mr. Frost, Lesley, and I were quite seasick for a few days. The younger children escaped with only a few hours of discomfort.

"The last day of the voyage we skirted along the north coast of Ireland, and thought the dark, wild-looking headlands and blue mountains very beautiful. We landed at Glasgow in the morning, and travelled all day across Scotland and England, arriving at London about seven o'clock. From the station we telephoned for rooms at the Premier Hotel, and after securing them, drove in a cab to the hotel, feeling greatly excited, you may imagine, at being all alone, without a single friend, in the biggest city in the world."[2]

Arriving in London on Monday, September 2, 1912, Frost and his family quite naturally found themselves overwhelmed at first, but the anxiety soon passed. Because of their number, they had to take two rooms at the Premier, a large hotel on Russell Square that had seen better days. The brown wallpaper with "a pattern of squirrels and flowers" was loose and musty, the carpets threadbare, and the gaslights dim. But everyone was excited by the notion of life in England. While Frost spent his days searching for a suitable house in the suburbs, Elinor toured the city with the children, who were fascinated by the huge buses which "glide[d] along hooting and tooting" as they threaded their way through the crowded streets. In the evenings, thirteen-year-old Lesley would baby-sit the younger children while her parents visited pubs, walked, or attended plays in the West End. Among the hottest hits in town was Bernard Shaw's deliciously ironic attack on the English bourgeoisie *Fanny's First Play*, which the Frosts both liked a great deal.

The house hunting was not easy; Elinor called it "a tiresome search." But Frost eventually found a suitable cottage in Beaconsfield, a village in Buckinghamshire, some twenty miles north of London—in those days a train journey of forty minutes from Marylebone Station. The place in question was a recently built cottage on Reynolds Road, a squat stucco house covered with dark green vines. The shingled roof sloped steeply, like something out of the Brothers Grimm. There was a large garden filled with pear and apple trees, as well as a good strawberry patch. Thick laurel and dogwood hedges circled the property, lending an aura of privacy, and a wall at the back of the garden separated this property from a large cherry orchard. Inside, the house was surprisingly spacious, with five bedrooms and a cozy sitting room. There was "room enough for all, if we push together," Elinor said in a letter home; and the price was right: twenty dollars a month, with a year's lease. It was called The Bungalow, an unimpressive name for a place that stood near houses called Kingboro, Denmill, Oakden, and Little Seeley's. But the Frosts did not hesitate to sign a year's lease.

The house was bare, so the Frosts purchased a number of pieces of used furniture from local shops. "We bought enough furniture to get along with for about $125," Elinor wrote home, "and shall sell it again when we leave." She added, "Our plan is to stay here for a year, and then go over to France for a year, if our courage holds out."[3] The sense that she and her husband were embarked on a perilous adventure is evident (at times overwhelming) especially during the first months of their English sojourn.

The goods brought on the ship from America soon arrived, having slowly made their way down from the docks in Glasgow: four crates of oddments that included several carpets as well as the family's trusty Blick typewriter. Frost quickly reassembled two favorite items, a long-cherished Morris chair, which he always used for writing (with a lap-board), and a rocker for Eleanor. Before long, everyone felt at home in The Bungalow.

This part of Buckinghamshire was rich in literary associations, as Frost noted. John Milton had written *Paradise Lost* only a couple of miles from their house, while Thomas Gray and Edmund Burke lay buried nearby. The poet Edmund Waller had once lived here, but the most prominent writer in the village now was G. K. Chesterton, the author of poems, mystery stories, literary criticism, and Christian apologetics; Frost knew his work well (he had recently read *The Heretics*) and often passed the older writer's house on Grove Road, only four streets over from Reynolds, although he never actually met Chesterton, much to his disappointment.

In many ways, life in The Bungalow resembled life in Derry. The

Frosts, especially in the early months, were thrown upon themselves. Family life blossomed, and the children felt well tended. Once again, the choice was made to educate at least the two younger children at home, largely because Frost himself disliked the crowded conditions in the local schools, where as many as forty pupils crammed into each classroom. The pupils themselves, the children of local farmers and shopkeepers, appeared "undernourished and without energy," he observed in one letter home. Writing to Harold Brown, an acquaintance who worked for the state school system back in New Hampshire, he offered an account of the school: "One would have to go to the slums of the city for their like in face and form in America. I did not see the sprinkling of bright eyes I should look for in the New England villages you and I grew up in. They were clean enough—the school sees to that. But some of them were pitiful little kids."[4] Lesley and Irma, the older daughters, were sent to St. Anne's, a private school located on Baring Road, not far from Reynolds Road—the sort of school commonly attended by middle-class children in those days. Elinor wrote home in October: "The children are having a very good time, but they are homesick sometimes. Of course it is quite an education for them to see another land and another people."[5]

According to Elinor, Frost settled quickly into a routine that left the morning free for his own writing. Apart from pulling together a collection of poems, he wanted to write a novel as well, a story about two generations of New Hampshire farmers. The plot was to revolve around a contrast between a young man recently out of college and an older farmhand who was skeptical of "book-learning." This novel quickly changed into a play, which was reduced and reframed in later years as a verse dialogue, appearing in *Steeple Bush* in 1947. (The notion of conflict between a college boy and an old farmhand had already been explored by Frost in "The Death of the Hired Man," one of his finest dramatic poems, which appeared in *North of Boston* but was written seven years earlier, in Derry.)

Walking again became one of Frost's favorite activities. He explored the countryside around Beaconsfield every afternoon, sometimes venturing to neighboring towns, such as High Wycombe, Jordans, or Gerrards Cross. He occasionally took the train into London; on one occasion he attended a meeting at Caxton Place, near Buckingham Palace, where the featured speaker was Bernard Shaw himself. The event was sponsored by the Women's Tax Resistance League, but Shaw was typically ironic in his speech; he apparently teased his earnest audience so mercilessly that they "didn't know whether he had come to help (as advertised) or hinder them," Frost recalled.

Most mornings, and often into the later afternoons, Frost worked on the manuscript of *A Boy's Will*, whose title came from Longfellow's famous poem "My Lost Youth" ("A boy's will is the wind's will / And the thoughts of youth are long, long thoughts"). Elinor worked closely beside him, helping her husband choose and order the poems. Writing to John Bartlett, Frost said that the book "comes pretty near being the story of five years of my life." The thirty-two poems in the collection (three were dropped at a later date, along with the explanatory glosses that appeared in the original edition in the table of contents) do, in a sense, describe the arc of a sad time, beginning with the abandonment of Dartmouth and his flight into the Dismal Swamp. He told one friend that the book reflected his retreat "into the wilderness." "The Tuft of Flowers," a poem that occurs near the end of the sequence, signals his return to society—the period in his life that began when he got the job at Pinkerton. But one is hard-pressed to find a genuine narrative in the sequence.

The settings of the poems shift from autumn through subsequent seasons and back to autumn, beginning with "Into My Own," which only in Frost's self-mythologizing retrospective sight could be seen as being about the flight from Dartmouth or into the Dismal Swamp. It is a poem about retreat, but a curiously rigid self-confidence suffuses the final couplet: "They would not find me changed from him they knew— / Only more sure of all I thought was true." This stubbornness lies at the heart of Frost's poetry: a willed resistance to mutability, to any external efforts to produce change. Experience, for him, was largely a mode of confirmation.

The fierce refusal to relinquish control of the self becomes, poem by poem, the unspoken subject of this collection. In looking for a larger narrative, Frost faced what all poets face when it comes to gathering a volume for publication. Poems are written sporadically, and rarely in sequence; while they may be related in theme or texture, there is rarely any "plot." The larger narrative that readers expect from a book of poems is often imposed, with more or less success. The lyrics of A Boy's Will do, however, play together rather well, tonally and stylistically. The poet-speaker generally assumes an implied listener, which lends a dramatic quality to their presentation. One can usually hear a dialectic at work as the poet-speaker attempts to reconcile his various moods, whether hopeful (as in "A Late Walk") or, more often, despairing (as in "Storm Fear"). The poet's nearly solipsistic reveries are, at times, interrupted by an intruder, as in "Love and a Question." Mostly, he is left to himself—as he prefers.

The poems often drift toward the interior, which is reflected in the isolation of the woods and fields. Even the heavens offer little but "Minerva's snow-white marble eyes / Without the gift of sight" ("Stars"). The most intense dramatic moment in the sequence occurs with "Storm Fear," where the poet and his family are boarded up inside their isolated house in the woods during a storm as the wind "works against us in the dark." Nature is hardly welcoming; instead, it poses a threat, wishing to unravel or undermine home and hearth. Even the warmer wind of "To the Thawing Wind" is unpredictable and threatening (although the poet here seems to catch the anarchic mood and almost welcome the wind's rough treatment, its urge to "Scatter poems on the floor").

A series of mild, late Victorian–sounding poems follows: "A Prayer in Spring," "Flower-Gathering," "Rose Pogonias," "In a Vale," and others. An important turn comes, however, midway through the book, with "The Vantage Point," where Frost declares: "If tired of trees I seek again mankind." He wanted his readers to see and feel that turning outward, to acknowledge the poet's reacquaintance with the social world. This is a far cry from that easy Romanticism wherein the natural world becomes a place of calm retreat from the madding crowd. But even "The Vantage Point" returns to the isolated self, with the poet smelling the earth, "the bruisèd plant," and gazing into "the crater of

the ant." This isolation is reinforced by the next poem, the magnificent "Mowing," where the poet cultivates a private motion, leaving
"the hay to make" and the chips to fall where they may. The speaker in
that poem, like Frost in general, knows that he cannot control the
world beyond the book.

Each of the poems in the original edition of *A Boy's Will* was given
an explanatory epigraph, but these glosses were regarded by Frost as
unnecessary in later editions. They did, however, serve their original
function, as William H. Pritchard has said, providing "both a teasingly
suggestive and gracefully reticent atmosphere in which to read the
poems."[6] Most of them were softly ironic: "The youth is persuaded that
he will be rather more than less himself for having forsworn the
world"; "He is in love with being misunderstood"; "He resolves to
become intelligible, at least to himself." These headings provided, as it
were, an innoculation against ruthless English reviewers who might
cry sentimentality. "But look," the glosses seem to say, "I am poking
fun at the poor young man!"

The sequence moves back to autumn with poems such as "October," and "Reluctance," where "The leaves are all dead on the ground /
Save those that the oak is keeping / To ravel them one by one." Ever
the observant naturalist, Frost knew that the oak is among the last
trees to release its leaves, and he uses the image to good effect here.
The tense "heart of man" does not want to give in, to scatter its leaves,
to abandon life. Nobody really wants to go "with the drift of things" or
"yield with a grace to reason." The life force is irrational (in the
Bergsonian sense of nondirected, vital) and overpowering. It refuses to
let "a love or a season" pass.

Frost often adopts a wistful tone commonly heard in Edwardian and
Georgian verse. But in the best of these poems, he rises above the
period manner, finding his own clear attitude toward the material at
hand. "Into My Own," "My November Guest," "A Late Walk," "Storm
Fear," "Mowing," "Revelation," "The Trial by Existence," "October,"
and "Reluctance" are each filled to the same brim, declaring to the
world that a genuine, highly distinct, and original poet has entered the
world. "We make ourselves a place apart," Frost wrote in "Revelation,"

and indeed he had made himself "a place apart" in this volume, if only somebody would notice.

With Elinor's encouragement, Frost approached the publishing house of David Nutt. It was a small but well-established firm, especially well known in the field of poetry. They published the late W. E. Henley, who remained among the popular poets of the day, as well as John Drinkwater, who served as poetry adviser to the firm's current head, a melancholy Frenchwoman called Mrs. M. L. Nutt, who had inherited this role from her late husband, Albert Trubner Nutt, whose father had founded the house. Frost personally carried the manuscript to Mrs. Nutt, "a woman dressed all in black, as if she had just risen from the sea."[7]

It must have taken considerable courage for him—an unknown foreign writer—to plunge into a London publisher's office and present himself as a poet worthy of publication. Mrs. Nutt emerged from a back room and took the manuscript from Frost, giving no encouragement but promising she would read the book carefully. She may have shown it to Drinkwater, although no record of this exists. In any case, Frost did not have long to wait for her response.

Lesley Frost later recalled the moment when Frost first learned that his book was taken. "It was not until a morning in 1912," she said, "when a card came . . . that we knew A Boy's Will had been accepted for publication. That was splendid. We were pleased because our elders seemed pleased. We couldn't comprehend . . . what resolve, what hope, what patience in waiting, had gone into that first book: what a climax, what a beginning, was signified by such a recognition coming at last."[8] The long and painful search for acknowledgment had finally come.

Frost was eager to settle the details of the contract with Mrs. Nutt as quickly as possible. It surprised him when she wanted an option to publish his next four books, poetry or prose; this suggested astounding faith in him. In those days, it was not uncommon for a publisher to insist on a subvention from the poet to cover the initial printing costs—just in case the book didn't sell. By contrast, Mrs. Nutt readily agreed to pay Frost a royalty of 12 percent after the first 250 of the first edition of 1,000 were sold—a generous offer.

As an American, Frost could not avoid certain misgivings about bringing out his work in England first; indeed, he could not help feeling some resentment that his work had not been eagerly greeted in his own country—even though he had never made significant attempts to get published there. In any case, it was gratifying to find such enthusiasm for his work in the country that had produced Chaucer, Shakespeare, Milton, and Wordsworth.

This encouragement from Mrs. Nutt's firm seemed to fuel his creativity. Back in Beaconsfield, he entered upon what in retrospect was his most sustained, productive stretch of composition. The poems that make up the core of North of Boston were written over the next eight months as Frost worked steadily, day after day, often beginning early and ending late. Elinor was amazed, as was Frost himself. The decision to move to England could not have been more compellingly affirmed. By late spring, nearly a dozen finished poems lay on his desk, including "Mending Wall," "Home Burial," "After Apple-Picking," and "Birches"—four of the best-known poems in the whole of American literature. (The latter remained in his file of unfinished poems until it was included in 1916 in Mountain Interval.)

The Frosts had made almost no friends in Beaconsfield during their first autumn in The Bungalow, apart from Effie Solomon, a young wife who lived four houses down the road. In later life, Solomon could still recall visiting the Frosts and hearing Robert read aloud from his new work.[9] For the most part, Frost had little contact with anyone outside his family in those early months abroad. A turning point came in the new year, however. After signing his contract with Nutt, a buoyant Frost decided to test the waters of literary England by attending the opening of the Poetry Bookshop on Devonshire Street in London.

On January 8, 1913, the opening was hosted by the shop's energetic owner, Harold Monro. It was an elegant bookstore, resembling a country drawing room, with thick carpets and built-in shelves of dark oak. The building itself was on three floors, and above the bookshop were meeting rooms and accommodations for writers and artists. Over three hundred people crowded the lower floor on the day of the opening—a mixture of writers, artists, critics, book editors, bohemians, and literary hangers-on. Almost immediately Frost met Frank (F. S.) Flint, a poet, and T. E. Hulme, a poet-critic. Both would have considerable influence on Frost. He also met Mary Gardner, another poet, who was married to Ernest Gardner, a professor of archaeology at University College, London.

Flint looked the part of a dry civil servant in his dark, pin-striped suit and wire-framed glasses. His first volume of poems, *In the Net of the Stars*, had appeared three years earlier to respectable reviews. When Frost told him, proudly, that his first book had just been accepted, Flint was duly interested. After Frost discovered Flint's book in the shop, he immediately bought it and asked for a signature. Flint was pleased by this attention, and asked Frost if he knew Ezra Pound, another American poet living in England. Frost replied that he did not, and Flint offered to bring them together. He also offered to review Frost's book when it appeared—a remarkable gesture of friendship on such brief acquaintance. Frost left Harold Monro's party dazzled by his good luck. In his first attempt to break into English literary life, he had succeeded beyond his hopes.

This was, in fact, a pivotal moment for the arts in London, as the novelist Ford Madox Ford later noted. Britain's capital, he said, "was unrivalled in its powers of assimilation—the great, easy-going, tolerant, lovable, old dressing-gown of a place that it was then, but was never more to be."[10] The two most recognized poets of the day were Yeats and Thomas Hardy; the latter's first poetry collection, *Wessex Poems*, had appeared in 1898 and was followed by several much-admired volumes. (*Time's Laughingstocks*, which appeared in 1909, was still much on the minds of poetry readers when Frost arrived in England, as were the three volumes of Hardy's epic drama in verse, *The Dynasts*—a sequence that made a strong impression on Frost, encouraging him to try his own hand at verse drama.) Among the more popular poets of the day were Rudyard Kipling, Chesterton, Alfred Noyes, John Masefield, Robert Bridges, Laurence Binyon, and Walter de la Mare—all cultivated writers of fairly traditional verse in the Edwardian manner. Younger poets of this era included James Elroy Flecker, Lascelles Abercrombie, Rupert Brooke, Wilfrid Gibson, W. H. Davies, Edward Thomas, Edmund Blunden, Wilfred Owen,

Robert Graves, and J. C. Squire—most of whom were included in Edward Marsh's popular anthology of 1912, *Georgian Poetry, 1911–1912*— a collection that went through several later editions. "English poetry is now once again putting on a new strength and beauty," Marsh wrote in his introduction. Indeed, Frost would find himself extremely comfortable among these poets, and would be considered by the English critics of this period a fairly typical "Georgian."

Much of the poetry in Marsh's Georgian anthologies was insipid, trading in facile imagery of rural life, with a kind of forced simplicity that made it the laughingstock of modernist writers. The world of this verse was largely cleansed of urban decay, spiritual angst, and psychological complication. But the best of it, represented by Owen and Thomas, for example, was sinewy and fresh. Frost's virtues—a roughhewn simplicity, an ear for dialect, a metaphysical edge—played well in this context, and it is not surprising that his work caught the interest of this school of poets, and that he was quickly assimilated.

A parallel movement had been developing for some years in America. Frost had come to England having read closely his more celebrated contemporaries: E. A. Robinson, Edgar Lee Masters, Vachel Lindsay, and Amy Lowell. These poets had taken a step forward from their predecessors, the "genteel" or late-Romantic poets, such as Richard Watson Gilder, Richard Hovey, Bliss Carman, and Louise Imogen Guiney. They favored a closer adherence to colloquial speech, greater realism in choice of subjects for poems, and a more muscular, direct approach. The poeticisms one saw in late-Victorian verse—flowery, artificial diction and distorted syntax, with a fairly circumscribed notion of what subjects were appropriate—were beginning to fade. One actually sees them fading throughout Frost's early verse.

Frost happened to land in England at exactly the right moment for modern poetry. Ezra Pound had brought with him from America certain principles (gathered mostly from his friend Amy Lowell) that came to be called imagism. The movement might be said to have formally come to England in 1912, when Pound met over tea and buns in a café in Kensington with H.D. (Hilda Doolittle) and Richard Aldington, and the group declared that they embodied a school called *imagisme*. The idea of belonging to a school that had an "ism" attached to it was fashionable, vaguely Gallic, and self-flattering. In the August 1912 issue of *Poetry Review*, an article by Flint celebrates contemporary French poetry, which included such startling movements as *unanisme*, *impulsionnisme*, and *paroxysme*.[11]

That October, Pound published *Ripostes*, a critical salvo that included five poems by T. E. Hulme as examples of pure imagism. Hulme, who had been talking for several years about imagism, had met irregularly for some years with several of the more interesting younger poets of the day at a restaurant in Soho called the Eiffel Tower, and Pound was able to thrust himself by force of personality into the center of an already burgeoning movement. In many ways a fierce traditionalist, having been trained in Romance languages at the University of Pennsylvania, Pound maintained that a poet's duty was to "modernize" himself. "Make it new," he famously said, taking upon himself the mission of teaching everyone around him to do so in a way that pleased him personally.

The March 1913 issue of *Poetry*, a little magazine published in Chicago by Harriet Monroe, carried Pound's imagist manifesto, where three basic principles were put forward:

1. Direct treatment of the "thing," whether subjective or objective.

2. To use absolutely no word that did not contribute to the presentation.

3. As regarding rhythm: to compose in sequence of the musical phrase, not in sequence of a metronome.

Pound was a fervent advocate of concreteness, warning that poets should "go in fear of abstraction." Richard Aldington, in the June 1914 *Egoist*, another influential little magazine, added that a poet should "use the language of common speech" and avoid "decorative" words. Poets should strive to "present an image," and to produce poetry that is "hard and clear, never blurred or indefinite." As it were, the best poets of the day were already moving in the directions outlined by Hulme, Pound, and Aldington, but these younger men took it upon themselves to formulate principles, to create the sense of a unified movement.

The connection between Frost and Pound would follow from that chance meeting with Flint; as soon as Frost returned to Beaconsfield, he wrote fetchingly to his new acquaintance: "I was only too childishly happy in being allowed to [be present] for a moment in company in which I hadn't to be ashamed of having written verse. Perhaps it will help you understand my state of mind if I tell you that I have lived for the most part in villages where it were better that a millstone were hanged about your neck than that you should own yourself a minor poet."[12]

Flint quickly told Ezra Pound about Frost, and a somewhat enigmatic card arrived in Beaconsfield from Pound inviting Frost to visit him in Kensington. "At home—sometimes," it said. It took Frost a couple of months to get up the courage to try his luck with Pound, but he did eventually call on his fellow countryman in early March, just as the daffodils were beginning to rise in clusters in the old graveyard that ran beside Church Walk, where Pound occupied a tiny flat in a three-story Victorian building near St. Mary Abbott's Church, at the end of a cul-de-sac.

An elderly landlady directed Frost to a narrow stairwell that led to Pound's flat at the top. He knocked at a heavy oak door, and Pound yelled in a high-pitched voice that the visitor—whoever he was—must wait; he was taking a "bird-bath," as he called it. When eventually the door opened, Pound was dressed flamboyantly in a blue-and-green silk dressing gown, sporting a ring in one ear; he was barefoot, with his carrot-colored hair brushed back like a waterfall going the wrong way, his red beard damp and glistening. He told Frost that he had been rude not to answer the card or visit him sooner. "Did you bring the book?" he asked, eager to see *A Boy's Will*. No, Frost said. It was still being bound, and he did not have a spare copy of the manuscript. Pound could not accept this and insisted that they go immediately to David Nutt's office to get a copy of the book.

They did so, and Frost that day got his first glimpse of the lovely book, with its pebble-grained covers. The two poets then returned to

Church Walk, where Pound began to read the book to himself at once, tossing Frost a magazine to keep himself busy. After a short while, a grinning Pound said, "You don't mind our liking this, do you?" Frost replied, "Oh, no, go right ahead."[13]

Relations between Pound and Frost were artificial and strained, with Pound playing the teacher (though he was eleven years younger than his latest catch) and Frost the slightly dazzled, even uncertain, student. He was smart enough to realize, however, that Pound was a useful connection. Indeed, Pound offered that very day to review *A Boy's Will*, and he kicked Frost out of the flat so that he could begin writing the review at once! A couple of days later Pound noted with typical bravura to Harriet Monroe in Chicago: "Have just discovered another Amur'k'n. VURRY Amur'k'n, with, I think, the seeds of grace."[14]

A few weeks later Pound invited Frost to meet Yeats, who had seen *A Boy's Will* courtesy of Pound. The Irish poet called this volume "the best poetry written in America for a long time," and said he was interested to meet "the young man from New England." With Pound as go-between, Frost and Yeats met at Yeats's apartment in the Woburn Buildings, just off Russell Square, on the evening of March 31, a Monday. Yeats had been living there for twenty years, occupying a small, candle-lit apartment. It was a thrilling moment for Frost, who had admired the great Irishman for many years.

Frost said to Yeats that he could usually tell if a poem had come quickly, or if it had been labored over. In his own experience, the best poems came swiftly, almost miraculously, riding like ice on a griddle "on their own melting," as he would often say. Frost ventured to suggest that "The Song of Wandering Aengus" was such a poem, one "given" to the poet by the Muse. Yeats demurred. No, he said. He had labored nine hours over that poem, and it had been the product of a terrible period in his life. At the end of the evening, Yeats told Frost that he often held gatherings on Monday evenings, when he was in London, and that Frost should always feel welcome. (Frost quickly reported all of this to John Bartlett in a letter in which he tried his best not to sound impressed with himself.)

A *Boy's Will* was not granted a resounding welcome in the world. "These poems are intended by the author to possess a certain sequence, and to depict the various stages of a young man's outlook on life," wrote a critic in the *Athenaeum*, on April 5, 1913. "The author is only half successful in this," the reviewer continued, suggesting that Frost's poems "do not rise above the ordinary, though here or there a happy line or phrase lingers gratefully in the memory." As the first review that Frost ever received, this must have been exceptionally disappointing. Five days later the *Times Literary Supplement* weighed in with a more cheerful assessment: "There is an agreeable individuality about these pieces: the writer is not afraid to voice the simplest of his thoughts and fancies, and these, springing from a capacity of complete absorption in the influences of nature and the open air, are often naively engaging. Sometimes, too, in a vein of reflection, he makes one stop and think, though the thought may be feebly or obscurely expressed." Not marvelous, but better.

Frost was outwardly stoic, suggesting in a letter to John Bartlett that he buy up twenty copies of the book to give the impression to the publisher that something was occurring, but he was described by Elinor in a letter to Margaret Bartlett as being "altogether discouraged." "I am very glad you and John like Robert's book," she said. "Of course I love it very much, and have been somewhat disappointed that the reviewers have not been more enthusiastic. How can they help seeing how exquisitely beautiful some of the poems are, and what an original music there is in most of them?"[15]

Pound's eagerly anticipated review in *Poetry* appeared in May, but the praise was not full-throated. These verses had in them "the tang of the New Hampshire woods," Pound wrote. He praised the "utter sincerity" of the poems, welcoming a poet who "has the good sense to speak naturally and to paint the thing, the thing as he sees it."[16] But the review was illogical, hastily written, and condescending. As Frost observed to Flint: "If any but a great man had written it, I should have called it vulgar." Fighting snideness with snideness, he referred to Pound as "that great intellect abloom in hair." But he perfectly understood the importance of this review for his career; he was now a player in the larger game of modern poetry, and having the backing of Ezra Pound—the ringmaster of modern literature—meant a lot.

A clutch of brief but complimentary reviews followed in both England and America, lifting Frost's spirits a little. But he was generally depressed by the lukewarm reception of his first volume. Nevertheless, the door to literary success was now ajar, and Frost could peer into that great sunlit room and imagine himself a genuine presence there.

The early spring of 1913 had been particularly chilling, with weeks of drizzle mirroring Frost's mood. A succession of sun-drenched, almost summery days in May, however, changed the atmosphere considerably. Elinor began to work each morning in the garden, and Frost often joined her. It was heartening to stand amidst flowering apple and pear trees. A long row of currant bushes in the back of the garden suddenly "went aflame," as Elinor wrote to a friend, their bloom "improbably bright." The Frosts had never been closer, it seemed, and they took long hikes in the countryside together. On weekends, the family often packed a lunch and set off merrily into the surrounding meadows and woodlands. Elinor would later refer to this period as "perhaps the best time ever."

Frost was not writing now at the same pace as earlier, but the poems continued to come, if more slowly. Meanwhile, his foothold in English literary society grew firmer. The friendship with Mary and Ernest Gardner, whom he had met at Harold Monro's party, had developed, with several visits back and forth between the two families; that summer, the Frosts were invited to spend a couple of weeks on the east coast of Scotland near the Gardners. Given Frost's heritage, this seemed like a fine idea, and they readily agreed to rent a small cottage in Kingsbarns, on the East Neuk of Fife, for the last two weeks in August.

The Frost family loved the setting. Kingsbarns is a coastal village near St. Andrews, which in medieval times was the ecclesiastical capital of Scotland. The tiny fishing villages along the East Neuk were them, as now, picturesque, with narrow stone houses and cobbled streets. Kingsbarns is particularly attractive, and the Frosts settled happily into life there, with long shoreline walks every morning. They often took their meals with the Gardners or picnicked with them on the furze-covered rocks overlooking the North Sea. Unfortunately, Frost soon began to resent the attitude of the Gardners, who felt they had "discovered" him, and his resentments are evident in letters to John Bartlett. "The Gardners don't like me anymore," he wrote. "They despise my judgement and resent my tactlessness."[17] He was eager to get back to Beaconsfield.

There was good news upon his return. Several new and highly laudatory reviews of A Boy's Will had appeared, including one in the Academy, an influential English journal, in which the anonymous reviewer singled out Frost among a clutch of other poets: "We wish we could fitly express the difference which marks off A Boy's Will from the other books here noticed. Perhaps it is best hinted by stating that the poems combine, with a rare sufficiency, the essential qualities of inevitability and surprise. We have read every line with that amazement and delight which are too seldom evoked by books of modern verse. Without need of qualification or trimming of epithets, it is undoubtedly the work of a true poet."[18]

Frost had every reason to imagine that his career as a poet was well under way, although he remained hesitant, uncertain—as though he could not shake off the sense of inferiority that had for more than a decade held him back. His next book, under contract to David Nutt, was still unfinished, and his financial situation was still shaky. Apart from everything else, Frost appeared to suffer from a growing sense of homesickness, a feeling that surfaced in his letters in late spring and seemed to worsen through the summer. As he wrote to Flint in June, whenever he walked about London he saw "lots of Americans . . . with their box-toed shoes." Even though he did not like their manner, he could not resist them: "I yearn towards them just the same. I'm a Yank from Yankville."[19] But he knew, in his heart of hearts, that he must not give in to such nostalgia. He had come to England to make his name as a poet, and he would not give up until he had done so.

8

IN A YELLOW WOOD
1914–1915

God help us not to take the English as the English take us.
—FROST, NOTEBOOK ENTRY, 1919

Throughout the summer and early fall of 1913, Frost worked hard assembling *North of Boston*, a second volume of poems. His working title, more descriptive than evocative, was *Farm Servants and Other People*. Among those given the poems for comment was T. E. Hulme, who met with Frost on July 1 in London to discuss the manuscript. Frost used this meeting to put forward his current ideas on poetry, especially his notion of "the sound of sense." He later reported to Flint that his theories "got just the rub they needed" from Hulme, whose sharp, critical mind had made him an important figure among the imagists.

Frost also gave a copy of the volume to Flint, whose response was warmly appreciative: "I have read your little dramas, and I like them very much. (It occurs to me typing this from a rough note that you might try your hand at a play later on when you are well known.) You have a lode there from which you ought to extract quantities of good clean ore." Flint offered a few minor criticisms, but was mainly enthusiastic: "I have nothing to say to you about these poems, except: go on!"[1]

That Frost was now brimming with ideas about poetry is evident from a letter to John Bartlett; though his rhetoric is self-congratulatory, it may be seen as Frost's way of cheering himself along: "To be perfectly frank with you I am one of the most notable craftsmen of my time. That will transpire presently. I am possibly the only person going who works on any but a worn out theory (principle I had better say) of versification. You see the great successes in recent poetry have been made on the assumption that the music of words was a matter of harmonized vowels and consonants. Both Swinburne and Tennyson arrived largely at effects in assonation. But they were on the wrong track or at any rate on a short length of it. Anyone else who goes that way must go after them. And that's where most are going. I alone of English writers have consciously set myself to make music out of what I may call the sound of sense."[2]

"The sound of sense" was an idea he would develop carefully in the coming year and return to throughout his life. Its chief formulation occurs in a letter to Bartlett written the following February:

> I give you a new definition of sentence:
>
> A sentence is a sound in itself on which other sounds called words may be strung.
>
> You may string words together without a sentence-sound to string them on just as you may tie clothes together by the sleeves and stretch them without a clothes line between two trees, but—it is bad for the clothes.
>
> The number of words you may string on one sentence-sound is not fixed but there is always danger of over loading.
>
> The sentence-sounds are very definite entities. (This is no literary mysticism I am preaching.) They are as definite as words. It is not impossible that they could be collected in a book though I don't at present see on what system they would be catalogued.
>
> They are apprehended by the ear. They are gathered by the ear from the vernacular and brought into books. Many of them are already familiar to us in books. I think no writer invents them. The most original writer only catches them fresh from talk, where they grow spontaneously.[3]

Frost continues for several pages, culminating in the "greatest test" of a piece of prose or a poem: "You listen for the sentence sounds. If you find some of those not bookish, caught fresh from the mouths of people, some of them striking, all of them definite and recognizable, so recognizable that with a little trouble you can place them and even name them, you know you have found a writer." He elaborates in another letter to Sidney Cox: "Just so many sentence sounds belong to a man as just so many vocal runs belong to one kind of bird. We come into the world with them and create none of them."[4]

Frost explained to Bartlett that the way to hear "the abstract sound of sense is from voices behind a door that cuts off the words." A poet must learn "to get cadences by skillfully breaking the sounds of sense with all their irregularity of accent across the regular beat of the metre." He was arguing here, implicitly, against Robert Bridges, the new British poet laureate, who believed in the fixed quantity of English syllables. Frost understood that the speaking voice is, somewhat paradoxically, both idiosyncratic and dependent upon the formal structures of English sound patterns. He praised "the abstract vitality of our speech"—a vitality that connects every speaker to the language itself, a community of shared signals. But what both separates and connects the true artist to this community is an original way of "breaking the sounds."

Two factors are always at work in a line of verse: the abstract possibility of the line and the poet's individual way of "breaking" words across it. The poetry, indeed, resides in the difference between these two possibilities. Thus, a line such as "There was never a sound beside the wood but one," the first line of "Mowing," can be scanned as iambic pentameter—in the abstract; in its vocalization, however, any number of different ways of scanning the line would seem more appropriate. Certainly, in reading the poem, a poet would be unlikely (and unwise) to stick to the strict iambic flow. The pleasure of poetry inheres in the contrast, then, between this abstract potential (the iambic regularity) and the vernacular embodiment of the line, which is governed by the poet's own voice and coded into the language. As Frost put it, "The living part of a poem is the intonation entangled somehow in the syntax, idiom, and meaning of a sentence. It is only there for those who have heard it previously in conversation. It is not for us in any Greek or Latin poem because our ears have not been filled with the tones of Greek and Roman talk. It is the most volatile and at the same time important part of poetry. It goes and the language becomes a dead language, the poetry dead poetry. . . . Words exist in the mouth, not in books."[5]

Having settled into Beaconsfield once again, with the older children in school and Elinor teaching the younger ones, Frost found himself on fire with the urge to write. The homesickness that had begun in late spring was now yielding marvelous fruit in poems such as "After Apple-Picking," "Mending Wall," and "Birches"—all written in Beaconsfield. The last one, inspired by a poem on the same subject by the American poet Lucy Larcom, began from a fragment about icicles dating back to 1906.[6] It opens fetchingly:

> *When I see birches bend to left and right*
> *Across the lines of straighter darker trees,*
> *I like to think some boy's been swinging them.*

Lesley, in the journal she kept when she was six, wrote alluringly about the New England game of swinging birches: "On the way home," she said, "i climbed up a hi birch and came down with it and i stopt in the air about three feet and pap cout me." Her father had been taught how to do this in the summer of 1886 by Charlie Peabody, a neighbor from Lawrence. The practice of climbing birches until your weight brought the trunk plunging to earth had caught his imagination, as it now caught Lesley's:

i like to climb trees very much but mam doesnt like me to becose i tare my stocings so i have to stop i do not like to but i have to at frst i was scared to swing with birchis but now i am not so much scared becose it wont hurt me. an i am not scared if it swings down with me if it does klere down with me i dont like it if it dosunt i climb uther threes but they downt swing as the birchis do so i dpwnt like them aswell i climb oak and mapel but with me they swing with me. i like that to but not as well but papa likes to swing beter. i climb apale trees but those dont swing a tall do they.[7]

Frost's later accounts of the writing of "Birches" were often misleading. He would tell admiring audiences that he wrote it one morning in Beaconsfield "with one stroke of the pen."[8] But he explained to Robert Penn Warren many years later that the poem was "two fragments soldered together so long ago I have forgotten where the joint is."[9] The poem, which was originally called "Swinging Birches," catches perfectly the "sound of sense" in poetry; while it is written in classic blank verse, one cannot help but hear Frost's grainy, idiosyncratic voice ushering the syllables into his own strong vernacular. He does not worry about shifting the blank verse line to meet the needs of the rhythm as he heard it building, as below:

> Soon the sun's warmth makes them shed crystal shells
> Shattering and avalanching on the snow-crust—
> Such heaps of broken glass to sweep away
> You'd think the inner dome of heaven had fallen.

These lines will not scan as iambic pentamenter unless you radically distort the language as it is spoken. Nobody, for instance, would accent the first line above as follows in reading it aloud:

> Soon thé sun's wármth makes thém shed crýstal shélls.

A more natural way of scanning the line would put stress on the first word, spreading the rest of the stresses more evenly throughout. In recorded versions of this line, Frost seems to emphasize virtually every syllable except the second ("the")—a kind of flattening out that is not untypical of New England folk dialects.

The poem has the rambling quality of everyday speech, a characteristic made explicit in the twenty-first and twenty-second lines: "But I was going to say when Truth broke in / With all her matter-of-fact about the ice-storm." Readers feel as though they are listening to a man talking away and likely to take any kind of sudden turn toward Truth—which may be defined here as any point of enlightenment that occurs in the poet's brain. But this rambling is deceptive; the poem, as soldered together in the final act of composition, is thoroughly unified, emphasizing the need that all human beings feel when "weary of considerations" to "get away from earth awhile."

Frost's commonplace theme of the wish to escape, to get away from his earthly troubles, is given perfect symbolic form in the trope of the boy climbing to heaven on the slender birch. Yet the greatness of this poem lies in the ending, where the poet emphasizes that he wants to come down before being snatched away. There is no desire for transcendental rapture that excludes a safe return to the mundane:

> *May no fate willfully misunderstand me*
> *And half grant what I wish and snatch me away*
> *Not to return. Earth's the right place for love:*
> *I don't know where it's likely to go better.*

The attractions of this poem are manifold, but its sensuousness is a crucial part of what holds the reader in thrall. The visual impact is strong, too, beginning with that image of the birches loaded with ice on "a sunny winter morning / After a rain." Here, as elsewhere in Frost, a covert sexual energy suffuses the imagery:

> *You may see their trunks arching in the woods*
> *Years afterwards, trailing their leaves on the ground*
> *Like girls on hands and knees that throw their hair*
> *Before them over their heads to dry in the sun.*

"Birches" is, as much as anything, a poem about onanistic fantasy, about an isolated boy with the urge to ride these trees to the ground, over and over again, "Until he took the stiffness out of them, / And not one but hung limp." The poem re-creates the curve of desire found in the sexual act, from anticipation, exhilaration, and fulfillment to the letting down at the end. That these sexual undertones are neatly buried in the literal imagery of birch-bending lends an element of metaphysical wit to the poem that is not the least of its appeal.

The idea for "Mending Wall" had come to him while in Scotland. Among the many people whom Frost had met in Kingsbarns was J. C. Smith, an inspector of schools from Edinburgh with a strong literary bent. Smith later recalled walking in the Fifeshire countryside with Frost and seeing "dry stone dykes" that reminded the New Englander of similar walls that had once absorbed so much of his time. Back in Beaconsfield, Frost's mind turned to a particular wall on the Derry farm that "I hadn't mended in several years and which must be in a terrible condition."[10]

"Mending Wall" was written in the fall of 1913, and it "contrasts two types of people," as Frost later said.[11] The poet-narrator observes rather quaintly: "He is all pine and I am apple orchard." The poem centers on the repair of a wall by two farmers, an activity initiated by the speaker:

> I let my neighbor know beyond the hill;
> And on a day we meet to walk the line
> And set the wall between us once again.

The poem rapidly becomes metaphorical. "Something there is that doesn't love a wall," it opens, and the line is repeated later as the narrator contemplates his own mischievous nature, which urges him to suggest to his neighbor that elves are responsible for the undoing of this wall. The taciturn neighbor will only mutter: "Good fences make good neighbors," a proverbial line quoted often in almanacs of the nineteenth century.[12] This catchy notion has often given readers pause, as Frost noted in 1962: "People are frequently misunderstanding it or misinterpreting it. The secret of what it means I keep."[13]

The secret is not so hard to fathom. Frost often emphasized the need for boundaries taken as liberating rather than confining limits. Richard Poirier observes that the real significance of "Mending Wall" is "that it suggests how much for Frost freedom is contingent upon some degree of restriction. More specifically, it can be said that restrictions, or forms, are a precondition for expression. Without them, even nature ceases to offer itself up for a reading."[14] Everywhere, in language and nature, Frost finds—or self-consciously erects—barriers that, as Marion Montgomery has noted, "serve as a framework for mutual understanding and respect."[15]

As in so many of Frost's best poems, various levels in the poem may be discerned, and these are often contradictory. This is especially so if one attempts to find an autobiographical strain in the poem. Frost himself made this point in later comments, as to Charles Foster at Bread Loaf in 1938, when he maintained: "I am both wall-builder and wall-destroyer."[16]

In "Mending Wall," it is, importantly, the speaker, not the "old-stone savage" living next door, who insists on the act of wall building. If hunters should come along at any time and undo the wall, he is quick to fix it. And he insists on the yearly ritual, as if civilization depends upon the collective activity of making barriers. There is a lot of "making" and "mending" in this poem, and it is more than a mere wall that is erected. One senses a profound commitment to the act of creating community in the speaker, who allies his voice with the "something" that sends frozen groundswells under the wall to disrupt it. (One could, perhaps, make something of the fact that the neighbor is capable of saying nothing himself except an old proverb.) The energy of the speaker's imagination unsettles and builds at the same time, a paradoxical notion that would seem to lie at the heart of the creative process itself.

It is intriguing to consider how many of Frost's best poems reflect on the act of creation, the process of breaking down the forms of reality given by the world and remaking them, restoring them to freshness. Frost's aesthetic was largely derived from the Romantics, especially Coleridge, who argued in the *Biographia Literaria* that the imagination of the poet "dissolves, diffuses, dissipates, in order to recreate." The enterprise of poetry, from Wordsworth on, was regarded as the work of defamiliarizing the familiar by freshening the vision: hence Pound's injunction to "make it new." For Coleridge and Wordsworth both, the chief opponent of making it new was "custom," and the work of the poet (in Coleridge's terminology) was to release "wonder" from the "familiar." In *The Prelude*, Wordsworth regularly condemns "habit," "use and custom," and "the regular action of the world," asking us to experience the miracle of being in the most commonplace objects:

> And the world's native produce, as it meets
> The sense with less habitual stretch of mind,
> Is ponder'd as a miracle.

The criterion for freshness is always "the child's sense of wonder and novelty."

"After Apple-Picking" was written in the same fall, and it takes up the workings of the imagination as an explicit theme. Frost's old Harvard professor George Santayana once defined the artist as "a person consenting to dream of reality." This poem centers on the idea of "the great harvest" of imaginative work that the narrator "himself desired," although a firm note of regret is attached to those experiences (poems) that were not brought across the line, translated, into poems:

> There were ten thousand thousand fruit to touch,
> Cherish in hand, lift down, and not let fall.

One can hardly imagine a better analogy for the gathering of poems from a poet's memory than this.

The poem begins quite realistically:

> My long two-pointed ladder's sticking through a tree
> Toward heaven still,
> And there's a barrel that I didn't fill
> Beside it, and there may be two or three
> Apples I didn't pick upon some bough.
> But I am done with apple-picking now.

Thus far the narrator provides a literal description of a commonplace farm activity, with only a hint at something metaphysical in the phrase "Toward heaven still." But the literalness dissolves in the next lines, as the speaker drowses off:

Essence of winter sleep is on the night,
The scent of apples: I am drowsing off.
I cannot rub the strangeness from my sight
I got from looking through a pane of glass
I skimmed this morning from the drinking trough
And held against the world of hoary grass.
It melted, and I let it fall and break.
But I was well
Upon my way to sleep before it fell,
And I could tell
What form my dreaming was about to take.

The tenses suddenly grow indistinct, and one cannot be sure where dream and reality intersect. The reader plunges through the looking glass of the ice into an imaginative world brimming with "load on load of apples coming in."

The form of the poem is itself unique in Frost, as Reuben A. Brower notes in his remarkable reading of this particular "lyric-idyll," as he calls it:

Everything said throughout the poem comes to the reader through sentences filled with incantatory repetitions and rhymes and in waves of sound linked by likeness of pattern. From the opening lines, apparently matter-of-fact talk falls into curious chain-like sentences, rich in end-rhymes and echoes of many sorts. But although the voice seems to be lapsing into the rhyming fits of insomnia, the fits shape themselves into distinct and subtly varied patterns.[17]

One can visualize Frost in his Morris chair in The Bungalow, his mind swirling with images of the life he left behind in New Hampshire. He was consciously making use of what he knew was extraordinary material, a bin stored with imagery that he could draw on. There seemed no end to the poems he might fashion from this experience, and even that material which had not yet been transformed into poetry was still there, waiting, like the apples that had struck the earth and been transported to the cider-apple heap—a hoard that would create a certain amount of anxiety in the poet until that time when he found the creative energy to raid it; thus, he could write: "One can see what will trouble / This sleep of mine, whatever sleep it is."

By the time Frost returned from Scotland, he was determined to get the new book into production as soon as possible. The date had been delayed from fall 1913 to spring 1914, which was itself an irritant. Frost had seen too many years flicker by without public recognition, and he was eager to get his recent poems before an audience. Even if the reviewers of the first book had not all been terribly enthusiastic, there was a warm response among his friends. J. C. Smith had written on September 15, 1913, from Edinburgh, for instance: "There's no doubt about it. You've got the poetic gift." He told Frost that his family had spent "two delightful evenings reading your book aloud after dinner." He added: "Let me know when to look for your second volume."[18]

By November, a fresh, feisty attitude toward his work seems to have taken over, as seen in a letter to John Bartlett:

> You musn't take me too seriously if I now proceed to brag a bit about my exploits as a poet. There is one qualifying fact always to bear in mind: there is a kind of success called "of esteem" and it butters no parsnips. It means a success with the critical few who are supposed to know. But really to arrive where I can stand on my legs as a poet and nothing else I must get outside that circle to the general reader who buys books in their thousands. I may not be able to do that. I believe in doing it—don't you doubt me there. I want to be a poet for all sorts and kinds. I could never make a merit of being caviare to the crowd the way my quasi-friend Pound does. I want to reach out, and would if it were a thing I could do by taking thought.[19]

Frost's resolve was marked by efforts to press himself upon English literary society. Through Hulme and others, he managed to befriend many of the leading poets of the day, such as Laurence Binyon, W. H. Davies, Ford Madox Ford, John Masefield, Wilfrid Gibson, and Robert Bridges. Harold Monro also helped, introducing Frost whenever he could to influential writers and critics. Gibson introduced Frost to Lascelles Abercrombie, a highly original critic and writer of dramatic poems not unlike those in Frost's *North of Boston*. Reading Abercrombie's recent sequence of dramatic poems, *Emblems of Love*, Frost quickly saw the parallels between them and worked to enlarge upon the acquaintance.

Another good contact, also urged upon him by Gibson, was W. H. Hudson. A sharp-witted, acerbic man with a good eye for poetry, Hudson was given a manuscript of one of the longer poems from the new manuscript (probably "The Death of the Hired Man"), and his response was heartening. "Forgive me for keeping your poem a day or two longer than I ought to have done," he wrote. "I very much like it, and imagine it must be unique in American poetry; it is like nothing I have seen from your country, and I foresee a welcome for it in ours. It was a great pleasure to meet you the other day. I owe Gibson a good turn for that."[20] Two weeks later, Frost was introduced to Edward Thomas over lunch at a restaurant in St. Martins Lane, near Trafalgar Square—an encounter that would lead to a friendship affecting both men profoundly.

One senses from his letters home that Frost felt at ease, if not at home, in England now. "The Englishmen are very charming," he wrote to Thomas Bird Mosher. "I begin to think I shall stay with them till I'm deported. If I weren't so poor I should plan to stay five years anyway."[21] Elsewhere, he writes to friends in America of "gadding" about at parties in Kensington with Elinor and attending long literary lunches at the Vienna Café in Soho. The Frosts also went to the theater as often as they could.

The family had a meager but happy Christmas in 1913. Frost made most of the toys for the children himself, fashioning them from wood. A tiny evergreen—nothing like the massive balsam firs that had been common on the farm in Derry—was brought in from a nearby copse and "decorated with cardboard ornaments and paper angels," as Elinor wrote home. In later years, none of the children would speak of this as a time of deprivation, however makeshift the arrangements.

The friendship with Gibson, who was four years younger than Frost, flourished this winter. Frost admired the stripped-down quality of Gibson's diction and the dramatic quality of his poems (Gibson wrote a good deal of full-scale drama in verse). Like Frost's, his poems often focused on working people, as in *Stonefolds* (1907), a collection of small verse dramas featuring the poor sheep farmers of Northumberland—a group who had much in common with the farmers of Frost's northern New England. The brooding, imagistic quality of this work appealed to Frost, as did the poems of Gibson's *Daily Bread* (1910), where dwellers in urban slums and mining towns were given a voice. He was also much taken by Gibson's popularity; here was a poet who had, indeed, managed to write "for all sorts and kinds." How quickly the friendship blossomed is made clear by Frost in a letter he wrote to an acquaintance back in the States in early December: "Gibson is my best friend. Probably you know his work. He is much talked of in America at the present time. He's just one of the plain folks with none of the marks of the literary poseur about him—none of the wrongheadedness of the professional literary man."[22]

For some time now, the Frosts had all been wanting to move away from Beaconsfield, which lacked the full charm of rural England. The idea of going into the Gloucester countryside, near Gibson, occurred in midwinter. Frost imagined it would be pleasant to live near "those who spoke our language and understood our thoughts."[23] Another reason may have been that the two elder daughters, Lesley and Irma, had begun to complain about the private school they were attending. After the first two terms were completed, they both refused to go back, and Elinor found herself having to instruct all four children every morning. The atmosphere in The Bungalow became altogether too claustrophobic.

In mid-January, Frost found tenants willing to wait upon his convenience. Urged on by Gibson and Abercrombie, he began searching for a cottage in Gloucestershire. Gibson had recently moved to the village of Greenway, and Abercrombie lived only a few miles away at Ryton.

After months of searching, Gibson found Little Iddens, a cottage in nearby Ledington—a classic west-country hamlet in the Dymock region. The last letter that Frost wrote from Beaconsfield was dated March 26, 1914, his fortieth birthday.

Little Iddens, about two miles from the Old Nailshop, where Gibson lived, was a small seventeenth-century cottage that bordered an undulating stretch of open fields. It was not a spacious house: much of the ground floor (made of smoothly worn brick) was taken up by a shed once used for cattle. The hearth-centered living room had a long oak table for dining pushed against one wall, and this adjoined a tiny kitchen; upstairs, reached by a steeply pitched staircase, were two bedrooms and a sleeping alcove. The low ceilings and tiny, leaded windows accentuated the cramped quality of the house.

For all these drawbacks, Little Iddens had many advantages, including charm. Its source of water was an old well by the side door, with a helmeted pump that splashed into a low tank. The views of the surrounding hay fields were idyllic, and each field was bordered by tall elms or bushes. An orchard of fruit trees lay beside the house itself, with apples, pears, and plums coming into flower just as the Frosts arrived. A fine vegetable garden was already going. Not a month after moving in, Frost wrote to Flint that he was "already up to my waist in peas and broadbeans, and holding up a hoe to mark the place of my disappearance."[24] The house struck everyone in the Frost family as an English equivalent of the farm in Derry.

Among the many good neighbors was John Haines, who was Abercrombie's distant cousin. A lawyer by profession, he loved poetry and eagerly devoured the latest journals. He was also an amateur botanist, like Frost, and adored long country walks. Haines described Frost at the time as "a very fine looking man indeed. He was of medium height but had a splendid physique and was especially broad-shouldered. His eyes were an attractive shade of jade blue, and extremely penetrating. . . . In disposition he was happy and cheerful. He talked much and well but liked occasional long silences and especially late at night enjoyed giving long, slow soliloquies on psychological and philosophical subjects. . . . His sense of humour pervaded all his talk and he could be sarcastic if he wanted to, though usually his humour was kindly and he had a great sense of fun."25

Edward Thomas, whom Frost had by now met several times, showed up with his son that spring. The Thomases had been cycling through Wales, and they spent a week at Little Iddens, sleeping in the loft with the two elder Frost children. This was a crucial time for this friendship, which from the first had been significant to both men. In later years, Helen Thomas would put her memories of first encountering Frost into her autobiography, recalling that

> Robert was a thickset man, not as tall as Edward, with a shock of grey hair. His face was tanned and weatherbeaten and his features powerful. His eyes, shaded by bushy grey eyebrows, were blue and clear. It was a striking and pleasing face, rugged and lined. He was dressed in an open-necked shirt and loose earth-stained trousers held up by a wide belt. His arms and chest were bare and very brown. His hands were hard and gnarled. He spoke with a slight American accent.26

What life was like at Little Iddens is perhaps best seen in a recollection by Eleanor Farjeon, a friend of Edward Thomas's who wrote a biography of him:

> The Frosts did not live by the clock, their clock conformed to the Frosts. There was always time for the thing in hand. Meals (bedtime too I believe) were when you felt like them. Irregular hours for children meant an extension of experience for them; it was more important for a child to go for a walk in the dark than to have an unbroken night's rest. By day, walks and talks were not shortened for the sake of things less interesting. When the children were hungry enough to be more interested in eating than in what they were doing, they came indoors and helped themselves to food that was left available in the small, pink-washed living room: bread, fruit, cold rice in a bowl. . . . The centre of the Frosts' life was out-of-doors and household stan-

dards mattered very little. If they had, Elinor struck me as too delicate to cope with them, indeed none of the family seemed especially robust; but though they were pale-complexioned they were lively and active, and too resourceful to be at a loose end.[27]

Elinor did suffer that spring and summer from the nervous condition that had plagued her for many years. Always keyed into the fluctuations of her husband's literary fortunes, her anxiety level soared after the publication of *North of Boston* on May 15, as two weeks of appalling silence from reviewers were followed by a brief mention in the *Times Literary Supplement*, where Frost was weakly commended for his "little pictures from ordinary life." What kept Frost from despair was the knowledge that his three new friends—Abercrombie, Gibson, and Thomas—had already written reviews on assignment that were bound to be favorable; Pound, too, had written a note to express interest in reviewing the book, although Frost considered this a mixed blessing, given Pound's response to *A Boy's Will*.

The first of the friendly reviews appeared in the *Nation* on June 13, a detailed and lengthy piece full of high praise by Abercrombie. "We find very little of the traditional manner of poetry in Mr. Frost's work," he wrote, "save a peculiar adaptation, as his usual form, of the pattern of blank verse. It is poetry which is not much more careful than good prose is to stress and extract the inmost values and suggestive force of words; it elaborates simile and metaphor scarcely more than good conversation does. But it is apt to treat the familiar images and acts of ordinary life much as poetry is usually inclined to treat words—to put them, that is to say, into such positions of relationship that some unexpected virtue comes out of them."

Abercrombie pointed out how difficult it was to locate Frost's originality, however unmistakable it might be; it owed something, he thought, to Frost's ability to get "poetry back again into touch with the living vigours of speech . . . the rise and fall, the stressed pauses and little hurries, of spoken language." He cited "Mending Wall," "Home Burial," and "A Hundred Collars" as examples of Frost's best work, noting that this poet had achieved distinction "by development rather

than by rebellion." His poetic ancestry could be traced back to Theocritus, Chaucer, and Wordsworth—a distinguished lineage.[28]

Frost had benefited immensely from being part of this informal
group, the Dymock poets—the only such group with whom he would
ever willingly associate. One catches a glimpse of what these gatherings were like in a poem called "The Golden Room," by Wilfrid
Gibson:

> Do you remember the still summer evening
> When in the cosy cream-washed living-room
> Of the Old Nailshop we all talked and laughed—
> Our neighbors from the Gallows, Catherine
> and Lascelles Abercromie; Rupert Brooke;
> Elinor and Robert Frost, living awhile
> At Little Iddens, who'd brought over with them
> Helen and Edward Thomas? In the lamplight
> We talked and laughed, but for the most part listened
> While Robert Frost kept on and on and on
> In his slow New England fashion for our delight,
> Holding us with shrewd turns and racy quips,
> And the rare twinkle of his grave blue eyes?
>
> We sat there in the lamplight while the day
> Died from rose-latticed casements, and the plovers
> Called over the low meadows till the owls
> Answered them from the elms; we sat and talked—
>
> Now a quick flash from Abercombie, now
> A murmured dry half-heard aside from Thomas,
> Now a clear, laughing word from Brooke, and then
> Again Frost's rich and ripe philosophy
> That had the body and tang of good draught-cider
> And poured as clear a stream.

This is not marvelous verse, but the portrait of Frost reveals something of the public manner he later perfected on platforms across the
United States. His homespun "rich and ripe philosophy" went down

well among the Dymock group, and it played well in England overall, as it would eventually in Frost's own country. The "shrewd turns and racy quips" would characterize Frost's later conversation, too, as a friend corroborates: "One expected the unexpected in Frost's conversation, the way he might change the subject abruptly or underscore something with a metaphor that took you by surprise. It kept you listening, on edge."[29]

Gibson's poem was written in 1926, and its nostalgia owes something to the fact that both Thomas and Brooke had been killed in the war—indeed, the war began that summer, with the assassination in Sarajevo of Archduke Francis Ferdinand. Oddly enough, none of Frost's letters of this summer refer to the darkening cloud across Europe. It was as if, once plunged into the bucolic world of Gloucestershire, Frost's heart and mind were fully absorbed by local details. The only news that really interested him was news of *North of Boston*.

A few good reviews arrived that summer, with Richard Aldington writing in the *Egoist*, Ford Madox Ford in *Outlook*, and Gibson in the *Bookman*. Not every word satisfied Frost, as might be expected; even the friendly reviews could rankle. Aldington, for instance, wrote: "It is in cumulative effect rather than in detail that Mr. Frost gets his results. He tells you a little or a big incident in rather stumbling blank verse, places two or three characters before you, and then tells you another incident with fresh characters, making you more interested all the time, until at the end of the book you realize that in a simple, unaffected sort of way he has put before you the whole life of the people 'North of Boston.' "[30]

A note of restraint in the Gibson review also caught Frost's attention, and he would later say to Haines, "I saw enough of his hypocritical joy over my good reviews last summer."[31] This friendship had obviously cooled, as scattered remarks throughout his correspondence suggest. He regarded Gibson's lack of direct exposure to the kinds of people and situations he wrote about a limitation resulting in superficiality and inauthenticity. Furthermore, he agreed with those critics (Pound among them) who dismissed Gibson on purely technical grounds as deficient.

The essential friendship was with Edward Thomas. A graduate of

Lincoln College, Oxford, the thirty-six-year-old writer had earned his living by his pen for a decade, publishing over two dozen travel books and biographies, as well as critical essays, reviews, and even one novel. It was at Frost's suggestion that Thomas began writing poems. "I referred him to paragraphs in his book *The Pursuit of Spring* and told him to write it in verse form in exactly the same cadence," Frost recalled.

One sees the Frostian influence on Thomas at first glance. The poems often recount a rural incident or focus on the natural world. The narrative style is plainspoken, unadorned, imagistic. One feels the strong grip of the poet's mind as he attempts to come to terms with some problem, a contradictory impulse, an idea. These are (to borrow a phrase of Stevens's) poems "of the mind / In the act of finding what will suffice." They move casually, but inexorably, toward moments of quiet illumination.

Thomas lived in the hamlet of Steep, southwest of London, with Helen, his wife of a dozen years, and their three children. Like Frost, he was given to dark periods. When he could not bear the clatter of family life, he would go off by himself, frequently staying for long periods with friends in London or elsewhere. In fact, when Frost first met him in 1913 he was staying with a friend in East Grinstead, where he had gone to get some work accomplished on a biography of Keats.

The two men made a vital connection. Indeed, Frost never got over this brief friendship. He felt that for the first time in his life he had been fully understood; for years afterward he mourned Thomas, who died in the war. Years later, Frost explained to a friend that he had not forced Thomas in his own direction: "The most our congeniality could do was confirm us both in what we were." He elaborates:

> I dragged him out from under the heap of his own work in prose
> he was buried alive under. He was throwing into his big perfunc-
> tory histories of Marlborough and the like, written to order, such
> poetry as would make him a name if he were but given credit for
> it. I made him see that he owed it to himself and to poetry to
> have it out by itself in poetic form where it must suffer itself to

be admired. It took me some time. I bantered, teased and bullied all the summer we were together at Ledington and Ryton. All he had to do was put his poetry in a form that declared itself. The theme must be the same, the accent exactly the same. He saw it and was tempted. It was plain that he had wanted to be a poet all the years he had been writing about poets not worth his little finger.[32]

In August 1914, the Thomas family rented a farmhouse within sight of Little Iddens that was owned by a farmer named Chandler. Though full of promise, the holiday began badly when Mr. Chandler (who was also a member of the army reserves) was summoned to active duty, leaving a good deal of chores behind for Frost and Thomas to accomplish on his behalf. Helen Thomas, meanwhile, found the isolation of Ledington confining, as did the children. Nor did she find the attraction of the Frost family quite as alluring as did her husband. She called Elinor "a rather nebulous personality" and looked askance at her housekeeping, which was "a very haphazard affair." She was also unimpressed by Elinor's cooking: "I remember that when dinner time approached in the middle of the day, she would take a bucket of potatoes into the field and sit on the grass to peel them—without water to my astonishment—and that, as far as I could see, was often the only preparation for a meal." Nevertheless, it was "obvious that Robert and Edward were very congenial to each other." She recalled long evenings of sitting around on the floor of Little Iddens, everyone with his or her back to the wall, singing folk songs and eating "cheap sugary biscuits" from a tin.[33]

The weather was blissful all summer, a succession of warm, breezy days that soon cheered the entire company, and a planned excursion to Wales was postponed. Frost's spirits were boosted by the three separate reviews that Thomas had written of *North of Boston*. "These poems are revolutionary because they lack the exaggeration of rhetoric," Thomas wrote in the *Daily News*, "and even at first sight appear to lack the poetic intensity of which rhetoric is an imitation. Their language is free from the poetical words and forms that are the chief material of secondary poets. The metre avoids not only the old-fashioned pomp and sweetness, but the later fashion also of discord and fuss." He saw that while many of the lines were plain in themselves, they were "bound together and made elements of beauty by a calm eagerness of emotion."[34] In the prestigious *English Review*, he described "The Death of the Hired Man," "Home Burial," "The Black Cottage," and "The Wood-Pile" as "masterpieces of deep and mysterious tenderness."

The relations between Thomas and Frost were mutually beneficial. Thomas was stimulated by Frost, who beckoned him toward writing poems, while Frost basked in the warm attention of a strong, critical mind. Frost's excitement at being taken seriously, especially with regard to the "sound of sense" idea, is evident in a letter home to Cox: "Thomas thinks he will write a book on what my definition of the sentence means for literary criticism." He added: "If I didn't drop into poetry every time I sat down to write I should be tempted to do a book on what it means for education."[35]

One first catches a glimpse of Thomas as a poet in a letter to Frost of December 15, 1914, where he talks about his new vocation: "I am in it & make no mistake."[36] He says that his writing habits, over the years, have prepared him well for his new art: "My bad habits and customs and duties of writing will make it rather easy to write when I've no business to. At the same time I find myself engrossed and conscious of a possible perfection as I never was in prose. Also I'm very impatient of my prose, and of reviews & of review books. And yet I have been uncommonly cheerful mostly. I have been rather pleased with some of the pieces, of course, but it's not wholly that. Still, I won't begin thanking you just yet, tho if you like I will put it down now that you are the only begetter right enough."

Early in September 1914, the Frosts left Little Iddens for The Gallows, a farmhouse in Ryton that rambled under a broad swath of thatch that had been leased from Lord Beauchamp by Lascelles and Catherine Abercrombie. The spacious house had recently been renovated, and there were essentially two separate parts to it. The Gallows would be empty for much of the fall because the Abercrombies were traveling with their two young children; when they returned, the idea was that both families could easily share the large house, thus saving on fuel costs.

The nudge had come from the owners of Little Iddens, who wanted it back. Frost did not mind, since now Elinor could fulfill her dream of living "under thatch." Another attraction of The Gallows was the game preserve of over a thousand acres that adjoined it. Abercrombie and his family, as tenants of the local lord, were at liberty to use these grounds for picnics and rambles, and the Frost family joined them on several occasions, usually after a long Sunday lunch.

Edward Thomas was a frequent visitor at The Gallows that fall, and he and Frost went on "botanizing" walks, as Frost put it. One quirk of Thomas was that he often regretted the particular path he had taken. Frost once said to him, "No matter which road you take, you'll always sigh, and wish you'd taken another." The image of Thomas stuck at a crossroads, uncertain about which branch to follow, inspired "The Road Not Taken," although Frost had been contemplating the image for a while. On February 10, 1912, for instance, he had written to Susan Hayes Ward: "Two lonely cross-roads that themselves cross each other I have walked several times this winter without meeting or over-taking so much as a single person on foot or on runners. The practically unbroken condition of both for several days after a snow or a blow proves that neither is much travelled."[37]

That poem, which opens Frost's third book of poetry, *Mountain Interval*, is one of the high crests of American poetry:

> *Two roads diverged in a yellow wood,*
> *And sorry I could not travel both*
> *And be one traveler, long I stood*
> *And looked down one as far as I could*
> *To where it bent in the undergrowth;*
>
> *Then took the other, as just as fair,*
> *And having perhaps the better claim,*

Because it was grassy and wanted wear;
Though as for that the passing there
Had worn them really about the same,

And both that morning equally lay
In leaves no step had trodden black.
Oh, I kept the first for another day!
Yet knowing how way leads on to way,
I doubted if I should ever come back.

I shall be telling this with a sigh
Somewhere ages and ages hence:
Two roads diverged in a wood, and I—
I took the one less traveled by,
And that has made all the difference.

The overpowering simplicity of the image is archetypal in its appeal: every reader has stood at some fork and wondered which might be the better path. Most will have wanted to take "the one less traveled by," and thus be thought a maverick or "lone striker." Yet the poem throws this desire into raw, ironic light: "I shall be telling this with a sigh," the narrator says, and the sigh reveals a certain sadness combined with a wan feeling of disingenuousness. One imagines the speaker looking back from old age, his grandchildren at his feet. He says, "I took the road less traveled by," while knowing—in his heart of hearts—that an element of posing is involved here.

There may well be no road less traveled by, as the poet has suggested in the three preceding stanzas. The road taken is "as just as fair," he notes: "Though as for that the passing there / Had worn them *really about the same*" (italics mine). In case the reader did not understand, the next line is more explicit: "And both that morning equally lay / In leaves no step had trodden black." Both paths, it would seem, are pristine, untrodden. This certainly puts a twist on the last, aphoristic couplet: "I took the one less traveled by, / And that has made all the difference." As frequently happens in Frost, the poet builds into his poem a fierce contradiction: the speaker of the poem gestures toward a simple, even simplistic, reading, while the poet himself demands a more complex, ironic reading. The play between these antithetical readings becomes an important part of the poem's dynamic.

One morning in late September, Frost and Thomas went for a long walk in the dense preserve beside The Gallows, and as they emerged from the woods a leathery-faced gamekeeper confronted them. These woods were not open to the public, he said. Frost snapped back at him, and was called "a damned cottager"—an insult that may have recalled Frost's having been called a "hen-man" back at Pinkerton. He was barely restrained by Thomas from hitting the man. Rather foolishly, Frost followed the gamekeeper home, while Thomas hovered behind him, terrified by his friend's temper. When the gamekeeper came to the door, Frost threatened him with a beating if he ever insulted him again.

The next day a constable called at The Gallows, saying that a complaint had been lodged. Frost was stunned, and livid. He appealed to Gibson for help, but there was no assistance there—a point that Frost would hold against him. ("You mustn't tell me a single thing about Gibson," he wrote to John Haines the next year from the States, "if you don't want to detract from the pleasure of your letters. . . . I can't help looking on him as the worst snob I met in England and I can't help blaming the snob he is for the most unpleasant memory I carried away from England: I mean my humiliating fight with the gamekeeper. Gibson is a coward and a snob not to have saved me from all that."[38]

Apparently Thomas felt that he had acted cowardly himself, refusing to stand up to the gamekeeper as Frost had. At least in Frost's later retelling, this sense of cowardice is what drove Thomas to enlist in the army. "That's why he went to war," Frost declared baldly in 1936.[39] The situation with the gamekeeper, as it were, was resolved when Abercrombie returned. The charges were quickly dropped, and Lord Beauchamp himself sent a personal note of apology to Frost (and a nasty note to the gamekeeper, telling him that if he wanted to fight he should join the army).

Early in the fall, a letter arrived from Henry Holt, a publisher in New York, at the office of David Nutt in London. Mrs. Holt, a Vermonter, had been given a copy of *North of Boston* by a friend. She had persuaded her husband to offer Frost a contract for the American rights, with options on his future work. After some haggling, an agreement was reached whereby Holt would take 150 copies of the unbound sheets of *North of Boston* for a trial run—not an auspicious beginning. Mrs. Nutt herself chided Holt: "Under present political circumstances, American publishers ought to show some willingness to help English publishers who have sufficient daring and intelligence to recognize the talent of one of their own countrymen."[40]

Frost learned of the arrangements in the beginning of November, and said to Elinor, "Now we can go home." The idea of returning to America became more urgent when Germany announced that it would soon blockade British ports. However much the Frosts liked England, they did not want to be marooned there for the duration of the war. There was also the question of finances: life in England had proved more expensive than he and Elinor had calculated, and even loans from various friends had failed to tide them over. In addition, the price of the passage home had risen significantly since their previous crossing, and there was no sign of its decreasing. All of these factors pointed toward an early departure.

Frost once again had to borrow money. This time he went to Abercrombie, Haines, and J. C. Smith. (Gibson was clearly not approachable in this regard.) All three offered Frost a loan without making the transaction difficult, and Frost gave each a promissory note. Tickets were booked on the American liner *St. Paul*, scheduled to leave from Liverpool on February 13. At this point in the war, it seemed a safer bet than a British liner, which might pose a more likely target for German subs.

Not surprisingly, Frost's mind turned anxiously toward home as winter deepened. He did not want to take another teaching job, although he knew this might be necessary. He dreamed of "a quiet job in a small college where I would be allowed to teach something a little new on the technique of writing and where I should have some honor for what I suppose myself to have done in poetry."[41] Shyly, he appended a footnote to the line where he asked for "some honor," saying "just a little bit." He wanted, rightly, to be recognized for who he was, for what he had accomplished. His self-confidence would soar and plunge, depending on the day; but a base level of reasonable assurance could now be counted on. He let his true feelings run free in an early-February letter to Cox in which he said, "The book [*North of Boston*] is epoch-making. I don't ask anyone to say so. All I ask now is to be allowed to live."[42]

That Frost was still uncertain about going back to America is evident from a conversation he had, sometime during the fall, with the young poet Robert Graves, whom he met in Harold Monro's bookshop. According to Graves, Frost was still actively debating whether or not to return home. He supposedly said that he might even enlist in the British army.[43] Since no mention of this plan is recorded elsewhere, it seems likely to have been a passing fancy, summoned expressly to impress Graves, who stood before him in an officer's uniform.

Back at The Gallows, Frost did manage to keep working. A number of poems for *Mountain Interval* were written in quick succession, including "The Sound of Trees," "A Patch of Old Snow," and "The Cow in Apple Time." Several older poems, such as "Putting in the Seed," were reworked. Frost was filled with a sense of his own power, and the responsiveness of editors to his new work confirmed these feelings. (Harold Monro, for example, took four of the new poems for his influential magazine *Poetry and Drama*.) It delighted Frost that much of this third volume was already in his notebooks, ready to be harvested.

The last month in England was taken up with packing and final arrangements, which included saying good-bye to many friends. Ezra Pound was not among them, however. Pound's review of *North of Boston*, while enthusiastic, had damned just about every other poet in America, and Frost worried that this would count against him when he got back. "I fear I am going to suffer a good deal at home by the support of Pound," he wrote to Sidney Cox. "Another such review as the one in *Poetry* and I shan't be admitted at Ellis Island."[44]

There was considerable fear of an impending German invasion throughout Britain, and Edward and Helen Thomas asked Frost to take their son Mervyn, who was fifteen, back with them to America, where he could board with a relative in Alstead, New Hampshire.

Helen had written to Elinor that this would be "the kindest of favors in this difficult time." The Frosts were happy to oblige.

Frost's feelings toward England on the eve of his departure are best seen in a farewell note to Harold Monro, whose support had been invaluable: "Thanks for everything. I had intended to see you before leaving but at the last moment we go rather precipitously; so that I am scanting duties. Anyway I don't want too much made of my going or I should feel as if I were never coming back. England has become half my native land—England the victorious. Good friends I have had here and hope to keep."[45]

In fact, Frost's mind and heart were now wholly trained on New England, that magical zone north of Boston which had been the source of so much poetry. He did not know exactly where he and his family would settle once they returned, but the general destination was New Hampshire, where he hoped to find a place high enough in the White Mountains so that his old hay fever complaints would not return. As he told Ernest Silver, he wanted to find "a farm in New England where I could live cheap and get Yankier and Yankier."[46] Nevertheless, the feelings of ambivalence were often overpowering. He said to Haines only a month before his departure: "We are on the move at last after all the threats. Life is once more one grand uncertainty, and I'd not be the one to lament the fact if I was sure I was well."[47]

The family left by train from the Dymock station, arriving in Liverpool on the night of February 12, 1915. By all accounts, Frost was deeply melancholy, worried that he was leaving behind the only community that had ever been supportive of his claims to being a poet. The uncertainty of his reception in America weighed heavily, and there must have been considerable anxiety about where and how he would live. On the evening of February 13, the *St. Paul* departed, with the family lying in their bunks fully clothed, in life jackets. The fear of German attacks on passenger ships was, quite rightly, perceived as real. Indeed, just over two months later, the British liner *Lusitania* was torpedoed by German submarines and went down, killing over a thousand civilians.

9

HOME AGAIN
1915–1916

Locality gives art. —FROST, NOTEBOOK ENTRY, 1910

The crossing from Liverpool to New York was unusually rough, with stormy seas and slantwise, icy rains. The *St. Paul* pitched and rolled, and the children were continually seasick. Nevertheless, Frost had every reason to feel optimistic about his prospects. He had made considerable headway in England as a poet, and his reputation had already filtered home. He could not, however, anticipate the full extent of the success that awaited him upon disembarkation.

As they departed, Frost's mind was on German submarines more than where the family would settle, but as the ship broke free of European waters, the debate over where they would live when they got home began in earnest. The children had fond memories of the farm in Derry (although Irma and Marjorie, now eleven and nine, were relying on their older siblings for impressions). Frost suggested a farm in the White Mountains of New Hampshire, where they had been so happy in previous summers. What better place to get "Yankier and Yankier"? The idea of going first to stay with John and Margaret Lynch in Bethlehem, an idyllic town in the Franconia region of New Hampshire, seemed a plausible course of action.

Once ashore, the Frosts checked into a hotel and went for a brisk walk. On Forty-second Street, Frost was leafing through a copy of the *New Republic* at a newsstand when, to his amazement, he discovered within its pages a prominent review of *North of Boston* by Amy Lowell; she called his book "the most American volume of poetry which has appeared for some time."[1] While there were caveats and chidings, Lowell essentially admired the volume for its realistic portrayal of rural New Englanders. Frost could not have been more pleasantly surprised.

He would have accompanied his family to New Hampshire at once were it not for the fact that Mervyn Thomas had been detained on Ellis Island because of immigration complications that might take a few days to sort through. Frost sent Elinor and the children ahead and decided to put his time in New York to good use. He went straight to Henry Holt's offices at 34 West Thirty-third Street, where he met Alfred Harcourt, head of the trade department. Harcourt informed Frost that not only did he have a check from the *New Republic* for "The Death of the Hired Man," which had been published a couple of weeks before, but that orders for *North of Boston* were coming in fast.

While in the city, Frost also met with Mrs. Henry Holt, who had been his advocate with her husband's firm. She had written an enthusiastic note to Frost in England, praising his poetry for its vivid sense of place, and he had responded warmly, well before there was any publishing connection between them. Mrs. Holt now urged Frost to consider Vermont as a place to settle, and her description of the Stowe region (where she and her husband owned a summer house) was so convincing that Frost scouted this area quite seriously in his pursuit of a farm.

With some difficulty, he managed to extricate poor Mervyn Thomas from Ellis Island and put him on a train to New Hampshire, where his relatives would meet him. Frost's own northbound journey was circuitous, with a brief detour to see his sister, Jeanie, in South Fork, Pennsylvania, where she was teaching. Frost had certain trepidations about seeing Jeanie again, given their erratic history, but the visit went extremely well, with Frost playing the role of big brother more generously and thoughtfully than he had in the past. He encouraged

Jeanie to return to college to finish her degree, and rather quixotically (for a man without an income) he offered to provide financial help if she needed it.

Stopping in Lawrence, Massachusetts, Frost paid a call on the family lawyer, Wilbur Rowell, and managed to extract an advance payment of two hundred dollars on his grandfather's annuity. In Boston, he called on the venerable editor of the *Atlantic Monthly*, Ellery Sedgwick—a literary gatekeeper of considerable power. Publication in Sedgwick's magazine had long been one of Frost's aspirations, and he had been rejected countless times over the past decade, often with vaguely snide notes. Now Sedgwick was all bonhomie, greeting Frost like an old friend. He had heard about the success of *North of Boston* from Amy Lowell, he explained. Frost told him about his English adventures, and Sedgwick was charmed; he invited the young man home for dinner that very night. One of the guests at his table was William Ernest Hocking, a Harvard philosopher, whom Frost liked immediately.

News of Frost's arrival in Boston circulated quickly, and soon two other Bostonians with literary inclinations were keen to meet him: Nathan Haskell Dole and Sylvester Baxter. They had both read *North of Boston* and, indeed, were going to talk about Frost at an upcoming meeting of the Boston Authors' Club. Sedgwick served as intermediary, and the next day Frost met both men.

Buoyed by the enthusiasm for his work that seemed to come from every quarter, Frost could not put a foot wrong. The charm that had served him so well in English literary circles seemed to be working at home, too. Nathan Dole became one of Frost's most ardent supporters, and he soon introduced Frost to William Stanley Braithwaite, a minor poet who edited the *Evening Transcript*, who leaped at the opportunity to interview Frost for his paper. (Braithwaite had just begun to edit the yearly *Anthology of Magazine Verse*, and he would regularly include Frost in this important collection.)

Quite by chance, Frost ran into Professor Hocking at the railway station in Boston and was immediately invited to come and spend the night in Cambridge. Though eager to get back to his family, Frost accepted. He was obviously making great headway in Boston literary society, and he rightly guessed that extending his trip a little further could be useful. The person he most wanted to meet was Amy Lowell, and at Hocking's suggestion he telephoned to thank her for the review in the *New Republic*. She insisted that he come to dinner that evening at her mansion in Brookline.

The sister of Harvard's president, Lowell belonged to an intellectual dynasty that included James Russell Lowell, one of the most popular poets of the previous century. She was imperious and eccentric but eager to gather younger poets into her circle. Among the handful of guests at her house that evening was John Gould Fletcher, a poet reared in Arkansas and educated at Harvard. Frost knew his work and was glad to make his acquaintance.

Though a formidable talker, Frost met his match in Amy Lowell, who held forth entertainingly the whole evening while Frost "sat on her sofa and said little," according to Fletcher. Perhaps listening was good for him that night, for he learned a great deal about the current poetry scene in the United States. The air was full of long-forgotten names, such as Gertrude Hall (who had recently died), George Sterling, Josephine Peabody, and Theodosia Garrison. Frost realized that his own work could not be easily classified, and that he was neither "modern" nor "conventional"—the pigeonholes into which Amy Lowell seemed determined to put everyone.

Frost enjoyed the evening with Lowell, and realized that he had made a definite mark in Boston literary society. Sylvester Baxter, for instance, wrote enthusiastically about his homecoming in the *Boston Herald*, reporting that Ellery Sedgwick was telling everyone that Frost was "another Masefield."[2] Baxter presented Frost to his readership as "a most agreeable personality," describing him as follows: "He is still in his thirties, but remains youthful in face and figure; dark brown hair, handsome gray-blue eyes, a well-modelled head and mobile features."

With a quiet sense of triumph, Frost made his way northward, arriving full of stories at the Lynch farm, where he spent several days walking in the local woods. It felt good to get away from the urban literary world, where jockeying for position was part of the daily routine.

"I wish I could describe the state I've been thrown into," Frost wrote to John Bartlett as the tasks of finding a suitable house and getting the children into local schools lay before him.

Slotting the children into schools would not be simple, since there was yet no certainty about where they would live. On the other hand, Frost—unlike Elinor—was quite willing to let the children stay out of school until the next fall, "safely out of the hands of schoolmarms," as he wrote to John Haines. Elinor proposed a school in Franconia, the largest town in the valley, but Frost's mind was on higher things: a house in the hills, with a view of Mount Lafayette's snowy peak. He wanted to look out over the whole Franconia Range, which included Garfield, Lincoln, Haystack, and Liberty peaks—a view much like the one described so crisply in " 'Out, Out—' ": "Five mountain ranges one behind the other / Under the sunset far into Vermont."

Within a matter of days, Frost found a little farm near the village of Sugar Hill—a resort town in summer—and knew immediately that this was for him. Unfortunately, the farm was owned by a man who had no mind, at first, to sell. After a brief conversation, however, the owner took to Frost, and agreed that for a thousand dollars, he would turn over the farm. Frost brought the whole family to inspect the property, and they responded well to the little house. It was primitive, with no indoor plumbing or electricity. A woodstove in the kitchen provided heat for the house, which was smaller than the house in Derry, and an uphill spring supplied water. There was an upper pasture and hay field, and a barn for hens and a few cows. Among several woodlots were stands of birch, maple (a sugar orchard), poplar, tamarack, and spruce. The deal was closed with a handshake, although the Frosts did not move in until June because a carpenter was busy with renovations.

Meanwhile, Frost found himself the continuing object of interest within the Boston literary community. Urged on by Dole and Baxter, Tufts College and the Boston Authors' Club both invited him to read his poetry in April. Frost used the opportunity to further his connections in the literary world. Among those he was eager to meet was Louis Untermeyer, a young poet and critic who was friendly with Lascelles Abercrombie. Abercrombie had told Untermeyer in a letter that he should "look out for Frost," a poet "whose work is pitched like that of nobody else."[3] Untermeyer duly wrote a warm letter to Frost in late February, and the two met at Sylvester Baxter's house in Malden, Massachusetts, when Frost came down to the Boston area in early April. This was the beginning of a long and close friendship between the two men; indeed, it would be the most sustained literary friendship of Frost's long life.

Untermeyer lived in New York, where he worked as a junior member in his family firm of jewelry manufacturers. He was also a prolific book reviewer and a contributing editor of the *Masses*, a socialist magazine published in Greenwich Village. Untermeyer was present at some of Frost's very early readings in the Boston area and later recalled, "He was painfully aware and somewhat frightened of audiences, a self-consciousness from which he rarely freed himself—he never would dine or even converse with his hosts before a lecture. Actually, he never lectured. He talked and, as he grew more at ease with people, talked in what seemed a haphazard assortment of comments that developed into a shrewd commentary on poetry as it related to the state of the world. He never 'recited' his poems, he 'said' them—sometimes, especially if they were new or short, he 'said' them twice. 'Would you like to hear me say that one again?' he would inquire."[4]

Untermeyer wrote a fiercely partisan review of *North of Boston* in the *Chicago Evening Post* on April 23, declaring, "I have little respect—literary respect—for anyone who can read the shortest of these poems without feeling the skill and power in them."[5] Frost realized, of course, that having a critic of Untermeyer's stature and enthusiasm on his side was a great boon, and he responded as one might expect, with appreciative letters. Untermeyer sent a copy of his own second volume of poems, *Challenge*, and Frost wrote back with enthusiasum; he was "full of the large spirit of it," he said.

In Boston, Frost gave two detailed interviews to Braithwaite for his newspaper. This was Frost's first opportunity to get across his notions of "the sound of sense" to a wider public, and he seized it. He talked about "writing with your ear to the voice," and singled out Wordsworth as a key predecessor: "This is what Wordsworth did himself in all his best poetry, proving that there can be no creative imagination unless there is a summoning up of experience, fresh from life, which has not hitherto been evoked."[6]

At Tufts College, after the reading, Frost met George H. Browne, from the Browne and Nichols School in Cambridge, who invited him to give a series of readings at four private schools in the Boston area for two hundred dollars. This was a fifth of the cost of the entire farm in the White Mountains, and Frost eagerly accepted. He also attended a meeting of the newly formed New England Poetry Society, where he met (for the second time) Edward Arlington Robinson, whose career had been steeply ascending for the past decade. Robinson was considered by most critics the leading poet of New England, and Frost felt keenly a sense of rivalry. Nevertheless, he admired Robinson, and a friendship based on mutual admiration began. (Robinson followed up this meeting by sending Frost his newly published play, *The Porcupine*, to which Frost replied, "It is good writing, or better than that, good speaking caught alive—every sentence of it."[7]

The reading at the Browne and Nichols School went extremely well. One of Mr. Browne's students was adept at speed-writing and kept a close account of Frost's performance. One gets the full flavor of Frost in performance in the student's verbatim record of Frost talking:

I want to call your attention to the function of the imagining ear. Your attention is too often called to the poet with extraordinarily vivid sight, and with the faculty of choosing exceptionally telling words for the sight. But equally valuable, even for schoolboy themes, is the use of the ear for material for compositions. When you listen to a speaker, you hear words, to be sure—but you also hear tones. The problem is to note them, to imagine them again, and to get them down in writing. But few of you probably ever thought of the possibility or of the necessity of doing this. You are generally told to distinguish simple, compound, and complex sentences—long and short—periodic and loose—to vary sentence structure. . . .

I always had a dream of getting away from it, when I was teaching school; and, in my own writing and teaching, of bringing in the living sounds of speech. For it is a fundamental fact that certain forms depend on the sound; e.g., note the various tones of irony, acquiescence, doubt, etc. in the farmer's "I guess so." And the great problem is, can you get those tones down on paper? How do you tell the tone? By the contact, by the animating spirit of the living voice. And how many tones do you think there are flying round? Hundreds of them—hundreds never brought to book. . . .

The vital thing, then, to consider in all composition, prose or verse, is the ACTION of the voice—sound-posturing, gesture. Get the stuff of life into the technique of your writing. That's the only escape from dry rhetoric.

When I began to teach, and long after I began to write, I didn't know what the matter was with me and my writing and with other people's writing. I recall distinctly the joy with which I had the first satisfaction of getting an expression adequate for my thought. I was so delighted that I had to cry. It was the second stanza of the little poem on the butterfly, written in my eighteenth year. And the sound in the mouths of men I found to be the basis of all effective expression—not merely words or phrases, but sentences—living things flying round, the vital parts of speech. And my poems are to be read in the appreciative tones of this live speech.[8]

When he got home, Frost wrote to Browne: "I see now that I could have gone a good deal deeper in my talk to the boys on images of sound and you would have had no quarrel with me. I can see a small textbook based on images of sound particularly on the kind I call vocal postures or vocal idioms that would revolutionize the teaching of English all the way up."[9] Frost's interest in pedagogy had not relented, although it had been several years since he had taught on a regular basis.

He now settled into life on his new farm, and began to listen once again to the "live speech" of local people. With work to be done, there was no excuse for his sitting on the porch with a lapboard across his knees, a pen in hand; this meant that, being Frost, he liked nothing better. "The whole point of farming was shirking duties," Frost later recalled. "You can't put your mind on farming. It won't stay there." He found he could work well, "as a poet, in the margins of farm life."[10]

The first summer in Franconia was memorable. Elinor liked having a home of her own again, after so many years, and the children immersed themselves in country pleasures: blueberry picking, long walks in the woods, swimming in the Ham Branch of the Gale River, which ran nearby. Frost often played baseball with the children, and he began playing sandlot ball again with local farmhands. Of course he also indulged in his private hobby, which he referred to as "botanizing."

He had not been writing poetry seriously for several months, ever since the return from England, but he quickly found his rhythm again. Among the poems written over the summer were "Brown's Descent," "The Gum-Gatherer," "The Vanishing Red," and " 'Out, Out—'." The latter, one of his most affecting poems, was based on a true story. In 1910, the tragedy at the core of the poem befell a neighbor's child on the South Road out of Bethlehem. The *Littleton Courier* reported the incident on March 31, 1910:

Raymond Tracy Fitzgerald, one of the twin sons of Michael G. and Margaret Fitzgerald of Bethlehem, died at his home Thursday afternoon, March 24, as a result of an accident by which one of his hands was badly hurt in a sawing machine. The young man was assisting in sawing up some wood in his own dooryard with a sawing machine and accidentally hit the loose pulley, causing the saw to descend upon his hand, cutting and lacerating it badly. Raymond was taken into the house and a physician was immediately summoned, but he died very suddenly from the effects of shock, which produced heart failure.

It's fascinating to see how Frost was able to dramatize this material. The poem opens lyrically, creating an idyll of New England life on a remote farm:

The buzz saw snarled and rattled in the yard
And made dust and dropped stove-length sticks of wood,
Sweet-scented stuff when the breeze drew across it.
And from there those that lifted eyes could count
Five mountain ranges one behind the other
Under the sunset far into Vermont.

A contrast between the mechanical saw that "snarled and rattled" and the gorgeous view (that nobody has the time to look at properly, given the pressures of survival) is neatly established, adding to the poignancy of the child's death. This "big boy / Doing a man's work, though a child at heart" has been denied many of the pleasures of boyhood.

In a brilliant sleight of thought, Frost declares that the saw "Leaped at the boy's hand, or seemed to leap." As ever, he seems to enjoy the ambiguity here, the suggestion that perhaps the saw was animate and malicious. "However it was," he goes on, "Neither refused the meeting." Frost appears to suggest that the boy has somehow wished, even willed, his own death. He has certainly made the world of technology, here symbolized by the buzz saw, ominous, even rapacious. In this, Frost can be seen reacting against the industrialization of farming.

The poem turns especially poignant in the immediate reaction to the accident:

> *The boy's first outcry was a rueful laugh,*
> *As he swung toward them holding up the hand,*
> *Half in appeal, but half as if to keep*
> *The life from spilling. . . .*

The "rue" in the boy's laugh is a familiar Frostian note: a wincing grin in which the fate of the boy is seen—by himself as much as the reader—as painfully ironic. The nakedness of the boy's gesture is at once pathetic and appalling.

"The boy saw all," we are told. What he saw was "all spoiled." His own life has been ruined, of course, but the family dynamic will hereafter be altered as well, "spoiled." The boy has subliminally come to understand that within the framework of a subsistence economy there is small room for a boy who cannot pull his weight. Circumstances are such that an extra "hand" is essential for survival.

The poem ends with cruel dispatch, clarity, and compression:

> *The doctor put him in the dark of ether.*
> *He lay and puffed his lips out with his breath.*
> *And then—the watcher at his pulse took fright.*
> *No one believed. They listened at his heart.*
> *Little—less—nothing!—and that ended it.*
> *No more to build on there. And they, since they*
> *Were not the one dead, turned to their affairs.*

One is reminded here of "Home Burial," where the husband who has lost his child turns immediately to the task of digging the grave. His mourning is severe, but it is worked out in the necessity of burying the child. There is a kind of cruelty in the last lines, especially in a time when grief is often unacknowledged, and when accepting the death of a child seems unimaginable. But in 1910, on a farm in rural New England, death was a frequent visitor, and the young were not spared. A cold practicality haunts the ending: "No more to build on there." Yet there is something noble in the acknowledgment that what has happened has happened, and that one must build where there is something to build on.

The title, of course, alludes to Shakespeare's famous lines in *Macbeth*:

> *Out, out, brief candle!*
> *Life's but a walking shadow, a poor player*
> *That struts and frets his hour upon the stage,*
> *And then is heard no more. It is a tale*
> *Told by an idiot, full of sound and fury,*
> *Signifying nothing.*

Frost uses this allusion to draw an important contrast between the life of a farm boy and that of a royal personage. The latter, it seems,

can see only the meaninglessness of existence, its noise and violence: death seems irrelevant, since life itself is—in a strange sense—
irrelevant. Macbeth hangs on to the prophecies of the witches at the
outset of the play—a sign of his neurosis and megalomania. He cannot
accept his own guilt in bringing about his wife's death, or in bringing
on his own demise.

The boy, on the other hand, lives in a society where mind and body
exist in harmonious relation. His work is essential for the community,
and for the family, who depends upon his contribution. When he cannot function as worker, his life loses a good deal of its meaning—a
point he gathers when he "sees all," intuitively, in a terrible flash. By
contrast, Macbeth, although born into the highest ranks, sees much
less. Frost is thus able to exalt the life of this small, organic community, where wisdom is commonplace, and pleasure is taken in small
things, such as the smell of the sawdust: "Sweet-scented stuff when the
breeze drew across it."

On the other hand, Frost also reveals the limitations of this rural
world, as John F. Lynen has noted: "The death, after all, is a bitter
thing; there is much to be said for a world in which one can survive an
accident such as the boy's. Ironically, it is the very advantages of the
rural world that make it, in other ways, inferior: the boy's conception
of life is such that any impairment is fatal; and the rural world is so
perfectly organized that any disruption of the natural order may lead to
catastrophe."[11]

It is part of Frost's modernity that he refuses to delimit meaning but
allows the poem to open into a complex and suggestive ambiguity.
" 'Out, Out—' " brings to the fore both the strengths and the weak-
nesses of pastoral life in this period. In a brief space, one gets a full
sense of the pleasures of working on such a farm as well as its obvious
burdens and liabilities. The comparison with *Macbeth* thrusts the
poem into a bracing perspective that neither belittles the "small"
world of the New England farm nor necessarily suggests that the boy's
world is superior to Macbeth's. The poem leaves a good deal of interpretive work for the reader to accomplish.

That first summer in the Franconia region was made all the more

pleasant by the news, from Ellery Sedgwick, that he was going to publish a laudatory essay on Frost in the *Atlantic*, as well as three poems:
"Birches," "The Road Not Taken," and "The Sound of Trees." There
was additional good news from Holt, saying that *North of Boston* was
rising steadily in sales. While Holt had originally imported only 150
copies from David Nutt in London, they quickly printed 1,300 more
copies of their own; a year later, after four printings, the book had
reached 20,000 sales—almost unheard of for a book of poetry.

Frost's ride was not entirely smooth, however. The trouble came
from Mrs. Nutt, who refused to let her newly popular American poet
publish some poems in a chapbook that Harold Monro proposed to
edit; furthermore, she ignored every request by Frost for a report of his
English sales, a clear breach of contract on her part. In frustration,
Frost turned to Alfred Harcourt, who tried without luck to get Mrs.
Nutt to let Frost go. Even after Frost wrote asserting that he considered their contract of December 16, 1912, void because she had
not paid royalties or provided an accounting of sales, she refused to
acknowledge an end to their partnership. Not until Mrs. Nutt's publishing house went bankrupt in 1921 was Frost ultimately free of all
her claims on him and his work.

Another bit of trouble came from a small handful of reviewers
who, as Frost had predicted, took offense that an American poet had
gone to England to seek affirmation. Among these was Jessie B.
Rittenhouse, an influential officer of the Poetry Society of America,
who wondered in her snide review of *North of Boston* in the *New York
Times Book Review* why "a made-in-England reputation is so coveted
by poets of this country."[12] Urged on by Frost, Alfred Harcourt
defended Frost in the same paper: "That Mr. Robert Frost's volume . . .
made its first appearance under the imprint of an English instead of an
American publisher has disturbed some of our reviewers and revived
the old complaint that we are unappreciative of true excellence when
it knocks at the door of our native literature. Mr. Frost's poems are pre-
eminently worth while, they are thoroughly original in theme and
treatment, they are genuinely interpretive of certain phases of American life—why, then, were they published first in England? The query

has suggested dire possibilities by way of answer. But now Mr. Frost himself comes to the rescue with an explanation the simplicity of which should allay at once any international jealousies or suspicions." Harcourt explained that Frost in fact had "never offered a book to an American publisher" before he went to England and "didn't cross the water seeking a British publisher."[13] This was literally true. Frost had never actually sent a book of poems to an American publisher and been rejected, although he had been turned down repeatedly by magazine editors; he had gone to England to seek an appreciative audience, though not explicitly to find a British publisher; that was merely a happy consequence of moving to England just as he was pulling together his first volume.

In September, a boost came from an unexpected source. William Dean Howells was the most influential man of letters in the country, a novelist and critic who had helped further the careers of Henry James and Mark Twain. He edited *Harper's*, and his "Editor's Easy Chair" was widely read. In a vigorous essay, he took a few sideswipes at vers libre poets, saying they "lacked all rigor," then turned his attack on both Amy Lowell and Edgar Lee Masters (whose *Spoon River Anthology* was popular at the time); he singled out Frost as one of the most promising developments in current poetry, praising his "very sweet rhyme and pleasant rhythm." With unusual insight, he noted Frost's ability to penetrate "to the heart of womanhood."[14] One sees this extraordinary empathy in the portrait of Mary in "The Death of the Hired Man," Estelle's mother in "The Housekeeper," and the mentally shaky farm wife in "A Servant to Servants." Indeed, Frost could enter a woman's consciousness with uncanny ease, intuit her needs and sympathies, find and exploit her vocal range.

Just half a year back in the United States, Frost found himself a real contender for that small quantity of attention devoted by the reading public to new poetry. Reviewers compared him, usually to his benefit, to Carl Sandburg (whose *Chicago Poems* had just been published), Edgar Lee Masters, and others. In Braithwaite's *Anthology of Magazine Verse for 1915*, he was among five poets singled out for special recognition (Wallace Stevens was another—one of his first appearances on the national scene). There seemed no stopping him.

But illness began to intrude as the fall deepened. At the end of October, Frost was feeling physically fragile, as one sees in a letter to George Browne of October 27: "It's not so much busy as sick with a cold I've been—though I've been a little busy helping Carol build the henhouse when I've felt able to be out of the wind. We got the house up and the roof onto it (and the hens into it) just before the rain came yesterday afternoon. This is something to have got off my mind. It leaves really very little to think of before winter but banking up and putting on a window or two."[15]

This was in part a form of sympathetic illness, as Elinor was herself extremely unwell. She had become pregnant again, accidentally—her seventh pregnancy. An old worry about her heart not being strong enough resurfaced, and she was forced to take to her bed. Frost wrote to Abercrombie in England: "You will be sorry to hear that Elinor is altogether out of health and we are in for our share of trouble."[16] The crisis ended when, in late November, she had a miscarriage.

Frost's life now took on a familiar pattern, combining farming, family life, writing, and lecturing. While he was not exactly beset with invitations to speak, these did come regularly, giving him that extra layer of income, making possible a fairly relaxed form of farming. "I like farming," he told a Boston reporter, "but I'm not much of a farmer." He elaborated: "I always go to farming when I can. I always make a failure of it, and then I have to go to teaching. I'm a good teacher, but it doesn't allow me time to write. I must either teach or write: can't do both together. But I have to live. . . . I've had a lazy, scrape-along life, and enjoyed it. I used to hate to write themes in school. I hate academic ways. I fight everything academic. The time we waste in trying to learn academically—the talent we starve with academic teaching!"[17]

In this interview, which appeared in the *Boston Post*, Frost was busily at work creating a self-myth that would accommodate and facilitate his writing life. He never mentioned that he had money from his grandfather, and he went out of his way to portray himself as lazy when, indeed, he worked hard enough to keep body and soul together, to keep the farm running and the poetry flowing. He was intensely ambitious, artistically; he wanted to make a name for himself, of course, but he also wanted to get his vision onto paper, to find a language adequate to experience. Having been neglected by the public for two decades, he also wanted an audience to confirm his vision.

In the winter and spring, Frost lectured widely. His various travels took him back to Dartmouth for the first time since he had left there years before. The high point of the spring was a lecture in Boston before the New England Association of Teachers of English, which took place on March 18, 1916. Frost reminisced about his own years as a teacher at Pinkerton, saying that he always encouraged students to write directly from experience. He worked by encouraging students, never discouraging them. Students should be shown to use their ears to gather information for essays, he suggested. His clear antipathy to the conventional forms of academic training rankled some members of the audience, and their hostility was evident in some of the questions—a development that took Frost by surprise. The whole experience of lecturing on the hoof was somewhat disorienting for him. "I wish I could remember where-all I've been in the past week or so and who-all I've baptized into my heresies," he wrote to Untermeyer upon his return.[18] The animosity in Boston had obviously not rattled his nerves, as it might have a few years earlier. He was rapidly building a stage presence and perfecting a mode of public address that satisfied him and much of his audience.

He was quite exhausted by the tour, however, and (according to Elinor) should have stayed put for a while, but an invitation to lecture in Philadelphia came from Cornelius Weygandt, a professor at the University of Pennsylvania whom he had met the previous summer. Frost read before nearly five hundred students at the College Hall Chapel at Pennsylvania on April 1, his biggest reading to date. He was interviewed the next day by the *Public Ledger*, a Philadelphia paper, and used this opportunity to expand on ideas developed in previous interviews. "You know, the Canadian woodchoppers [make their own] axe-handles, following the curve of the grain, and they're strong and beautiful. Art should follow lines in nature, like the grain of an axe-handle," he maintained.[19]

On his way home, he stopped to read his poems at Amherst College, thus making the most crucial academic contact of his life. A group of students had invited Frost, supported by their professor, Stark Young—a brilliant young author himself. Young had been brought to Amherst by Alexander Meiklejohn, Amherst's energetic and original new president. Having spent two days at Amherst, Frost was impressed by the physical surroundings and intellectual atmosphere. It occurred to him that here was the kind of small college where he might like to teach one day.

As word spread of Frost's memorable public appearances, the demand for his presence only increased; indeed, Harvard asked him to attend its commencement in June and to read a poem as the Phi Beta Kappa poet—a great honor for anyone but especially for a man who had himself dropped out of Harvard. Frost accepted this invitation happily. He and Elinor left the children with their neighbors, Reverend Joseph Warner Fobes and his wife, Edith, who spent their summers at a nearby farm. Mrs. Fobes, in particular, became a very close friend of Elinor's.

Alfred Harcourt had been wondering when he might expect the next book of poems, and Frost had reassured him that he was almost ready. That summer, he set to work on assembling *Mountain Interval*. It was not difficult work, since he had come back from England with a fairly complete manuscript. The poems he had written since moving to Franconia filled out the book nicely. It was merely a question of arranging the poems in a satisfying sequence.

In the middle of the summer, two visitors arrived unexpectedly: Stark Young and Alexander Meiklejohn. They came with an offer that Frost, though he briefly hesitated, could not refuse. He was invited to join the faculty at Amherst for the spring semester of 1917 for $2,000. He would be expected to teach only two courses. Meiklejohn, a maverick in American education, assured Frost that his brand of anti-academicism would be welcome at Amherst, where he was trying to do something different.

Among the factors that played into Frost's decision to accept this offer was the climate of Franconia. In winter, the cold was so bracing that the Frost family often found themselves bedridden with colds and lung ailments. Carol, in particular, seemed always on the edge of something serious, such as tuberculosis. The idea of finding a farm in some more hospitable part of New England dawned on Frost, and he told John Bartlett that he hoped one day to use Franconia merely as a summer home when he was "rich enough to let it lie idle all but two or three months in the year."[20]

Frost accepted the offer formally after making another trip to Amherst to confirm his original impression and discuss the terms of the appointment in greater detail. President Meiklejohn was pleased by Frost's response and wrote to tell him that he had read "The Road Not Taken" in college chapel to the delight of the students, who applauded vigorously. "I can assure you of an eager and hearty welcome by the community," he said.[21] Little did Frost know, of course, that this association with Amherst would become a more-or-less permanent aspect of his life until his death in 1963.

10

A PERSON OF GOOD
ASPIRATIONS
1917–1919

I came to live in the house of a professor who was off in Europe having what a professor would call a good time. He had left all his books for me to have a good time with, but had taken good care that I shouldn't have too good a time with them. He had marked them all and with a pencil whenever he had found a mistake of any kind—just as if they were written exercises of pupils. He had never praised anything (I should have loathed his praise), but he had never contributed an idea or interesting commentary. —FROST, NOTEBOOK ENTRY, 1919

Frost had originally responded to the news that Edward Thomas had enlisted in the Royal Garrison Artillery with sympathy, telling him, "I am within a hair of being precisely as sorry and as glad as you are." He added, in noble tones: "You are doing it for the self-same reason I shall hope to do it for if my time ever comes and I am brave enough, namely, because there seems nothing else for a man to do. I have never seen anything more exquisite than the pain you have made of it. You are a terror and I admire you. For what has a man locomotion if it isn't to take him into things he is between barely and not quite standing."[1]

An odd, contradictory mix of motives went into Thomas's decision to go to war, and Frost was only too familiar with this sort of internal conflict. Since coming back to the United States, he had looked on with trepidation from afar as Thomas moved from camp to camp in

England, noting with satisfaction that his friend always found a little time to write poems (many of which he sent to Frost for comment). By the time he arrived in France in the winter of 1917, he had already published over half a dozen poems in periodicals (under the pseudonym Edward Eastaway), and a volume of Eastaway poems had just been accepted by a London publisher—a collection dedicated to Frost, who had urged him to turn to poetry.

Thomas's letters from the front arrived irregularly at the tiny post office in Franconia, describing the dismal conditions under which this war in France was being fought. Thomas was stationed in the village of Arras, where he served as adjutant to a colonel. His duties included long bouts of observation work from a high post overlooking the scene of battle. In one letter, he described to Frost "the moan of the approaching & hovering shell & the black grisly flap that it seems to make as it bursts." He often seems eerily detached from the terrible scenes he describes, as if he were himself in no danger.

Frost, meanwhile, persuaded Alfred Harcourt to issue the Thomas poems in the United States. In these negotiations, Helen Thomas acted as agent for her husband, striking up a regular correspondence with Frost, who had recently urged her to let the American edition appear under the name of Edward Thomas and not a pseudonym. Knowing her husband's wishes, Helen insisted that "Eastaway will not be Thomas & that's that." Her description of his soldiering is memorable: "He's back on his battery now in the thick of it as he wanted to be, firing 400 rounds a day from his gun, listening to the men talking, & getting on well with his fellow officers. He's had little time for depression and homesickness. He says, 'I cannot think of ever being home again, & dare not think of never being there again.'"

The letter contained a shattering, though matter-of-fact, postscript: "This letter was returned by the Censor ages after I posted it. I have had to take out the photographs. But lately I have just received the news of Edward's death. He was killed on Easter Monday by a shell."

Frost was devastated. "I knew from the moment when I first met him at his unhappiest that he would some day clear his mind and save his life," he wrote back to Helen. "I have had four wonderful years with him. I know he has done this all for you: he is all yours. But you must let me cry my cry for him as if he were *almost* all mine too."[2] In a letter to Edward Garnett, he said, "Edward Thomas was the only brother I ever had. I fail to see how we can have been so much to each other, he an Englishman and I an American and our first meeting put off till we were both in middle life. I hadn't a plan for the future that didn't include him."[3]

The death of Thomas was so overwhelming that Frost could not immediately respond—as a poet. "I find he was too near to me," he said. "Some time I shall write about him. Perhaps it will come to me to write in verse. As yet I feel too much the loss of the best friend I ever had. And by that I don't mean I am overwhelmed with grief. Something in me refuses to take the risk—angrily refuses to take the risk— of seeming to use grief for literary purposes. When I care less, I can do more."[4] Thirty years later, in an essay called "A Romantic Chasm," he mused: "I wish Edward Thomas (that poet) were here to ponder gulfs in general with me as in the days when he and I tired the sun with talking on the footpaths and stiles of Ledington and Ryton."

Eventually, he managed to get his feelings onto paper, in a poem called "To E.T.," which first appeared in the *Yale Review* in April 1920:

> *I slumbered with your poems on my breast,*
> *Spread open as I dropped them half-read through*
> *Like dove wings on a figure on a tomb*
> *To see if in a dream they brought of you,*
>
> *I might not have the chance I missed in life*
> *Through some delay, and call you to your face*
> *First soldier, and then poet, and then both,*
> *Who died a soldier-poet of your race.*
>
> *I meant, you meant, that nothing should remain*
> *Unsaid between us, brother, and this remained—*
> *And one thing more that was not then to say:*
> *The Victory for what it lost and gained.*

You went to meet the shell's embrace of fire
On Vimy Ridge; and when you fell that day
The war seemed over more for you than me,
But now for me than you—the other way.

How over, though, for even me who knew
The foe thrust back unsafe beyond the Rhine,
If I was not to speak of it to you
And see you pleased once more with words of mine?

Frost addresses the deceased directly, regretting that in life, to his face, he had "Through some delay" not called Thomas "First soldier, and then poet, and then both." The tone is complex, beginning with that odd admission by the speaker that he had fallen asleep with the poems on his breast "half-read." This poem, as William Pritchard has noted, "seems undistinguished by Frost's usual range of tone and wit."[5] On the other hand, there is subtleness here; the opening itself, with its admission of laziness with regard to reading Thomas, detours around any idealization of Thomas that might threaten to obliterate the poem with sentiment. Even so, Frost succumbs to a kind of sentimentality when he calls Thomas "a soldier-poet of your race."

In the third stanza, one feels the pressure of conflicting emotions: "I meant, you meant that nothing should remain / Unsaid between us." He and Thomas were roughly the same age, and oddly similar in temperament, even family circumstances. In fact, this is a fairly rare example in Frost's life of an equal relationship. For the most part, he preferred to spend time with younger men who looked up to him; if they were writers, they were poets of lesser talent, such as Untermeyer, or teachers, such as Sidney Cox.

The memorably concise third stanza gives way to a concluding stanza of lesser power. Indeed, "How over" is a distracting way to begin a stanza, and the next line (about the "foe thrust back unsafe beyond the Rhine") is slack and rhetorical. The final question rescues the poem, however, with a quiet pathos, embodied in an intimate appeal to Thomas for sympathy.

Louis Untermeyer admitted to Frost that he disliked "To E.T." and received this response some years later: "You know, you old skeezicks, you never managed to dislike heartily any poem I ever wrote except the one to E.T. and that is complicated with the war in such a way that you are afraid it may be a tract in favor of heroism. (But it isn't.)"[6] In the end, Frost was never quite able to express his deepest feelings about Thomas in poetry.

Among the poems Frost wrote in Franconia in the summer of 1917 was "For Once, Then, Something." It is one of his most intriguing poems:

> Others taunt me with having knelt at well-curbs
> Always wrong to the light, so never seeing
> Deeper down in the well than where the water
> Gives me back in a shining surface picture
> Me myself in the summer heaven godlike
> Looking out of a wreath of fern and cloud puffs
> Once, when trying with a chin against a well-curb,
> I discerned, as I thought, beyond the picture,
> Through the picture, a something white, uncertain,
> Something more of the depths—and then I lost it.
> Water came to rebuke the too clear water.
> One drop fell from a fern, and lo, a ripple
> Shook whatever it was lay there at bottom,
> Blurred it, blotted it out. What was that whiteness?
> Truth? A pebble of quartz? For once, then, something.

The poem employs a hendecasyllabic meter that vaguely imitates a meter used by Catullus, one of Frost's favorite Latin poets (whom, according to Reuben Brower, he was fond of quoting in the original). As a poem, it ranks with "Spring Pools" and "The Silken Tent" as one of Frost's most intricate pieces of verse making, one that intimately marries his poetic vision and personal philosophy; to a degree, it represents his response to critics who saw him as a country bumpkin whose poems did not see much beyond the "shining surface" of rural life, with himself at its center. The image of Narcissus is implied, with the poet looking into the well (of memory?) and seeing himself "in the summer heaven godlike" while wearing a poet's crown of laurels, his head poking through the proverbial clouds.

The poem turns on the word *"Once"*; with the ironic italics, Frost is cutting himself a bit of critical slack, as if to say: How about it, friends? Grant me that once in a great while I see more than the surface, more than my own reflection. But even here, he admits the impossibility of finding "truth," that mysterious something that lies "at bottom." "Water came to rebuke the too clear water." That biblical word "rebuke" suggests that perhaps some higher (or lower) spiritual force has connived to prevent a human being from catching more than a glimpse of Reality (in the Platonic sense). The biblical texture is reinforced in the next line, where "and lo" precedes the ripple that finally scrambles the image. The last line is deeply ironic, in that the "something" might well be "nothing." The uncertainty of the poem is reinforced by the feminine (i.e., unaccented) endings of each line, which suffuse the poem with a feeling of inconclusiveness.

Frost had a number of unfinished poems on his desk, including "Paul's Wife," "To Earthward," "The Aim Was Song," and many others that would eventually appear in *New Hampshire* (1923). Some of these poems had been lingering in his folder marked "Unfinished Poems" for a decade or more. Typically, Frost would suddenly recall a poem and return to it, striking out lines, adding more. Some poems stayed in rough draft for decades on end. "Dust of Snow," for example, was finally published (in the *London Mercury*) in 1920, but early versions seem to date back to 1896.[7]

During the fall of 1917, Frost felt as though he were just beginning to hear the sound of his voice again, but Amherst called, and he could not resist.

In a time when most colleges have a poet on campus, if not several, it seems difficult to imagine how odd it was for Amherst College to have hired Robert Frost in the winter of 1917. The initial work of Stark Young and Alexander Meiklejohn had resulted in Frost's becoming a temporary member of the Amherst faculty as a replacement for George Bosworth Churchill, who had been elected to the Massachusetts Senate. Exactly how he might fit in was an open question—one that Frost himself entertained quite frankly. In the recesses of his heart, he wondered if teaching was a good way to support his avocation. "My object in living is to unite / My avocation and my vocation," he would write in "Two Tramps in Mud Time." A poet first and last, he often said that teaching distracted him from the real work of making poems. But a reliable income was sorely needed, especially now, the English sojourn having utterly depleted his savings. Furthermore, the lure of Amherst was considerable.

It was an obvious place for Frost to go. President Meiklejohn—an Englishman by birth who had come to America in 1880, at the age of eight—had been at the college since 1912, having previously taught philosophy at Brown (which had been his own undergraduate college). He was drawn to innovative approaches in education, and the appointment of Frost was a bold stroke in this direction. "The college is primarily not a place of the body, nor of the feelings, nor even of the will; it is, first of all, a place of mind," Meiklejohn had written. He hoped to plunge students into "the problems of philosophy" from the outset, promoting the "fun of reading and conversing and investigating and reflecting."[8] These were all good signs for Frost, who liked nothing better than "conversing and investigating and reflecting."

Frost had written to Untermeyer that "you get more credit for thinking if you restate formulae or cite cases that fall in easily under formulae, but all the fun is outside saying things that suggest formulae that won't formulate—that almost but don't quite formulate. I should like to be so subtle at this game as to seem to the casual person altogether obvious."[9] On Amherst College letterhead a few days after arriving on campus, he wrote to Untermeyer: "I seize this department stationery to give you a new sense of what a merely important person I am become in my decline from greatness."[10]

As a place to live, Amherst appealed to Frost and his family. It was a tiny New England village of classic proportions, with a broad common surrounded by tall elms. The college—one of the oldest and most respectable in the country—lay at the southern end of the common, a cluster of redbrick and gray granite buildings constructed along the crest of a hill. From the highest vantage, one got a panoramic view across miles of fertile valley. The Frosts moved into a yellow wood-frame house on Dana Street, a short walk from the campus. The children were enrolled in local schools. A warm welcome came from their neighbors Otto and Ethel Manthey-Zorn, who would soon become close friends. When Elinor discovered that the house was devoid of blankets, Ethel quickly produced an armful of her own.

In his first semester, Frost was responsible for teaching a seminar on reading and writing poetry and a larger class on English drama before Shakespeare. The former was his favorite; it met one night each week in an upper room of the Beta Theta Pi fraternity house, which faced the common. The students gathered in worn leather armchairs around a log fire, and Frost held forth entertainingly on pet topics, such as the sound of sense. "He often appeared in the room with a clutch of slim volumes in his briefcase," one student recalled, and he would usually begin by reading aloud from Dickinson, Herbert, Wordsworth, and assorted contemporaries. Students presented their own poems in class, and Frost reacted generously to their work; he encouraged the class to remain long after the two prescribed hours were over. He rarely got home to Dana Street before midnight, and he would often be so revved up by the night's conversation that he would sit in the kitchen until dawn, reading and writing.

The drama course proved taxing. Frost was not an expert on the subject, and he spent much of his spare time reading Heywood, Kyd, Lyly, Greene, Peele, and Marlowe—staying one step ahead of the students. Whereas his predecessor in the course, Professor Churchill, had stressed the historical background to these playwrights, Frost kept the emphasis squarely on the texts. He also stressed the basic principles of drama: the importance of situation, the use of tone in the creation of emotion, and aspects of voice. These were all subjects he had talked about at length before, although never in a classroom setting.

Frost was frustrated by the rigid approach to writing already in place at Amherst, and fought his own battle against this conventionality. He insisted that students write from the heart about subjects that genuinely mattered to them, emphasizing the importance of close personal observation of the world. "I'll never correct a paper for style," he told his classes. "I'm looking for subject matter, substance in yourself."[11] He noted in his journals: "What we do in college is to get over our little-mindedness. Education—to get it you have to hang around till you catch on."[12]

Reports from students suggest that Frost was easygoing to the point of being disorganized. One student, for instance, reported that his drama course was "the most loosely run and undisciplined class of any of the classes I attended in college."[13] Another remembered that Frost was "headstrong with his own ideas" but "always stimulating." He usually began class with "a long ramble about whatever subject was of interest that day," making no attempt to interest students who did not already share his enthusiasm for the subject. A rude handful of students in the drama course would actually play cards in the back of the room, unchallenged by Frost, who did not want to adopt the role of disciplinarian.

One might have expected Frost to feel grateful to both Stark Young and Alexander Meiklejohn for their support, but this was not the case. He took against their liberalism at once, seeing himself as a rugged Emersonian individualist who rebuffed any notions of collectivism. He felt isolated in the academy and struck back with characteristic force at those who disagreed with him, making scathing remarks to his students about certain colleagues. "He had violent prejudices and hatreds," recalled Henry A. Ladd, a member of the Class of 1918.[14] For the most part, there was little opportunity in his classes to disagree with him, largely because he did most of the talking himself.

Much of his animosity was directed toward Young, a sophisticated, urbane southerner whose effete, openly homosexual manner unnerved Frost. When he heard from one of his favorite students that Young had unabashedly tried to entice him into sexual relations, Frost reported this to Meiklejohn. But Stark Young was well published, and hugely popular as a teacher; what is more, Meiklejohn considered Young a close friend. This was of course long before the days when sexual harassment claims were routine, and Meiklejohn was not about to dismiss such a valuable member of the faculty based on indirect accusations. Meiklejohn's stance clearly hardened Frost against him. Never one to hold his tongue, Frost was unguarded in his criticisms of the president with both students and faculty.

Before the term was over, the United States had finally entered the war against Germany, and many of Frost's students dropped everything to enlist. He cheered them on. As ever, he had great sympathy for students who wanted to drop out of college for any reason. War, in particular, struck him as a very good reason. "I don't see why the fact that I can't be in a fight should keep me from liking the fight," he wrote to one of his English department colleagues, George Whicher.[15] He often said that only age and family responsibilities kept him home.

The Stark Young affair wore at his nerves, and he began to regret having taken the job at Amherst in the first place. He wondered if it were right, after all, for a poet to spend precious reserves of imaginative energy in the classroom, where the rewards were so intangible. He had been productive in England, as a poet, and it was obvious to him that while he was teaching he was not writing.

In March, he spent a week in the Chicago area as the guest of Harriet Moody (widow of the poet William Vaughn Moody), who had arranged for him to read and lecture at several local colleges and poetry societies. These public performances seem to have recalled him to his vocation, as a poet, and by late spring he longed for the peace and freedom of Franconia. He wanted to get back to gardening and mild chores, to sitting on the porch with his mountain view, and to writing poems. He also looked forward to putting the abrasions of Amherst politics well behind him.

The summer came and went too quickly, however. Frost was back on the Amherst campus in the fall of 1917, having been lured back by Meiklejohn—who admired Frost despite his prickly behavior. To sweeten the deal, Meiklejohn saw that Frost was granted full professorial status, with a commensurate salary ($2,500 for the upcoming academic year). Given his precarious finances, Frost believed he had no choice but to return.

The money was important, since *Mountain Interval* had not sold anything like as well as *North of Boston*. Indeed, this little book— somewhat hurried into print by Alfred Harcourt—had not made the kind of impact Frost had wished for it. Nevertheless, it contains half a dozen poems that rank among Frost's absolute best: "The Road Not Taken," "An Old Man's Winter Night," "Hyla Brook," "Birches," "Putting in the Seed," "The Hill Wife," and "The Sound of Trees." Most of these were actually written in Derry long before and hoarded in his notebooks, although Frost would occasionally trim or add lines before final publication.

The second stint at Amherst proved no more satisfying to Frost than his first. The poems certainly did not come; indeed, Frost complained that he couldn't write well "with somebody looking over my shoulder." President Meiklejohn, as a figure of authority, took on the character of the disapproving father in Frost's imagination, and relations between them seemed only to get worse—if that was possible. The situation with Stark Young also deteriorated, especially now that Young was fully aware of Frost's attempts to subvert him.

Frost took comfort, however, in his growing fame. "The Ax-Helve" appeared in October in the *Atlantic Monthly*, attracting compliments from friends and colleagues. It was another of Frost's remarkable poems about the nature of poetry itself. The Canadian woodsman in the poem, Baptiste, becomes distraught when he sees that the narrator is chopping wood with a bad ax. He offers to carve a good handle (or "helve") for him, free of charge. That night, at Baptiste's home, the process of carving becomes an ingenious metaphor for the act of poetic composition:

> *Needlessly soon he had his ax-helves out,*
> *A quiverful to choose from, since he wished me*
> *To have the best he had, or had to spare—*
> *Not for me to ask which, when what he took*
> *Had beauties he had to point me out at length*
> *To insure their not being wasted on me.*
> *He liked to have it slender as a whipstock,*

> Free from the least knot, equal to the strain
> Of bending like a sword across the knee.
> He showed me that the lines of a good helve
> Were native to the grain before the knife
> Expressed them, and its curves were no false curves
> Put on it from without. And there its strength lay
> For the hard work. He chafed its long white body
> From end to end with his rough hand shut round it.
> He tried it at the eye-hole in the ax-head.
> "Hahn, hahn," he mused, "don't need much taking down."
> Baptiste knew how to make a short job long
> For love of it, and yet not waste time either.

In the margins of a friend's book, next to this poem, Frost wrote in pencil: "This is as near as I like to come to talking about art, in a work of art—such as it is."[16] Once again, Frost had found a metaphor of universal significance in a local image.

That fall, Amy Lowell chose to focus on him in a widely noticed book, *Tendencies in Modern American Poetry*, where she included Frost among Robinson, Sandburg, Masters, John Gould Fletcher, and H.D.—elite company for a man who, only a few years earlier, had been virtually unknown in his own country. Lowell, unfortunately, was prone to sentimental caricature when it came to Frost, and she spoke of him as "all compounded as he seems to be of the granite and gentians of our Northern mountains."

Not surprisingly, Frost was annoyed by the way Lowell found his regionalism a form of limitation. On December 2, 1917, he wrote to her in a sly, bemused fashion that nevertheless impressed upon her that he was no hick from the woods:

I must see you before long if only to put it to you while the business is still before the house why I am not by your own showing the least provincial, the most national, of American poets—why I ought not to be, anyway. Doesn't the wonder grow that I have never written anything or as you say never published anything except about New England farms when you consider the jumble I am? Mother, Scotch immigrant. Father oldest New England stock unmixed. Ten years in West. Thirty years in East. Three years in England. Not less than six months in any of these: San Francisco, New York, Boston, Cambridge, Lawrence, London. Lived in Maine, N.H., Vt., Mass. Twenty-five years in cities, nine in villages, nine on farms. Saw the South on foot. Dartmouth, Harvard two years. Shoe-worker, mill-hand, farm-hand, editor, reporter, insurance agent, agent for Shakespearean reader, reader myself, teacher in every kind of school public and private including psychological normal school and college. Prize for running at Caledonia Club picnic: prizes for assumed parts at masquerade balls; medals for goodness in high school; detour for scholarship at Harvard; money for verse. Knew Henry George well and saw much at one time (by way of contrast) of a noted boss [Christopher "Boss" Buckley in San Francisco]. Presbyterian, Unitarian, Swedenborgian, Nothing. All the vices but disloyalty and chewing gum or tobacco.[17]

Frost put himself forward boldly and cleverly. Although he continued to play the role of the Yankee farmer-poet, especially when reading his poems in public, he did not want to be mistaken for a rube, especially by sophisticated critics of poetry.

Lesley Frost had by now gone off to Wellesley College, where her professors made demands that she considered pedantic and petty. She had, of course, been educated in unusual circumstances, often at home by her parents; conventional education was perhaps bound to grate on her. Furthermore, she was as headstrong and willful as her father. She did not take happily to college life, which struck her as regimented and pointless. After one year, with her father's support, she dropped out with the hopes of becoming an airplane pilot—a prospect that unsettled her parents. Flying was not womanly work, especially in these early days of aviation.

In the fall of 1918, Amherst was "part military camp, part college," as one student recalled. The American entry into the war had changed the tone of college life, and Frost could not avoid getting into arguments with colleagues and students about the wisdom of the war. More to irritate his antiwar colleagues than because he really believed in this particular war, Frost maintained an unwaveringly hawkish stance.

His manner in the classroom in the fall semester of 1918 was recorded by E. A. Richards, a member of the Class of 1921:

> During those months it was good to be even remotely in acquaintance with Mr. Frost . . . for here was a man more deeply sentient, more solidly intellectual, with those qualities in finer and more equable balance than we had heretofore known. . . .
>
> We were glad to go to his house at ten or eleven at night and sit somewhat uneasily in his sitting room until he came in from some depth of the dwelling and sprawled out on a lounge. He read from this poet and that, throwing the book aside when he had reached what seemed to him the furthest reach of luminous expression in some particular poem. And then he would say what occurred to him in relation to that poem, going from there to the general considerations of poetry.
>
> He never, or rarely, talked about his own work.[18]

President Meiklejohn continued to believe that having Frost on his faculty was good for the college, and he was aware that it might be difficult to keep him. Frost would often express his doubts about teaching, wondering aloud if he shouldn't return to Franconia and resume farming. But Meiklejohn appealed to Frost's vanity, offering him an honorary degree at the 1918 commencement; Frost was reappointed to a professorship with the understanding that he would teach only in the fall semester, leaving him free to write and travel the rest of the year, as he saw fit. It was a remarkable deal.

The fall of 1918 was infamous for a flu epidemic that killed thousands in the month of October alone. Frost, who was always susceptible to colds and flus, fell desperately ill during the second week of classes and could not teach for over ten weeks—missing most of the term. He was even too unwell to celebrate the end of the war on

November 11. Elinor, meanwhile, was also under considerable strain, having to look after her sick husband and take care of the children.

Frost stayed at Amherst through the spring of 1920, but remained unhappy about Stark Young, who grew increasingly bitter about Frost's attempts to unseat him. Young believed that Meiklejohn had been manipulated by Frost, against his own better judgment, into extending the poet's contract at the college. A situation developed in which some members of the faculty sided with Frost, while others (the majority) stood by Young. In the end, there can be no doubt that Frost behaved ungratefully toward Young, who had been instrumental in bringing him to Amherst in the first place. This academic feuding utterly destroyed Frost's peace of mind, and he could not write.

The fact that Frost was not writing troubled him greatly, and he blamed Amherst for distracting him from his real work. He had always found it easier to write when he was farming, and he wanted to get back to the farm in Franconia as soon as possible. Needing a good excuse to resign, he kept pushing the Stark Young issue with Meiklejohn, insisting that Young be fired on grounds of "immorality." The president was not about to fire Young, of course, and he made this plain to Frost, who then suggested that he must resign himself in protest. He did so, in January, although he stayed on through the graduation. As he explained to one alumnus, he felt "too much out of sympathy with what the present administration seems bent on doing with this old New England college" to continue as a member of the faculty. But he was honest enough to admit that he had enjoyed "the 'academic freedom' to be entirely myself under Mr. Meiklejohn." In a somewhat self-dramatizing vein, he claimed that the president hated his "dangerous rationalistic and anti-intellectualistic philosophy."[19] In truth, Meiklejohn was more than willing to let Frost be Frost.

There can be no doubt, however, that Frost intensely disliked the liberal atmosphere at Amherst, where ideas of every stripe were tolerated, even encouraged. As he wrote to Wilbur Cross at the *Yale Review*: "I am too much a creature of prejudice to stay and listen to such stuff" as Amherst put forward.[20] He was also busy erecting his reputation for cantankerousness, and in his first major foray into the public arena, he had certainly laid a solid foundation. As usual, he was well aware of his calculations; he would tell Untermeyer, "Nothing I do or say is as yet due to anything but a strong determination to have my own way. . . . I cut up no ructions but with design to gain my ends even as aforetime when I was a child in San Francisco I played sick to get out of going to school. There's a vigorous devil in me that raises me above or drops me below the level of pity."[21] Yet he was, he maintained, "a person of good aspirations." Everything was based on that, and his friends ultimately agreed. "He could be contrary and difficult," recalled Victor Reichert, "but you always knew Frost meant well. His standards were very high, personally and professionally, even though he pretended otherwise at times—even played at being worse than he was."[22]

II

LIVING IN VERMONT
1920–1922

I have moved a good part of the way to a stone cottage on a hill at South Shaftsbury in southern Vermont on the New York side near the historic town of Bennington where if I have any money left after repairing the roof in the spring I mean to plant a new Garden of Eden with a thousand apple trees of some unforbidden variety.

—FROST TO G. R. ELLIOT, OCTOBER 23, 1920

Frost explained his leaving Amherst to Sidney Cox in a letter of July 17, 1920:

I've kicked myself out of Amherst and settled down to revising old poems when I am not making new ones.

Teaching is all right, and I don't mean to speak of it with condescension. I shall have another go at it before the last employee is fired. I believe in teaching, but I don't believe in going to school. Every day I feel bound to save my consistency by advising my pupils to leave school. Then if they insist on coming to school, it is not my fault: I can teach them with a clear conscience.

We seem on the point of leaving Franconia. The hawser is cast off, in fact, though we lie still against the wharf. They say when you run away from a place it is yourself you are generally running away from and that goes with you and is the first thing you meet in the next place you turn up. In this case it is Frosts we are running away from and Frosts can hardly help going with us since Frosts we are ourselves. If you ever see any talk of me in print you may notice that it is my frostiness that is more and more played up. I am cold, snow-dusted, and all that. I can see that I am in a way or I would write to my best friends oftener. Don't say amen too fervently if you don't want to hurt my feelings and your own prospects.[1]

Frost was desperate for the peace and freedom of country life after leaving Amherst, convinced that his poetry had suffered while he toiled in the academy. He was suddenly intent upon hurling "fistfuls [of poems] right and left," as he wrote to Wilbur Cross. The Amherst experience had stifled him, as a poet—although he admitted that it had appealed to his "philosopher" side. Now that he had liberated himself from "care and intellectuality," he could face the blank page again, and listen to the inner voice that was caught, at times accidentally, as he walked in the woods or sat, idly, expecting nothing.

It was a cold, clear summer in Franconia, with ice-blue skies and almost no rain. Frost had wanted to return to growing fruits and vegetables, but the summer's breezy chill reminded him that northern New Hampshire was not an especially hospitable place for farming. The land was rocky, and the growing season painfully short. He began to think that what he really wanted was fruit trees—apples, in particular, the crop he had most enjoyed harvesting during the years in Derry.

Apple orchards dotted the landscape of southern Vermont, and Frost (with the aid of the novelist Dorothy Canfield Fisher) began searching for a better place to farm. Fisher herself—a stocky, gray-haired woman of forty-one—had a farm just outside of Arlington, Vermont, and she recommended the little towns near Bennington.

After several scouting missions, Frost found a farm near Fisher in the village of South Shaftsbury, halfway between Bennington and Arlington. The Peleg Cole place was a ninety-acre farm, with a rough-hewn house (circa 1779) made of large granite chunks and pine clapboard; a slate roof was pitched steeply to discard the heavy snow. A gable and window hung out over the front door, while the other windows were neatly recessed, with red trimming. Perched on a small rise, the house had views of the Green Mountains to the east and the Taconics to the west. Large maples, oaks, and chestnuts shaded the house in the summer—an attractive feature that appealed at once to Frost. He was most taken by the ancient apple orchard on the property—"as good as they get," he said. There was also a substantial maple grove, with a small sugar shack for boiling down the precious sap into syrup, a good cash crop. The property also included a brook and plenty of good pastureland, as well as two small barns.

The house itself was in poor condition, without running water or a furnace. Elinor hesitated when she saw the house, but Fisher urged her and Frost to go ahead, offering the temporary use of a house she owned in Arlington called The Manse (where she had lived before her marriage). Marjorie, who was fifteen, could enroll in the ninth grade in North Bennington that fall—a prospect that encouraged Elinor, who (like Marjorie) was unhappy with the school in Franconia. Frost was deeply affected by the natural surroundings, and felt that he could write there. It was much like going back to Derry.

Exactly how Frost saw the move himself is evident from a letter to his English friend John Haines, written on October 10, 1920:

I have been leaving Franconia, New Hampshire (a German-English combination of names) to go and live in South Shaftsbury, Vermont (an English-French combination). Our motives for making the change were not political, however, but agricultural. We seek a better place to farm and especially grow apples. Franconia's winter killed apple trees—and some years even in July and August frosted gardens. The beautiful White Mountains were too near for warmth. A hundred miles further south and out of the higher peaks as we shall be, we think we ought to be safer.

Arlington, Shaftsbury, Rupert, Sunderland, Manchester, Dorset, Rutland: the towns all round us are named after courtiers of Charles the Second. It looks as if some gunpowder plot had blown them up at a ball and scattered them over our map. I might wish they rang a little more Puritanically to my ear, but as you know I make a point about not being too fastidious about anything but the main issue.[2]

The old problem of how to make a living also returned, now that Frost had thrown over his Amherst job (which, in his last academic year, had brought in $4,000). Although he was greatly in demand as a lecturer, these performances rarely netted more than a hundred dollars; published poems brought in anywhere from fifteen to thirty dollars, but Frost had not been prolific in the past few years: under half a dozen poems had appeared between 1917 and 1920.

Frost's immediate financial crisis was relieved by a well-off young man called Raymond Holden, a New Yorker who summered in Franconia. Holden had known Frost for a few years, and he had shared his own poetry with the older poet. They had corresponded for several years while Holden was serving with the cavalry sent by President Woodrow Wilson to protect the Mexican border during the uprising of Pancho Villa. When he (and his new wife) returned to Franconia in 1919, he bought half of the Frost farm in Franconia for $2,500, with a promise to buy the other half for the same price if Frost should decide to move. Thus, Frost increased his original investment in the Franconia farm fivefold; he had plenty of money left to buy the Peleg Cole place, with cash to spare. Lawrance Thompson, ever eager to impugn Frost's motives, suggests that the poet took advantage of young Holden, who admired him and certainly hoped to settle near him.

But Holden was hardly forced to buy the Frost property—and there is plenty of correspondence to suggest that Frost genuinely liked Holden and acted as a kind of mentor to him. Holden remained a great admirer to the end, although he briefly felt that Frost had used him for his convenience.[3] In an unpublished memoir, he recalled:

The happiest and most memorable days of my friendship with Robert were in spite of the difficulties which arose there for me and for him—those at Franconia between 1915 and 1920. I can point to many of his poems and say, "This was written after we did such-and-such." He had the habit, when he finished a new poem, of writing out a copy of it in longhand, signing it, and giving it to me. I remember particularly the appearance of one called "Evening in a Sugar Orchard," and of another entitled "A Hillside Thaw," both of which were written in the early spring of 1919 [Holden may mean 1920], after he and I had sat up all one night tending the fire and keeping the sap flowing in the sugar orchard close to Robert's house.[4]

In his search for capital to fund his move to South Shaftsbury, Frost also borrowed $1,000 from Louis Untermeyer. This loan, which is more a sign of Frost's deep anxiety about money than an indication of genuine need, was repaid a few months later. As usual, Untermeyer was glad to be of use to Frost, and he encouraged the man he admired to depend on him in this way.

The release from academic life appears to have worked at once. Frost wrote half a dozen important poems in the summer and fall of 1920, including "A Star in a Stoneboat," "The Star-Splitter," "Maple," "The Grindstone," "Two Witches" (which includes "The Witch of Coös" and "The Pauper Witch of Grafton"), "Wild Grapes," and "Fire and Ice"—a remarkable run of creativity. He was also able to complete several poems begun earlier, such as "Paul's Wife," a fanciful poem about Mrs. Paul Bunyan, wife of the legendary lumberjack, which had been started in 1912 and left unfinished. Within a few months, he had a good start on a new collection.

The range of this work is startling, from the narrative invention of "Paul's Wife" to the lively verse drama of "The Witch of Coös" to the fierce, aphoristic compactness of "Fire and Ice." This latter—an attempt to write in the epigramatic style of the classical poets—is rightly celebrated:

> *Some say the world will end in fire,*
> *Some say in ice.*
> *From what I've tasted of desire*
> *I hold with those who favor fire.*
> *But if it had to perish twice,*

I think I know enough of hate
To say that for destruction ice
Is also great
And would suffice.

The poem was roughed out in Amherst the previous fall, but in July Frost pulled it together, lacing the rhymes as tightly as a boot. At once whimsical and fierce, the poem contains a bold admission: "I think I know enough of hate." Indeed, Frost delighted in his own prejudices, these "hatreds" that were his way of staking out the boundaries of self-hood. William Pritchard quotes a letter Frost wrote to B. F. Skinner (a recent college graduate) in 1926: "All that makes a writer is the ability to write strongly and directly from some unaccountable and almost invicible personal prejudice."[5]

In "Fire and Ice," the poet-narrator seems to have been through the torrid and frigid zones, to have loved and hated. The Yankee pose is apparent in the easy generalizations ("Some say") and the self-consciously elevated diction one might hear at a Vermont town meeting ("I hold with those"). The speaker uses reticence at times ("From what I've tasted of desire") to imply vast worlds of experience, but there is also the hint that he has experienced great bitterness ("I think I know enough of hate"). Rhyming with "hate," the word "great" in the penultimate line is wonderfully general, even offhand, given the context: "To say that for destruction ice / Is also great / And would suffice." He is even wryly comic, wittily rhyming "ice" with "suffice." One can scarely imagine a more complex linking of tones in such a short space, or such compacted fury combining with such quiet, effective comedy.

By 1920, Frost had become thoroughly at ease in the role of spokesman for rural New England, getting (as he said) "Yankier and Yankier" as he aged. He had begun to understand the range of subjects and tonalities possible within his tiny territory, seeing there were few limits to where he could go in this persona, or how deeply he could inhabit it. By now—he was forty-seven—the mask and the man were closely bound. From this point on Frost would rarely distance himself from the mask, and would wear it freely—even defiantly—in public.

He could play at being something that, in fact, he was, taking pleasure in the possibilities of his persona. As Seamus Heaney has noted, his "appetite for his own independence was fierce and expressed itself in a reiterated belief in his right to limits: his defenses, his fences, and his freedom were all interdependent."[6] Yet he also recognized that his fear of chaos, of the abyss into which he periodically fell, urged upon him these limits, and that self-containment was a kind of defense against those darker, threatening forces barely held in abeyance.

Frost's relationship with his sister, Jeanie, had taken an unhappy turn the previous spring. A letter from Wilbur Rowell, the family attorney (who had remained in closer touch with Jeanie than had her brother), was full of bad news: "Last Thursday morning the Police Department of Portland, Maine, telephoned to me saying that they had Jeanie Frost in confinement and that she was demented. They wanted me to come there and take her off their hands. This I declined to do. I have neither the authority nor the means to take care of her."[7] Rowell explained that she had been moving from place to place, drawing advances on her grandfather's annual annuity. The money was almost gone by now, and Frost would have to step in.

He had come to his sister's aid when, in 1916, she'd enrolled as a mature student at the University of Michigan, following up on his promise to assist her in getting some credentials. By chance, he had recently met, in Franconia, an English professor from Michigan called Morris P. Tilley, whom he had asked to help his sister in any way possible. Tilley later reported to Frost that Jeanie had "made last year upon two of her instructors and two of the college officers . . . the impression of extreme eccentricity."[8] One senses a degree of delicacy in Tilley's phrasing.

Jeanie had been quite unable to adjust to college life—or life in general, as her police detention suggests; by April 1920 she was a permanent resident of the State Hospital in Augusta, Maine, where she would spend the last nine years of her life in a confused state, dying in 1929 at the age of fifty-three. It was an abiding tragedy for her brother, who saw traces of insanity in himself and his children that often led to fits of anxiety. As it was, he rarely saw her again, finding visits too painful to withstand. As he later confided to John Bartlett, he believed the situation with Jeanie was brought on partly by her own "poor choices in life." He thought that everyone's sanity, or "soul," as he liked to call it, hung by a thread—not literally, as his New England ancestor Jonathan Edwards argued in "Sinners in the Hands of an Angry God," but figuratively. It is up to each of us, as Frost once wrote, to "save ourselves unaided." Jeanie had (by her brother's reckoning) made the wrong decisions, and she had paid dearly with her sanity.[9]

The renovations were completed on the house in South Shaftsbury by mid-November, and the Frosts moved in. There was no real farming to be done at this time of year, so Frost settled into a sustained period of writing; he was self-consciously trying to recapture the feeling he had had in Derry, and in Beaconsfield. He began, as usual, by revising poems that had long sat in rough form in his notebooks. These included "Nothing Gold Can Stay"—one of his most affecting lyrics:

> Nature's first green is gold,
> Her hardest hue to hold.
> Her early leaf's a flower;
> But only so an hour.
> Then leaf subsides to leaf.
> So Eden sank to grief,
> So dawn goes down to day.
> Nothing gold can stay.

A poem like this is the product of close natural observation, a passionate sympathy for the processes of nature, and a finely tuned awarness of nature's metaphorical potential. There is an aphoristic brilliance in the first line, compounded by the subsequent lines. The poem takes a remarkable turn in the fifth and sixth lines: "Then leaf subsides to leaf. / So Eden sank to grief." Here is the Emersonian move: to associate patterns of natural imagery with the cycles of human life, to find the correspondences between these parallel worlds. The minute natural observation of the first four lines gives way, suddenly, to the

Fall of Man—a dramatic widening of the poem's sphere of meaning as Frost appears to suggest that the mere passage of time, and the organic unfolding of "leaf subsid[ing] to leaf," brings about this disaster. In the last two lines, the sphere widens to include the cycles of the cosmos: "So dawn goes down to day." The poet takes the reader to a rarely visited place—the slide from dawn (often associated in classical poetry with the color of gold) to day. Everything is flux, the poem suggests; the bloom of Eden withers. The gold of beginnings becomes the more durable green of summer, which is nothing but a stage on the way to autumnal fire and wintery blankness.

This arresting lyric was coaxed from a fragment written in 1900. A version was sent on March 20, 1920, to George Roy Elliott, a recent friend who in 1919 had written an article on Frost in the *Nation* that he'd liked a great deal and that had sparked a lifelong friendship between the two men (indeed, the last letter Frost ever wrote was to Elliott).[10] This version contained twenty-four lines, divided into three octets. The first two octets were compacted into the current poem. The final octet was rescued and expanded decades later to be published in *A Witness Tree* as "It Is Almost the Year Two Thousand":

> To start the world of old
> We had one age of gold
> Not labored out of mines,
> And some say there are signs
> The second such has come,
> The true Millennium,
> The final golden glow
> To end it. And if so
> (And science ought to know)
> We well may raise our heads
> From weeding garden beds
> And annotating books
> To watch this end de luxe.

A fatal cuteness ("this end de luxe") makes the later poem so much less affecting and interesting than "Nothing Gold Can Stay," although something of the original fire still smolders here and there, especially in the aphoristic first four lines.

Another important poem of this period was "Two Look at Two." Frost had managed a rough draft during his last year at Amherst, and he sent a version of the poem to Cox in a letter of July 17, 1920.[11] It is one of Frost's most successful ventures into dramatic poetry, complicated by the presence of a narrator who at times conflates with the characters in the poem, a couple who are wandering in the woods:

> Love and forgetting might have carried them
> A little further up the mountainside
> With night so near, but not much further up.
> They must have halted soon in any case
> With thoughts of the path back, how rough it was
> With rock and washout, and unsafe in darkness;
> When they were halted by a tumbled wall
> With barbed-wire binding. . . .

Note how the poem opens with four lines of conventional blank verse (made somewhat less regular by the reversal of the first foot). It's that jagged fifth line that upsets the rhythmical motion, setting up a complex range of rhythmical expectations and possibilities. As in "The Road Not Taken" and "Birches," Frost is good at portraying indecision; when the couple meet the barbed wire and "tumbled wall," they hesitate:

> They stood facing this,
> Spending what onward impulse they still had
> In one last look the way they must not go,
> On up the failing path, where, if a stone
> Or earthslide moved at night, it moved itself;
> No footstep moved it. . . .

One could not hear a more Frostian note than "Spending what onward impulse they still had / In one last look the way they must not go." These lines recall the pivotal moment in "Storm Fear," one of his earliest poems: "It costs no inward struggle not to go, / Ah, no!" Frost's characters, literally as well as figuratively, seem endlessly forced to calculate the costs of movement, trying to predict the weight of various consequences that can only be guessed at.

The couple think their journey is over, when suddenly a doe "from round a spruce stood looking at them / Across the wall, as near the wall as they." The drama is heightened when a buck appears, too:

> "This, then, is all. What more is there to ask?"
> But no, not yet. A snort to bid them wait.
> A buck from round the spruce stood looking at them.

Frost dares repeat "from round the spruce stood looking at them / Across the wall, as near the wall as they." This repetition, or echo, contributes to the wavelike motion of the narrative, with its rise and fall. "But no, not yet" is spoken by the invisible narrator, but it might as well be contained in the quotation that precedes it. The poem moves toward an intense lyrical denouement in which the Emersonian correspondence is fully satisfied, as if inner and outer worlds have merged in a moment of affirmation quite unusual in Frost (and powerfully rebutted in a later poem, "The Most of It," from *A Witness Tree*). "It was all," Frost writes:

> A great wave from it going over them,
> As if the earth in one unlooked-for favor
> Had made them certain earth returned their love.

"At such moments," says Seamus Heaney, "a fullness rebounds back upon itself, or it rebounds off something or someone else and thereby creates a wave capable of lifting the burden of our knowledge and the experience to a new, refreshing plane."[12]

Meanwhile, Frost's money problems were further subdued in November by an offer from Holt to serve as consulting editor for a salary of a hundred dollars a month, an amount that Frost acknowledged to another friend was "small but large for a poet."[13] This had been the idea of Lincoln MacVeagh, a young Harvard graduate who had taken over as Frost's editor from Alfred Harcourt, who had left Holt to found his own company with Donald Brace, another colleague from Holt. (Harcourt had vigorously tried to take Frost with him, but Frost—though sympathetic at first—finally stayed with Holt because the company owned the rights to his earlier volumes, and he had been warned that Holt would not let these books appear in any future collected edition issued by another publisher.)

Frost had been "barding around," as he put it, through the Amherst years, but now he pursued this course aggressively. The South Shaftsbury home became a base of operations, and Frost traveled to far-flung corners of the continent, reading poems wherever anybody was willing to invite him: Bryn Mawr, New York City, Texas, Michigan, Princeton. At Princeton, in March, he met Paul Elmer More, author of the *Shelburne Essays*. More's biographer, Arthur Hazard Dakin, records a letter from More that recalls the encounter with Frost:

> I have always rather admired his poetry, which is modern in some respects, but has balance and measure and deals with the real things of life. It was a pleasure to talk with him—we sat up until about one—and hear how sound his views on art and human nature are. He knows all the wild men now snorting up the sides of Parnassus, has heard the infinite scandals of their life, and can prick them out in epigrams to the king's taste. It was rather exhilarating to listen to him, and I think too he went away somewhat encouraged from his contact with a kindred soul.[14]

Frost occasionally stayed overnight in Manhattan at Mrs. William Vaughn Moody's redbrick townhouse in Greenwich Village, which she maintained as a kind of watering hole for writers. There, in 1919, he had met the midwestern poet Ridgely Torrence, who became a good friend. (Torrence was appointed as poetry editor of the *New Republic* in 1920, and Frost wrote to him jestingly: "You'll begin to think I don't see the beauty of having a friend on the editorial staff of the *New Republic*. But I do and I mean to show it by sending you some poems I have on hand just as soon as I can.")[15]

Perhaps inevitably, Frost began to cast about for another academic affiliation almost as soon as he was free of Amherst. What he had in mind was something extremely free-floating: a poet-in-residence position. He had recently heard that Middlebury College had just begun a new School of English at Bread Loaf Mountain, on a glorious summer campus roughly eight miles from the main campus in the village of Middlebury. Professor Wilfred E. Davison was the head of the program, which offered graduate study in English and American literature. Frost wrote to Davison suggesting that he come and lecture for a week or so: "I might fit into your summer plan with a course on the Responsibilities of Teachers of Composition," he wrote.[16] This inquiry led to a visit to Stone Cottage (as the Frosts now called their house in South Shaftsbury), and—after some haggling over money—an arrangement was made for Frost to visit the School of English the following summer. Thus began Robert Frost's connection to Bread Loaf, which would remain a vital aspect of his life.

Not quite out of the blue came an offer from the University of Michigan for Frost to spend a year as visiting fellow for $5,000—a tidy sum for very little work. Frost had been recommended for this fellowship by Percy MacKaye, a poet and dramatist who was also a friend of Ridgely Torrence's. The invitation was not unwelcome, though it would mean that the Frost family would again have to uproot itself; furthermore, Frost was anxious about cutting himself off from the region that had been his home for so long. Despite these objections, he was also becoming conscious of his need for a live audience and a community of intelligent friends. He had sorely missed those aspects of the Amherst job since coming to South Shaftsbury.

The Frosts planned to return to Franconia during the August hay-fever season. "I am beginning to sniff the air suspiciously, on the point of taking flight from these weedy regions," he wrote to Raymond Holden. "It can't be long before you hear me come crashing through the woods in your direction."[17] The period of awkwardness between

Frost and Holden had passed, and in Franconia they quickly resumed the friendship, taking long walks together into the nearby forests and spending late nights on the open porch of Holden's house "discussing poetry and philosophy, history and natural science," as Holden recalled. Frost's mind was "all sparks, fanning wide."

The Frosts returned to South Shaftsbury in September to make arrangements for the Michigan adventure. Marjorie was to stay in North Bennington with her best friend, Lillian LaBatt, during her junior year at North Bennington High School. Carol would stay at the farm, tending to the crop of apples, although he would soon join his parents in Ann Arbor. Lesley, who had been working in New York, decided to accompany her parents to Michigan and audit a few courses at the university. Irma would also audit courses, although she planned to focus on her painting and sculpture, working at home in a studio at the top of their large Victorian house at 1523 Washtenaw Avenue—a furnished house owned by the widow of a deceased professor of classics. The most substantial house that the Frost family had thus far occupied, it gave Frost a sense of his importance as a visiting fellow.

Exactly what Frost would do was left open by the president of the university, Dr. Marion L. Burton. Because the job of poet-in-residence was still highly experimental in American education, there was no clear vision of how Frost might function with the university. To his credit, Frost was able to invent this role for himself, and for generations of writers-in-residence to follow. He understood that the point of having a writer on a campus was "to say something to the world for keeping the creative and erudite together in education."[18]

Having made his way at Amherst bumpily, he was prepared for the pitfalls and possibilities of the Michigan fellowship. He knew perfectly well that certain members of the faculty would resent him; indeed, a few complained that the university was wasting $5,000 on a poet who sat around doing nothing while they slaved in the classroom. But these voices were insignificant, dwarfed by the general enthusiasm for Frost, who proceeded carefully, taking considerable pains to get to know faculty and students alike.

He was guided through the thickets of faculty politics by Morris P.

Tilley, his old friend from summers in Franconia. One member of the English department, Roy Cowden, took the trouble to introduce Frost to undergraduate writers, especially those associated with the school literary magazine, *Whimsies*. Frost was also careful to make himself available to the townspeople, and gave regular public readings and lectures, using his considerable charm to good effect.

An important function of any writer within a university setting is to bring other writers to the campus, and Frost worked hard behind the scenes to see that Michigan had a strong series of visiting speakers, including Carl Sandburg (whom he vaguely disliked, joking that he spent most of his time "washing his white hair" and strumming his "mandolin," as Frost referred to the poet's guitar), Amy Lowell, Vachel Lindsay, Padraic Colum, Witter Bynner, and—of course—Louis Untermeyer. On these occasions Frost played the role of host energetically, often keeping the visitors up well past their bedtimes.

One of the essential features of the Michigan fellowship was that Frost should have time to work on his own poems, and—as at Amherst—he found the distractions of the position such that relatively little free time for writing could be uncovered. He did, however, revise some poems to his satisfaction. "Evening in a Sugar Orchard" (which he gave to *Whimsies* to publish in their issue of November 1921) and "A Hillside Thaw" were among these—two vivid snapshots of rural New England life. Frost had in mind a new collection, and spent time contemplating its arrangement, but he lacked a central poem or defining notion for this hypothetical volume.

Carol, Lesley, and Irma decamped from Ann Arbor in the spring, for various reasons (Carol had quarreled with his father over his farming plans and stormed out of the house without even saying that he was going home to South Shaftsbury). Frost and Elinor were left to close up the house and say good-byes. President Burton had already intimated that he hoped Frost might return for another year of this "fine experiment" and suggested that Frost was as popular in the town as the university's well-known football coach, "Hurry-Up" Yost. Frost, amusingly, then suggested that this comparison be put to the test, and that Burton schedule a poetry reading by Frost at the same time as a

Michigan football game. He added, "If you come to my poetry reading, you will be the only one there, because I shall be at the football
game!"[19]

Frost made it clear to Burton that he would accept an offer to
extend the fellowship at Michigan. Nevertheless, by the time he
arrived back in South Shaftsbury, in mid-June 1922, he was tired of
academic life and toyed with the idea of giving it up altogether. He
wanted to reconnect to the farm, to turn over the soil, to sit under a
tree with a notebook on his lap. As on the farm at Derry, he often
worked at the kitchen table late at night, enjoying the solitude of a
house in which everyone else was asleep, "with the crickets outside,
like a metronome." He recalled one vivid night when two of his most
celebrated poems, "New Hampshire" and "Stopping by Woods on a
Snowy Evening," came in one great rush. He later recalled to Louis
Mertins:

> There had been days of terrific strain on the farm. You see, I can
> manage a poem in the singular very well and not feel the strain,
> not too much. In the midst of my work at the farm I could han-
> dle such a task. Sometimes one would grow out of an idea, leav-
> ing me relaxed. At other times the idea would produce a second
> growth, coercing itself as a Siamese twin on its predecessor.
> That would bring trouble of spirit, and more than likely right in
> harvest time. I would be in a terrible stew, fever, likely. My legs
> would ache, my head would ache. Eating was out of the ques-
> tion. Sleep? There wasn't any. . . . "Stopping by Woods on a
> Snowy Evening" was written just about that way, after I had
> been working all night long on "New Hampshire." But I must
> admit, it was written in a few minutes without any strain.[20]

The whole poem may have come to Frost in a flash, but he had
great trouble with the last stanza. It was some time before he thought
of solving the problem by simply repeating the last line: "And miles to
go before I sleep." This famous repetition gives the poem a peculiar,
haunting quality.

"New Hampshire" is an important poem in the Frost canon, not so much for its effectiveness as poetry but for its sly cogence in putting forward a theory of poetry. It falls into a mode of satirical verse that would, in the later years, seem to overwhelm the more serious lyrics— which remain the best of Frost. Nevertheless, one must pay careful attention to these satires, and to "New Hampshire" in particular. It was not for nothing that Frost chose to put it first in his next collection, *New Hampshire*, and to make the rest of the poems seem (perhaps in satirical response to Eliot's *The Waste Land*) mere "Notes and Grace Notes" in attendance on the title poem.

The slyness is there from the outset. Frost, in the manner of the Roman poet Horace, whom he admired, takes on the role of playful rustic philosopher:

> *I met a lady from the South who said*
> *(You won't believe she said it, but she said it):*
> *"None of my family ever worked, or had*
> *A thing to sell.".* . .

Thus begins the first movement of the poem (up to line 60), where Frost argues wittily that only in New Hampshire do people understand the proper relationship between labor, actual goods, and that great, damnable abstraction—money. Frost gives comic examples of false attitudes toward the creation of wealth from California to Arkansas. Only New Hampshire, it seems, has got it right. "The having anything to sell is what / Is the disgrace in man or state or nation," Frost says. Selling is an activity that suggests, to the wary New Hampshirite, an illegitimate prodigality.

In a shrewd turn, Frost transforms the material poverty of New Hampshire into spiritual wealth. He argues that one can find within these parsimonious state borders "One each of everything," which makes it a little but perfect world: a Platonic heaven-on-earth. In an age bent on "getting and spending" (as Wordsworth put it), one is relieved to find in New Hampshire such spareness and universality. Indeed, "New Hampshire" moves slowly but inexorably into a meditation on the relationship between the universal and the particular in the context of regionalism.

Typically, Frost embraces every paradox, and wants everything both ways at once. (Katherine Kearns notes that Frost's joking allusiveness in "New Hampshire" often "countermands the confident, assertive tone" of the poem, providing a dark after-echo. She also notes the dizzying effect of this technique: "For the reader who is in on the joke, the effect is not to reorient meaning but to undermine it.")[21] With regard to regionalism, Frost wants New Hampshire to be utterly distinct yet representative, professing an immersion in the local, an escape into the particulars of a given region, implying that all of life can be found in this specific place.

The central section of the poem dwells on the New Hampshire mountains as suggestive of the imagination as a whole. Frost upbraids Emerson for disparaging New Hampshire and using the mountains to belittle the residents of the state themselves; he chides Amy Lowell for a similar attitude. (Frost is still responding here to Lowell's chapter on him in her 1917 book, *Tendencies in Modern Poetry*, where she sees Frost's rural types as mired in a narrow-mindedness that amounts to degeneracy. "His people are left-overs of the old stock," she wrote, "morbid, pursued by phantoms, slowly sinking to insanity.")[22]

In a clever move that brings his own aesthetic to the fore, Frost examines the idea of New Hampshire in relation to both universals and particulars in lines 228–47, proclaiming himself "the author / Of several books against the world in general." Any narrow regionalist view of his poetic project is openly denounced because it "restrict[s] my meaning." His meaning is wide, even universal. "I'm what is called a sensibilitist, / Or otherwise an environmentalist," he proclaims. While the use of these abstract terms mocks the academic critics who would seek to characterize him, Frost—as always—wants it both ways here as well. He is "an environmentalist" in the sense that he writes out of a specific environment and admits to being shaped by it; that is part and parcel of being a regionalist. But he also affects his environment, even shapes it himself:

> I make a virtue of my suffering
> From nearly everything that goes on round me.

> *In other words, I know wherever I am,*
> *Being the creature of literature I am,*
> *I shall not lack for pain to keep me awake.*

That is, no matter what is "really" happening around him, Frost is determined to see that it conforms to his own imagination, becomes an extension of his ongoing self-mythification (to an extent reversing the Darwinian idea that the environment shapes the individual). The theme of personal progress through trial and suffering, "the trial by existence," recurs in many of Frost's best poems, but here it is absorbed into his private *ars poetica*.

The mountains of New Hampshire are elevated in this poem to the level of a poetic symbol as Frost contemplates (with increasing fury) Emerson's remark that "The God who made New Hampshire / Taunted the lofty land with little men." Frost does not wish to belittle the people of New Hampshire but to raise the mountains even higher. All that is required, he suggests, is enough imagination to get the job accomplished. The distance that must be crossed between reality (the actual mountains) and Reality (the imagined mountains) becomes, in Frost's aesthetic, a point of honor. The poet challenges reality, then modifies it; he "cannot rest from planning day or night / How high I'd thrust the peaks in summer snow."

The poem concludes with an elaborately comic musing on the use of realism in literature, the argument put forward in the context of an argument between the poet and a "New York alec / About the new school of the pseudo-phallic." This urban intellectual supposedly makes the case that the writer must describe reality warts and all or retreat into "prudery." Frost responds frostily: " 'Me for the hills where I don't have to choose.' " That is, he will escape to his region, and to regionalism-as-universal-ground, a place where he can have it both ways: the concreteness of locality and the universality of a world where things are typical.

There is nothing escapist about this attitude. Frost actually dismisses the prudery of those who wish to escape from nature, making fun of those who run "for shelter" from nature "quoting Matthew

Arnold"—who represents (to Frost) a kind of disembodied, bloodless humanism. "I choose to be a plain New Hampshire farmer," the poet declares toward the end of the poem. But even here, he backs off this statement with a wry parenthetical remark suggesting that his money would come from "a publisher in New York City." The last three lines are, in fact, a model of wryness:

> It's restful to arrive at a decision,
> And restful just to think about New Hampshire.
> At present I am living in Vermont.

This is called having your cake and eating it, too.

While not one of Frost's best poems, "New Hampshire" is central to the poet's work of this period, typifying the ironic use of the pastoral mode in his work and laying out an argument for a poetry that at once celebrates the specifics of rural life while maintaining a certain rueful distance. The doubleness of Frost's vision is put forward explicitly, as Kearns suggests, by the joking references throughout, which create a counterargument. The narrative proceeds by anecdote and rumination, a mode that again suggests a rural persona; as if to confound this mode, the range of allusion (from Greek metaphysics to Matthew Arnold) is such that nobody would mistake this for an uneducated farmer's voice. New England is taken as representative, but there is nothing subjective about this choice; Frost moves through the local into the universal.

The morning after the all-night session in which Frost wrote "New Hampshire" at his kitchen table in South Shaftsbury, he wrote "Stopping by Woods on a Snowy Evening," his most famous lyric. "Having finished 'New Hampshire,'" he said, "I went outdoors, got out sideways and didn't disturb anybody in the house, and about nine or ten o'clock went back in and wrote the piece about the snowy evening and the little horse as if I'd had an hallucination."[23] "Stopping by Woods" represents the perfection of Frost's art in the straight lyric mode, his "best bid for remembrance," as he told Louis Untermeyer. He remarked to Reginald Cook that it contained "all I ever knew." And in countless readings of the poem in public, he would leave it open to the listener to decide what was meant by the poem's suggestive final stanza:

> *The woods are lovely, dark and deep,*
> *But I have promises to keep,*
> *And miles to go before I sleep,*
> *And miles to go before I sleep.*

To an audience at Bread Loaf, he once said that the ominous-seeming last lines don't necessarily mean that "you're going to do anything bad" when you get home. On the contrary, he found something comforting in those lines, a promise of coming in from the cold, from the solitude, threat, and wilderness of icy woods, into good company.

The aphoristic quality of this little poem, which seems so natural that one cannot imagine its having been invented, is such that one can hardly *not* memorize it. Even thematically, it is typical of Frost's art: a poem about a loner, a man against nature, in the dark, on a frozen winter night. He stops suddenly, mystifying his horse, who "gives his harness bells a shake / To ask if there is some mistake." In a brilliantly compressed image of rural winter, Frost writes: "The only other sound's the sweep / Of easy wind and downy flake." Those lines, with their strange, alluring modulation of vowels and consonants, possess an eerie perfection. The final stanza, with its haunting repetitions, gives the poem that doubleness required of all good Frostian lyrics; had Frost written the line once, the reader might have taken it to mean only that the traveler had a long way to go that night; the repetition adds an element of wonder, giving the line a numinous glow. One begins to question what Frost really meant, which is the point: Frost's traveler in "Stopping by Woods" does not know where he is ultimately heading, just as travelers in life are often uncertain of their final destination. The sigh heard in the last stanza of "The Road Not Taken" ("I shall be telling this with a sigh / Somewhere ages and ages hence") recurs, invisibly but unmistakably, between the last two lines here, signaling a shift of tone, a slight modulation into doubleness and irony.

12

THE MIND
SKATING CIRCLES
1923–1925

Since last I saw you I have come to the conclusion that style in prose or verse is that which indicates how the writer takes himself and what he is saying. —FROST TO UNTERMEYER, JUNE 9, 1923

The summer of 1922 ended with an ambitious hike on the Long Trail, beginning in Bennington and following the Green Mountains northward to the Canadian border. Frost eagerly joined Carol, Lesley, Marjorie, and Marjorie's closest friend, Lillian LaBatt, for the 225-mile trek. They planned to sleep in mountain shelters, and they carried on their backs all the supplies they would need for the journey. Frost kept a small notebook in his pocket for making what he called "wood-notes."

Like Wordsworth and Dickens before him, Frost was an avid walker, but at Pico Peak he developed a problem with his feet (which he attributed to his boots), so he temporarily abandoned the group and went by train from Rutland to Middlebury. Having bought another pair of boots, he rejoined the hikers at Lake Pleiad—a deep, spring-fed pond in the middle of the woods. He stayed with the younger set for a few more days, making it to Mount Mansfield, where his feet at last gave out, even with fresh boots. The rest of the pack managed to get to the Canadian border without him.

Despite having bailed out early, Frost found the experience a memorable one, and he wrote enthusiastically to John Haines in England: "I did something like 200 miles, most of them painful to the feet, but all beautiful to the eye and mind."[1] He resolved to keep up his interest in hiking, noting that regular movement "stilled the mind" in a way that was productive of poetry.

This heady dose of wilderness was just what Frost needed before plunging back into the academic world of Michigan. Even so, he reentered the academy at his own gingerly pace, attending a reception in his honor held by President Burton on October 11, but then skipping out for a few weeks of "barding around" the country, as he always put it. Having been elected poet laureate of Vermont, he appeared in Rutland and elsewhere in this new guise, prompting a snide piece about his appointment in the *New York Times*: "Mr. Frost was born in California, and his college days were spent partly at Dartmouth and partly at Harvard. He was a farmer for a while, or *Who's Who* says so, though one wonders, and then, after teaching in several New Hampshire schools he finally landed a post as Professor of English Literature in Amherst. His home is set down as Franconia, N.H., but he does have a summer place in South Shaftsbury, Vt., and that seems to be his only connection with the Green Mountain State."[2]

Frost also read his poems to a group in Boston, and at Wellesley College, where a professor (who also wrote poetry) named Katherine Lee Bates invited him to read. Another friend at Wellesley was the writer Gamaliel Bradford, whom Frost had met on a visit to Wellesley three years before. He had taken to Bradford, and tried unsuccessfully to get his poetry, plays, and novels published. In his later years, one often sees Frost in the role one associates with Ezra Pound: friend and aide to writers. He regularly went out of his way to help those whose work he admired (although, unlike Pound, he seems to have chosen to promote writers several rungs below him in talent and therefore unlikely to become rivals).

A heated topic for discussion between Bradford and Frost was the anonymously published *A Critical Fable*, which had recently set tongues wagging in the world of letters. It was modeled on James Russell Lowell's *A Fable for Critics*, which had made lighthearted fun of

Emerson, Longfellow, Holmes, Whittier, Poe, and even Lowell himself. Frost knew at once that Amy Lowell had written it, in imitation of her famous ancestor; he had heard enough of her opinions on her contemporaries to recognize them here. It slightly annoyed him to see himself pictured as a "foggy benignity wandering in space / With a stray wisp of moonlight just touching his face." On the other hand, Miss Lowell had placed Frost among the poets worth teasing—the peer of Robinson, Sandburg, Masters, Lindsay, and herself (Eliot and Stevens, among others, were relegated to a lesser category). One suspects that Frost was not *too* peeved.

Before returning to Ann Arbor, he ventured as far south as Louisiana, Texas, and Missouri to read and lecture. By now, his confidence had grown to a point where he rarely showed any degree of nervousness in public, although he privately fretted over each performance. The student paper at one southern college where he spoke reported, "Not only did he give selections from his own works, but he also explained the origin and characteristics of modern poetry, including references to other modern poets, thus giving the audience an intimate glimpse of every contemporary in the art. And besides these things, and something which many will remember longer probably than the context of his lecture, his charming sense of humor."[3]

Robert Penn Warren recalled that "Frost came to Vanderbilt to lecture [in 1922], invited by [John Crowe] Ransom. Ransom and Frost admired each other—they were both traditionalists at heart. Frost's poetics—his unconventional use of conventional meters and forms—appealed to us. He made a strong impression, very open and sincere, but sharp-witted, too. He met Merrill Moore on that visit, and Moore later settled in Boston. That friendship kept going. The same thing happened with Donald Davidson, who went so far as to buy a house at Bread Loaf to be near Frost, who had this way of attracting people."[4]

Meanwhile, Frost was working with Lincoln MacVeagh, his new editor at Holt, to pull together his fourth volume, to be called simply *New Hampshire*. MacVeagh had another idea for a book, too: a selection of the best of the first three volumes. He planned to publish this selection in March 1923. The double impact of a substantial new book of poems with a volume of selected poems was carefully calculated to present Frost as a major contemporary figure.

The reading tour of the South had been more exhausting than Frost had bargained for, however, and he succumbed to influenza upon his return to Ann Arbor. Nevertheless, it was a relief to be home. He and Elinor had moved into a house on Washtenaw Avenue across the street from the larger one they had occupied the year before, but it was more to their liking, "more cheerful and homelike," Elinor reported. Her dislike of housework was such that she much preferred less space. Furthermore, the children were back in Vermont, "involved with their own comings and goings," as she wrote to her friend in Franconia, Edith Fobes, who became a regular correspondent.

Frost was not expected to teach any formal classes at the university, but there were still demands on his time: teas and faculty receptions, student plays, dinner parties. He wrote to George Whicher of Amherst that he was "not Mr. Frost formerly of Michigan but Mr. Frost formally of Michigan." Already planning to play hooky from Michigan, he added: "I expect to spend a lot of my time in South Shaftsbury this year, writing little verses."[5]

In November, "The Witch of Coös" won a prize of two hundred dollars from *Poetry Magazine*—a foretaste of good things to come. "I don't care what people think of my poetry so long as they award it prizes," he wrote with some wryness to the editor Harriet Monroe.[6] His taste for accolades was whetted, and he seems to have enjoyed the spectacle of his own enjoyment of these approbations. He was ever the fondest spectator at his own show, and was more than willing to forgive himself the occasional lapse in behavior. "I am bad as you imply or openly assert," he wrote to John Haines, who had teased him about his "wickedness."[7]

A good example of this was Frost's behavior to Joseph Warren Beach, a young scholar from the University of Minnesota who had come to visit him several years before in Franconia. Beach and Frost went for long walks in the woods, and the younger man quickly realized that Frost relished good anecdotes, especially those with a slightly outrageous or lascivious bent. Beach presented himself as a young Don Juan, bragging about his exploits with young women in the university.

A year later, Frost was invited to read at Minnesota, and during this visit he listened to Beach's tales of adventures with a beautiful young graduate assistant called Dagmar Doneghy, who was considering marriage to the owner of a local circus. Frost (perhaps tongue-in-cheek) insisted that Beach marry the woman at once—or at least propose to her. Beach hesitated, explaining that Dagmar was difficult even to meet these days. When Frost suggested kidnapping her, Beach agreed to go visit her—with Frost tagging along as mentor. They drove (in Beach's car) up and down the Minneapolis street where Dagmar lived, and when she emerged from the house, they asked her to come with them for a ride. Innocently, she agreed. Soon they were driving deep into the country together. Poor Dagmar had been "kidnapped."

Beach pulled to the side of a deserted country road and asked the confused Dagmar to go for a little walk. When they returned (a considerable amount of time later), Beach announced to Frost that they were engaged. "Good," Frost declared. "Let's get you married today." They protested that Minnesota law prevented such hastiness, but Frost said Indiana was close enough; you could get married there without delay. Astoundingly, the couple agreed, and they set off for Indiana together, where Frost officially witnessed the marriage before a justice of the peace the very next day. It was a bit of lark for Frost, although as one friend later observed, "He seemed to delight in the company of young couples, and encouraged their relationships, taking an almost proprietary interest in their affairs."[8]

Frost delighted in retelling the story of Dagmar's kidnapping and the abrupt wedding, exaggerating what was already a fantastic tale. He especially enjoyed painting Beach as the worst sort of rake and scoundrel; eventually these tales got back to the English department at Minnesota, where Beach was coming up for tenure. A friend of Beach's, as well as Beach himself, pleaded with Frost to curtail his gossip. The friend went so far as to visit Frost in Ann Arbor to ask him to write directly to the chair of the English department to reassure him that Beach was an upstanding fellow. Frost complied, confessing that in his gossiping he had done Beach "a grave injustice." He added: "This is merely a hasty note to undo at once any harm I may have done him in your estimation."[9]

Frost adored playing the Lord of Misrule and caused a little trouble whenever he could. This occasionally brought hard feelings (as it did in the case of Joseph Warren Beach, who broke off relations with Frost from that point on), although these hard feelings often seem to have surprised and hurt Frost, who always claimed he meant no harm.

Another tiff, this one of a literary nature, occurred in midwinter. Frost went to New York to visit Louis Untermeyer and Ridgely Torrence, and was taken to a cocktail party where he encountered Burton Rascoe, a well-known columnist for the *New York Tribune*. This was 1922, of course: the annus mirabilis of modernist literature. T. S. Eliot had just published *The Waste Land*, and Joyce had brought out *Ulysses*. Frost had never liked the work of either, and he got into a furious debate with Rascoe at the party over the "modern school" of writers. To Frost's chagrin, Rascoe repeated their conversation in his column the next week.

"Robert Frost in voice and demeanor reminds me much of Sherwood Anderson," Rascoe said. "He has the same deliberate and ingenuous way of speaking; he is earnest, earthy, humorous, without put-on, very real, likable, genuine. I admire him very much as a person. I regret that I find almost nothing to interest me in his poems. They are deft, they are competent, they are of the soil; but they are not distinctive.

"Frost and I left the party together and went to Grand Central Station, where we talked for half an hour about Ezra Pound, T. S. Eliot, Conrad Aiken, and Amy Lowell. . . . Frost has little sympathy with Eliot's work, but then he wouldn't naturally; his own aesthetic problem is radically different from that of Eliot's. . . . 'I don't like obscurity in poetry,' he told me. 'I don't think a thing has to be obvious before it is said, but it ought to be obvious when it is said. I like to read Eliot because it is fun seeing the way he does things, but I am always glad it is his way and not mine.'"[10]

In a pique, Frost wrote a scathing letter to the columnist, calling him "You Little Rascol." Fortunately, he sent the letter to Untermeyer first, who talked him out of responding at all. It was Untermeyer's sound opinion that Frost should not respond to critics; the only fit reaction, Untermeyer said, was "to write poems and more poems."

Frost noted to Untermeyer: "You and Jean [Untermeyer] think such wrath ill becomes me. I'm over it now anyway."[11]

Frost understood that keeping his poetry before the public was essential to keeping his reputation alive, and he determined to finish soon the volume he was calling *New Hampshire*. He huddled with his family in South Shaftsbury through December and January, working on the manuscript, which now seemed destined for a November 1923 publication date. Unfortunately, he was hampered by what Elinor described to a friend as "wracking coughs and fevers." Ill health of a minor sort would often interfere with his work in the coming decade.

Frost spent as little time as possible in Ann Arbor, returning in February and leaving in April (although he reappeared in late May to give a farewell reading to a full, enthusiastic audience at Sarah Caswell Angell Hall). Even when he was supposedly in residence, he took countless side trips for readings and lectures. His peripatetic life was now established, and he actively sought well-paid public appearances. Elinor commonly acted as his agent, responding to those who invited him to speak, negotiating the fees, making arrangements for his travel.

Back in Amherst, the crisis over the presidency of Alexander Meiklejohn finally came to a head, and he was dismissed by the Board of Trustees. The chief complaint against him (made by a phalanx of conservative professors and trustees) was that he discouraged religion on campus—a complaint often voiced by Frost himself (who, despite his personal rejection of all forms of conventional worship, at least notionally supported the idea of traditional religious practice).[12] Meiklejohn also suffered from embarrassing financial problems: he was heavily in debt, having borrowed large sums from wealthy trustees, and could not repay these loans. Nor had he looked after the college's finances well. "He could inspire but could not manage," observed Walter Lippmann in the *New York World*.

Fourteen of the college's fifty faculty members resigned in protest (including Stark Young), and thirteen seniors refused to accept their diplomas at the graduation ceremony. A large portion of the junior class announced that they would not return in the fall for their senior year. This was a shattering situation, but Frost was elated by the news, aligning himself firmly with the anti-Meiklejohn group. It did, however, surprise him when a telegram arrived from the trustees offering him another job at Amherst, on similar terms to the one he had previously held there; with the resignations of so many faculty members, there was obviously a great need to replenish the ranks.

A venerable member of the classics department, George Daniel Olds, was selected as the new president, and he personally drove up to see Frost in South Shaftsbury in May, hoping to entice him back to Amherst. Olds and Frost knew each other well, and Frost admired him for his commitment to educational norms that Meiklejohn had been determined to ignore or subvert. Olds sweetened the offer by saying that Frost could teach any two courses he liked each semester; otherwise, he would serve as poet-in-residence, and his chief duty would be to write his own poems.

With this offer, the same old conflicts arose in Frost, as might have been expected. "I ought to have been poet enough to stay away," he wrote to Wilbur Cross.[13] But he explained that he found the opportunity to shape the direction of a liberal arts college irresistible. In general, he and Elinor simply preferred being in Massachusetts to Michigan; it was, after all, closer to home.

In June, Frost received an honorary degree from the University of Vermont. This degree meant more to him than the ones from Amherst and Michigan, he said, because the others had "strings attached." He had intimate connections with those institutions, and the degrees were part of the wooing process. The University of Vermont had nothing to gain by giving Frost this degree, and he was pleased. The public recognition of Robert Frost was now under way with a vengeance.

In September, the Frosts moved into a faculty house in Amherst at 10 Dana Street, a wood-frame dwelling with a glorious western view, surrounded by maple, oak, and apple trees. Huge lilacs bushed against the southern side, just below the Frosts' bedroom window. Elinor liked the new place, considering it "spacious enough but easy to look after," as she wrote to Edith Fobes. The house was sparsely furnished, but this appealed to the Frosts, who liked the bare, hardwood floors and the abundant woodwork throughout the house. Frost's study window was shaded by the apple trees.

As promised by the new president, he was assigned two courses of his own devising that fall: one a writing course (a small seminar of carefully selected students), the other simply called "Readings." The literature course gave free range to his imagination, and he assigned a variety of texts that included Melville's *Typee* and Thoreau's *Walden*—always a favorite book. The former is a thinly disguised autobiographical memoir about a young man who jumps ship in the South Seas to investigate life among the cannibals; the latter, of course, is the classic American memoir of retreat and self-discovery, subtitled *Life in the Woods*. On a deep level, Frost identified with these rebels and iconoclasts, Melville and Thoreau, men of quirky independence, fierce opinions, and unconventional approaches to what Emerson called "the conduct of life." Another interesting choice for this course was Edward Gibbon's *Autobiography*, which includes a detailed account of his eccentric education.

As usual, Frost preached independence of mind and unconventionality in all his classes—ironically, he remained very much in the Meiklejohn mold, despite his objections to the man and his frequent complaint that Amherst was still suffering from "Meiklejaundice." As President John Sloan Dickey of Dartmouth later recalled, "I don't think Frost realized how out-of-the-mainstream his approach was. He was highly eccentric, highly original, as a teacher. He encouraged a kind of rebellion against the standard approaches to life. He was almost aggressively self-determined, self-determining."[14]

A good deal of Frost's thinking in the fall of 1923 concerned the relationship between a man's writing style and his sense of himself. In a letter to Untermeyer, Frost explained the evolution of his philosophy on this topic: "Many sensitive natures have plainly shown by their style that they took themselves lightly in self-defense. They are the ironists. Some fair to good writers have no style and so leave us ignorant of how to take themselves. But that is the one important thing to know: because on it depends our likes and dislikes." He did not regard the Wildean notion that the style is the man as adequate, however. "The man's ideas would be some element then of his style. So would his deeds.

But I would narrow the definition. His deeds are his deeds; his ideas are his ideas. His style is the way he carries himself toward his ideas and deeds. . . . It is the mind skating circles round itself as it moves forward."[15]

Frost was obviously describing himself here: his mind seemed to swirl, skating circles around itself as it moved forward. Many recalled the fascination of listening to him in class, how he "would take an idea, play with it, knock it around, retreat, often picking up on earlier themes that one thought he'd forgotten, but gently progressing toward some further point."[16] Thus Frost began to take himself a certain way, to carry himself toward his ideas, even his deeds, with a certain bemused, canny self-confidence that might, ungenerously, be taken for arrogance. Even in conversation, his approach to thinking stood out. "He sees ideas from many angles," noted an early colleague at Bread Loaf, "and he illustrates everything to himself as he thinks, in specific instances and anecdotes. His talk is full of digressions, as one thing suggests another to him."[17]

One of the major events of 1923 for the Frost family was the marriage of Carol and Lillian LaBatt. Lillian, of course, had been Marjorie's closest friend, but she and Carol had gotten to know each other well in the past year. Hiking the Long Trail had added to their closeness. Now, after Lillian's abrupt decision to drop out of college before her first semester was over (she had been attending the University of Vermont), Carol decided to push for an immediate wedding. Frost explained the situation in a letter to Lincoln MacVeagh: "It was all done in a week. I may be frosty, but I rather like to look on at such things. And I like children to be terribly in love. They are a nice pair. Lillian is an uncommonly pretty little girl. She is pretty, quiet and unpractical. She has been a great friend of the girls in the family for some years. All she has done is transfer herself from the girls to the boy. We'll see how completely she deserts the girls."[18]

Leaving the children to themselves on the farm in South Shaftsbury, the Frosts returned to Amherst. The invitations to lecture and read his poems hither and yonder continued to pour in, although Frost felt he could not easily abandon his classes at Amherst. He did, however, manage to get away half a dozen times, reading or lecturing in

Boston, Philadelphia, and Baltimore. In 1924 he spent spring break as the special guest in Ann Arbor of President Burton, who reported to Frost that he was authorized by the Board of Regents to offer him an astounding deal: a permanent position as fellow in letters. He would be required to teach no courses at all, just to give occasional seminars or private conferences. The salary would be $5,000 a year.

Frost, after much agonizing, accepted this offer on the condition that it would not be announced until the following autumn; he needed time to work things out with Amherst. In effect, he would teach a further year at Amherst; that way, he could leave with a clear conscience—although few at Amherst, including President Olds, would see it this way, as he knew only too well.

Meanwhile, *New Hampshire* was making its way among readers. It had been published on November 15, 1923, in an edition of 5,350 copies, with another 350 copies appearing in a limited signed edition. The book, wittily organized in three sections, was subtitled *A Poem with Notes and Grace Notes* and carried woodcuts by J. J. Lankes. The structure was meant as a satirical jab at Eliot's *The Waste Land*, published the previous year with famously pedantic footnotes. Among the notable lyrics in this collection are "Fire and Ice," "Dust of Snow," "Nothing Gold Can Stay," "The Aim Was Song," "Stopping by Woods on a Snowy Evening," "For Once, Then, Something," "To Earthward," and "The Need of Being Versed in Country Things." Each of these poems is distinct and peerless, representing another crest in Frost's development—like a jagged mountain range with numerous peaks.

"To Earthward," in Frost's mind, had been a pivotal poem. "One of the greatest changes my nature has undergone is of record in 'To Earthward,'" he said.[19] He remembered that in his school days he could not proceed with a copybook if he had once blotted it; that perfectionism had led to great misery. Now he found himself able to accept the imperfect, even to "crave the flaws of human handiwork."

The poem itself, which Frost virtually never read in public because he found it too painful, is astonishing:

> Love at the lips was touch
> As sweet as I could bear;

And once that seemed too much;
I lived on air

That crossed me from sweet things,
The flow of—was it musk
From hidden grapevine springs
Down hill at dusk?

I had the swirl and ache
From sprays of honeysuckle
That when they're gathered shake
Dew on the knuckle.

I craved strong sweets, but those
Seemed strong when I was young;
The petal of the rose
It was that stung.

Now no joy but lacks salt
That is not dashed with pain
And weariness and fault;
I crave the stain

Of tears, the aftermark
Of almost too much love,
The sweet of bitter bark
And burning clove.

When stiff and sore and scarred
I take away my hand
From leaning on it hard
In grass and sand,

The hurt is not enough:
I long for weight and strength
To feel the earth as rough
To all my length.

The poem swerves, as Seamus Heaney notes, "from living and walking on air to living and enduring on earth," a motion in contrast to that of "Birches," where the boy climbed up in order to descend. In the complex gravity of this poem, the lover is buoyed even as he attempts to descend; the more he submits to the gravitational force, the more he is lifted. In the last stanza, the paradox is exquisitely balanced, as Heaney says: "Pictorially, we are offered an image of the body hugging the earth, seeking to penetrate to the very *humus* in humility, wishing the ground were a penitential bed. But the paradoxical result of this drive toward abasement is a marvel of levitation: in spite of the physical push to earthward, the psychic direction is skyward."[20]

There are also a number of narrative poems that count among Frost's best: "The Grindstone," "The Ax-Helve," "The Witch of Coös," and "Wild Grapes." The voices in the narrative poems are vivid and fresh, ready to engage the reader with wit, as in the opening of "The Grindstone":

> *Having a wheel and four legs of its own*
> *Has never availed the cumbersome grindstone*
> *To get it anywhere that I can see.*
> *These hands have helped it go, and even race;*
> *Not all the motion, though, they ever lent,*
> *Not all the miles it may have thought it went,*
> *Have got it one step from the starting place.*

Frost dwells on the nature of his pastoral art in this poem, picking up and elaborating themes raised in the title poem, "New Hampshire." His overall use of colloquial, regional language reached new heights in this collection. In a poet of lesser talents, this language might well have seemed no more than a turn on the idea of regionalism. Yet "Frost understood that the colloquial language was something more than pungent and something greater than quaint," says James M. Cox. He points out that Frost understood in a deep way the sense of free play characteristic of the dialect spoken by people in the northern New England region: "This free play, which seems to me close to the heart of so much colloquial speech, is surely the sign of a deep grace of life residing in those who naturally speak such language. Frost heard better than any American poet the sound of that deeper sense."[21]

New Hampshire was respectfully reviewed by many of Frost's acquaintances in the literary world: Padraic Colum, Mark Van Doren, Mark De Wolfe Howe, and—as always—Louis Untermeyer. (A negative review in the *Freeman* prompted Frost to write to Untermeyer with his suspicions that somebody was consciously out to get him: "It just shows how hard it is for an American publication, however lofty its pretensions, to keep from lending itself to blackmail and corruption.")[22] Among the shrewdest responses was one by John Farrar, who wrote of *New Hampshire* that it contained "the loveliest of his lyrics. . . . An almost rigid adherence to the colloquial prevails; where Lowell and Whittier observed and reported the New England peasant, Frost has become one. He writes stories of their most vivid moments with unswerving power of dramatic presentation. Some of the best pictures are of grim and terrible events, and the whole body of his writing indubitably shows a decaying and degenerating New England. That he fails to see the other side of life is untrue. Passages of great beauty shine from drabness. His events and his characters have moments of warmth and happiness. Always, however, is manifest the sense of fairness to events as he sees them."[23]

Frost was awarded the Pulitzer Prize for Poetry in 1924—a major turning point in the public recognition of a poet whose reputation would continue to grow by extraordinary leaps throughout the next few decades. This Pulitzer was the first of four that he would be awarded in his lifetime—a record number, in fact. *New Hampshire* was, by any standard, a success in its day, though in subsequent years it has attracted less attention than Frost's other collections.

As usual, the Frosts returned to South Shaftsbury for the summer of 1924. Frost wrote very little poetry that summer but spent a good deal of time with Carol, whose talent for farming impressed him mightily. "The farm goes rip-roaring as no farm ever went with me," he wrote to Untermeyer. "Carol has hired almost nothing done this year. He has ploughed and done all the haying himself. Fun to look on at—I always dreamed of being a real farmer: and seeing him one is almost the same as being one myself. My heart's in it with him."[24]

Frost did make a short trip north that summer to Ripton (near

Middlebury), where he read his poetry and lectured at the Bread Loaf Graduate School of English. (After 1939, he would habitually spend his summers in Ripton near the Bread Loaf campus.) Among the members of the summer faculty whom Frost knew was George Whicher of Amherst College, but Frost apparently felt awkward in his presence, perhaps because he was soon to abandon Amherst for Michigan.

He returned to Amherst in the fall with a certain nostalgia, knowing (as none of his colleagues yet did) that he would soon be gone. He was also tense about carrying such a big secret, although some relief came in November when the nature of the post at Michigan was made public. "His fellowship at the University of Michigan has been created especially for him," reported the *Boston Evening Transcript*, "and will exist for life. The fellowship entails no obligations of teaching and it provides for all living expenses. He will have his entire freedom to work and write." Nobody at Amherst could possibly chide him for accepting an offer this bountiful.

On March 26, 1925, a dinner was held in celebration of his fiftieth birthday at the Hotel Brevoort in New York City.[25] It was arranged by Frederic G. Melcher, a New Englander who had migrated to Indianapolis, where he set up a bookstore. (He later edited *Publishers Weekly*.) At Frost's bidding, Melcher worked with Untermeyer to bring together the appropriate friends. Carl Van Doren acted as master of ceremonies. Other speakers included Dorothy Canfield Fisher and Wilbur Cross. A message from Amy Lowell was read aloud; in it, she described her "profound attachment to the man" and her admiration for his work. Lowell was terribly ill at this time, and would die six weeks later, but Frost did not realize how badly off she was and resented her absence. It was Amy Lowell, after all, who had written that important, early American review in the *New Republic*—the one that had greeted Frost on his first day back in America after the British sojourn.

Somewhat spitefully, Frost decided not to attend a dinner in Boston the next month in honor of Lowell, who had recently published a two-volume biography of John Keats to great acclaim (it had already gone into a fourth printing by the time of the dinner). Frost had Elinor write to Lowell and claim exhaustion on his part. When Lowell died shortly thereafter, Frost felt guilty. Covering over the guilt with levity, however, he wrote to Untermeyer (who had also not attended what Frost called her "Keats Eats"): "She got it on us rather by dying just at a moment when we could be made to feel that we had perhaps judged her too hardly."[26]

Frost actively disliked Amy Lowell's poetry, and said so in private, but now the need for public tributes to her verse was upon him, and he rose on several occasions to the task. His formal statement to the press is memorable:

> It is absurd to think that the only way to tell if a poem is lasting is to wait and see if it lasts. The right reader of a good poem can tell the moment it strikes him that he has taken an immortal wound, that he will never get over it. That is to say, permanence in poetry as in love is perceived instantly. It has not to wait the test of time. The proof of a poem is not that we have never forgotten it, but that we knew at sight that we never could forget it. There was a barb to it and a toxin that we owned to at once. How often I have heard it in the voice and seen it in the eyes of this generation that Amy Lowell had lodged poetry with them to stay.[27]

The truth is that Frost admired few of his contemporaries and felt certain rivalries more keenly than others. One can also see that Frost (having suffered decades of near-total eclipse) was especially eager for the spotlight. He did not, however, have much to worry about in this regard. Recognition came in wave after wave, including honorary degrees from Middlebury College and Yale in 1924 and another from Bowdoin College (offered in 1925 but delayed until 1926 because of Elinor's health).

Elinor's illness in the spring of 1925 added a new element of uncertainty to family life. Frost sent a telegram to explain to the president of Bowdoin his forthcoming absence at the graduation ceremony. "Elinor had a serious nervous collapse early last week," he wrote. He put the blame for her condition on himself: "The amount of it is, my way of life lately has put too much strain on her. All this campaigning goes against her better nature and so also does some of this fancy teaching, my perpetual at-home charity clinic for incipient poesis, for instance. Time we got back into the quiet from which we came."[28]

The astonishing fact is that Elinor, herself over fifty, had suffered a miscarriage—much to the surprise of everyone concerned. Her nerves were quite bad, too; she found the pace of life, with the constant travel, the demands of people coming and going from the house, and the general hubbub connected with Frost's "campaigning," almost too much to bear. She longed for the days on the farm at Derry, when nobody knew who Robert Frost was, and when the longest trip was the occasional visit to a neighboring village. Elinor was hesitant about the Michigan appointment, which she feared would result in only more public activity of the kind she disliked. Furthermore, she did not like being away from her children. But she lacked the will to go against her husband's wishes.

At least the summer of 1925 was a pleasant one on the farm in South Shaftsbury, with Irma and Marjorie gathering around. Carol and Lillian were present, as always, and Lesley was a frequent visitor; she was now working as a bookseller in Pittsfield, Massachusetts, some forty miles to the south. Frost wrote to John Haines in late July: "Yesterday we were haying in America. We got in about two tons of timothy not unmixed with clover. We sold to people passing in their cars some five hundred stems of sweet peas at a cent a piece."[29]

In August, the Frosts accepted an invitation from Joseph and Edith Fobes to use their guest cottage on their summer estate in Franconia— an attractive offer, since Frost was desperate at this time of year to get as high into the mountains as possible because of his hay fever. This was the first of what would prove an annual retreat to the Fobes' cottage in Franconia at this time of year. They remained in Franconia until the last week in August, when they set off (with considerable regret at leaving the children and abandoning the farm in South Shaftsbury just as the fruit trees were heavy with apples, cherries, and pears). They had barely started on their journey when Frost, quietly, resolved to stay in Michigan for a limited period.

William Prescott Frost, 1872
(*Courtesy Dartmouth College Library*)

Belle Moody Frost, 1876
(*Courtesy Dartmouth
College Library*)

Frost and sister, Jeanie, 1876
(*Courtesy Dartmouth College Library*)

Elinor Miriam White, 1892
(*Courtesy Dartmouth College Library*)

Frost, 1892 (*Courtesy Dartmouth College Library*)

Frost children at Derry Farm, 1908 (*Courtesy Dartmouth College Library*)

Frost at Pinkerton Academy, 1910
(*Courtesy Mrs. Grace S. Pettengill*)

John Bartlett, 1910
(*Courtesy Amherst College Library*)

Frost and Elinor at Plymouth, 1911
(*Courtesy Lesley Lee Francis*)

The Frost children, 1911
(*Courtesy Lesley Lee Francis*)

Frost in England, 1913 (*Courtesy Dartmouth College Library*)

Little Iddens, home of the Frost family in Ledington, Gloucester, 1914
(*Courtesy Dartmouth College Library*)

Edward Thomas, 1914
(*Courtesy Myfanny Thomas*)

Frost in Franconia, New Hampshire, 1915 (*Courtesy Dartmouth College Library*)

Frost and son, Carol, in Franconia, New Hampshire, 1916–1917
(*Courtesy Lesley Lee Francis*)

Frost home at Sunset Avenue in Amherst (*Courtesy of Dartmouth College Library*)

Frost in South Shaftsbury, Vermont, 1921 (*Courtesy Dartmouth College Library*)

Stone Cottage in South Shaftsbury, Vermont (*Courtesy of Dartmouth College Library*)

Frost with Dartmouth students, late 1940s (*Courtesy Dartmouth College Library*)

Frost and his granddaughter, Robin, at her graduation, 1952 (*Courtesy Robin Hudnut*)

The Homer Noble farm, Ripton (*Courtesy Dartmouth College Library*)

The Frost cabin in Ripton, Vermont (*Courtesy of Dartmouth College Library*)

Frost's eightieth birthday dinner, Amherst, Massachusetts, 1954. Left to right: Charles Cole, Thornton Wilder, Frost, Archibald MacLeish, Louis Untermeyer, Hyde Cox, and Curtis Canfield. (*Courtesy Dartmouth College Library*)

Frost in Ripton with Lawrence Thompson and Reginald "Doc" Cook
(*Courtesy Lesley Lee Francis*)

Frost with Ted and Kay Morrison at Bread Loaf
(*Courtesy Dartmouth College Library*)

Frost at Camp Keewaydin, Vermont, 1959 (*Courtesy Harold Curtiss*)

Frost, Lesley, and her daughters
(*Courtesy Dartmouth College Library*)

W. H. Auden and Frost in Oxford, 1957 (*Courtesy Dartmouth College Library*)

Frost at the Kennedy inauguration, 1961 (*Courtesy Lesley Lee Francis*)

Frost and his dog, Gillie, in Vermont, 1961 (*Courtesy of Dartmouth College Library*)

Frost with Nikita Khrushchev, in Russia, 1962 (*Courtesy Dartmouth College Library*)

13

TAKEN AND TOSSED
1926–1927

In those days there were wonders. From one of these wonders we have our breath—from the other our faith by a long descent.

—FROST, NOTEBOOK ENTRY, 1926

Carol and Lillian were left in charge of the farm in South Shaftsbury, while Marjorie joined Lesley in Pittsfield at her bookstore, The Open Book. Irma was back in New York again after having stayed with her family in Franconia during the hay-fever season (she, like her father, suffered terribly from the allergy). Irma had resumed studies at the Art Students League, although the plan was for her to join her parents as soon as possible in Michigan.

The new address in Ann Arbor was 1223 Pontiac Road, a small colonial house far enough from the campus so that students and colleagues could not drop in casually. The Frosts had made a gesture toward permanence in Michigan by having all their furniture shipped from Amherst, but it was several weeks before the furniture arrived. They were forced to stay temporarily with Dean and Mrs. Joseph A. Bursley, who were now their best friends in Ann Arbor, since President Burton had died the previous spring.

The new president of Michigan was Clarence Cool Little, a New Englander who had once taught biology at Harvard; most recently, he had served as president of the University of Maine. His wife wrote poetry, and she found Frost's presence in Ann Arbor especially attractive. She had recently formed a group of poetry enthusiasts, and she invited Frost to join them. He agreed to come now and then, but he was always wary of these kinds of meetings. Furthermore, he did not want to have his time soaked up in this manner, given that part of the attraction of the Michigan job was the promise of freedom from distractions.

The absence of formal teaching responsibilities certainly came as a relief. "I [am] a poetic radiator," he said, in describing his duties at Michigan to a friend, "I just sit around and radiate poetry."[1] Indeed, it looked as though the Michigan appointment might really provide a quiet space for Frost to work, but the invitations to read his poetry at various campuses around the country continued to pour in, and Frost could not resist them—in part because he was still supporting his children financially. In October, he returned to New England for an extensive tour that took him from Hanover, New Hampshire, to New York, to Chapel Hill, North Carolina, all within a two-week stretch. (Elinor had accompanied him on the initial swing east, making her way to South Shaftsbury for a brief visit with Carol and Lillian.) When Frost returned to Ann Arbor he was so exhausted that he collapsed with a severe influenza.

Like his father, Carol had weak lungs, and his health was a continuing worry for his parents, who kept in close touch with him by letter and telephone. The situation with Carol worsened suddenly in November, and the Frosts suggested that he seek a higher, drier climate for rest and recuperation throughout the winter; they suggested sternly that he go to Colorado to visit the Bartletts, who were always obliging. On the other hand, Frost understood that Carol was loath to admit to being sick at all. "He has something of my father in him that won't own up sick," Frost wrote to John Bartlett.[2]

Marjorie was another worry. She had been suffering from anxiety and nervous prostration for the past year, and her condition grew worse as winter approached. This was exacerbated by chronic appendicitis, for which she would soon need an operation. Elinor found herself fretting over her, and she left Ann Arbor for Pittsfield, hoping to help. Frost wrote to his friend Otto Manthey-Zorn, "I may follow if she

[Elinor] gives the word. It wouldn't be long anyway before we began to think of heading for Amherst. But I rather wanted to stay still where I was for a few weeks. Elinor may bring Marj out here if she is well enough to move. I'm weary of this scattered way of living. Either I mean to become an explorer and live homeless entirely or to settle down and raise chickens with a single post office address."[3] He did follow Elinor to Pittsfield, but speaking commitments meant that he could not stay at his daughter's side for long.

In early February he wrote to Untermeyer from Michigan: "We have been East two whole months with a sick Marjorie and are now divided over her, Elinor having stayed on to take care of her and I having come to Ann Arbor to make some show of teaching a little for my year's pay. I'm sad enough about Marj, but I am more busted up than sad. All this sickness and scatteration of the family is our fault and not our misfortune or I wouldn't admit it. It's a result and a judgment on us. We ought to have gone back farming years ago or we ought to have stayed farming when we knew we were well off."[4]

Frost would be teaching just one class a week this spring at Michigan, an informal seminar on writing that he had volunteered to conduct. With Elinor back in New England, he felt lonely, and was beginning to worry about his lack of productivity. "I have done four small books in twenty-eight years," he noted to John Bartlett, "one in seven."[5] Frost was not one to confuse quantity with quality, however, and he was fully aware that he had written a dozen or more poems as good as any that had yet been written in the United States; nevertheless, he was afraid for his career. He understood that it was essential for a writer to publish good work at regular, even frequent, intervals or be dismissed by critics as a "has-been." He had seen many promising poets come and go, often with amazing speed.

With Elinor away, he abandoned all pretense of having a schedule and often slept until early afternoon and stayed up late into the night. One student recalled having stopped by to see Frost just before dinner and not being let go until three in the morning. This life of well-cultivated leisure was just right for creativity, and Frost's muse responded well. He wrote "Spring Pools" in early spring:

These pools that, though in forests, still reflect
The total sky almost without defect,
And like the flowers beside them, chill and shiver,
Will like the flowers beside them soon be gone,
And yet not out by any brook or river,
But up by roots to bring dark foliage on.

The trees that have it in their pent-up buds
To darken nature and be summer woods—
Let them think twice before they use their powers
To blot out and drink up and sweep away
These flowery waters and these watery flowers
From snow that melted only yesterday.

The identically patterned stanzas, like the subject they mirror, reflect each other—even as the penultimate line comes close to mocking the reflectiveness of this poem: "These flowery waters and these watery flowers." As in many of his best lyrics, "Spring Pools" is about poetry, about the process of creativity. Water, here as elsewhere in Frost, can be taken to mean a substance into which one dips for inspiration. Yet the poem is more complicated than this. Frost is covertly playing in the first line with the old notion of art as an imitation of nature—an idea that, in various forms, can be traced back to Plato's *Republic* and Aristotle's *Poetics*.

Horace, who derived a good deal from Aristotle, coined the phrase *ut pictura poesis*, making the analogy between poetry and painting. The notion that "painting is mute poetry, and poetry a speaking picture" was originally formulated by Simonides, and the suggestiveness of this idea was such that, as Irving Babbitt points out, "It is rare to read through a critical treatise on either art or literature, written between the middle of the sixteenth and middle of the eighteenth century, without finding an approving mention of the Horatian simile."[6]

Frost, himself a classicist, would have had in mind the whole range of this discussion. The subject of the poem is the nature of reflection and the way it is absorbed into a larger organic whole. The poem must first be read on a literal plane as being about how leaves and flowers are "brought on" by the act of sucking up spring pools through the roots of trees—a natural phenomenon known to most readers. But Frost gives clear signals that he wants us to read beyond the natural phenomenon, to search for its symbolic implications.

The roots that suck the pools dry are somewhat menacing; they do, after all, obliterate the reflection, the original vision, which was "almost without defect" (even here, Frost hedges with "almost"); the roots "bring dark foliage on," which may be taken in different ways, not all pleasing; this point is made all the more explicit in the first lines of the second stanza: "The trees that have it in their pent-up buds / To darken nature" are distinctly threatening; they can "blot out and drink up and sweep away" a powerful reflection. Here Frost again subscribes to the Romantic notion (the Germans, especially J. G. Herder, were fond of this idea) of natural or organic violence as part of the dialectic of the imagination.

In another familiar gesture, Frost commands: "Let them think twice" before doing what they do. How serious is he? On some level, he is dead serious; he resists this destruction of easy and near-perfect correspondence—the sky reflected in the spring pools, or art mirroring nature. On a deeper level, however, he does not really want the trees to think twice about the process; the "pent-up buds" must be fed, just as the artist must destroy in order to create, or (in terms Coleridge put forward that Frost would have approved) to re-create. Frost always wants to reach for a more complicated vision, one arrived at after much pain, much "sucking up" of passive, reflected beauty. Although the sucked-up pools will go on to give new life to foliage, "Frost sees that transformation as loss rather than gain," as George F. Bagby says.[7]

The poet's imagination takes the beautiful world and scrambles it, remakes it; there is something dark in the final foliage of the completed art object, perhaps, but this is necessary. As Coleridge put it, "Images, however beautiful, though faithfully copied from nature, and as accurately represented in words, do not of themselves characterize the poet. They became proofs of original genius only as far as they are modified by a predominant passion; or when they have the effect of reducing multitude to unity, or succession to an instant; or lastly, when a human or intellectual life is transferred to them from the poet's own spirit."[8]

Frost was, in fact, obsessed by what is called the heterocosmic ana-
logue, defined by the critic M. H. Abrams as "the parallel between
writing poetry and creating the universe."[9] He saw the poet as a kind
of god, capable of mixing the given elements of the universe to invent
a parallel world. The act of poetic imagination is one of transformation, which must at times verge on the destructive; it can, that is, "blot
out and drink up and sweep away" the world's image of itself. But the
result of this act is sublime, at once beautiful and frightening.

Another poem written in Ann Arbor around this time was "A
Winter Eden," in which Frost celebrates "A winter garden in an alder
swamp." It is another of his meticulously observed nature poems,
although one begins to see what happens when Frost relies too heavily
on mannerisms. The winter garden is said to elevate existence:

> It lifts existence on a plane of snow
> One level higher than the earth below,
> One level nearer heaven overhead,
> And last year's berries shining scarlet red.

The parallelism here seems forced, a point of charm rather than a
focus. Frost seems unable to move the poem beyond the surface level,
the literal description of place, however evocative.

What remains interesting, however, is Frost's consistent use of
imagery taken from rural New England; even living in Ann Arbor did
not distract him from his regional preoccupation. If anything, being
away from New England stimulated his memory and spurred his imagination of that region. "I never write about a place in New England, if I
am there," he said. "I always write about it when I am away. In Michigan I shall be composing poetry about New Hampshire and Vermont
with longing and homesickness better than I would if I were there, just
as in England."[10]

Frost was getting more and more eager to assemble a new collection. In his folder of old poems, he found many pieces that, with a little dusting off, would meet the standard of his best work. There was,
perhaps, some hoarding instinct at work here; this secret bank of
poems was a stake in the future, a way of ensuring that if his creativity

entered a period of drought, there was always something in reserve—a deep pool into which he could put his roots.

Among the poems held back was "Tree at My Window," which he apparently revised in Michigan. The locale of the poem is unspecific, but Frost told Lawrance Thompson that it was inspired by a memory of the Derry farm, where a big tree would scrape against the window of his house in summer. The poem opens with an address to the tree:

> *Tree at my window, window tree,*
> *My sash is lowered when night comes on;*
> *But let there never be curtain drawn*
> *Between you and me.*

Frost's interest in the world of Emersonian correspondences becomes the central subject of this poem. The implicit question posed by the poet concerns the relation of inner and outer worlds, described here as "weathers." This idea is distinctly Coleridgean (by way of the German aesthetician F. W. J. von Schelling, whom Coleridge had been reading closely); Coleridge's article "On Poesy or Art" (1818) arises from Schelling's idea of parallelism between the mental world and the physical world. Essences found within nature are seen to have a corresponding life in the mind; in this metaphysics, art is seen by Coleridge as "the mediatress between, and reconciler of, nature and man. It is, therefore, the power of humanizing nature, of infusing the thoughts and passions of man into everything which is the object of his contemplation."

Frost, of course, cannot resist making fun of the tree as a "Vague dream-head lifted out of the ground," with the leaves as "light tongues talking aloud." He is aware that not everything in nature is profound, and that much of what he experiences in listening to this tree is mere chatter. Nevertheless, his identification with the tree becomes complex in the third stanza:

> *But, tree, I have seen you taken and tossed,*
> *And if you have seen me when I slept,*
> *You have seen me when I was taken and swept*
> *And all but lost.*

The strange, startling beauty of this stanza compares favorably with any other lines in Frost. The rigidity of the rhythm breaks down artfully into a more colloquial rhythm in those two middle lines, with its poetic feet boldly syncopated (iambs becoming anapests at just the right moments); the swaying of the lines seems to mimic the motion of the branches in a slight wind as they reach for the house.

The poem ends, perhaps a little cutely, but with undeniable aphoristic brilliance:

> *That day she put our heads together,*
> *Fate had her imagination about her,*
> *Your head so much concerned with outer,*
> *Mine with inner, weather.*

Even Frost was dazzled by his own technical prowess in this last stanza: "No matter what I think it means," he said, "I'm infatuated with the way the rhymes come off here."[11]

A surprise visit from President Olds of Amherst in the spring lifted Frost's spirits: a continuation of the old tug-of-war between Amherst and Michigan for Frost's presence. Olds offered Frost $5,000 for ten weeks of teaching per year, a remarkably high sum in those days for anyone in the teaching profession. Frost accepted the offer at once, relieved to put the Michigan experience behind him. He wrote to Roy Elliott (who had mentioned to Olds that Frost might be open to a fresh offer), "Think of the untold acres I can spade up in the forty weeks of every year I am going to have free for farming. Suppose I live like [Walter Savage] Landor till ninety. That will give me one thousand six hundred weeks all to myself to put in at any thing I like."[12] As it were, Frost did live almost to the age of ninety, getting most of those coveted "one thousand six hundred weeks."

If there were any hard feelings in Michigan about his departure, Frost did not care. He was glad to rejoin his family in South Shaftsbury, and to put the Midwest behind him. Elinor had already gone ahead of him, and she was busily helping Carol and Lillian with Prescott, their son, who was just beginning to walk. Carol had recently made significant improvements to the property, adding a hundred dwarf Astrachan apple trees and a large patch of blueberry bushes. One small hillside had been set aside to grow flowers, and there was talk of setting up a greenhouse to supply flowers for the newly established Bennington College, which was only four miles away.

Elinor was quite overworked, even overwhelmed. Both Lillian and Marjorie had been ill, and they could hardly be expected to help with the farm chores. Lillian's condition turned perilous in July, requiring surgery in Bennington. Elinor wrote to her friend Edith Fobes about the situation: "I have had an anxious and busy time since our return. I found Lillian not feeling well, and felt puzzled about her. Her doctor didn't seem to know and finally advised an examination by the surgeon that comes to the Bennington hospital from Albany once a week. This surgeon advised an exploratory incision, and probably other things. It was most fortunate he advised it. She was operated on last Thursday, and they found a tubal pregnancy. It would surely have ruptured sometime during the next two weeks, and would have caused her death in all probability. The uterus was bound down in such a way that they could not diagnose it."[13]

On top of everything, Irma had decided to get married. She and her prospective husband, John Paine Cone, were busy making wedding plans. Cone had grown up in Kansas, on a wheat farm, and hoped to return home with Irma after the wedding to help his elderly parents run their farm. This plan gave Elinor some distress: she liked her children nearby. The whole scene at Stone Cottage made Frost extremely nervous, and Elinor decided it was best for them both to get away to Franconia for much of August. "Robert has become very nervous," she wrote to Mrs. Fobes, "and it is necessary for us to be by ourselves, without the children, for a little while, so that he may recover his equanimity."[14] One is struck by the degree to which Elinor, by now, had completely identified with Frost, ploughing under her own needs and early ambitions for herself; for the rest of her life, she served the family as protector, facilitator, and go-between.

The Frosts stayed in Franconia for three months, through the end of October. It proved a remarkably good place to work. Frost picked up a poem begun in 1920 called "West-Running Brook" and found himself inspired to revise it thoroughly. It had been started in response to an Amherst student who'd published, in the *Amherst Monthly* (March 1920), a poem called "Joe Wright's Brook." That poem was about two lovers discussing the name of a brook. Frost told the student, Edward Richards, that he would have done it quite differently; the poem, he said, brought to mind a brook on his Derry farm that defied its natural parameters and flowed west instead of east, toward the Atlantic. In 1937, Frost explained in a letter that "West-Running Brook" was connected, in his mind, with "Reluctance," "The Tuft of Flowers," and "The Death of the Hired Man," in being about "the same subject," which he described as "my position . . . between socialism and individualism."[15]

Frost often seemed to think he was talking about these great abstractions, but there is little in "West-Running Brook" to make one think about either of these terms except in the most general, uninteresting way. The poem has more in common with a very early poem, "Hyla Brook," where a stream is likewise the symbol of poetic inspiration, or a very late poem, "Directive," which ends: "Here are your waters and your watering place. / Drink and be whole again beyond confusion."

The poem inhabits the dialogue form that one saw frequently used in *North of Boston*, but there is nothing dramatic about "West-Running Brook." Frost attempts something quite different, a kind of meditative lyric couched in the spoken voice. The husband-wife dialogue has none of the edginess of the dramatic lyrics (as in "Home Burial," where the dramatic tension is brought to a fierce climax). Fred, the husband, seems to get carried away by the sound of his own voice. He asks at the outset:

> *What does it think it's doing running west*
> *When all the other country brooks flow east*
> *To reach the ocean?"* . . .

His answer is the point of the poem: " 'It must be the brook / Can trust itself to go by contraries.' "

These are not, however, the violent contraries of William Blake's *The Marriage of Heaven and Hell.* ("Without contraries is no progression," wrote Blake.) Frost's contraries are mere motions against the grain, formulated as a resistance to going with "the drift of things," as he said in "Reluctance." In addition, the moral dimension in Frost's poem is, as Robert Faggen notes, "more ambiguous" than in Blake, "drawn across lines of male and female, the rational and the intuitive, the ethereal and the telluric, in this case a man named Fred (how worldly!) and his mate."[16]

Overall, the unnamed wife in the poem operates mostly as a sounding board for her husband, who gets most of the good lines. And they are good lines indeed:

> *"Speaking of contraries, see how the brook*
> *In that white wave runs counter to itself.*
> *It is from that in water we were from*
> *Long, long before we were from any creature.*
> *Here we, in our impatience of the steps,*
> *Get back to the beginning of beginnings,*
> *The stream of everything that runs away."*

Frost seems much taken by the Darwinian idea that the human race began in a primitive, aquatic environment, then evolved landward, skyward. The stream, of course, is a familiar symbol of life in Western literature from Lucretius on, and one of Frost's recurrent images. In this poem, the symbol is refined and beautifully nuanced:

> *"It is this backward motion toward the source,*
> *Against the stream, that most we see ourselves in,*
> *The tribute of the current to the source.*
> *It is from this in nature we are from.*
> *It is most us."*

William H. Pritchard sees his final peroration by Fred as "eloquent, perhaps rather too much so." He adds that the unnamed spouse "might justifiably have wondered what came over Fred that he could suddenly rise to such heights or depths of profundity."[17] That Frost's speakers notice their excess of eloquence is acknowledged in the last exchange: "Today will be the day / You said so," the wife remarks, wryly. Fred counters: "No, today will be the day / You said the brook was called West-Running Brook." Importantly, the wife has the last word, and plays the role of reconciler: "Today will be the day of what we both said."

I place this poem higher in Frost's canon than Pritchard does, largely because so many of the poet's preoccupations converge here. The symbol of the stream is nowhere in Frost more carefully construed; as Rueben Brower says, "The rebellious flowing of the stream is a figure for the loving trust of husband and wife in the other's difference, the expected and desired contraries that make a marriage." With severe compactness, Frost manages to talk about this particular marriage in terms of the stream, but to talk about matters of life and death as well. "In explaining why the brook runs west," says Brower, "the wife had given her husband the metaphor that has shaped all the rest of his thinking."[18]

There is also the fact that Frost's two chief forms of poetry, dramatic and lyric, merge in "West-Running Brook." As in most of his bucolic lyrics, the poet begins with close observation of a natural phenomenon; he moves from that to analysis by metaphor. Fred might well have spun into the ether too quickly had not his wife been there, gently tugging him back to earth. (Brower, oddly, sees it the other way around, with his wife being less down-to-earth.) It must also be said that Fred's eloquence is, at times, ear-catching, as when he talks with Shakespearean fluidity about "The universal cataract of death / That spends to nothingness."

In the end, Frost seems to suggest that what ultimately redeems us, as human beings, is our natural resistance in the face of extinction. The poet's identification with nature is, in effect, his own quiet tribute to the source, which might be seen as the Universal Ground, or perhaps even God. "It is most us," he says; that is, the kingdom of God is within us, whether we like it or not.

One is tempted to overread such a poem, but Frost—always the sly and canny poet—never gives too much away, is never explicit. The reader is left tantalized, drawn ineluctably forward, expectant but never satisfied. Schooled in imagism by Pound and Hulme, Frost believed in the adequacy, the self-sufficiency, of the symbol. A little bit of faith, in poetry, goes a long way. As Frost put it, "Why literature is the next thing to religion in which as you know or believe an ounce of faith is worth all the theology ever written. Sight and insight, give us those."[19]

Irma's wedding was the primary event of the fall, followed by a lecture tour that began in early December. A two-week visit to Wesleyan University in Connecticut was eventually to be followed, in spring, by brief residencies at Michigan, Dartmouth, and Bowdoin—an exhausting string of assignments for a man who had supposedly given up teaching for farming and writing poetry.

His promised ten-week term at Amherst began in January, and he settled in happily at the college that had been important in his life thus far. "It was always Amherst that mattered to him," recalled Jack W. C. Hagstrom, a student from Amherst in the early 1950s who became a friend.[20] "Wherever else he taught, it felt temporary. Amherst was always home." Among those whom Frost was especially glad to see again was Otto Manthey-Zorn. One afternoon, Manthey-Zorn asked Frost to visit his seminar on German philosophy, which met from four until six in the evening. One student in the class remembered vividly the impression the poet made: "Frost began to discuss metaphors in an easy way, asking occasional questions to bring out our ideas. Gradually the evening shadows lengthened and after a while Frost alone was talking. The room grew darker and darker until we could not see each others' faces. But no one even thought of turning on the light. The dinner hour came and went, and still no one of that half score of hungry boys dreamed of leaving. We dared not even stir for fear of interrupting. Finally, long after seven, Frost stopped and said, 'Well, I guess that's enough.' We thanked him and left as if under a spell."[21]

Despite many happy experiences in the classroom, Frost had constantly to deal with family problems, which became increasingly intense. Marjorie had been ill throughout the winter, and she stayed in Amherst with her parents at their house on Amity Street, even though—as Elinor wrote to Edith Fobes on February 22, 1927—"she really ought to have been in some warmer climate for the winter."[22] The Frosts began to see that part, perhaps the largest part, of Marjorie's illness was psychological. She seemed horribly fragile, and the strain of dealing with her wore on both parents. Frost himself would plunge into dark moods periodically. What kept him going was the public occasions. "I think he needed these obligations," a friend recalled. "One could easily imagine him subsiding, never leaving his bedroom. But teaching, and the public readings—these demands were crucial. They kept him from withdrawing. He knew that, of course. He was self-protective in this way. He used the demands of his public career to keep himself afloat."[23]

Meanwhile, the next volume of poems was taking shape. Frost did not want his book to be a mere miscellany; he felt, quite sensibly, that a collection of verse should be read whole, and that it was important to arrange his poems in some thematic way. Just as New Hampshire had a long title poem that served as a principle of organization, Frost realized that "West-Running Brook" was exactly the right poem for the new collection, with its theme of progression by contraries. Indeed, this poem became his title poem.

The volume moves through six sections, beginning with Frost's strongest poem, "Spring Pools." This section ends with "Acceptance," a poem about the eerie silence that follows even the most spectacular defeats in nature, as when the "spent sun" goes down "burning into the gulf below" and still "No voice in nature is heard to cry aloud / At what has happened." Echoing a famous line by Alexander Pope, the poem ends with a declaration (in ironic quotes): "Let what will be, be."

Frost takes up that line again as a preface to the second section, "Fiat Nox" or "Let There Be Darkness." He writes again: "Let the night be too dark for me to see / Into the future. Let what will be, be."

There follows a sequence of poems which follow, in part, the Via Negativa—the dark way of knowledge. "Once by the Pacific" and "Bereft" are here—two strong poems rescued from earlier days. The former has one of Frost's finest rhetorical swells at the opening:

> *The shattered water made a misty din.*
> *Great waves looked over others coming in,*
> *And thought of doing something to the shore*
> *That water never did to land before.*

Later in the sonnet, Frost says: "It looked as if a night of dark intent / Was coming, and not only a night, an age." He follows this depressing thought with: "Someone had better be prepared for rage." Like Dylan Thomas after him, Frost was prepared to "rage against the dying of the light."

Intriguingly, Frost places "Tree at My Window" in this section, suggesting an even darker interpretation than one might have guessed for this poem about being "taken and swept / And all but lost." Nobody writes about near misses with deep depression better than Frost, and this poem might be taken as a self-rebuke, with the poet scolded by the tree as it scratches the window, the poet's own head too much obsessed by inner weather.

The section ends with "Acquainted with the Night," which had been written in Ann Arbor:

> *I have been one acquainted with the night.*
> *I have walked out in rain—and back in rain.*
> *I have outwalked the furthest city light.*
>
> *I have looked down the saddest city lane.*
> *I have passed by the watchman on his beat*
> *And dropped my eyes, unwilling to explain.*
>
> *I have stood still and stopped the sound of feet*
> *When far away an interrupted cry*
> *Came over houses from another street,*

> *But not to call me back or say good-by;*
> *And further still at an unearthly height,*
> *One luminary clock against the sky*
>
> *Proclaimed the time was neither wrong nor right.*
> *I have been one acquainted with the night.*

What first strikes the reader here is the sound of the poem, its insistent and peculiar rhythms. The poem was, Frost later suggested, "written for the tune." Although a sonnet by form, with a closing couplet, the poem has the fluid, repetitive aspect of a villanelle, with the three-line stanzas mimicking the terza rima of Dante—appropriate for a poem about the descent into darkness.

One unusual feature of this poem is the urban setting, with the speaker as a troubled visionary who has "outwalked the furthest city light" and plunged into dark regions around the city, the ghostly suburbs. One is reminded, indeed, of the Unreal City evoked in *The Waste Land*, especially where Frost writes of the "One luminary clock against the sky" proclaiming that the time "was neither wrong nor right." (The clock, Frost once said, was in the tower of the old Washtenaw County Courthouse.)[24] Time, in Frost, is neutral, amoral; Frost's theology, as ever, is concealed—his truth is difficult to place. The protagonist of the poem is a solitary wanderer of sad city lanes, someone who averts his eyes from other human beings. As Harold H. Watts has noted: "To be responsive to the pressures of nature or process, man must live with the pressures that come from other men (modern society, traditional culture) reduced to a minimum."[25]

I find this poem overwhelmingly melancholy, but oddly compelling. The rhythms seem inescapable, and the deft rhyming and consistent, well-defined images all work together. The poem makes a unified, definite impression on the reader, preparing the way for "West-Running Brook," the title poem, which is ultimately a poem about resistance, about the human need to overcome the downward drift toward darkness, the natural disintegration of the organic universe. Just as the riffles in the water "send up" something to the source, so human beings—those who have the gumption and gift—are called upon to "send up" something to the source, too. (Again, the metaphysics of Henri Bergson are fairly explicit here.)

After the huge swell of "West-Running Brook," with its curlicues of philosophy and rhetoric all placed in a slightly ironic context by the figure of Fred's wife, who indulges his flights of fancy but keeps bringing him back to reality, tugging gently at the margins of his speech, the last two sections of the collection open a broader base of irony, culminating in "Riders" and "The Bear," two of Frost's shrewdest, though little-read, poems. In the former, Frost writes:

> *The surest thing there is is we are riders,*
> *And though none too successful at it, guiders,*
> *Through everything presented, land and tide*
> *And now the very air, of what we ride.*

Human beings are at once passive (riders) and active (guiders), depending on the angle of vision. History is regarded as a bareback ride on earth's headless horse. The ride is terrifying, though comic, too. The one good thing Frost can think of to say is that "We have ideas yet that we haven't tried," and so there is hope.

That hope is restrained, wittily, in the last poem of the book, "The Bear," where Frost writes in rhyming couplets (occasionally expanding into triplets), the favorite form of the English Augustan poets, whose tone Frost emulates. He celebrates "the uncaged progress of the bear" as it roams the natural world, noting with irony that while "The world has room to make a bear feel free; / The universe seems cramped to you and me." People are, in effect, caged—by each other, and by conventions of one kind or another; our mode of vision is limited, though we try to extend it with "The telescope at one end of his beat, / And at the other end the microscope, / Two instruments of nearly equal hope, / And in conjunction giving quite a spread." In his witty conclusion, Frost offers a portrait of the human being as a caged animal:

> *He sits back on his fundamental butt*
> *With lifted snout and eyes (if any) shut,*
> *(He almost looks religious but he's not),*

And back and forth he sways from cheek to cheek,
At one extreme agreeing with one Greek,
At the other agreeing with another Greek
Which may be thought, but only so to speak.
A baggy figure, equally pathetic
When sedentary and when peripatetic.

West-Running Brook is not evenly first-rate as a collection, though it is filled with luminous moments—even whole poems, such as "Acquainted with the Night" and "Once by the Pacific," that are small miracles of perfection. The ironic note so often sounded here has been heard earlier, especially in *New Hampshire*; but Frost is not a poet who developed in any obvious ways from book to book, as did Yeats or Eliot or Stevens. Instead, he grew by accretion. His peculiar method of hoarding poems (going back to them, often decades later, to revise) only adds to the difficulty of discerning "development." In a sense, Frost achieved his vision early, and he restates, re-creates, refigures this original vision in book after book. There are no great leaps forward, only deepenings, confirmations, and subtle extensions.

Frost lost another editor when Lincoln MacVeagh resigned from the firm of Henry Holt, but he was soon replaced by Richard H. Thornton, who came to see Frost in South Shaftsbury. Frost was not tempted to leave Holt, which had done a fine job with *New Hampshire* and his *Selected Poems*. Now, with a Pulitzer Prize to his credit and a new volume of poems in hand, Frost felt in a good position to drive a bargain.

Much to his surprise, Holt did not resist his request for higher royalties and a monthly payment of $250 over the next five years. They would publish *West-Running Brook* in the fall of 1928, with woodcuts by Frost's favorite illustrator, J. J. Lankes, who had now become a good friend. (Frost and Lankes were linked, over four decades, by "subject, theme, tone and perspective," says Welford Dunaway Taylor in a study of this long and fruitful collaboration.)[26] There would be an advance of $2,000. Furthermore, Holt would reissue his *Selected Poems* with added material, and they would publish a *Collected Poems* in a year or two. What more could a poet ask for?

Frost's reputation had been steadily growing in other ways. The New York firm of George H. Doran published a well-known series of monographs on American writers, and an editor whom Frost had met at Bread Loaf, John Farrar, decided to have someone write on Frost and offered him the chance to select his own profiler. One possibility, in Frost's mind, was Edward Davison, a young English poet who had moved permanently to the United States in 1925; Frost had met Davison at Bread Loaf and liked him. Somewhat impulsively, he asked Davison to write the monograph, and Davison showed interest.

At the same time, an article on Frost appeared in the *Saturday Review of Literature* in which Frost was celebrated by Gorham B. Munson as "the purest classical poet in America today."[27] Munson was fascinated by the lines in "New Hampshire" where Frost talks about "being a good Greek." The idea of himself as a classical poet appealed to Frost, and he suddenly wanted Munson as his biographer, not Davison. After some delicate backtracking with Davison, Munson was elected for the job and given access to several of Frost's closest friends, including Louis Untermeyer and John Bartlett. He produced a little volume in November 1927 called *Robert Frost: A Study in Sensibility and Good Sense.*

The same month the book appeared, Frost wrote amusingly to Bartlett, "The first report I have had on the biographical sketch speaks chiefly of your contribution to it. I ain't a-going to thank you. It was an inspiration of mine to give Munson direct access to my past through two or three of my independent friends. I thought it would be fun to take the risk of his hearing something to my discredit. The worst you could [reveal] was my Indian vindictiveness. Really I am awful there. I am worse than you know. I can never seem to forgive people that scare me within an inch of my life. I am going to try to be good and cease from strife."[28]

Munson's book remains a fascinating volume, although it puts forward the unsustainable thesis that Frost was somehow more "classical" than "romantic" as a poet and thinker, invoking Irving Babbitt (the Harvard critic and humanist) as Frost's spiritual mentor. Frost actually disliked Babbitt's version of humanism, which was antireligious, and rejected Munson's book as simplistic and wrongheaded. On the other hand, aspects of Frost's thinking have something in common with Babbitt's: namely, a commitment to common sense and moderation as a corrective to the fashionable nihilism that Babbitt saw around him and decried. Babbitt, however, was strictly anti-Platonic, and had no use for a spiritual realm. This did not settle well with the son of a Swedenborgian who maintained a quiet belief in traditional religious values.

"Frost often appeared to side with religion," says Peter J. Stanlis. "He admired Darwin, but did not like Darwin's supporters, such as T. H. Huxley, or any brand of rationalism or humanism. In general, Frost believed that religion and science, including scientific theories such as Darwin's on evolution, were two different metaphorical ways of perceiving the same reality, and were 'contraries,' and not to be set against each other in ways that forced one to choose between them. The final harmony of the wife and Fred in their dialogue in 'West-Running Brook' is a fine example of this point. She presents a religious and idealistic view of the brook; he a scientific account of the origins of life out of matter and water. In the end they are harmonized though still distinct in what they said."[29]

Munson's account of Frost was highly influential, however, and it set in place a vision of Frost as a crusty Yankee with a sharply antiromantic side. As one critic would say, "It would take a good while for readers to get Munson, or Munson's version of Frost, out of their heads."[30]

14 ORIGINAL RESPONSE
1928–1930

There are a lot of things I could say to you about the art [of poetry] if we were talking, and one of them is that it should be of major adventures only, outward and inward—important things that happen to you, or important things that occur to you. Mere poeticality won't suffice. —FROST TO KIMBALL FLACCUS, 1928

With his renewed appointment at Amherst, Frost entered into a pattern in the 1926–27 academic year that would remain in place for over a decade. He would be in residence at Amherst for a limited period each year, during which time he would teach informally, offering seminars or lectures as he saw fit. "What I teach," he once said, "is myself, my way of seeing the world, of knowing the world."[1] It was an unusual and privileged position for a poet to occupy.

With Vermont as his base of operations, he would travel far and wide in the United States, giving readings and lectures, often for considerable sums of money. "Frost never prepared much, either for class or for a lecture," one friend recalls. "He was what you might call an intuitionalist. He preferred to talk about what came to him spontaneously."[2] For the most part, he would read his poems and digress in the spaces between them, offering witty remarks or wisecracks interspersed with nuggets of wisdom.

A huge gap opened in this decade between Frost's private and public lives, with the public life so glitteringly full of achievements and honors, and the private life increasingly laden with grief—illness, family crises. One is especially struck by the Frost children's dependence on their parents well into their adult lives. Only Lesley seemed able to make her way strongly in the world, although now that Irma was married she became somewhat more settled. Marjorie's physical and psychological problems only grew more intense as she matured. Carol and Lillian, though hardworking and devoted to each other, were consistently plagued by financial and health problems that seemed out of their control.

The Frosts had for some time halfheartedly entertained the notion of returning to Europe, but it would take them until August 1928 to organize the trip. They were spurred on by Marjorie, who wanted to learn French and gain some experience abroad. Arrangements for this adventure were made by Dorothy Canfield Fisher, the Frosts' neighbor in South Shaftsbury, who had spent several months near Sèvres during the First World War. She knew a family there who would play host to Marjorie for a limited period.

The Frosts sailed from Quebec to Le Havre on August 4, arriving a week later in Paris, where they lingered for a few days of sightseeing (and a visit to the opera) before taking Marjorie to Sèvres. Frost found himself miserable in France, where everything seemed utterly strange to him. He was looking forward to getting to England, where he intended to visit his old friend John Haines. He wrote to Haines on August 28:

Thus far I have nothing to report of this expedition but bad. We came to France in the hope that it might improve our invalid Marjorie by awakening interest in her to learn the French language. That hope has failed and the disappointment has been almost too much for Elinor on top of everything else she has had to bear for the last two years. I can't tell you how she has lost courage and strength as I have watched her. She is in a serious condition—much more serious at this moment than Marjorie. We ought by right to abandon our campaign and baggage and retreat to America, but that seems cruel to contemplate with nothing done, none of our friends seen that we wanted to see and have been wanting to see for so long. I have one last resource. I am going to try to find a sort of travelling-companion-nurse for Marjorie to take her off her mother's hands for a few weeks.[3]

Frost added; "Of course it is to see you more than anything else that I made this desperate journey across the Atlantic in our old age and worn-out condition. Elinor has had too much on her. I am afraid it will take her a long time to recover. Something radical will have to be done for her, and I will have to be the one to do it. She is in a state past doing anything for herself."

It annoyed Frost, in France, that he could not speak French, especially when it came to the newspapers. He was vividly aware, however, that U.S. Secretary of State Frank B. Kellogg was in Paris negotiating a treaty that was called the Pact of Paris. This document was full of idealism in the tradition of Woodrow Wilson, who (unlike Frost) was deeply skeptical of the use of force in international relations. Frost, if anything, was a populist in the vein of Teddy Roosevelt, and he denounced this latest treaty to Elinor and other friends, convinced that one should avoid promises about not wielding a big stick when necessary. Nevertheless, he could not help but admire Wilson's character: "He had calibre," he wrote home to Otto Manthey-Zorn on August 20, "he saw as vastly as anyone that ever lived."[4]

In September, with Marjorie safely in the hands of her French guardians, the Frosts left for England. They rested in London, keeping to themselves, before going on to visit Haines in Gloucestershire. Frost wrote home to John Bartlett that he was "no real traveller." He was, however, extremely eager to see Haines, and to reminisce with him about Edward Thomas. Haines recalled that they took "walks in the Cotswolds together, and, later, sat on Churchdown Hill whilst he expounded the inner origin of his poetical themes, and, once again, we climbed May Hill and gazed round that astounding ring of country from the Brecon Beacons to Shropshire, and from the northernmost Cotswold to the Channel's rim . . . but the wraith of that dead friend was ever before us."[5]

It had long been a wish of Frost's to visit Ireland, and he did so not long after arriving in London. He took a steamer across the Irish Sea by himself, leaving Elinor (who was feverish with a mild case of what she called "the usual British influenza") behind; he was met by Padraic Colum and George William Russell (who wrote under the initials A.E.), two Irish poets whom he had known for some years. (He stayed in Dublin with the poet Constantine P. Curran, Colum's friend.) The high point of this sojourn was a dinner with Yeats, whom Frost had admired for so many years (but encountered only once before, in 1913). Yeats recognized Frost, in both senses, and greeted him warmly.

The dinner with Yeats included A.E., and Frost later told Mertins that "he had his first experience in listening to genuine conversation when he heard A.E. and Yeats talk together in Ireland." Mertins points out that the link between poetry and conversation was essential to Yeats: "Whenever Frost in after years had occasion to refer to that visit to Eire [in 1928], it was not of the Irish landscape, or of Irish farming, or of the Irish peasantry, or of the Sinn Feiners, or of the Eire Republic, or of de Valera that he talked. These things scarcely formed a backdrop. It was always of the other-worldly conversation he held with the two Irish mystics—men of the older Ireland—such talk, he said, 'as nowhere else on earth have I ever heard the like of. These men took ordinary conversation and lifted it into the realm of pure literature.' "[6]

Frost later said: "During the meal Yeats spoke up and said, 'You know I was the first poet in modern times to put that colloquial everyday speech of yours into poetry. I did it in my poetic play *The Land of Heart's Desire.*' "[7] This sort of comment, from a lesser poet, might have stirred a sense of rivalry; Frost, however, had nothing but admiration for Yeats, and he understood that his remark was meant as a gesture of solidarity.

Back in England, Frost made the literary rounds, visiting such old friends and acquaintances as Lascelles Abercrombie (who had grown old and diabetic), Wilfrid Gibson, John Cournos, John Gould Fletcher, F. S. Flint, and Edward Garnett—the latter a critic who had championed both Frost and Thomas. He and Elinor also spent a night with the old poet Walter de la Mare and his wife. "De la Mare is the best of the best," he wrote back to Ted Morrison.[8] For old times' sake, they went out of their way to visit Helen Thomas, whose memoir of her life with Edward Thomas had recently been a minor sensation—largely because of her accounts of their marital troubles. Frost, as might be expected, found the memoir distasteful, although he was polite about it. Writing home to Cox, he said the book was "a good piece of work in a way, but it took a good [deal] of squirming on her part to justify it." He wondered if Helen "wasn't in danger of making E.T. look ridiculous in the innocence she credited him with."[9]

Frost wrote to John Haines about these comings and goings in his usual wry voice:

> We saw Helen Thomas and that ended one passage in our lives. She delivered herself of several choice things. The reason she didn't want Edward's letters published was because he wasn't interesting in his letters. She sometimes rejoiced he wasn't alive to see the state England was in. She needn't be afraid I shall ever publish his letters to me. She may be right about the state of England; it seems a poor sort of country where a woman has to give up living with a man married to someone else for fear of losing her pension. I decided before I had lectured to her long that Edward had worse enemies to his memory than poor old Wilfrid [Gibson]. It needed only that decision to make it easy to visit Wilfrid at Letchworth. He has since sent me a poem in which he stoutly excuses us all for looking so horribly old after such a terrible war. I couldn't see that he had aged much. He must have meant his wife and us. I don't want to be excused for looking horribly old. I want it denied I look horribly old.[10]

While staying in London in early October, Frost telephoned Harold Monro at his Poetry Bookshop, now moved to Great Russell Street (near the British Museum); the normally reserved Monro seemed both surprised and thrilled to hear from him, and proposed that Frost read at the bookshop. As an enticement, he promised that T. S. Eliot would attend the performance. Frost, who had been scornful of Eliot's poetry in public for years, was nonetheless intrigued and agreed to read on the evening of October 18. Unfortunately, Eliot sent his regrets on the day of the reading. An embarrassed Monro hastily arranged a dinner party with Eliot for the following night.

The conversation at the dinner centered on Monro, who had done a good deal to promote the careers of both Frost and Eliot (although, in Eliot's case, he had been reluctant at first). Frost was polite throughout the dinner, as was Eliot, but Eliot's put-on English accent and Anglophile manners did not impress Frost; indeed, it only fueled his distaste for Eliot, encouraging him in later years to make derogatory remarks about the poetry and the man. "He was always against Eliot," Richard Eberhart recalled. "He considered him a snob, and a fake. Those were the worst things you could be in Frost's way of thinking."

Elinor, meanwhile, had gone back to Sèvres by herself to get Marjorie, returning just in time for two dinners that had been scheduled in Frost's honor, one by the English Speaking Union and another by the P.E.N. Club. Unfortunately, he fell ill just before the dinners; as often happened when he was either overworked or stressed by too much contact with the public, he succumbed to what he and Elinor usually called "the grippe"—a complaint marked by a tightening of the chest, a racking cough, and night sweats. In the days preceding these bouts, Frost would usually plunge into a state of depression, whereupon his body's resistance would fall; the grippe would then come on, and he would take to his bed for a week or more. This is what happened in London, and Elinor (herself still in poor health) was forced to look after him. "Robert and I are both struggling," she wrote home to Edith Fobes. "We can hardly wait to return."

In all, the European trip was something of a failure, given that its purpose had been to give a boost to Marjorie and Elinor. Both had proved unequal to the demanding aspects of travel. In early November, in a note to John Haines, Frost foresaw an early conclusion to their journey: "This may as well end the expedition. It has been too much of a strain anyway. I wish I could promise to see you again, but it wouldn't be honest as things are. I've made Elinor unhappier . . . than I think I ever made her before. She's too sick for a jaunting party and I should not have dragged her out of her home."[11]

Before sailing home, on November 15, Frost called on the current poet laureate, Robert Bridges, at his home in Boars Hill, near Oxford. He had met Bridges before, most recently in Michigan in 1925. The English poet, however, was now eighty-four, and weak; much to Frost's disappointment, he showed little interest in him or his theories of poetry. They sat before a coal fire with "lukewarm cups of tea on their laps" as Bridges talked at length about his own final book, which he proposed to call *The Testament of Beauty*. Frost thanked Bridges for his hospitality but took his leave as quickly as was polite—an anticlimactic end to a less than perfect journey.

After a rough crossing on the SS *Olympic*, Frost parted company with Elinor and Marjorie, who went back to South Shaftsbury while he turned south from New York to lecture in Baltimore and North Carolina. On his way back, he stopped to see his editor in New York, where *West-Running Brook* had only just been published. By the time he got back to Vermont, in early December, he was thoroughly exhausted. He arrived in South Shaftsbury as the winter's first serious snowfall was just beginning.

The situation at home was even more complicated than usual. Marjorie had suddenly decided that she should study nursing and had written off to the well-regarded Johns Hopkins Nurse Training School, in Baltimore; the school immediately accepted her for the winter term, beginning in February. Her parents, of course, wondered if she could possibly manage a demanding course of study. In any case, carried forward by her enthusiasm, they agreed to support her financially.

Irma, who had been married now for two years, had left her husband and returned home to Vermont with a baby son in the spring of 1928. Her husband had later followed her east, hoping to patch things up. He agreed to remain in Vermont, and the Frosts decided to help them out by buying a small farm near Bennington. Now, as Christmas of 1928 approached, Irma's troubled marriage once again upset everyone as she complained to her parents that life with John Paine Cone was barely tolerable. She predicted that soon everything would collapse on her.

Lesley, too, was having marital problems; she had married

(somewhat defiantly) while her parents were abroad. Dwight Francis had been married before. His daughter Lesley Francis recalls: "My father was the son of Henry Francis, a well-to-do industrialist. Before the family lost all their wealth in the Depression, they had given Dwight a good deal of money to start his own business. He was very good-looking, very handsome, Harvard-educated; he had been a flyer in Canada, and had married a woman called Kay, who was only seventeen, in Paris. The marriage lasted just one year, and there were no children. He was something of a playboy, but that oversimplifies it; he was quite serious about each of his marriages. But he was out of my life before I was born. He went on to marry several more times—and each love was the love of his life. With my mother, he hit upon a very bad time; with the Depression, he lost all his money, as did his father, who was completely devastated. My father suddenly had to go to work and found a job in real estate. Things eventually got a little better for him, and he had three sons by his third wife, all of whom did well.

"Lesley, my mother, was terribly in love with him, but the marriage only lasted from 1929 until 1931. Apparently my father would suddenly want to go skiing in the Alps or do something frivolous, and my mother got tired of this. She said, 'Go ahead, but don't come back.' He didn't. Mother got no alimony, nor any child support, but she had total custody of her children. Father was banished from our existence, and I didn't actually meet him until I was a teenager. My mother didn't remarry until 1952, when she married Joseph W. Ballantine—a diplomat and China expert."[12]

Frost was barely settled again when Lesley appeared in South Shaftsbury with tales of marital woe, saying she might soon get divorced. Although neither she nor Irma got divorced at this time, it was clear—much to their parents' chagrin—that in both cases it was inevitable. Frost was a self-professed believer in monogamy who was always distressed when news of divorce surfaced among his acquaintances. Indeed, it was during this period that Louis Untermeyer and his wife, Jean, underwent a rocky patch that led to a divorce. They remarried a short while later, but not before Untermeyer had married and quickly divorced another woman—a bizarre interval that displeased Frost, who had written scoldingly to Untermeyer from England, "My judgment on you is that you have wronged yourself in all this business of alternating between two wives. You have been acting against your nature under pressure of the bad smart talk you have listened to and learned to share in the society you have cultivated in your own New York salons (so to call them.) I've heard the mocking when I have been there and heard you lend yourself to it till I was ready to bet what would happen. None of it was right or wise or real. What I dread most now is that you will go on the assumption that, though it was folly and landed you in tragedy, it was on the way somewhere and somehow prepared you for a greater and fuller life. Shut up. To hell with such comforts. It was all time and energy lost, as I have said before."[13] He gave similar warnings to both Lesley and Irma, but to no avail.

Frost often went on long walks with a local mail clerk and beekeeper named Charles Monroe, and it was on one of their walks in 1928 that Monroe showed him a little farm that he could not resist, "a poor little cottage of five rooms, two ordinary fireplaces, and one large kitchen fireplace all in one central chimney as it was in the beginning." It was located on 153 acres, with fifty in woods (mixed stands of maple, pine, and paper birches), the rest rolling pastureland. As Lawrance Thompson notes, "There was a special fascination, for Frost, in any country real estate with a 'for sale' sign posted on it."[14]

The tiny eighteenth-century house had a lovely view to the west, toward New York. It was not far from Buck's Cobble, a well-known local promontory with astounding views of the Green Mountains and the Taconics. Looking east, one could actually see the peak of Mount Equinox. The asking price for the farm was only $5,000—a price Frost could easily afford, even as the rest of the country was going bankrupt. His fortunes had, indeed, risen in marked contrast to those around him, now that he was making a sound income from the combination of his Amherst salary, his royalties, and the substantial fees he could command on the lecture circuit. The Depression was not, for him, a significant factor, although he could see its effects on his children, which meant that he experienced this dark period in American economic history indirectly.

The reasons for moving to a new farm at this time were clear: Stone Cottage had been given to Carol and Lillian, and it was unseemly for the elder Frosts to remain there indefinitely. They had rented a place called Shingle Cottage, in North Bennington, for the past year, as a way of staying out of the way, but they wanted a place of their own. Stone Cottage had also become a frequent gathering place for the whole Frost clan, and the noise and commotion there were such that Frost's nerves were often strained. He wanted peace, and he could afford it now.

A poet and friend, Wade Van Dore, was offered a chance to live in the house and make some repairs—although professional carpenters would be working to add a bathroom and do the necessary renovations. Van Dore took the offer, anticipating a lot of free time for his own writing. It was in response to a poem by Van Dore that Frost wrote "The Most of It," one of his most complex and interesting poems. Van Dore was a lover of nature in the most conventional sense, and had written a poem called "The Echo" in which he lamented that the only response he could manage to rouse in nature was the faint echo of his own. Van Dore recalled, "I often confided in him my strange adventures in silence and loneliness in the lake country northwest of Lake Superior; but, aside from a great answer I might have desired from nature, was I crying out for his and not someone else's sympathy after failing to find complete fulfillment in a great wilderness? The dark and primitive feeling of his poem suggests that he took my seeking as something that touched him personally."[15]

Frost wrote his poetic response to Van Dore in an inspired blaze of composition, "all in one afternoon," as he later said:

> He thought he kept the universe alone;
> For all the voice in answer he could wake
> Was but the mocking echo of his own
> From some tree-hidden cliff across the lake.
> Some morning from the boulder-broken beach

> *He would cry out on life, that what it wants*
> *Is not its own love back in copy speech,*
> *But counter-love, original response.*
> *And nothing ever came of what he cried*
> *Unless it was the embodiment that crashed*
> *In the cliff's talus on the other side,*
> *And then in the far-distant water splashed,*
> *But after a time allowed for it to swim,*
> *Instead of proving human when it neared*
> *And someone else additional to him,*
> *As a great buck it powerfully appeared,*
> *Pushing the crumpled water up ahead,*
> *And landed pouring like a waterfall,*
> *And stumbled through the rocks with horny tread,*
> *And forced the underbrush—and that was all.*

This richly textured poem appears, on the surface, to turn the notion of correspondence (which Frost originally got from Swedenborg—who was also an important source for Emerson, who reframed the idea for American readers) on its head; the speaker wants more than his "own love back in copy speech" when he calls across a lake—as did Van Dore in "The Echo." Echo is not enough. Frost—or the speaker in the poem—seeks "counter-love, original response," but no response is forthcoming except the "embodiment" which comes "As a great buck"—a mystifying "as" if ever one existed.[16] This embodiment charges out of the water "with horny tread" and lands "pouring like a waterfall"—a terrifying force, utterly inhuman.

This is certainly one of Frost's darker poems, especially with "and that was all" coming as the final utterance. Randall Jarrell called it "a poem which indicates as well as any I can think of Frost's stubborn truthfulness, his willingness to admit both the falseness in the cliché and the falseness in the contradiction of the cliché; if the universe never gives us either a black or a white answer, but only a black-and-white one that is somehow not an answer at all, still its inhuman not-answer exceeds any answer that we human beings could have thought of or wished for."[17] In its beautifully controlled, argumentative compactness, matched by a wonderful spareness and ingenuity, "The Most of It" stands well above the usual run of Frost poems from this period. It is worth noting that Frost decided to sit on this poem, holding it in reserve for a later date. It finally came to light in A Witness Tree (1942). As ever, this habit of holding back poems for a later volume makes it virtually impossible to analyze Frost in terms of his progressive development: he did not, like most poets, grow and shift; rather, like a tree, he added rings.

Meanwhile, J. J. Lankes, the woodcut artist whose illustrations had so greatly enhanced the physical aspect of Frost's books, was allowed to build himself a small shack on the new property for the summer. Lankes needed to get away from his large family for a while to get some work done. But he would have to share the farm with Van Dore—a juxtaposition bound to create sparks. Indeed, the two housesitters did not get along at all. Lankes wrote home to his wife in Virginia, "Just now 3 stonemasons are working, 1 teamster, two plumbers . . . then there is Wade. Altogether not a quiet place. I've been lending a hand . . . unloading stone, doing a little mowing—and such. Frost comes every day (except Sunday—he does not show up at all). He always comes into the studio and work is impossible for all the talk."[18]

Frost spent his usual ten weeks in residence at Amherst early in the year, then spent a month on the road in the late spring, lecturing and reading his poems at college campuses. The crowds everywhere were "large and more than respectful," he noted, as if amazed by his own success. Returning to Shingle Cottage in May, he was eager to enjoy a summer in the out-of-doors. The call of the new farm was irresistible, and he eagerly supervised Van Dore in the planting of five hundred red pine seedlings bought from the state of Vermont for a nominal fee. He helped the younger man transplant young elm and maple trees near the house itself, and worked intermittently with the stone masons. He also spent a good deal of time with Carol at his old farm, often doing errands in town for his son. Lankes records one particularly nice story about going with Frost into Bennington to deliver an order of sweet peas to the Catamount Inn. The doorman curtly told Frost that he was not to enter through the front door but to use the delivery door. Lankes remarked, "I'll bet that particular hostelry never had a guest nearly as important as Frost enter the main gate."[19]

Frost was not, in the late twenties, writing many poems, or many good ones. He was highly conscious of this, and fretted over his lack of productiveness, blaming it on "all the teaching and lecturing I do" and on family troubles. His *Collected Poems* was scheduled for publication in 1930, and he grew more anxious as the months passed, wondering how the critics would regard it. He understood only too well that taste is fickle, and that poets with huge reputations in one decade can pass into oblivion the next. The success of the modernist movement, especially of Eliot and Pound, threatened him. He must also have measured himself against Edna St. Vincent Millay, E. A. Robinson, Vachel Lindsay, Edgar Lee Masters, Carl Sandburg, and dozens of other well-known poets, including Don Marquis, Anna Hempstead Branch, Odell Shepard, and Dana Burnet—all Frost's immediate contemporaries and rivals. If one examines William Bliss Carman's popular *Oxford Book of American Verse* (1927), one sees that Frost is struggling to hold his own with the above names. (An interesting side note is the fact that Wallace Stevens, now regarded as Frost's chief contemporary, was not even represented in Carman's book; it would take at least another two decades for his achievement to be fully recognized.)

As the thirties approached, so did an interest in radical politics. The case of Sacco and Vanzetti had become a focus, and intellectuals rallied around these anarchist-idealists who were to be executed for murder in 1927; among those rushing to support them was Edna St. Vincent Millay, who wrote a famous poem in their defense called "Justice Denied in Massachusetts." Genevieve Taggard, an influential critic and poet and a friend of Frost's, had also joined the Sacco-Vanzetti protest. Frost felt distinctly at odds with his times, and worried that his conservative political ideas would damage his reception as a poet. As ever, he wanted to think of himself as a "lone striker," and could not bear the notion of being associated with any school or "ism." He claimed to loathe socialism, communism, anarchism, and even humanism.

But he understood more than most writers the importance of keeping his name afloat in certain circles, so—with great reservations—he accepted an invitation to lecture at the New School for Social Research. The lectures were scheduled for the first three months of 1931, but Frost worried in advance about sitting cheek-by-jowl with so many leftist intellectuals (he assumed, quite rightly, that the New School was a hotbed of radicals and progressives of one kind or another). In a letter to Frederic G. Melcher, he said: "I'm not afraid of the radicals . . . nor of the Jews. I may be a radical myself and there is a theory that the Scotch were Jews and another that the Yankees were Jews. I am a Scotch Yankee."[20]

Frost was not, like T. S. Eliot or Ezra Pound, a genuine anti-Semite, but he shared the attitudes of his generation of Yankee populists toward both Jews and blacks. He was also suspicious of nearly all foreigners, a prejudice reinforced by his most recent visit to France. Party affiliations just do not apply to Frost, who was neither a Republican nor a Democrat in any consistent or recognizable way. But one cringes to see him making remarks that, by the standards of today, would be judged either racist or anti-Semitic.

On the subject of Frost's prejudices, Peter J. Stanlis is helpful: "You may recall a famous remark that Jonathan Swift says in a letter to Alexander Pope (September 29, 1725): 'I have ever hated all nations, professions, and communities, and all my love is toward individuals: For instance, I hate the tribe of lawyers, but I love Counsellor Such-a-one, and Judge Such-a-one: so with physicians—I will not speak of my own trade—soldiers, English, Scotch, French, and the rest. But principally I hate and detest that animal called man, although I heartily love John, Peter, Thomas, and so forth. This is the system upon which I have governed myself for many years.' I think that Frost is very much like Swift; he loved particulars and disliked abstract categories. This is at heart the basis of his hatred of all sentimental responses to life. It also underscored his belief in self-interest far above claims of social benevolence."[21]

While Frost was not writing poems as regularly as he had when he was younger, his mind now turned powerfully to the art of poetry. He delivered a lecture called "Education by Poetry" to the Alumni Council at Amherst College, on November 15, 1930. It was recorded stenographically, then revised by Frost before publication in the Amherst *Graduates' Quarterly* (February 1931). Based on a lecture he had given at Bryn Mawr College a few years before, it represented Frost's most complete and suggestive statement on the use of poetry to date.

"Poetry begins in trivial metaphors," he says, "pretty metaphors, 'grace' metaphors, and goes on to the profoundest thinking that we have. Poetry provides the one permissible way of saying one thing and meaning another." He cautions his listeners that "unless you have had your proper poetical education in the metaphor, you are not safe anywhere. Because you are not at ease with figurative values: you don't know the metaphor in its strength and its weakness. You don't know how far you may expect to ride it and when it may break down with you. You are not safe in science; you are not safe in history." Interestingly, Frost cannot even talk about metaphor without employing it himself.

Frost believed that the "greatest of all attempts to say one thing in terms of another is the philosophical attempt to say matter in terms of spirit, or spirit in terms of matter." In formulating this, he (consciously or not) is redeploying an aesthetic common to the German Romantics, especially Goethe, who famously wrote: "Whoever has truly grasped the meaning of history will realize in thousands of examples that the materialization of the spirit or the spiritualization of matter never rests, but always breaks out, among prophets, believer, poets, orators, artists, and lovers of art."[22] Frost is not, in his thinking on metaphor, an innovator, but he grapples seriously with ideas and reformulates them in his own Yankee style. His core ideas are, in essence, Romantic—often with an Emersonian tinge, although even here Frost's natural melancholy and resistance to enthusiasm of a certain kind have a darkening effect on his Emersonian streak. Metaphor is, for him, transformative but not a form of religious alchemy holding out a transcendental promise of redemption. Earth is always "the right place for love."

"I have wanted in late years to go further and further in making metaphor the whole of thinking," Frost says. Anticipating what scientists have increasingly been saying about their own discipline, he is convinced that even scientific thinking depends on metaphor. With typical whimsy, he writes:

> The other day we had a visit here, a noted scientist, whose latest word to the world has been that the more accurately you know where a thing is, the less accurately you are able to state how fast it is moving. You can see why that would be so, without going back to Zeno's problem of the arrow's flight. In carrying numbers into the realm of space and at the same time into the realm of time you are mixing metaphors, that is all, and you are in trouble. They won't mix. The two don't go together.

Frost also understands the connection between metaphor and belief: "The person who gets close enough to poetry, he is going to know more about the word *belief* than anybody else knows, even in religion nowadays." He outlines the various forms of belief as *self-belief*, as when a young person is convinced of his own value, even though he has not yet shown it to the world; *love-belief*, as when one has a belief in someone else, and in the relationship that will (one firmly believes) follow from that situation; and *literary-belief*. The latter is what must occur every time a poem or story is written: the author trusts in the thing-to-come, which is "more felt than known."

These three forms of belief, in Frost's argument, are closely related to *God-belief*: "the belief in God is a relationship you enter into with Him to bring about the future," he suggests. Here he comes about as close to stating explicitly his religious feelings as anywhere else in his writing. For him, religion, like art, is an opportunity for belief, a structure that allows the possibility of creation, which begins in emptiness and absence but ends in wholeness and presence.

Frost was at the height of his intellectual powers as 1930 approached, although much of his best work lay behind him. He seemed to know this, which made the reception of his *Collected Poems* so much more vexing. The book collected *him*, and if critics didn't like it, he might have fewer and fewer opportunities to impress them in the future. The situation was made worse by the fact that E. A. Robinson's *Collected Poems* had won a Pulitzer the previous year, and the critics often played Robinson against Frost, sometimes to the detriment of Frost.

He had been seriously upset by some of the reviews of *West-Running Brook*, where the suggestion had been put forward that he was an escapist, a poet out of touch with his times. One critic attacked "Acquainted with the Night," for instance, because of the "one luminary clock" that "proclaimed the time was neither wrong nor right." "Frost evidently believes it is the artist himself that matters and not the time in which he happens to live," this anonymous reviewer wrote.[23] As might be expected, Frost was annoyed by the suggestion that he was out of step, or that he was burying his head in the sand. He regarded his poems as fierce gestures in the direction of sanity, as attempts to wrest a "momentary stay against confusion" from the chaos of life. For him personally, each poem was a victory over depression, anxiety, fear, and sloth.

A number of the early reviews of his *Collected Poems* picked up on the anti-Frost line that had begun to emerge with *West-Running Brook*. In the *New Republic*, Granville Hicks—an important voice in critical circles—maintained that Frost's poetry ran "counter to the consensus of opinion of the critics of all ages as well as to the temper of his own era." He complained that the poems contained "nothing of industrialism" and failed to note the "disruptive effect that scientific hypotheses have had on modern thought." There was no mention of Freud anywhere, or even a sense that Frost had absorbed any Freudian ideas. These apparent blind spots in Frost meant he could not "contribute directly to the unification, in imaginative terms, of our culture. He cannot give us the sense of belonging in the industrial, scientific, Freudian world in which we find ourselves."[24]

Fortunately, a phalanx of supporters, led by Genevieve Taggard in the *New York Herald Tribune*, rose to Frost's defense, seeing in his work "universal experience portrayed concretely, in locality, in Yankee accent."[25] In the end, this capacious book solidified his reputation, appealing to a wide range of readers with varying degrees of critical sophistication. Much to his surprise, he was awarded his second Pulitzer Prize for this collection. And on November 13, he was elected to the American Academy of Arts and Letters, sponsored by Paul Elmer More, Irving Babbitt, and Wilbur Cross (over the objections of Robert Underwood Johnson, who had long disliked Frost and his poetry). This was an important milestone for Frost, who had belonged for many years to the lesser National Institute of Arts and Letters. At last, it seemed, the heights of Parnassus had been scaled.

15

BUILDING SOIL

1931–1934

All experience ever is is confirmation anyway.
—FROST TO THEODORE MORRISON, JUNE 27, 1930

I am just starting to write letters again, letters or anything else, after a long sickness of public life," Frost had explained to Untermeyer in the summer of 1930. "I hardly know my own handwriting. I hardly know myself seated at a desk." Continuing in this meditative vein, he wondered what had become of the years between 1912, when he left for England, and the present. It had all seemed "no very real dream." While awaiting the publication of his *Collected Poems*, he'd said, "I wonder what next. I don't want to raise sheep; I don't want to keep cows; I don't want to be called a farmer." He groused that an acquaintance had recently asked him if he'd written anything in the past two months. "Me! Write anything in two months! It used to take me ten years to write anything." He guessed it would take him twice as long now.[1]

Frost had spent so much time before the public in the past decade, reading and lecturing, that he seemed to have lost track of the inner self that formed poems. It would, as he predicted, be a slow haul to his next slim volume, which would not appear until 1936. In the meantime, Frost would see, if anything, a widening of his role as public poet.

The demands for his presence on platforms around the country seemed only to grow as word of his remarkable performing abilities spread. "If you got wind of a Frost reading, you changed whatever plans you had and went to see him," Richard Eberhart recalled. "I saw him in the late twenties, and again in the early thirties. He seemed to get better each time. He had a way of taking a word and turning it on its head, making witty comments, seizing an old New England saying and making it sound twice as profound as it was. There was always a sparkle in him, an impish quality. It was tremendously charming, and very self-conscious, though nobody minded that. It was a performance, and taken as such."

One of the main stages from now until Frost's death would be Bread Loaf Mountain in Ripton, Vermont. In 1921, Wilfred Davison of Middlebury College had founded the Bread Loaf School of English on the mountain campus of the college, twelve miles from the center of Middlebury itself. Five years later, at Frost's suggestion, the Bread Loaf Writers' Conference had been started by John Farrar, a New York publisher. (Frost once referred to the conference as the Two Weeks Manuscript Sales Fair—a sign that he resented the commercial aspects of the conference, which had been promoted by John Farrar.) Frost's presence on the mountain became a huge part of its attraction to would-be writers, and he would lure to Bread Loaf many of his friends, including Untermeyer, who seemed never far behind whenever Frost appeared somewhere.

Untermeyer had become a student, not only of Frost's verse, but of his lecturing. He declared (somewhat prematurely, in fact) that his friend had long since "overcome the nervousness preliminary to mounting the platform. . . . Feeling his way through a talk until it assumed the shape of an essay, [Frost] could not help enjoying the rapprochement and the response with which audiences enjoyed him. His remarks between the reading of his poems were peppered with epigrams. Some of them found their way into poems; some of them came from fragments of midnight conversations—he was at his voluble best after 11:00 P.M. Others were suggested by letters he had been writing."[2] Untermeyer lists some examples of these nocturnal Frostian epigrams:

I am not an escapist; on the contrary, I am a pursuitist. I would rather cast an idea by implication than cast a ballot.

I am also a separatist. You can't mix things properly until you have separated them, unscrambled them from their original chaotic mixture and held them separate long enough to test their qualities and values.

Sometimes it strikes me that the writers of free verse got their idea from incorrect proof pages.

I am against all the isms as being merely ideas in and out of favor. The latest ideologies are formidable equations that resolve themselves into nothing more startling than that nothing equals nothing.

There are three ages of man: first, when he learns to let go with his hands; second, when he learns to let go with his heart; third, when he learns to let go with his head.

Frost liked to create schemas—an aspect of his love of form; the process was part of his method as a thinker, and this thinking eventually settled into lines of poetry. Increasingly his poems dealt with social themes, and these often went over well with audiences, since they were easy to follow and often amusing. "Departmental," for example, was written in the thirties and remained a favorite at readings. The public liked it, though it was not among Frost's better work. On the other hand, some of his discursive, political poems—"Build Soil," written in 1932, is a good example of this—brought a discursive element into American poetry that had long been missing.

One of the impediments to Frost's progress as a poet was the siege of bad health that would increasingly afflict him and his family throughout the thirties. In October 1930, the Frosts learned that Marjorie had contracted tuberculosis—still a dreaded illness, although contemporary treatments were increasingly effective and offered victims of the disease real hope for recovery. For Marjorie, this diagnosis meant that she must end her nursing studies at Johns Hopkins and go into a sanatorium.

Through the Bartletts, the Frosts heard about the Mesa Verde Sanatorium in Boulder, Colorado. This sanatorium was only a few blocks from the Bartlett home, and John and Margaret willingly took on the responsibility of looking after Marjorie while she was there. Almost coincidentally, Frost had agreed to attend the Rocky Mountain Writers' Conference in Boulder during the following summer.

With Marjorie heavily on their minds, the Frosts moved to Amherst, as usual, for the winter months (when Frost would teach); in April, Elinor returned to South Shaftsbury while her husband "trooped the country as a poet," as she wrote to Edith Fobes. He gave readings and lectures at various institutions, including Wesleyan, Yale, Harvard, Clark, Bates, and Bowdoin. He also delivered the six promised lectures at the New School for Social Research in New York, where he found the audience "more sympathetic and less radical" than he had anticipated. The poet Marianne Moore attended these lectures and in a letter to Ezra Pound called him "one of the best speakers I have ever listened to."[3] This lecture stint was hard on Frost, however, and precipitated a severe case of influenza that kept him in bed for nearly two weeks in May.

Making matters even worse, Lillian was diagnosed with tuberculosis in May. She having been one of Marjorie's closest friends in high school, it seemed like bizarre bad luck that both of them should be stricken by the same disease at the same time. Now Carol became frantic, and he decided that he must take Lillian and Prescott to California, where the weather would improve her health. The journey, by car, would be accomplished in slow stages, with long rest stops along the way so that Lillian would not get overly tired; a visit to Marjorie at Mesa Verde would be part of the itinerary.

As if these problems were not enough to preoccupy the elder Frosts, there was the added fact that Lesley, now living in Montauk, at the farthest point out on Long Island, was pregnant for the second time and unwell. Given the fragility of her marriage, it seemed appropriate for her parents to venture out to Montauk to assist her, or at least to lend moral support. They did so, and found her in considerable pain. Frost wrote to Untermeyer from the Southampton hospital, "I am in no mood to estimate myself or anything I ever did. Lesley is . . . in ineffectual pain and has been for three days now. We don't understand what's the matter."[4] As it turned out, there was nothing terribly wrong, and the child—Lesley Lee Francis—was born without complications on June 20, 1931.

In July, the Frosts visited Marjorie in Colorado. Elinor wrote to Edith Fobes: "Marjorie looks beautiful—she weighs 120 pounds and her skin is clear and firm. It was a most fortunate decision—to bring her here. The doctors think she has had T.B. for eight or ten years, and only six weeks ago the tuberculin test gave a very positive reaction. She intends to stay in this climate another year, at least, though not in the sanatorium. She will board somewhere and take a course at the University."[5]

They took their daughter to Evergreen, a small town in the mountains—some eight thousand feet above sea level, where Frost spent ten days "botanizing" and stretching his lungs. The weather was perfect: fiercely blue skies, the air hot and dry. Frost went off by himself most days, a notebook in his pocket; it was a glorious, if brief, time, and he began work on several new poems.

He could not, however, stay away from his family troubles for long. Elinor was increasingly worried about Lillian and had anxieties about what might become of Carol and Prescott should her daughter-in-law require long-term hospitalization. Her original optimism about Marjorie also proved short-lived; now as she spent time with her daughter, she realized that her health was still extremely shaky. "Why are we so unfortunate?" she asked Edith Fobes in a letter from Evergreen. "I have worked so hard for my family all these years, and now everything seems tumbling around me."[6]

From Colorado, the Frosts ventured to California to see Carol's family; they had arrived, as planned, in San Bernardino. En route, by train, from Denver to Utah, Frost got the idea for "On the Heart's Beginning to Cloud the Mind," one of the often overlooked poems in *A Further Range*. "I was looking out of a train window away out in Utah and way in the night, and I saw one lonely light way off, you know, far from any other all around. I made a whole poem out of that," he later remembered.[7] The poem is written in couplets, a form that sometimes brought out the worst in Frost, perhaps because it forced him into a stance of cuteness as he reached for witty effects. In this poem, however, he manages to avoid posturing and cuteness; he is writing in his most skeptical mood, deriding the common habit of identifying with other people too easily, assuming too much about their motives. This all plays into the general political drift of the poems in A *Further Range*, which if not conservative in tone are distinctly antiliberal. The poet-narrator stares from his train window into the night and sees a light:

> Something I saw or thought I saw
> In the desert at midnight in Utah,
> Looking out of my lower berth
> At moonlight sky and moonlit earth.
> The sky had here and there a star;
> The earth had a single light afar,
> A flickering, human pathetic light,
> That was maintained against the night,
> It seemed to me, by the people there,
> With a God-forsaken brute despair.
> It would flutter and fall in half an hour
> Like the last petal off a flower.

With its thudding tetrameter, the poem mimics the sway of the train. The narrative swerves from the scene set in the above lines, however, moving toward a recognition that one cannot know what is really going on with other people, why they might light a fire or put it out. The heart, with its liberal sentiments (bordering on sentimentalities), was beginning to cloud the mind, where cool reason suggests that you cannot know another person's heart. This theme would preoccupy Frost through the early thirties and dominate the poems of A *Further Range*, some of which can be read as a response to the New Deal, which Frost abhorred.[8]

"The Figure in the Doorway" is another train poem, based on the traveler's observations. But this poem, despite several fetching lines, rarely moves beyond the level of light verse. The train in the poem passes a house with a "great gaunt figure" in a cabin door, and Frost is simply struck by the man's isolation, "The miles and miles he lived from anywhere." But the man's existence was "evidently something he could bear." Frost is guessing about this, of course—letting his own heart cloud his mind.

Frost was clearly struggling to rediscover his way as poet. "The way doesn't get easier," he told Reginald Cook, "only harder to find, what with so much underbrush growing."9 The great temptation, of course, was to repeat himself (and, like most poets, he did plenty of this), but he also felt a need to go beyond what he had done, to explore a further range of thought and feeling.

The Frosts arrived on the West Coast to find Carol and his family staying at the California Hotel in San Bernardino. Carol was searching for a house to rent, and Frost helped him; they soon located a bungalow in Monrovia, near Pasadena, with a view of the San Gabriel Mountains. Carol would plant flowers and vegetables, and Lillian would recuperate there, under the care of a local TB specialist. The rent was cheap ($27.50 per month), and Frost would pay it. He was also paying for all of Marjorie's care back in Colorado, and sending regular checks to Irma, too. It struck him as a particular piece of bad luck that he should have to be supporting his grown children in this fashion, but there was obviously no choice. The need to earn a living for his family, at this late stage, actually spurred him on. He could not simply retreat into depression, old age, lethargy, the shadows. He must get up and do something.

Frost had long been looking forward to returning to his native state. He was especially keen to revisit San Francisco, and he did so eagerly now with Elinor, although she was too unwell to accompany him on his walks. He was quite shocked by the degree of change in the city. In many instances, he could recognize nothing at all on a street that had once been familiar. One place he made sure to visit was the beach below Cliff House, not far from one end of what is now the

Golden Gate Bridge: this was the setting for the poem "Once by the Pacific." He stood looking out to sea on that pebbled beach, and he was overwhelmed by memories of his father and mother, of a lost and irrecoverable world. "You probably shouldn't go back to places you knew when you were younger," he later said after a reading of "Once by the Pacific." "It brings on trouble, strange thoughts, dreams."[10]

Before leaving for New England, the Frosts returned for a couple of final weeks with Carol, Lillian, and Prescott. From there, Elinor explained to Edith Fobes that Carol had rented Stone Cottage "for a year for $500 to people who will probably buy it before the year is over for $8,000." She also noted that "if Lillian is cured he [Carol] may want to buy a small piece of land here. We can spare them $150 a month for at least two years, so they will be all right financially for a while, and I am greatly hoping that she will be well on the road to recovery by the end of two years."[11]

They returned, by train, to South Shaftsbury in mid-September, whereupon Frost immediately set out for another lecture tour that took him from Maine to Philadelphia. He was determined to get his bank account as full as possible, especially now that ill-health was making the lives of his children terribly uncertain.

The grim health of the family, as of February 2, 1932, is suggested by one of Elinor's letters to Mrs. Fobes:

I must tell you about Marjorie and Lillian. Marjorie has been declared by the specialist to be entirely free from the tuberculous "process," and yet—she has twice had a spell of pleurisy—not with *effusion*—since the cold weather came on. She is still in the sanatorium, but has a good many callers, and goes out with friends she has made in the town and the University. She liked Boulder and the Colorado people very much indeed, and has had many kindnesses. . . .

Lillian has not improved as we hoped and expected she would when we left Monrovia. She seemed to gain for a few weeks, then quite suddenly, when some cloudy, damp weather came on, she went downhill very fast, so that her doctors easily

persuaded her to go into a sanatorium and begin the pneumo-
thorax treatment which means deflating her bad lung, you
know, by pumping air into the pleural cavity. There were adhe-
sions from previous scars of T.B. so that it was a little doubtful if
the treatment would be effective. Fortunately, it has been very
successful. From twenty treatments in thirty days, they have
been gradually reduced to one each week, and the coughing has
practically ceased. The doctor gives her every encouragement
that she will live, but it will be a long and expensive fight and
this of course leaves Carol and Prescott bereft. It may be that
after five or six months of sanatorium treatment, she can go to
the house with a practical nurse, and have the treatments there.
I think she probably can. I am hoping though, that she and
Carol will be willing to have me take Prescott for a year. The
California schools are so much superior to ours, that in one way
I would regret taking him out of the best, cheerful school he is
in and bring him east, to our dingy dirty-brick buildings.[12]

Elinor also had to contend with her husband's mania for buying real
estate. He was tired of renting in Amherst, and real estate prices
(because of the Depression) were low. In November, with Elinor's nervous blessing, Frost purchased 15 Sunset Avenue, a substantial Victorian home that had belonged to a former president of Massachusetts
State College. It was by far the grandest house that the Frosts had ever
owned. He had it furnished in Victorian style by a decorator, complete
with horsehair sofas, damask drapes, and an Axminster rug. Whimsically, Frost wrote to Marjorie that he and Elinor were "in possession of
our Big Home and overwhelmed with the responsibilities of taste it
lays upon us."[13]

Much to the surprise of her parents, Marjorie had fallen in love
with a student at the University of Colorado, Willard E. Fraser; Marjorie described him to her father as "a dear, kind, and considerate man,
another real Victorian." Fraser himself wrote to the Frosts to explain
that he was hoping to marry Marjorie and that he planned to become
an archaeologist. Frost was elated, and wrote back, "I am particularly

glad you are bringing archaeology into the family. Archaeology is one of the four things I wanted most to go into in life, archaeology, astronomy, farming, and teaching Latin."[14] The Frosts made immediate plans to visit Colorado and California again the following summer, as soon as Frost dispensed with an obligation to deliver the Phi Beta Kappa poem at Columbia University, from which he would that year receive his ninth honorary degree.

His poem was "Build Soil." To utter aloud this somewhat reactionary poem in this setting at the beginning of the Great Depression took courage. It contained none of the quasi-socialist sympathies current among intellectuals and artists in the United States at the moment. On the contrary, Frost explicitly makes an argument against socialism, or any form of group thinking. The poem is, for me, one of Frost's most successful forays into the realm of political verse. As a format, he chose a well-known pastoral mode, writing in superficial imitation of Virgil's "First Eclogue," which takes the shape of a dialogue between two stock figures: the farmer (Tityrus) and the farmer-poet (Meliboeus). Lest anyone miss the Virgilian echo, Frost adopts their names, though he has them talking in distinctly twentieth-century terms:

> Why, Tityrus! But you've forgotten me.
> I'm Meliboeus the potato man,
> The one you had the talk with, you remember,
> Here on this very campus years ago.
> Hard times have struck me and I'm on the move.

Meliboeus has had to "give [his] interval farm up"—an interval being a New England dialect term for land in a valley (as in the title of Frost's *Mountain Interval*, where the term carries a double meaning, suggesting a pause in a journey as well as a dip in the landscape). He has taken to stony, uphill pastureland, where he can raise sheep. His attitude toward the farmer-poet is ambivalent: "You live by writing / Your poems on a farm and call that farming." Frost's blank verse is fluent and wonderfully simple. As W. H. Auden said of his style, "The music is always that of the speaking voice, quiet and sensible, and I cannot think of any modern poet, except Cavafy, who uses language more simply."[15]

Tityrus (who represents Frost) confesses to being tempted to turn his poetic gifts to politics: "I have half a mind / To take a writing hand in politics." It has, he notes, been done well before. He admits to thinking that the "times seem revolutionary bad."

Meliboeus wonders how bad the times have become, and whether or not they warrant the poet leaving off the traditional themes of poetry for politics—themes such as "love's alternations, joy and grief, / The weather's alternations, summer and winter." Then the talk turns to socialism as a possible solution to the crisis, and Tityrus suggests calmly that "socialism is / An element in any government." But he is against the more general use of "love" as a concept in these political arrangements, as in love of the people. "There is no love" of this general kind, he argues: "There's only love of men and women, love / Of children, love of friends, of men, of God."

The poem meanders through an ingenious, utterly Frostian examination of the concept of freedom. "Everyone asks freedom for himself," Frost muses, "The man free love, the business man free trade, / The writer and talker free speech and free press." Everything, in Frost's view, comes down to self-interest. The argument moves quickly into the concept of greed, which is intimately related to self-interest:

> Greed has been taught a little abnegation
> And shall be more before we're done with it.
> It is just fool enough to think itself
> Self-taught. But our brute snarling and lashing taught it.
> None shall be as ambitious as he can.
> None should be as ingenious as he could.

That is, our "brute snarling and lashing" in the marketplace have brought on greed, which is bad because it ultimately limits ambition and ingenuity—an argument that is highly original and runs against the typical conservative grain.

Indeed, Frost is hardly a typical conservative; he is not, in fact, a conservative in the contemporary sense. He is an agrarian freethinker, a democrat with a small "d," with isolationist and libertarian tendencies. "My friends all know I'm interpersonal," Tityrus says. But long before "I'm interpersonal / Away 'way down inside I'm personal." The poem goes on to talk about national identities:

> Just so before we're international
> We're national and act as nationals.
> The colors are kept unmixed on the palette,
> Or better on dish plates all around the room,
> So the effect when they are mixed on canvas
> May seem almost exclusively designed.
> Some minds are so confounded intermental
> They remind me of pictures on a palette.

Frost had used similar language in his talk to the Amherst Alumni Council, "Education by Poetry," in which he spoke of the internationalists:

I should want to say to anyone like that: "Look! First I want to be a person. And I want you to be a person, and then we can be as interpersonal as you please. . . . But, first, you have got to have the personality. First of all, you have got to have the nations and then they can be as international as they please with each other."

I should like to use another metaphor on them. I want my palette, if I am a painter, I want my palette on my thumb or on my chair, all clean, pure, separate colors. Then I will do the mixing on the canvas. The canvas is where the work of art is, where we make the conquest. But we want the nations all separate, pure, distinct, things as separate as we can make them; and then in our thoughts, in our arts, and so on, we can do what we please about it.

In this period Frost often moved from prose to poetry, formulating his ideas in lectures and letters, then putting them into verse. In fact, much of the central thinking that went into "Build Soil" is found in a letter to Louis Untermeyer that was sent from South Shaftsbury on May 13, 1931. It was headed by a motto from Tennyson's "The Lotos-Eaters": "Courage he said and pointed toward the *land*" (Frost's italics). The letter was written to encourage Untermeyer, who had just purchased a farm in the Adirondacks:

> The land be your strength and refuge. But at the same time I say this so consonant with your own sentiments of the moment, let me utter a word of warning against the land as an affectation. What determines the population of the world is not at all the amount of tillable land it affords: but it is something in the nature of the people themselves that limits the size of the globulate mass they are socially capable of. There is always, there will always be, a lot, many lots of land left out of the system. I dedicate these lots to the stray souls who from incohesiveness feel rarely the need of the forum for their thoughts of the market for their wares and produce. They raise a crop of rye, we'll say. To them it is green manure. They plow it under. They raise a crop of endives in their cellar. They eat it themselves. That is they turn it under. They have an idea. Instead of rushing into print with it, they turn it under to enrich the soil. Out of that idea they have another idea. Still they turn that under. What they finally venture doubtfully to publication with is an idea of an idea of an idea.

There is Frostian brilliance here, an example of the way he can extend metaphor further and further into thought. The essential point of "Build Soil" concerns plowing under the first crops, of letting the land go fallow, of not stripping the soil but enriching it. It makes good sense in both farming and writing, and Frost was perpetually drawn to the figurative alliance between these two arts. Thus, Tityrus condemns those poets who rush into print, just as he chastises those farmers who rush to market:

> More that should be kept back—the soil for instance
> In my opinion,—though we both know poets

> *Who fall all over each other to bring soil*
> *And even subsoil and hardpan to market.*
> *To sell the hay off, let alone the soil,*
> *Is an unpardonable sin in farming.*
> *The moral is, make a late start to market.*

The poem builds to a fine frenzy of oracular didacticism as Tityrus gives his best advice to Meliboeus:

> *You shall go to your run-out mountain farm,*
> *Poor castaway of commerce, and so live*
> *That none shall ever see you come to market—*
> *Not for a long long time. Plant, breed, produce,*
> *But what you raise or grow, why feed it out,*
> *Eat it or plow it under where it stands*
> *To build the soil. For what is more accursed*
> *Than an impoverished soil, pale and metallic?*
> *What cries more to our kind for sympathy?*

"Build Soil" is an Emersonian plea for self-reliance, a quirky caution against excessive reliance on the market economy, a warning about the rush to internationalism, or socialism, or any "ism." It is the lone striker's grand testament. As Frost's Tityrus says at the end:

> *Steal away and stay away.*
> *Don't join too many gangs. Join few if any.*
> *Join the United States and join the family—*
> *But not much in between unless a college.*

Independence of thought, for Frost, goes hand in hand with financial and ideological independence.

Frost actually took his own advice, spending many years, even decades, "plowing it under" and building soil—in Derry, for example, the years when so much was sown and very little reaped or sent to market. He let ideas come, but felt no compulsion to rush into print with

them; he let them play in his head, play on his tongue in endless conversations; he put them into letters, into prose, which formed a kind of
halfway stage between speech and poetry. What reached print was "an
idea of an idea of an idea." When it finally emerged, it was fully formed
and richly developed.

The Frosts left for California soon after he received another honorary
degree, this time from Williams College, on June 20. He had hoped to
duck out of sight for a few months in order to work on his poems, and
California seemed a good place for this. He had few friends or connections there, apart from Carol's family. His son had found him a
house in Monrovia that afforded a majestic view of the mountains—
something Frost always appreciated—and it was within walking distance of Carol's place, so that Elinor could easily move back and forth
between the two houses. A three-month lease was signed. He wrote to
Otto Manthey-Zorn on July 4, 1932, "Here we are just moved into the
fifth house owned or rented by the Frosts in this year of our Independence 157. The question is how independent anyone can be with so
many houses to live in."[16]

En route to California, the Frosts had stopped in Colorado to visit
with Marjorie and meet their prospective son-in-law, Willard Fraser,
for the first time. They had of course already heard a good deal about
him from their daughter, and had corresponded with him. He was "as
good as his letters," Frost observed. A firm bond—one that lasted—
was struck.

Willard was about to leave on an archaeological expedition to
Mexico, where he had previously done research. While he was gone,
Marjorie would go to California to stay with her parents. She planned
to remain there, with Carol and Lillian, for a little while after her parents left, then go to visit Willard's family in Montana before coming
back, ultimately, to the Vermont house for Christmas.

The Frosts made a zigzag journey home in October, stopping for
lectures and readings in various places, including Boulder, Omaha,
and Ann Arbor. The next big event on Frost's schedule was a meeting
with T. S. Eliot at the St. Botolph Club in Boston on November 15.

Eliot was delivering the prestigious Charles Eliot Norton lectures at Harvard, where he was being lionized by faculty and students. At the St. Botolph Club meeting that Frost attended, he addressed a small circle of younger admirers (many of them poets, including Robert Hillyer and John Brooks Wheelwright). Asked to read a poem at one point, Eliot agreed, on the condition that Frost also read one. Frost agreed, but said he would have to write one on the spot while Eliot recited his. He immediately took out a small notebook and began to scribble. Eliot was confused but went ahead with a recital of "The Hippopotamus." When Frost's turn came, he read "My Olympic Record Stride," a poem actually written some months before in California and memorized (indeed, Frost had recited it from memory to an audience a few weeks before, so it was fresh in his mind). He pretended to improvise the last stanza on the spot. There was dutiful applause, and nobody but Frost seemed to understand—or appreciate—the joke.

Christmas in Vermont was a dismal affair. Marjorie was there, with Irma and her husband, John, and their son, Jacky. Everyone except Elinor came down with the flu, and poor Elinor was run ragged looking after them. Frost himself took to his bed, though he joined everyone for meals, where much of the conversation centered on Marjorie's upcoming wedding in the summer. It would take another month or so before it was finally agreed that Billings, Montana—Willard's hometown—was the appropriate setting. (Frost himself did not like family ceremonies, and was relieved to have the occasion off his and Elinor's shoulders.)

After the New Year, the Frosts returned to their home in Amherst. Frost plunged into teaching, then in April set off for the usual round of readings and lectures. On May 31, 1933, Elinor wrote to Richard Thornton:

We are still in Amherst. We have lingered here because of Robert's health. Two days after he was in New York, he came down with a bad cold. It was a queer cold, with a temperature, and has been followed by a prolonged period of temperature and prostration. He has very little appetite, and is intensely nervous.

The doctor is watching him, with tuberculosis in mind, and advises absolute quiet for an indefinite period, that is, an avoidance of whatever might be a physical or nervous strain. He stays in bed until dinner time, and then dresses and wanders around the house, and if it is sunny, sits a little while outdoors.[17]

One is amazed by the endless succession of illnesses recorded by Elinor, month after month. These bouts of flu may have been related to the depression that Frost was always, on some level, fending off. Elinor often notes in her letters that "Robert has taken to his bed," with or without obvious cause. He went through prolonged periods when he could not teach, or travel, or write.

Frost barely made it through the wedding in Montana, which took place in June, and spent much of the summer ailing. He found himself short of breath, easily tired, and prone to fevers and racking coughs. The suspicion arose that he might have contracted tuberculosis, an old fear that seems never to have left him. His doctor in South Shaftsbury suggested that he think about spending the winters in a warm climate, such as Florida. (In later years, Frost would in fact follow this advice, eventually buying a place in South Miami.) The current illness was exacerbated by his annual bout with hay fever. All previously arranged readings and lectures were canceled in the late summer and early fall of 1933.

One of the few good things to come out of this period was the poem "Desert Places," which Frost claimed (as usual) to have written straight through from beginning to end "without fumbling a sentence."[18] The poem opens with a breathless moment of realization:

> *Snow falling and night falling fast, oh, fast*
> *In a field I looked into going past.*
> *And the ground almost covered smooth in snow,*
> *But a few weeds and stubble showing last.*

Frost notes that the "animals are smothered in their lairs," a striking image of claustrophobic despair. Then he goes on, shockingly:

> *I am too absent-spirited to count;*
> *The loneliness includes me unawares.*

It would be hard to overpraise the stark brilliance of the last line above, with its suggestion of the mingling of interior and exterior realities. The snow-covered landscape, so muffled and blank, mirrors an inner feeling of isolation and spiritual poverty:

> *And lonely as it is that loneliness*
> *Will be more lonely ere it will be less—*
> *A blanker whiteness of benighted snow*
> *With no expression, nothing to express.*

For equal severity, one would have to turn to Gerard Manley Hopkins's so-called Terrible Sonnets, especially the one that opens: "No worst, there is none. Pitched past pitch of grief, / More pangs will, schooled at forepangs, wilder wring." Like Hopkins, Frost would sink into a deep melancholy, then cast his thoughts upon the landscape around him, finding in that external reality a corresponding vision of bleakness.

The poet in "Desert Places" looks up at the stars and says: "They cannot scare me with their empty spaces / Between stars," alluding to Pascal, who spoke of the "infinite silent spaces between the stars." In the chilling final couplet, Frost concludes: "I have it in me so much nearer home / To scare myself with my own desert places."

"Provide, Provide," which Randall Jarrell has justly called "an immortal masterpiece," was also written during this dark time. One cannot imagine a less sentimental, wiser poem, or one that makes such an expedient, minimalist suggestion about how we should live our lives. The poem is, at once, a wry commentary on Roosevelt's New Deal (and its bureaucracy) and a paean to self-sufficiency; it opens with an allusion to Abishag, who is mentioned in 1 Kings 1:3 as a beautiful Shunammite maiden who came to attend the dying King David. But Abishag is now "the withered hag," and is pictured washing the steps "with pail and rag." All beauty fades. As Frost notes: "Too many fall from great and good / For you to doubt the likelihood."

The poem is written in strong, four-beat (tetrameter) rhyming triplets, with "plenty of tune," as Frost said before reading it at Bread Loaf one summer. The poet advises people to die early and "avoid the fate" of Abishag or, if you must die late, "Make up your mind to die in state." With breathtaking cynicism, he says, "Make the whole stock exchange your own! / If need be occupy a throne, / Where nobody can call *you* crone." The last three stanzas are among Frost's most compressed and startling:

> *Some have relied on what they knew,*
> *Others on being simply true.*
> *What worked for them might work for you.*
>
> *No memory of having starred*
> *Atones for later disregard*
> *Or keeps the end from being hard.*
>
> *Better to go down dignified*
> *With boughten friendship at your side*
> *Than none at all. Provide, provide!*

In other words, provide for yourself (rather than let somebody else provide for you—and probably provide something you do not really want). You cannot rely on memory of past stardom or success; these simply do not help. Rely on experience, or your sense of truth, if you can.

Frost's poetry in the early thirties ran deeply against the grain of what was being said and written in intellectual circles, as Stanley Burnshaw says in *Robert Frost Himself.* Burnshaw notes that people were often overheard talking about "where Frost stood" with regard to the current political scene. They were aware he was not a leftist or a liberal, but they found him difficult to read. "No poet alive could be more elusive," Burnshaw says, "though we granted from all that was argued about 'Build Soil' that Frost's views were not our views and his faith—whatever it was—differed from ours. And in terms of political practice and program, we were probably on opposing sides."[19]

By "we" Burnshaw refers to that group of urban intellectuals who

subscribed to such journals as the weekly *New Masses*, which Burnshaw edited. Oddly enough, Burnshaw and Frost became good friends,
which suggests that Frost was not prickly about the politics of those
around him; he was quite happy to surround himself with people who
thought differently from himself. (Untermeyer, for instance, was a
man of the left—and he was Frost's closest intellectual companion
through much of his adult life.)

Two other major poems of this period were "Neither Out Far nor In
Deep," which had actually been written a year earlier, in California,
and was revised for publication in the fall of 1933, and "Two Tramps in
Mud Time," which has long been a favorite of anthologists. The latter
was based on an incident that happened several years before on the
farm in Franconia. The poem has an almost mythic opening:

> Out of the mud two strangers came
> And caught me splitting wood in the yard.
> And one of them put me off my aim
> By hailing cheerily "Hit them hard!"
> I knew pretty well why he dropped behind
> And let the other go on a way.
> I knew pretty well what he had in mind:
> He wanted to take my job for pay.

These were stressful economic times, and tramps were everywhere—
honest men, mostly, in search of a meager living. Frost's narrator, as
the second stanza makes clear, is enjoying his work: "every piece I
squarely hit / Fell splinterless as a cloven rock." Few poets in the history of English verse have written so well about work, or the pleasure
of doing physical chores.

"The sun was warm but the wind was chill," he writes in the third
stanza, describing with freshness and particularity the feel of a volatile
April day in northern New England, when you hover between March
and May, depending on the wind and sun. The narrator notes that the
mere fact of these two tramps showing up and wanting his job makes
him enjoy the job even more. He does not want to relinquish it, even

though he knows he should. The penultimate stanza puts the matter frankly: "My right [to work] might be love but theirs was need." And when it came down to love against need, "Theirs was the better right—agreed."

Agreed. That's the final political or moral point. But Frost's speaker in the poem cannot leave off there. He concludes:

> *But yield who will to their separation,*
> *My object in living is to unite*
> *My avocation and my vocation*
> *As my two eyes make one in sight.*
> *Only where love and need are one,*
> *And the work is play for mortal stakes,*
> *Is the deed ever really done*
> *For Heaven and the future's sakes.*

"I am philosophically opposed to having one Iseult for my vocation and another for my avocation," Frost said, echoing his poem, in a letter to R. P. T. Coffin.[20] As usual, the poet takes away with one hand what he has given with the other, suggesting that, with his head, he knows that need overrides love in situations such as that posed in this poem. Yet he refuses to let it rest there. He wants to make a generalization about how, ideally, "love and need are one," even though the concrete situation of the poem seems to contradict this notion. As always in Frost's best work, various levels of argument swirl below the surface. It is pointless to complain, as Malcolm Cowley does, that the speaker in the poem should have offered these homeless men some other work if he was too selfish to give up the chopping himself.[21]

If the poem is based on a real incident (as Frost suggested it was), he may well have offered the men work. Nevertheless, the literal truth of any poem is subordinate to its imaginative truth, so it becomes pointless to worry about what "did" or "didn't" happen. "You never know where a poem comes from," Frost said, "but where it's gone, that you can tell. You can see the tail, the trace of the comet, after it's gone."[22]

. . .

Marjorie was expecting a baby in March, so Elinor set out alone in February to be with her during the final weeks before the birth. She left her husband to his teaching duties at Amherst, though she was uneasy about his weakened condition. He did, however, seem better now, and had resumed his regular level of activity. The baby was born on March 16, a daughter called Marjorie Robin Fraser, and two weeks later Elinor rushed back to Amherst because Frost appeared to have suffered a relapse. He was coughing again, and had taken to his bed with a fever.

But Elinor was no sooner home than word came that Marjorie had taken a bad turn. She had come down with puerperal fever, as a complication of childbirth, and was delirious. As soon as they could, the Frosts went together back to Billings, to Marjorie's side. Six weeks later, the doctors suggested that Marjorie be flown by private plane to the Mayo Clinic in Rochester, Minnesota. Puerperal fever was often fatal, but doctors at the Mayo Clinic had recently developed some new and promising treatments. It was Marjorie's best hope for survival, and Frost decided to spare no expense. They were themselves driven to the clinic by Willard, while the baby was left in the care of a nurse.

It was all to no avail, however, and Marjorie died on May 2, 1934. "I told you by telegram what was hanging over us," Frost wrote to Untermeyer. "So you know what to expect. Well, the blow has fallen. The noblest of us all is dead and has taken our hearts out of the world with her."[23] In a similar vein, Elinor wrote to Edith Fobes, "Poor darling child—it seems too heart-breaking, that after achieving good health, and finding perfect happiness in life, she had to lose it all so soon."[24] The family now entered a period of dark, seemingly endless, mourning.

16

HIS OWN
STRATEGIC RETREAT
1935–1938

*I should hate to spend the only life I was going to have here
in being annoyed with the time I happened to live in.*

—FROST, NOTEBOOK ENTRY, 1935

The strain of Marjorie's death took its toll in many different ways.
For a start, Willard Fraser was devasted, and was at first unable to
look after baby Robin by himself. He was helped in the painful summer after his wife's death by Lillian, who had made a remarkably
strong recovery from tuberculosis. Elinor, too, pitched in, but this put
so much extra strain on her that she suffered a serious heart attack in
November. Frost thought, briefly, that he had lost his wife. He was, he
told Untermeyer, "all fear for Elinor."

His own pulmonary problems continued, with repeated bouts of
coughing and fevers. The Frosts decided to follow their doctor's
orders and go to Florida in December with Lillian, Carol, and
Prescott. The elder Frosts traveled by train to Key West, followed by
Carol's family in their car. In those days, Key West was an isolated,
untrendy place, a nearly tropical island that had recently lost almost
half its population when the cigar business, which had been its chief
industry, moved to Tampa. It was still, as Frost noted, "fairly dense
with population, equal parts Negro, Cuban, and American."[1] The
island was, by comparison with the mainland, primitive, with no

public sewers or running water, and few amenities. Key West's most famous resident was Ernest Hemingway, although Frost did not run into him.

Frost did, however, run into Wallace Stevens, who was staying at a nearby hotel, the Casa Marina. Stevens and Frost had never met, but they encountered each other several times now, and Stevens invited Frost to have dinner one night at the hotel with himself and a well-known southern judge, Arthur Powell, a friend of Stevens's. Frost was mildly suspicious of Stevens, who was vice president of an insurance company in Hartford and every inch a country club man. John Bartlett later recalled Frost's account of this meeting, which was doubtless exaggerated for effect: "[Frost] told a story of an evening, much of a night, spent in Florida with a New Englander, vice-president of a big Connecticut insurance company, but also a poet—kept the two lives absolutely separate. . . . The vice-president-poet drank heavily at dinner, offended by making passes at the waitresses, and in the hotel room was very drunk. He would order the judge to tell the same story over and over again."[2] Frost apparently enjoyed telling this story, and word eventually got back to Stevens, who was displeased. Some notes were exchanged between them, concluding the following summer with this from Frost:

It relieves me to know that you haven't minded my public levity about our great talk in Key West. I'm never so serious as when playful. I was in a better condition than you to appreciate that talk. I shall treasure the memory of it. Take it from me there was no conflict at all, but the prettiest kind of stand-off. You and I and the judge found we liked one another, I think. And you and I really like each other's works. At least down underneath I suspect we do. We should. We must. If I'm somewhat academic (I'm more agricultural) and you are somewhat executive, so much the better: it is so we are saved from being literary and deployers of words derived from words. Our poetry comes choppy, in well-separated poems, well interrupted by time, sleep, and events. Hurrah for us in private![3]

Stevens himself put the matter like this to Harriet Monroe: "I have only recently returned to the office after a visit to Key West. Robert Frost was spending the winter there. We had a number of pleasant meetings, after which I invited him to come to dinner one evening. It so happened that on the afternoon of that day Judge Powell and I were giving a cocktail party. The cocktail party, the dinner with Frost, and several other things became all mixed up, and I imagine that Frost has been purifying himself by various exorcisms ever since. However, it was nice to meet him, particularly since he was a classmate of mine at college, although we did not know each other at Cambridge."[4]

While in Key West, Frost occupied himself by writing an introduction to Sarah Cleghorn's autobiography (she was a Vermont neighbor). Cleghorn was a reform-minded progressive thinker—thus antithetical to Frost—but he liked her personally and, as usual, threw his support behind his friends regardless of their political leanings. His own politics were of course distinctly conservative in character, although with a quirkiness that made it difficult to place him. The truth was, he was merely annoyed by the politics of the present. "Only dull clods live in the present," he scribbled in his notebook in Key West. "They alone have the nerves to stand the impact of things."[5]

That winter, Key West had become one of Roosevelt's pet projects for emergency relief. In fact, two-thirds of the island was currently on relief, and the local government was in bankruptcy. Municipal authority temporarily lay with the Florida Emergency Relief Administration. Frost was distressed by what he saw and considered the town a "safe place for slackers." He wrote to Otto Manthey-Zorn: "So help me I didn't know the safety I was getting into in coming to Key West. Elinor will absolve me of having got her involved more or less personally in the New Deal on purpose. But it is a portentous fact that I have brought her to the pet salvation project of her President and mine. It's the damnedest joke yet."[6]

Frost's response to the political situation is seen in the poetry he wrote this winter in Key West. "A Drumlin Woodchuck" and "Departmental" were begun there, and both reflect (however indirectly) Frost's current political concerns. While "Departmental" is extremely light, and seems to make no real point except to chide bureaucratic efficiency, "A Drumlin Woodchuck" can be taken on many levels as a poem about Frost's own "strategic retreat" from national politics. The poem (which takes up in a public way a theme treated more personally in "The Ovenbird" some years before) comes from the mouth of a woodchuck (which is also a colloquial way of referring to a local person in Vermont) who lives in an oval hill that has been carved out by glacial drifting (a "drumlin"). "My own strategic retreat," the animal says, "Is where two rocks almost meet, / And still more secure and snug, / A two-door burrow I dug."

As a political loner, Frost worried about being attacked, and the drumlin woodchuck seems just as concerned about protecting himself from his enemies, although he "shrewdly pretends / That he and the world are friends." But he and the world are not friends, or so the poet implies. The woodchuck is endlessly alert, ready to attack if necessary, but preferring to retreat, to protect his flanks. "We take occasion to think," says the clever woodchuck:

> And if after the hunt goes past
> And the double-barreled blast
> (Like war and pestilence
> And the loss of common sense),
>
> If I can with confidence say
> That still for another day,
> Or even another year,
> I will be there for you, my dear,
>
> It will be because, though small
> As measured against the All,
> I have been so instinctively thorough
> About my crevice and burrow.

The roots of Frost's idiosyncratic politics are nicely exposed here. What motivated him, and engendered his stance of embattlement, was the need to take care of himself, and his own, and to protect his independence in a time when the government threatened to deprive him, and his fellow-countrymen, of it. The self-protectiveness arose from a fear of survival, and he regarded this as common sense. "I keep my head down most of the time," Frost once told an audience, "like a woodchuck. I keep to my hole. I play it safe." And he did, most of the time, keeping two rocks behind him and escape routes at either end of his hole.

Elinor felt exhausted during their time in Key West, and the good weather helped only a little. Her heart seemed to race whenever she climbed stairs, and she became dizzy whenever she attempted to clean the house or cook. She wrote to Natalie Davison, the wife of Edward Davison, on February 8: "I do not seem to gain much strength. When I try to do anything, my arms are as heavy as lead, and if I overdo it at all, I begin to tremble all over."[7]

Because of Elinor's illness, Frost did not teach as planned during the late winter at Amherst; he had written to Stanley King, the current president of the college, to explain his inability to perform his usual duties, and King had been fully sympathetic; when Frost returned to Amherst in April from Key West, however, he plunged into a series of public readings and lectures at the college to compensate for his absence. These occasions were widely attended by students and faculty, and reporters from both the student and town newspapers gave detailed accounts of the poet's manner, which delighted the audiences: "The character, wit, and chatty informal style" of the poet was noted. In his usual manner, he digressed eagerly as "the muse led him in unexpected directions." In one lecture, he attacked "the modern way of writing poetry," detecting the baleful influence of Ezra Pound, who encouraged his followers to "seek originality by subtracting meter and meaning from their work." When he ventured into politics, as he would often do, he could never resist making jabs at the current mania for utopian thinking. "There are too many things to be done before Utopia can be attained," he said in his final lecture, which was held during commencement week in the college chapel, "yet writers from Plato to [Herbert] Spencer and ever later have crusaded in this seemingly hopeless cause."[8]

Soon after his return to the farm in South Shaftsbury that summer, Frost began work on an unusual assignment: to write an introduction to *King Jasper*, a posthumous volume of poems by his old (but never close) friend E. A. Robinson, who had only recently died. He and Frost had gotten on well in the past few years, although they rarely saw each other. Robinson made no secret of his admiration for Frost, and this softened Frost toward the man whom he often regarded as his chief rival; he agreed to write the introduction in part because it was a good opportunity for him to put a word in for the kind of poetry he himself wrote.

The introduction became a platform for Frost to air many of his pet peeves. "It may come to the notice of posterity (and then again it may not) that this our age ran wild in the quest of new ways to be new," he complained. He rehashed a number of the themes that had been raised in his Amherst lectures a few weeks before. Poets had vainly attempted to seem original by omitting punctuation, capital letters, metrics, images, and so forth. They had eliminated "phrase, epigram, coherence, logic, and consistency." But to what end? Where was the real originality in all of this?

In a moving turn, Frost wrote, "The utmost ambition is to lodge a few poems where they will be hard to get rid of, to lodge a few irreducible bits, where Robinson lodged more than his share." He added, beautifully, "The style is the man. Rather say the style is the way the man takes himself; and to be at all charming or even bearable, the way is almost rigidly prescribed. If it is with outer seriousness, it must be with inner humor. If it is with outer humor, it must be with inner seriousness. Neither one alone without the other under it will do."

The Frosts traveled west in July to visit Marjorie's grave and to see both Willard and the baby. It was a painful journey, but Frost distracted himself by putting in an appearance at the Rocky Mountain Writers' Conference, which was now directed by Edward Davison, his old friend. (Davison still hoped one day to write Frost's biography, although Frost was now cooperating with Robert S. Newdick of Ohio State University, who had been working assiduously on a biography of

Frost since 1935—a project interrupted by Newdick's untimely death in 1939.) One gets a sense of the mood of the Colorado visit from the recollections of Margaret B. Anderson, the daughter of John and Margaret Bartlett:

> We were barely settled in our Pine Street house when Rob and Elinor came for the Writers' Conference again. It was the first time since Marjorie's death that John had seen them, and Willard came down from Billings with Robin, his mother, and brother Jack. Robin had spent some time in the East with Carol and Lillian, but the tearing of the emotions, shifting her back and forth, was too much for the family to bear. Rob decided it was better to have her brought up in Montana with Willard and her grandmother. The Frasers stayed with us, Rob and Elinor at the Boulderado Hotel.
>
> I remember sitting on the bench under our apple tree talking to Elinor. Her voice was quiet, her eyes tearful, but without tears. In her hands she clutched a ball of a handkerchief and an abused pack of cigarettes. She seemed cool, distant, and her smile was only a remote suggestion, as if she meant "some other time, not now."
>
> But Rob, John noted as soon as he greeted the Frosts at the station in Denver, looked fresh, vigorous, and happy, "never more so."[9]

Among those on the faculty at the Writers' Conference was Robert Penn Warren, who gave a lecture entitled "The Recent Southern Novel," which Frost attended. Warren recalled, "He was unhappy with my subject. The novel did not interest him, and the Southern novel least of all. He couldn't read Faulkner, he said. Never read much fiction, except when his students wrote it." It pleased Frost, however, that so many students and people from the community were eager to meet him. Warren said that "he gave a series of lectures on poetry that were held in the largest auditorium at the University, and the hall was jammed. People stood up and down the aisles. Frost was never more winning: his humor fresh, funny. His manner was engaging. He read his poems with a deep, grainy voice, sometimes twice. He'd say, 'I'll say that one again, in case you missed it the first time around.' "

Warren found Frost highly sympathetic. "He was genuinely appreciative of other writers. He had an interest in the Southern Agrarians, and he called himself a Yankee Agrarian."[10] Indeed, Frost had much in common with that school of southern intellectuals identified with the Southern Agrarians, who were essentially anti-industrialists, believers in agriculture as the basis for culture. Their conservatism also applied to the natural world, which they wished to preserve from the ravages of commercialism, creeping suburbia, and the kind of mindless growth that had ruined so much of the industrial north in the late nineteenth and early twentieth centuries. In their famous manifesto of 1930, *I'll Take My Stand*, a dozen leading Agrarians defined their movement. Donald Davidson wrote that "the making of an industrialized society will extinguish the meaning of the arts, as humanity has known them in the past, by changing the conditions of life that have given art a meaning. For they have been produced in societies which were for the most part stable, religious, and agrarian; where the goodness of life was measured by a scale of values having little to do with the material values of industrialism; where men were never too far removed from nature to forget that the chief subject of art, in the final sense, is nature."[11]

One of the doctrines that the Agrarians, like Frost, disliked intensely was the idea of progress. "The concept of Progress," wrote John Crowe Ransom, "is the concept of man's increasing command, and eventually perfect command, over the forces of nature; a concept which enhances too readily our conceit, and brutalizes our life. I believe there is possible no deep sense of beauty, no heroism of conduct, and no sublimity of religion, which is not informed by the humble sense of man's precarious position in the universe."[12] This might well have been written by Frost; as Warren said, "Frost's lectures in Colorado were deeply in harmony with what the Southern Agrarians were saying, although he put everything in his own very personal and memorable way, usually playing concepts off one another, pairing them and switching them. His performances were occasions for wit, playful, although marked by an underlying seriousness."

One of the things that the Southern Agrarians emphasized was that a society as a whole must be disciplined, regulated according to established principles. Frost strongly concurred; he wrote in his notebooks that summer, "I heard a false progressive say that self-discipline was the only discipline, and I was tempted to say that he who has had only *self*-discipline knows no discipline at all."[13] In his usual wayward, self-deconstructing manner, Frost added: "One of the hardest disciplines is having to learn the meaningless," by which he apparently meant the meaninglessness of life, that sense of a universe without design or obvious purpose.

After the Colorado conference, the Frosts traveled with the Bartletts to New Mexico, where the poet Witter Bynner presided over a local poetry group in Santa Fe. Frost had always admired Bynner from a distance, as a poet and cultural force, although he knew that Bynner was headstrong and prickly. He nevertheless agreed to speak to the group. It was both an occasion for him to see the famous Pueblo Indian ruins and an opportunity to forge an alliance with Bynner. The day the Frosts went to visit the Pueblo site, however, was also the day that Bynner had arranged a large lunch for Frost at his home.

Frost arrived late, annoying Bynner from the outset. A tense discussion soon followed over a recent book of poetry by Horatio Colony, one of Bynner's Harvard classmates. The book was full of thinly veiled celebrations of homosexuality—a subject that Frost found distasteful. Bynner praised the book as one of the best things he had read since first encountering A. E. Housman (another poet whose work had a vivid strain of homoeroticism). This comment insulted Frost, and in his impish vein he pretended that he, too, was a great admirer of Colony's book; indeed, he asked to read one of his favorite poems aloud. Bynner was briefly deceived and passed the book to Frost, who read an obviously charged passage in which the implications of the poem were clear. Frost then teased Bynner by saying he was "too young and innocent to understand such verse." Seeing that he had been had, Bynner exploded, pouring a whole mug of beer over Frost's snowy head. Far from recoiling, Frost actually enjoyed Bynner's outburst and remained calm and smiling; he had made his point and provoked a scene. As a friend later remarked, "Robert took great pleasure in setting the cat among the pigeons. He was childlike in this, not really malicious, although sometimes the situation would get out of hand."[14]

After reading his poems to a huge audience in Santa Fe, Frost returned to South Shaftsbury, where he began to think about a new book of poems. Thus far, he had put little attention on this subject. Fugitive poems had appeared here and there, but he had not been thinking about the poems in relation to one another. "Two Tramps in Mud Time" had recently been published in the *Saturday Review of Literature*, "On the Heart's Beginning to Cloud the Mind" came out in *Scribner's Magazine*, and "Desert Places" appeared in the *American Mercury*; there were also numerous poems in various degrees of revision. Frost was suddenly quite astonished by how much finished work he had in hand. Since his last collection was published in 1928, it was certainly time for a new book.

Frost spent much of the fall pulling together poems and sending them out to editors at magazines. The fruits of these efforts would emerge throughout 1936, when approximately half of the poems from *A Further Range* appeared in major periodicals, including "A Blue Ribbon at Amesbury," "A Record Stride," "A Drumlin Woodchuck," and "A Roadside Stand" in the *Atlantic Monthly*, "The White-Tailed Hornet," "The Master Speed," "Voice Ways," and "Departmental" in the *Yale Review*, "In Time of Cloudburst" and "The Figure in the Doorway" in the *Virginia Quarterly*, "At Woodward's Gardens" and several sections from the aphoristic sequence called "Ten Mills" in *Poetry*, and "The Strong Are Saying Nothing" in the *American Mercury*. "You see, I have to keep reminding them I'm here," Frost told Untermeyer coyly.

The Frosts were still grieving for Marjorie throughout the fall, and they stayed close to home until obligations drew them to such disparate places as Rockford, Illinois (where Lesley was now teaching in the Department of English), and Decatur, Georgia. In Georgia, he read his poems on November 7, 1935, at Agnes Scott College for the sum of five hundred dollars—enormous for a poetry reading in the middle of the Depression. Frost was, in fact, so favorably impressed by Agnes

Scott College that he would visit that college nineteen more times, the last in 1962. (Another draw was Emma May Laney, a faculty member at Agnes Scott whom he liked a great deal.)

Elinor found it much harder than her husband to recover her balance, and she began to experience chest pains in October that seemed, to her doctor, more ominous than the previous ones. He urged her to go south again for the winter, and Frost agreed. Having recently fallen prey to another bout of influenza upon returning from Georgia, he could not face the prospect of a bitterly cold winter in Amherst. He wrote to President King to explain the situation, and King was (as usual) sympathetic—even though there was some resistance to Frost on the faculty, a small number of whom felt that he was getting a substantial salary for no work. For the most part, however, there was general support for Frost at Amherst.

Just after Christmas, the Frosts set off for Miami, where they rented a house in nearby Coconut Grove. An invitation to participate in the Winter Institute of Literature at the University of Miami had come, and Frost thought that some minor affiliation would be useful. He agreed to give a reading and a talk, and to meet some of the local writers. But despite the change of climate, he was soon ill, and he spent much of January in bed with a fever and cold. Elinor was forced to look after him, although her own health was hardly resplendent. One cannot help but think that Frost often took advantage of his wife— indeed, he would say as much himself in later years.

Frost had recently agreed to return in March to give the Charles Eliot Norton lectures at Harvard—a major honor, and something that he could not turn down, especially coming from one of his own undergraduate colleges. He was asked to deliver six public lectures that Harvard's press would publish afterward. Frost was hesitant about the latter part of the deal; he customarily lectured without notes, speaking from the top of his head, and it would be an unusual chore to have to write out the lectures. He decided that the only way he could manage was for a stenographer to take down his talks, which he could then rework into printable shape.

He was also invited to read a Phi Beta Kappa poem at Harvard in the following autumn, as part of its tercentenary celebration. He accepted again, but was not happy about writing a poem to order. As Elinor put it, "he hates to know that he *must* write."[15] Having to produce something at someone's request took the mystery out of it, and he liked, even required, that mystery to produce decent work. "You don't know when a poem will come, or from where," he said. "And that's a good thing. A poet doesn't want to know too much, not while he's writing anyway. The knowing can come later."[16]

By now, Frost had acquired a fairly complete picture of himself; that is, he understood the complex nature of his evolving self-portrait. In March, he wrote to Sidney Cox, "You have to remember I'm a family man, a professor, a farmer, a lecturer, a contributor to magazines, a publisher's author, and a diner-out when I am where they have dinners. I am also as I forgot to say a resorter northward for hay fever and southward for influenza. I think I keep my head pretty well in all this for such an old slow coach."[17]

The Norton lectures began on March 4, when Frost addressed a crowd of more than a thousand students, faculty members, and others. His talk in the New Lecture Hall, "The Old Way to Be New," was the first in a series of lectures generally titled "The Renewal of Words." According to one listener, he "seemed to make it up as he went along, although it was obviously well planned."[18] Frost was at the height of his form as a performer, able to summon phrases that had been gathering on his tongue for decades. He could illustrate points with his own poems or draw on countless others from his favorite poets, often reciting lines from memory. Indeed, Frost had memorized countless poems, in Latin and English.

His familiar brand of raw Yankee humor went down well, and he looked every inch a bard: whitish-gray hair flying in wisps, blue eyes piercing, squinting. His body was thickset, sturdy. His voice was deep, the accent perfectly rural—an act he had long ago mastered. His continuous flow of aphorisms had about them the quality of folk sayings.

Among the enthusiastic audience that night were Harvard President James Bryant Conant and his wife, who found the performance electrifying. Conant invited the Frosts to dinner the following week, and Frost was convinced that Harvard would soon offer him a professorship. Unfortunately, there were extreme political differences between Conant and Frost, and this emerged at the dinner. Frost, at the table, denounced Roosevelt at length, and Conant responded curtly to the poet, "You have a bitter tongue."

In Florida some months before, Frost had met Bernard DeVoto, a Harvard tutor and novelist-critic. DeVoto now devoted himself to the poet, helping him find somewhere to live in Cambridge and introducing him to the Harvard community. (DeVoto, whose lack of a doctorate made him an unlikely candidate for a permanent job at Harvard, would soon leave to edit the *Saturday Review of Literature*.)

An older acquaintance, Theodore Morrison, was also on the faculty, and Frost often dined with him and his wife, Kathleen (known as Kay). Morrison was now running the Bread Loaf Writers' Conference, and Frost had often seen him in recent summers. The Morrisons realized that Harvard was not going to play host to Frost in a proper way, so they held a reception for him at their home on Mason Street after five of the six lectures. This gesture cemented a relationship that would become crucial for Frost in his later years.

Kay Morrison, formerly Kay Johnston, had been an undergraduate at Bryn Mawr, where she'd served as editor in chief of the student newspaper. She had first met Frost in 1918, and had invited him to lecture there in 1920, during her senior year.[19] Since then, she and Frost had remained vaguely in touch; now, the friendship blossomed. Kay was beautiful, charming, and sophisticated in a way that Frost had rarely seen in a woman. She was strikingly independent as well, a "woman of tremendous vitality and strong views, who could hold her own with Frost. She didn't let him get away with anything, but was always attentive, respectful. He liked the independence in her, and encouraged her to speak her mind."[20] It is worth noting that Frost found Kay's independence appealing—unusual for this time. She may well, in this regard, have reminded him of Elinor, who always maintained a certain emotional separateness from her husband, even though she observed the traditional role of subservience in public.

Frost had come ahead of Elinor from Florida, but Elinor soon followed. She had not been well throughout the winter, and there was no evidence of improvement in her health—a fact that worried Frost. "A

bad cold had housed her for the first weeks [of Frost's Norton presenta-
tions]," recalled Kay Morrison, "but even in the succeeding ones she
followed her established pattern of not going to [her husband's] lecture
but waiting up eagerly at home to hear how it had been received."21

The second Norton lecture was entitled "Vocal Imagination—the
Merger of Form and Content." This theme had interested him for
decades: the way a poem comes alive in colloquial intonations, in
patches where a poet manages to entangle syntax and idiom in a manner that connects to living speech. In essence, Frost reformulated his
old arguments about the "sound of sense."

The third lecture was called "Does Wisdom Signify?" This topic
was so general that it allowed Frost to ramble mightily on subjects dear
to his heart. He began with the old notion that the manner of expression is more important in a poem than its meaning; he went on to
object to this kind of superficial writing, suggesting that words were
deeds, and that trivial arguments in a poem irritated him. According
to one reporter who was there, he drifted from joke to joke, from perception to perception, with little in the way of overall pattern or argument, although the audience seemed not to care. There was always
plenty to admire.22

The last lectures bore these titles: "Poetry as Prowess (Feat of
Words)," "Before the Beginning of a Poem," and "After the End of a
Poem." Again, the topics were general enough to allow Frost the room
he liked for meandering and free association. Having recently given
some talks on the craft of poetry at the Winter Institute in Florida, he
was prepared to pepper his arguments with deft quotations from a
range of English and American poets. He conveyed "the importance of
poetry as speech that was somehow essential, and when he recited
lines of verse, his own or that of other poets, you understood exactly
what he meant. He had a way of 'saying' a poem that struck you
between the eyes, and in the heart. The audience was appropriately
dazzled."23

Frost also found time to mingle with a small number of Harvard
students. One undergraduate who came to see him was Robert Lowell,
whose cousin Amy had been among Frost's earliest supporters. Lowell

brought a long poem in an envelope and asked Frost's advice. Lowell recalled:

> I'd gone to call on Frost with a huge epic poem on the First Cru-sade, all written out in clumsy longhand on lined paper. He read a page of that and said, "You have no compression." Then he read me a very short poem of Collins, "How Sleep the Brave," and he said, "That's not a great poem, but it's not too long." He was very kindly about it. . . . [He then read the opening of "The Fall of] Hyperion"; the line about the Naiad, something about her pressing a cold finger to her cold lips, which wouldn't seem like a voice passage at all. And he said, "Now Keats comes alive here." That was a revelation to me.[24]

As ever, Frost had a good eye for talent, and he followed Lowell's career closely. When *Lord Weary's Castle* (1946) won the Pulitzer Prize, Frost wrote to Lowell, "Isn't it fine that the young promise I began to entertain hopes of when it visited me on Fayerweather Street, Cambridge, in 1936, should have come to so much and to so much promise for the future?"[25] Later, Frost would prove a sympathetic friend when Lowell was plagued by mental illness. Frost even visited him in a mental hospital outside of Boston in 1949, and in 1957 he played an important role in helping to calm an agitated Lowell. Hear-ing of his crisis, he came at once to the younger poet's house to see if he could help; as the poet William Alfred recalled, "Mr. Frost went up into [Lowell's] study . . . on the top floor, and tried to engage him in conversation. . . . He tried to calm him down. That's what I mean about Mr. Frost. He was just a very good man. He didn't have to do that."[26]

In June, *A Further Range* was published. It was taken by the Book-of-the-Month Club as a selection, which meant a sale of fifty thousand copies right off the top; the publisher, Holt, was thus guaranteed a success. It also meant that Frost would have solid royalty payments. But he was more worried about the reception of the book than the sales figures, and he understood that his conservative politics clashed with the prevailing interests in proletarian literature, in socialism, in all manner of progressive thinking. As expected, he did not have to wait long for the attacks to begin.

Newton Arvin, a well-known scholar and critic, launched a major volley in the *Partisan Review*, suggesting that Frost's philosophy of "strategic retreat" now seemed "as profitless as a dried-up well." He took Frost to task for writing once again about a dismal New England full of "unpainted farmhouses and so many frostbitten villages and so many arid sitting-rooms."[27] This was followed quickly by further attacks: a mauling by Horace Gregory in the *New Republic*, another by R. P. Blackmur in the *Nation*, and another by Rolfe Humphries in the *New Masses*. Humphries wrote, "The further range to which Frost invited himself is an excursion into the field of political didactic, and his address is unbecoming. . . . *A Further Range?* A further shrinking."[28]

The attacks continued into the fall, with a review in *New England Quarterly* in which Dudley Fitts praised some of the lyrics but derided the political poems; of "Build Soil," for instance, he commented, "The voice is still the voice of Frost, it is true, and all the tricks are here; but the diction is faded, the expression imprecise, and the tone extraordinarily tired and uneasy. It is a strange thing that Robert Frost, pondering the problem of a sick society, should suddenly become ineffectual, should seem unable to deal abstractly with matter that he has powerfully suggested in many of his best lyrics."[29]

Frost recoiled from these criticisms, spiraling downward into depression, even though a number of his friends, including Louis Untermeyer and E. Merrill Root, weighed in with extremely positive reviews. Needing to make another strategic retreat, Frost decided not to deliver the Phi Beta Kappa poem at Harvard as promised; he also canceled most of his public lectures and readings scheduled for late summer and early fall. He even ducked out of a fall stint at Amherst that he had promised to President King in exchange for being allowed to give the Norton lectures at Harvard in the spring.

In August, as usual, the Frosts spent the hay-fever season at the Fobes's cottage in Franconia, and Elinor wrote to Mrs. Fobes, "Robert is awake so late at night, and is apt to feel like a walk even after midnight."[30] Depression often precipitated physical ailments, and soon an attack of shingles brought him tumbling further. Frost's doctor said he was suffering from "nervous exhaustion," Elinor reported, and that "if he didn't stop trying to work he would get into a condition that might take a year to recover from. He couldn't work, anyway, the pain in his head was so acute."[31]

Frost's dark mood, in late November, is reflected in a letter to DeVoto in which he complains of being unable to write letters. "Too much has happened to me this year. I am stopped in my tracks as if everybody in the opposing eleven had concentrated on me. No, not as bad as that. But I haven't dared look at paper. This is the first letter I have written in four months—absolutely the first. I prescribed loafing for myself. I may have been wrong. At any rate herewith I start again (though in bed again) and quit whining and shirking."[32] Here is Frost once again pulling himself out of depression, forcing himself into the world: the poet-as-survivor.

The Frosts planned a major family reunion in the South as part of the recovery program. Florida was dismissed as a destination: Elinor had bad memories of the previous winter, when her husband had been ill through most of their stay. They chose San Antonio, Texas, somewhat arbitrarily, on the advice of a friend. Carol, Lillian, and Prescott eagerly came, as did Lesley and her two children, who were living in Mexico City. Irma was still struggling in her marriage, and she decided not to come, but Willard came down from Montana with young Robin. After the holidays, the Frosts and Carol's family found apartments to rent for the winter.

In the meanwhile, a reaction against the harsh reviews of *A Further Range* began, with a clutch of extremely positive reviews coming in. More important, Richard Thornton, Frost's editor at Holt, put together a collection of essays called *Recognition of Robert Frost: Twenty-fifth Anniversary*. It was a substantial book, containing excerpts of critical appraisals going back to James Maurice Thompson's private letter of praise for Frost to William Hayes Ward in November 1894. Thompson had found "some secret of genius between the lines, an appeal to sympathy lying deep in one's sources of tenderness." He thought Frost's art "singular and biting."

But the first essay in the book was of more recent vintage, and suggested the way Frost was taken by his contemporaries. "The Permanence of Robert Frost" offered an overview by Mark Van Doren, an important young critic and poet. He considered Frost's place in American literature to be "singularly central," saying that he could be appreciated on many levels. "If he is not all things to all men he is something to almost anybody—to posterity, one supposes, as well as to us." He concluded by calling Frost "a poet of and for the world" whose voice "is immediately recognizable as a human voice, and recognizable for the much that it has to say." Essay upon essay celebrated the poet, and the sum was impressive. It was impossible not to realize that Frost had a secure place in the world of American poetry.

This view was confirmed in May 1937 when Frost was awarded his third Pulitzer Prize, for A Further Range—an unprecedented achievement (although Louis Untermeyer's presence on the prize committee had not diminished his chances). The book continued to sell extremely well, too, making Frost by far the best-selling American poet since Longfellow.

These accolades and affirmations encouraged Frost, and Elinor urged him to go back into the world. Tentatively, he began to accept invitations to read and lecture in New England in the fall of 1937. He had hoped to resume his old relationship with Amherst College, too, but Elinor's health seemed only to grow worse. Frost wrote to Ted Morrison on October 2, "You haven't heard, but Elinor has been very seriously ill. She is home from the hospital and about the house a little. That's all that can be said for her. I shall be taking her south soon. She needs a long long rest."[33]

The Frosts had, in retrospect, been disappointed by the sojourn in Texas, and they decided to return to Florida and to rent an apartment at 743 Bay Street in the university town of Gainesville in early December. They had visited there before and liked its openness and accessibility. Lesley had agreed to take a neighboring apartment so that she could help her mother, who was in no condition to look after the apartment by herself or prepare meals. A nearby house for Carol and his family was soon found, too. As usual, the Frosts footed the bill, and did so willingly.

Christmas of 1937 went well enough, despite Elinor's bad health. A large Christmas dinner was served at Carol's house, and the children "played all day without quarrelling," Elinor wrote to a friend. "We have all been very well so far. I rest a great deal, of course. The nights here are cool, almost cold, even after warm days."[34]

In the first week of January, Frost received from Bernard DeVoto a long-awaited article he had written for the *Saturday Review*. DeVoto used the Thornton collection as an occasion to strike a blow at Frost's most recent critics. He described some of these reviewers as "screamingly silly." Arvin, Gregory, and Blackmur were characterized as "a group of muddled minds" who deigned to "tell us about Mr. Frost without bothering to read him." Blackmur's piece was singled out as "the most idiotic review since the invention of movable type." DeVoto separated the critics of Frost into various camps. Some "see Mr. Frost escaping from reality into nature or idea or distance or the unknown." Others "assert that he never escapes but instead holds fast to the fact which is the sweetest dream that labor knows." Another contrast was developed between the left-wing critics for whom "the only right way to write poetry now was to revolt in it against private ownership of the means of production" and those who regarded Frost as "a complete proletarian" himself. Frost was, according to DeVoto, "the only pure proletarian poet of our time. His is the only body of poetry of this age which originates in the experience of humble people, treated with the profound respect of identification, and used as the sole measure of the reality and value of all experience."[35]

According to Elinor, her husband was "deeply gratified and relieved" by the DeVoto piece, but he was also savvy enough to see that DeVoto had gone overboard, writing in the manner of his hero, H. L. Mencken, without Mencken's wit or genuine originality of style. Nevertheless, the piece offered Frost a counterbalancing voice to play in his head and helped to muffle the noise of the critical voices against him. By March, in fact, Frost told Untermeyer that he felt "quite himself again" and was eager to begin writing.

He was also pleased by Gainesville. Carol often took him on long drives in the surrounding countryside, which was flat but agreeably rural. There were warm lakes for swimming, and lots of woods for "botanizing." Frost became excited about the prospect of learning to identify a whole new range of flora and fauna. He drove with Lesley one day in February over to Stetson University, where he addressed a packed auditorium. When one student quizzed him about the underlying politics of his work, Frost told him "not to attach to his poems undue political and philosophical importance."[36]

As often happened, his mania for real estate reappeared, and he decided to buy a house in Gainesville so that he and Elinor could be assured of a regular place to go back to each winter. After a careful search, he and Carol found a likely property and took Elinor to inspect it; she liked it very much, and they discussed making an offer on the way home.

On their return to Bay Street Elinor walked ahead of her husband up the stairs to their second floor apartment, but halfway up she suffered a severe heart attack and dropped to her knees. Frost and his son carried her to a bedroom, where she quickly lost consciousness. A local doctor, John Henry Thomas, was summoned, and he pronounced the situation grave. Elinor was not to be moved. Frost became so agitated that the doctor banished him from the room, forcing him to stand outside the door.

A sequence of seven further attacks occurred in two days, and Frost was kept away from his wife, although he could hear her muffled responses to the doctor through the closed door. It was feared that contact with her obviously agitated husband would drain what little energy she had left. But this was all to no avail. Elinor died on March 20, two days after the first attack, of "an acute coronary occlusion." Frost's wife of forty-three years, and the only woman he had ever loved, was gone.

17 DEPTHS BELOW DEPTHS
1939–1940

The poem must have as good a point as an anecdote or a joke. It is more effective if it has something analogous to the practical joke: an action, a "put up job" such as being carried out as a serenade or valentine or requiem. . . . The sentences must spring from each other and talk to each other, even when the thing is only one character speaking. —FROST, NOTEBOOK ENTRY, 1939

Frost was pitched into turmoil by Elinor's sudden death in Florida. Making things worse, Lesley now accused him of hastening her mother's death by allowing her to live in the upstairs apartment in Gainesville, rather than insisting that they take the ground floor—thus forcing her to climb stairs several times each day. Lesley also suggested that her father had selfishly put his own career before Elinor's welfare. Frost was unable to defend himself or do much of anything as Lesley and Clifford Lyons, a recent friend, took Elinor's body to Jacksonville for cremation, leaving Frost to sit in his apartment with the shades drawn. As often happened when depression struck, Frost succumbed to a racking cough and fever; he was so ill, in fact, that the memorial service that had been planned was postponed, and the doctor warned that he might easily lapse into pneumonia if he didn't have a period of complete rest.

In a notebook, Frost had recently mentioned "Elinor's wish that our hope of life hereafter depended on something else *as well* as religion."[1]

Although he was a man of deep spirituality, and always spoke well of conventional religion, he was not himself conventional in his beliefs. He could not, in other words, rely on any literal belief in the hereafter to comfort him after Elinor's death. The Swedenborgian faith of his mother was of no use to him now.

By any standards, Frost's dedication to his wife and family were extraordinary. With regard to Elinor, he was positively uxorious. Most of his poems, he said, were written to her; all of his books thus far had been dedicated to her. That he had been a devoted father cannot be questioned: the children had grown up with him in the house as a vivid, consistent presence. Even into adulthood, they had spent unusual amounts of time with their father, who showed continued interest in their lives and fortunes. Unfortunately, the impression that Frost was a bad father has spread widely, largely because of Lawrance Thompson's biography, which quite distorts the overall picture by placing undue emphasis on Frost's failures despite the fact that they were within the range of normal behavior. No parent or spouse is ever perfect, and Frost—a man who fought with depression and anxiety throughout his life—struggled with his family responsibilities; for the most part, he bore them well.

After Elinor's death, he found himself surrounded by friends wanting to help. Hervey Allen, a popular novelist, rushed up from Miami to assist in any way he could. Untermeyer came down from New York. Even Stanley King, the president of Amherst, came to Florida to offer emotional support—a remarkable fact, given Frost's lack of enthusiasm for the King presidency. With King's help, arrangements were made for a memorial service to be held in the Johnson Chapel at Amherst.

Frost wrote to his son on April 15, "Well, you're hard at work up there and that must be some comfort. I hope you have an interesting summer. You'll be getting new trees and baby chicks and I suppose putting on the dormant spray. There was nothing Elinor wanted more than to have you take satisfaction out of that home and farm. I wish you would remember it every day of your life."[2]

To Benny DeVoto, Frost wrote movingly about the role Elinor had played in warding off his loneliness: "I expect to have to go depths below depths in thinking before I catch myself and can say what I want to be while I last. I shall be all right in public, but I can't tell you how I am going to behave when I am alone. She could always be present to govern my loneliness without making me feel less alone. It is now running into more than a week longer than I was ever away from her since June 1895. You can see how I might have doubts of myself. I am going to work very hard in May and be on the go with people so as not to try myself solitary too soon."[3]

Frost would make being "on the go with people" the rest of his life's work, and would fight his loneliness by "making sure that there were people around, lots of people, and that somebody was there at night so that he could talk himself to sleep."[4]

The memorial service at Amherst closed a chapter in Frost's life. He had told President King of his intentions to resign, and King had tried to dissuade him, but Frost was more determined now than ever. He did not want to live in the house on Sunset Avenue any longer, nor did he want any formal relationship with Amherst College. He was aware that several faculty members believed he had shirked his duties, and he wanted not to have to worry about this. Elinor's death had, in a sense, changed everything; Frost wanted to make some public split as a way of recognizing an inner truth. Things would never be the same again.

To make it easy for Frost, Stanley King agreed that Amherst College should acquire the house, and at a price higher than he had paid for it. Frost's resignation was accepted with regrets, and he was told to "come to Amherst as frequently as possible." King was effusive in his letter: "Personally, I shall miss you keenly as a member of our college family. I have often said that in the field of human understanding you are one of the wisest men I have ever met. Our talks together at your house and at our house are one of the happiest memories of the six years I have spent at Amherst. I have learned from you many things which I cannot put on paper."[5]

Frost returned to South Shaftsbury, going first to the house he called Gully Gulch, the last dwelling that he and Elinor had shared in Vermont. He found it impossibly lonely there, "too full of Elinor to withstand," and moved temporarily into Stone Cottage with Carol and his family. In June, he made a private excursion to Derry to visit the farm that had provided so much inspiration for so many of his best poems. Elinor had wished to have her ashes spread along Hyla Brook, and Frost was hoping to arrange for this with the current owners; he was, however, met with indifference at the Derry farm, and did not have the heart to bury Elinor there. He would bury her ashes in Vermont, which now felt more like home than New Hampshire.

The death of Elinor is a major curtain that fell in the play of Frost's life, signaling the final act. The conditions, even the setting, for his life changed significantly from this point on. Instead of moving between South Shaftsbury and Amherst, he would shift among three residences: the Homer Noble farm in Ripton, an apartment in Boston (later, a duplex in Cambridge), and South Miami, where he would spend the worst months of winter.

The relationship with Bread Loaf began in earnest after Elinor's death in 1938. Through the late spring and summer, Frost was wild with grief. He wrote to Untermeyer from Amherst in May, "I don't know myself yet and won't for a long time, if I ever do. I am so quickened by what has happened that I can't touch my mind with a memory of any kind. I can't touch my skin anywhere with my finger but it hurts like a sad inspiration. In such like condition I spent all of yesterday packing deadly personal things in the desolate house on Sunset Avenue."[6] He was intent upon staying with his children "till I can decide who I am now, and what I have to go on with."[7]

Frost's letters from this summer suggest that he was in a deep state of self-recrimination with regard to Elinor: "I'm afraid I dragged her through pretty much of a life for one as frail as she," he confessed to J. J. Lankes. "Too many children, too many habitations, too many vicissitudes. And a faith required that would have exhausted most women. God damn me when he gets around to it."[8]

In "(Re)Figuring Love: Robert Frost in Crisis, 1938–1942," Donald G. Sheehy writes brilliantly about this horrendous period, when Frost sailed close to the shores of madness. It was Sheehy, in fact, who first discovered the extent of Frost's relationship with Kay Morrison, who signed on during the summer of 1938 as his secretary and would remain his closest companion until his death twenty-five years later.

Sheehy comments, "Grief had been compounded by guilt. Disturbed by Lesley's emotional indictment that his artistic self-interest had caused much of her mother's suffering, Frost retrospectively heard in the silence of Elinor's final hours a tenor of renunciation."[9]

As Sheehy notes, Kay Morrison (whom Frost had grown exceptionally fond of during the recent stint at Harvard) was visiting friends in Vermont in July 1938 and came to see him in South Shaftsbury. Seeing that he was in rough emotional shape, she invited him to spend some time with her and her children at the house where she was staying. He accepted, and soon fell utterly under her spell. "Their relationship had an original flash point, which was probably sexual," says Lesley Lee Francis, the poet's granddaughter. "But too much can be made of that. The relationship very quickly subsided into one of close friendship and mutual respect."[10]

In an unguarded moment, Frost asked Kay Morrison to marry him: the impulsive behavior of a grief-stricken man. Kay was already married, of course, and not unhappily so; she patiently explained this to Frost. "She was a tremendously sophisticated and usually sensible and sensitive woman," recalls Louise Reichert, a friend of Frost's, "but probably should not have gotten involved with Frost in an intimate way. I think she regretted this, but she was devoted to him, and to her husband. A peculiar triangle was in place there, with Ted and Kay definitely married, looking after their children, but with Frost on hand as a kind of uncle, as a close relative. They made up a family of sorts. Ted was a gentleman, and he must have known what was happening—or had happened—between Frost and his wife, but he trusted Kay. He was also deeply respectful of Frost's genius, and he was willing to let a great deal pass unnoticed, unremarked on." She adds, "I don't think that Ted would have let the relationship continue if he thought Kay was physically involved with Robert. I spent a lot of time in their company, and that tension just wasn't there. It was full of mutual respect."[11] Peter J. Stanlis adds, "As far as one could tell, there was no visible tension between the Morrisons and Frost. On several occasions when I came to the farm for an evening talk with Frost, if I arrived a bit early, and they were finishing dinner, they would invite me in for dessert and coffee. They always appeared to be in close harmony."[12]

Ted Morrison had invited Frost to lecture at the Writers' Conference that summer, and the poet eagerly accepted now that he and Kay were involved. But Frost understood on some deep level that Kay was devoted to Ted, and his attitude is reflected in a letter written shortly after the conference ended that August: "You two rescued me from a very dangerous self when you had the idea of keeping me for the whole session at Bread Loaf. I am still infinitely restless, but I came away from you as good as saved. I had had a lover's quarrel with the world. I loved the world, but you might never have guessed it from the things I thought and said. Now the quarrel is made up."[13]

The notion that the quarrel was made up might be placed in a folder called "wishful thinking," but Frost was definitely feeling better, however temporarily. The grieving over Elinor's death would, indeed, take years. Deep inside, he would never get over it. But Kay Morrison's intervention could not have occurred at a more critical moment.

While the relationship between Frost and Kay appears to have slipped into the platonic realm rather quickly, Frost could not abide the concept. His fury over the notion of a "platonic" affair was on his mind throughout the conference at Bread Loaf, and he could often be overheard in the dining hall on the subject. Indeed, over dinner he told the young poet Charles Foster (who had recently become a regular correspondent and friend) that "he was against Plato—declaiming that Platonism came down to preferring the woman in somebody else's bed to the wife in your own." Frost had the idea of married love heavily on his mind—a thing he had valued and lost so recently—and he said to Foster, "Man and woman are married by lasting affection or they are never married. Only such a humanly beautiful tie deserves respect. All others are mockeries of it, hypocrisies to hide some base gain." Somewhat shockingly, he added, "Adultery and fornications are generalizations. Each human case should be tried independently. And does this lead to license? I do not think so. Let the affection be deep and it can only be for one person."[14] Frost was thinking of both Elinor and Kay here, celebrating his long marriage to Elinor, and wishing he could marry Kay.

The experience of being with the Morrisons at Bread Loaf renewed Frost. Foster wrote in his journal, "I noticed all the old wit and richness back again. Yesterday morning, I took him for a long ride. . . . He sees that the world is not frozen mentally, but is moving and growing like him." Frost turned to Foster and said, "Only poetry comes close to catching the fast flowing world and holding it. Poetry is the height of knowledge." And he was ready to plunge into this kind of knowledge again.

Nevertheless, Frost was sailing between sharp rocks every day now. A certain wildness was evident in his manner at Bread Loaf; he behaved oddly, even outrageously, at times. In his biography of DeVoto, Wallace Stegner recounts an infamous scene where Frost began "playing around like an idle, inattentive schoolboy in a classroom."[15] During a poetry reading at the Little Theater by Archibald MacLeish, Frost lit a match, setting fire (accidentally on purpose) to a wad of papers that he had crumpled on the chair beside him. He thus drew attention away from MacLeish, whom he had always considered pompous and second-rate. Later that same night, in Treman Cottage (where the faculty at Bread Loaf often retreated after a reading for further conversation), Frost baited MacLeish by making rude remarks as the latter attempted to read aloud from a new play. An angry DeVoto shouted at Frost, "You're a good poet, Robert, but you're a bad man."[16]

It was Stegner's opinion, some years later, that Frost was clearly in distress that summer of 1938. He was doing everything he could to draw attention to his pain. It was his odd, even impossible, way of grieving. He hated himself that summer, and he wanted "those around him to hate him," and this acting out with MacLeish was part of the perverse process. Stegner noted, "One knew that Elinor had just died, and felt pity. There was that halo of sadness on Frost. He had been singled out that year for particular anguish, and most of us understood this."[17]

As often before, Frost sought comfort in his art, writing "Carpe Diem" and "The Wind and the Rain" in the harrowing months after Elinor's death. The former (an echo of poems by Horace and Herrick) describes the present moment as "too much for the senses / Too crowding, too confusing," while the latter is elegiac in tone, with its title reminiscent of Thomas Hardy. "That far-off day the leaves in flight / Were letting in the colder light," Frost says, recalling the way he would rashly thrust himself into the destructive element as a young man:

> I leaned on with a singing trust
> And let it drive me deathward too.
> With breaking step I stabbed the dust,
> Yet did not much to shorten stride.
> I sang of death—but had I known
> The many deaths one must have died
> Before he came to meet his own!
> Oh, should a child be left unwarned
> That any song in which he mourned
> Would be as if he prophesied?

"There is no more naked an exclamation or unanswerable a question to be found in Frost's poetry," William H. Pritchard says.[18] The mere act of writing poems ("song") would seem to tempt fate—a point made explicitly by the last three lines of the first part:

> And yet 'twould seem that what is sung
> In happy sadness by the young,
> Fate has no choice but to fulfill.

As Emerson suggested in his essay "Fate": "They who talk much of destiny, invite the evils they fear."

The first of the two sections is centered on wind, the second on rain. In the second, Frost observes that "there is always more than should be said." He was, as he once said, "a believer in silences." The poem ends, hauntingly, with internal and external realities strangely interacting:

> I have been one no dwelling could contain
> When there was rain;
> But I must forth at dusk, my time of day,
> To see to the unburdening of skies.

Rain was the tears adopted by my eyes
That have none left to stay.

After the Bread Loaf Conference of 1938, Frost visited Untermeyer at his farm in upstate New York, then returned to Amherst to settle his bank account and say good-bye to various friends before moving to Boston, where he could be near Kay. She had agreed to act as his secretary, and the arrangement was a unique one. Kay would serve as business manager, agent, closest friend, object of adoration, scold, and typist. To take on these multiple tasks, she quit her part-time job as a reader for the Atlantic Monthly Press.

At first, the job was established on a trial basis, although it was soon apparent to everyone that she was here to stay. "I don't think he could have managed without her," Hyde Cox recalls. "She knew where everything was, where he had to go next, who was expecting him to give this reading or that lecture. Frost's correspondence had grown unmanageable, and Kay was able to bring some discipline to bear."

In Boston, Frost moved from the stuffy St. Botolph Club on Newbury Street to the Ritz-Carlton Hotel, which overlooks the Public Garden. But his old pulmonary troubles started up again, and he was briefly hospitalized in September. Kay had found him an apartment at 88 Mount Vernon Street, and this was being refurbished. It was small, but Frost considered it no more than a base from which he could pursue what would be his last career, that of full-time bard. He expected now to earn a living by lecturing and reading—a role he had virtually invented for himself. "A few poets may have traveled the country and read their poems aloud," said Allen Ginsberg, "but Frost was relentless, and professional. He created an audience for poetry readings, and a role for the poet, that hadn't been there before. It was easier for those who came after him. He was the first voyager, a kind of pioneer, the original entrepreneur of poetry."[19]

Frost liked the idea of being attached to some college or university, and he was now keen to make contact with Harvard. Several friends in Cambridge—David McCord, Merrill Moore, and Robert Hillyer—approached some wealthy alumni to see if a fellowship for Frost might not be funded from without. Moore wrote to an influential member of the Harvard board, "Here is what might be considered a golden opportunity [for Harvard]. Here is the greatest living poet writing in English, in his declining years, it is true, but sane, mellow and sound. He is alone now and his needs are simple. He has a great deal of usefulness and a great deal of charm. Might it not be possible that some one single person would 'grubstake' him for the University for a number of years or something like that? He brings great credit wherever he comes and has a gift of stimulating people in a way that is creative and nonacademic."[20]

Not long after moving into the new apartment, Frost set off for Columbus, Ohio, where he stopped to visit with Robert S. Newdick, his biographer. He gave readings and lectures at Ohio State (where Newdick taught) and other colleges in the Columbus area. He then traveled to Iowa City, where he spoke to a group of writers at the University of Iowa. Charles Foster was present and wrote in his notebook, "Robert Frost was here yesterday and spoke to the writers. He was a tired man; the old snap was gone."[21] Even so, the poet returned to Boston by way of Buffalo, where he gave another reading to a large crowd.

Frost was eager to settle down to writing again. He had a solid file of poems in draft that needed revision, some of them dating from many years before, and he had several new poems in rough form. One of the finest poems written (or revised) somewhere in this period was "The Silken Tent," which he gave to Kay as though it was written for her, although Lesley later claimed to have typed a version of this poem while her mother was still alive. Jeffrey Cramer notes, "Although Kay Morrison was indeed presented with the poem, there is no reason to believe that she was ultimately its original inspiration. In all likelihood, the poem was written to Elinor, but after Elinor's death, the increased respect and love he felt for Kay prompted Frost to present this sonnet to her."[22] Given Frost's habit of putting poems away for months, even years or decades, before revising them, it seems quite possible that this poem was written earlier, then revised for Kay. In any case, it remains a centerpiece of Frost's poetry and one of the finest sonnets written in English in this century. The whole is a single, gorgeously elaborated, sentence:

She is as in a field a silken tent
At midday when a sunny summer breeze
Has dried the dew and all its ropes relent,
So that in guys it gently sways at ease,
And its supporting central cedar pole,
That is its pinnacle to heavenward
And signifies the sureness of the soul,
Seems to owe naught to any single cord,
But strictly held by none, is loosely bound
By countless silken ties of love and thought
To everything on earth the compass round,
And only by one's going slightly taut
In the capriciousness of summer air
Is of the slightest bondage made aware.

As Richard Poirier remarks, "The whole poem is a performance, a display for the beloved while also being an exemplification of what it is like for a poem, as well as a tent or a person, to exist within the constrictions of space ('a field') and time ('at midday') wherein the greatest possible freedom is consistent with the intricacies of form and inseparable from them."[23]

The sentence, as a syntactic unit, is grammatically complete after the first two words: "She is." The poet matter-of-factly declares her presence, her being: the idealized lover who needs no elaboration. But as the impulse toward figurative thinking quickly overwhelms, the third word of the poem, "as"—perhaps the most important word in poetry—takes over, and the conceit begins. The tent is mysteriously "silken," giving the metaphor a vaguely biblical feel, as in the "Song of Songs," where the bride is beautiful "as the tents of Kedar, as the curtains of Solomon." (One would not literally expect to see a silken tent, unless one thinks of silken as meaning "shiny" or "shimmering.")

The action of the poem (or nonaction) takes place at high noon, in the prime of the love object's life, so to speak; the "silken ties of love and thought" that bind her to "everything on earth" are loose, although the crucial point is that they are loosely *bound*. The phrase indirectly celebrates a married love in which the beloved is "tied" but not "tied down," just as in a poem one encounters limits, but these limits are liberating. Indeed, the poem, as a poem in form, enacts the limits of the sonnet and demonstrates by its very performance the act of being freed by strictures: the marvelous paradox of poetic form.

The woman-as-tree is an interesting figure in the poem: the cedar pole that supports the tent is both a correlative evoking the "soul" of the woman and "is its pinnacle to heavenward." This line reaches back to "Birches," where the boy-hero climbed heavenward on the trunk of the tree but was ultimately dropped back to earth, "the right place for love." Here, too, Frost does not want his love object to get too platonized; "airy nothings," as Shakespeare suggests, must give way to "a local habitation and a name" for love to occur in its proper fullness. Hence, at the end of the poem, when the breeze strikes—a metaphor for the tugs of pain, loss, grieving, and all forms of resistance in life that one necessarily encounters as the precondition of being alive— the "silken ties" are drawn ever so slightly, suggesting the form of this particular love (much as the lines of the poem are made visible by the flexing in form that occurs through the writing of the sonnet). Frost's gift for finding the right, as well as unexpected, word is never more visible than in that penultimate line, when he writes about the "capriciousness" of summer air, with its aura of malicious abandon tempered by that sense of sprightliness which is part of its connotation. The figure of the wind tightening the "silken ties" and making "the slightest bondage" visible itself embodies the paradox of freedom and control.

Frost regarded the ties of community as well as the ties of marriage as productive, liberating attachments. "What is man but all his connections?" he said elsewhere. "He's just a tiny invisible knot so that he can't discern it himself: the knot where all his connections meet."[24] And in his notebooks, he wrote, "Connections and community—the basis of love, and the product."[25]

The poem slithers through its form, the lines quietly enjambed so that one is only slightly aware of the five-foot line or the strict rhymes. The form is a classic Elizabethan sonnet, and this particular example owes a good deal to the love sonnets of Shakespeare, which Frost admired. ("He often quoted the sonnets," recalled one friend, "and always from memory. He said he could happily pass the time on train or car journeys by reciting these poems in his head.")26 "The Silken Tent" also owes something to Frost's consistent interest in form itself, which gives shape to or "informs" ideas and experience. As Frost wrote in his notebooks, "Inform is a good word. Let us inform with idea and measuring all we can of works and life."27

While "The Silken Tent" is a crest in this period of Frost's writing, there is also "Never Again Would Birds' Song Be the Same" to consider, a poem that was certainly written for Kay. It opens grandly:

> *He would declare and could himself believe*
> *That the birds there in all the garden round*
> *From having heard the daylong voice of Eve*
> *Had added to their own an oversound,*
> *Her tone of meaning but without the words.*

The influence of Shakespeare's love sonnets is again present here, especially in that first line, which echoes a line from the first scene in *Hamlet*: "So have I heard and do in part believe it." (Frost once called this line "the most beautiful single line of English verse.")28

Pritchard has called this poem "the quietest and most discreet of his sonnets," saying that it "has about it the air of a tour de force."29 Like all of Frost's best poems, it is at least on some metaphorical level about poetry itself. Like Eve, or the subject of the poem (Kay?), Frost has himself created "an oversound," adding something to the universal bank of emotional and verbal music. The poem is also a fascinating account of how human language and nature's nonhuman sounds intermingle to forge meaning:

> *Moreover her voice upon their voices crossed*
> *Had now persisted in the woods so long*
> *That probably it never would be lost.*
> *Never again would birds' song be the same.*
> *And to do that to birds was why she came.*

The witty couplet that brings the sonnet to a close might well be taken as a gloss of Blake's famous observation that "Without man, nature is barren."

Meanwhile, Frost's editor at Holt, Richard Thornton, fell out of favor with Herbert G. Bristol, the chairman of the board. The ramification of this corporate squabbling was felt by Frost. Thornton was urged to reduce the poet's guaranteed monthly payment of $250, though he refused to do so. Frost came close to leaving Holt when Thornton was fired, but he was quickly appeased by Bristol and a new editor, T. J. Wilson. A fresh contract was drawn up that pleased Frost immensely: he was guaranteed $300 monthly, for life. He would also receive a 20 percent royalty payment on future work—a rare accession to a poet.

Frost was also pleased that Holt wished to bring out a volume of his collected poems in 1939. A cheaper version of this collection would be coming out with another publisher, under a special arrangement with Holt—an arrangement that would "widen the circle of your readers considerably," Bristol suggested to the poet in a conciliatory letter. To distinguish the cheaper edition from Holt's more expensive version, Frost was asked to supply a short preface. What he provided was entitled "The Figure a Poem Makes."

This brief, charming essay brings into play many of the notes Frost had been sounding for years as he mined his lectures and notebooks for ideas and particular phrases. In its most widely quoted paragraph, the poet declares that a poem "begins in delight and ends in wisdom."

> The figure is the same as for love. No one can really hold that the ecstasy should be static and stand still in one place. It begins in delight, it inclines to the impulse, it assumes direction with the first line laid down, it runs a course of lucky events, and ends in a clarification of life—not necessarily a great clarification, such as sects and cults are founded on, but in a momentary stay against confusion.

Frost finished this memorable, intensely suggestive, and compact essay in January, and was aware he had succeeded in bringing together in a short space many of his favorite notions, such as the idea of "wildness"—a subject much on his mind since Elinor's death, which had brought him into a wild space of his own. The poet's wildness must be "pure," he wrote, the poet "wild with nothing to be wild about." T. J. Wilson was delighted to have the essay, and he reassured Frost that it was "a perfect preface for the *Collected*, and a fine piece in itself, almost a poem in prose."[30]

Frost was making plans for going to Florida for the winter, and was already scheduling lectures and readings in the South, when he received word that he would be awarded the Gold Medal "for distinguished work in poetry" by the National Institute of Arts and Letters at their annual banquet in New York on January 18. This meant he would have to hover in the Northeast for longer than usual.

Soon after the award ceremony, he set off for Key West, where he joined the Morrisons at the Casa Marina Hotel. From there, he returned to the Miami area, where he stayed with Hervey Allen, whose company he found highly entertaining. Allen was a voluble, large man with a huge income from his best-selling novels, such as *Anthony Adverse*. Frost's friendship with Allen, whom he first met in 1927 at Bread Loaf, would figure increasingly in his life in Florida.

Frost was joined in early February by Carol and his family, who rented a house near the Allens, in Coconut Grove, for two months, through March. It gave Frost considerable pause to see, and fully understand, the extent to which Carol was suffering from psychological problems. Subsistence farming in New England had done nothing to bolster his ego, and he felt embarrassingly dependent on his father, who continued to pay for such things as this winter trip to Florida. Carol was, in fact, eager to abandon the life of a Vermont farmer and move to Florida, where he imagined he might be able to break free of what felt to him like overwhelming ties to his father and his past. Somewhat disastrously, he also hoped to pursue a career in writing poetry.

After the Morrisons left for Cambridge in early February, Frost became increasingly gloomy. Hervey Allen grew quite panicky about his condition and suggested that his other houseguests, the poet Paul Engle and his wife, Mary, take Frost by seaplane to Cuba. Grimly, Frost acquiesced. "We went down to Camaguey, saw several cities besides Havana and plenty of sugar cane and royal palms," he wrote to Lesley. "The land is rich: the people are miserably poor. Everywhere beggars and beggar-vendors. We saw one great beach to beat the world and on it a car with a Vermont license which on inquiry proved to belong to a friend of yours, the head of the art department at Bennington College. . . . I am not much on foreign parts. . . . To me the best of the excursion was the flight both ways in the big Pan American plane and especially the swoop and mighty splash into the bays on arrival."[31]

Frost wrote to Lesley in late February about Carol's condition, which seemed to be improving, although he worried generally about the survival of his son's family: "Carol came down perverse and surly, but he improved on being let alone. Or so I imagine. I have played cards with them [Carol, Lillian, and Prescott] six or eight nights and had a couple of long rides with them. They have been fishing on their own considerably. They are not lucky so far in life. They catch no fish. The mongrel dog has just brought forth eight more . . . mongrel pups for them to drown. Nobody else's experience profits them the least. I told them they couldn't take care of a bitch. I couldn't."[32]

Frost returned to Cambridge in March, although he soon traveled to his old hometown of Lawrence to give a series of lectures. In April, he read his poems at the University of Iowa, where he visited both Charles Foster and Norman Foerster. The latter was host of the event, and he incurred the wrath of Frost for scheduling the reading in a room that held only three hundred people. The place was so overflowing that Frost had to fight his way to the podium; after the reading, he vented his frustration to Foerster, demanding, "Who do you think I am, a rural schoolteacher that nobody wants to hear?"[33] Foster, in his notes, recorded this impression: "Frost highly irritable, though always interesting to hear." He discerned "a look of exhaustion in his eyes, in his voice," wondering "what pressures he must be under."

Though obviously exhausted, Frost pressed on to visit the Bartletts in Colorado, then on to further lecture assignments in the West. It was

May before he arrived back in Cambridge. Much to his surprise, there was a letter awaiting him from President Conant of Harvard, inviting him to become Ralph Waldo Emerson Fellow—a two-year appointment invented specifically for Frost and paid for by a number of Harvard alumni who called themselves the "Friends of Robert Frost." President Conant later recalled that he noticed some reluctance in Frost about accepting this position, a feeling that to get involved in another responsibility might not be the best thing for him. Frost had, of course, been attached to colleges and universities for many years. It was, perhaps, time to break free.

Aware, however, that several friends had gone to considerable lengths to create this position, Frost decided to accept it. His misgivings are nevertheless evident in the letter he wrote to Conant, wondering if he were really "fitted for the duties of a fellow." He felt free to express his general anti-academic bias: "I am a peculiarly advanced case of what I am, good or bad. Much of education in school I have never believed in. At the first serious suggestion of my pretending to Latinity or any other kind of scholarship I am struck as schoolshy as in the nineties when I fled uneducated to the Philistines. What has brought me back in and partly disarmed me is the kindness the colleges have shown my poetry. I find myself even anxious to be useful to them in requital."[34] Nevertheless, he did accept the appointment, especially since Conant had made it clear that there were no formal duties attached to it. It was merely hoped that Frost would occasionally meet with students and offer public lectures now and then.

That summer, Frost returned to Bread Loaf, "teaming up" (as he put it) with Louis Untermeyer to teach a class in the criticism of poetry. He also bought the house that would remain his summer home until his death over two decades later: the Homer Noble Farm in Ripton, two miles from the Bread Loaf campus. Mrs. Noble had been renting the farm to faculty members at Bread Loaf for several years, and she was willing to sell it. The property delighted Frost: a small, wood-frame farmhouse on just over 150 acres surrounded by the Green Mountain National Forest. The privacy of the place was perfect: the gravel drive leading to the farm was itself over half a mile long, so that nobody would stop by accidentally. There were open fields behind the house, with an astounding view of the mountains. A few minutes' walk uphill, on the edge of the woods, was a self-contained cabin with a living room, a bedroom, a bath, and a kitchen. The stone fireplace in the living room was alluring, and there was a pleasant screened-in porch with dramatic views to the southwest across a meadow.

Frost knew that the Morrisons loved the farmhouse and would be happy to live there while he occupied the cabin. There was a phone in the main farmhouse communicating with the cabin—an early version of an intercom; Kay could cook the meals and ring Frost to come down. The three of them would form a unique clan. One friend remembers, "It was an odd but interesting arrangement. The three of them actually got along very well, and the house and cabin were close enough yet far enough apart so that everyone was happy. Kay would come up in the morning and work with Robert on his letters and arrangements. There was plenty of solitude for Robert, but when he needed company, it was there."[35]

The proximity to Bread Loaf was a bonus. Over the years, a steady stream of young writers made the pilgrimage to the Homer Noble Farm and, often with their own manuscripts in hand, walked along the maple-lined path to the cabin, where Frost sat in his Morris chair, usually with a glass of iced tea in hand. But one Bread Loafer of this era registered the downside of a visit to Frost: "His love of conversation was such that you might go to visit him at eight, just after dinner, and find yourself listening to him talk until two or three in the morning. He would get wound up, and keep talking. It was marvelous talk, but there was a lot of it. Sometimes there was a little desperation there, as if a lapse into silence would have terrible consequences."[36]

Frost returned to Boston in the fall of 1939, plunging headlong into teaching at Harvard. His single course was called Poetry. The first classes went well, but he soon developed a severe infection of the kidney that interrupted the term; indeed, he was forced to move temporarily into the Morrison home on Walker Street, where Kay employed two nurses to help look after him. He was also, as he readily admitted in a letter to Louis Untermeyer, suffering from depression.[37]

Having sold the house in South Shaftsbury, Frost was easily able to afford the Homer Noble farm. With his usual mania for real estate, he was also intent upon buying something in Florida, where he had been forced to depend on the hospitality of friends. His finances were more than ample for these needs, but he felt the urge for more security. He had, after all, a large family to think about.

A temporary financial boost came in the shape of one Earle J. Bernheimer, a wealthy collector. Bernheimer had been collecting Frost's books and manuscripts since 1936, and he visited Frost at the Homer Noble farm in the summer of 1939 to ask if he might "rent" the little volume called *Twilight* that Frost had had privately printed as a gift for Elinor in 1894 (in an edition of two copies). He explained to Frost that upon his (Bernheimer's) death, the book would be given to any library that Frost designated. The concept of "renting" a book for one's own lifetime was a peculiar one, and Frost at first balked; he distrusted Bernheimer, but eventually decided that if the man would pay enough "rent" on the book, he was willing to part with it. For remuneration, he asked the collector to give a thousand dollars to each of his four children, and Bernheimer quickly agreed. To possess this one-of-a-kind object was a collector's dream.

As winter approached, illness followed illness, and Frost wound up in Massachusetts General Hospital in the second week of the new year. It was a bad start to what would seem, in retrospect, a particularly dark year. Explaining his illness to Sidney Cox, Frost said: "I have been very sick largely we now think from some very drastic medicine that doctors tried on me for cystitis. I went crazy with it one night alone and broke chairs ad lib till a friend [Merrill Moore, who was a poet-psychiatrist] happened to save me."[38] Moore had stopped in to see Frost, quite by chance, and found him barely conscious in his apartment; he called an ambulance, and Frost was hospitalized for a week.

On February 1, later than usual, he left for Key West with Kay Morrison and her son, Bobby. They stayed as before at the Casa Marina. Kay was planning to remain with Frost for two weeks, to be replaced by Lawrance Thompson, who would look after the ailing poet for another month. Thompson, who taught at Princeton, had recently been named by Frost as his official biographer—a relationship that would last until Frost's death, with many repercussions, not least of which was a three-volume assault on Frost's character in the shape of a literary biography.

In the dining room at the Casa Marina, Frost encountered a soft-spoken, highly intelligent man in his early twenties. Frost had been standing beside the stone fireplace in the main dining room when the fellow approached and introduced himself as Hyde Cox, a Harvard graduate who had attended Frost's Norton lectures in 1936. "I explained to him that I had inherited enough money from my grandfather so that I didn't have to worry about making a living," Cox recalls.[39] He further explained that he had sought "real experience of the world" by hawking newspapers on street corners and taking other similar jobs around the country. He had been traveling for the past six months in a brand-new Chevrolet coupe, but recently a bout of influenza had laid him low, and he'd decided to recover by spending a few days at the Casa Marina.

"Mr. Frost took me on a long walk," Cox remembers. "We talked well into the night, and found that we shared many experiences. I was, of course, four decades younger, but we were both at loose ends just now." Cox was invited for breakfast the next morning, and Frost insisted that the young man call on him when he returned to the Boston area. (Cox lived on the north shore, in Manchester, in a magnificent house on the sea called Crow Island.) This friendship would continue until Frost's death and would be extremely important to both men. Indeed, Cox became a surrogate son of sorts.

Frost also saw Wallace Stevens again at the Casa Marina, and they exchanged some teasing remarks. "The trouble with you, Robert, is that you're too academic," Stevens remarked. Frost replied that Stevens was, indeed, "too executive." Then Stevens said, with mock horror: "But you, you write about . . . subjects." Frost came back: "And you, Wallace, you write about bric-a-brac."[40] The fact is, these two major American poets of the first half of the twentieth century worked from such contradictory, even exclusive, aesthetics that neither could really read the other with much satisfaction.

Frost spent the rest of his time in Florida with Hervey Allen, who encouraged him to look for local real estate. Always eager to buy another house, Frost spent several weeks with realtors. After many disappointments, he finally agreed to purchase a five-acre plot of scrubby pineland in Coconut Grove. It was undeveloped land, so it cost only $1,500. There were some legal problems, but these were resolved within a few months, whereupon Frost would begin building two small, prefabricated houses there that he called Pencil Pines.[41]

One reason Frost determined to build in Florida was that Carol still planned to move there for good. The farm in South Shaftsbury had not been financially viable, and Carol had been forced to borrow more and more money from his father. Frost's hope was that his son, who had acquired construction skills over the years, would supervise the building of the houses for him. This would provide a legitimate form of work and, of course, an income, a maneuver designed to increase Carol's self-respect. Soon after taking possession of the land, Frost wrote eagerly from Boston to Allen, asking about the best places to buy lumber and other building supplies.

But Carol was in no position to build houses for his father, or even to maintain his own household. For many years now, he had been plagued by wild fears, anxiety attacks, and bouts of depression. He had grown increasingly paranoid over the years as well, complaining that his neighbors and friends were plotting against him. His wife's health problems, which kept shifting (she was soon to undergo a hysterectomy), frightened him; he could not imagine looking after teenage Prescott by himself. On top of everything, the death of Elinor, who had been his protector for so many years, had cruelly undermined his confidence.

Frost was summoned to South Shaftsbury by Lillian in early October. She was going into the hospital for her operation and was afraid to leave Carol on his own with Prescott. Frost dutifully arrived, finding his son in a state of unusually deep depression. Having regularly experienced depression himself, Frost at once understood the seriousness of the problem. When Lillian explained that Carol had spoken of suicide several times, he grew alarmed.

He stayed with his son for several days, talking to him, often late into the night. Convinced that Carol had pulled himself together, he returned to Ripton. A day later, on October 9, he received a call from his grandson at seven in the morning. Prescott said that Carol had shot himself in the head with a deer rifle early that morning. He had been wakened by the shot, and had discovered his father sprawled in a pool of blood on the kitchen floor.

Prescott had, in fact, stayed up most of the night with his father, aware of the precarious state of his mind. But exhaustion had forced him to bed. When he heard the rifle shot, soon after dawn, he knew what had happened. With admirable cool, he had telephoned the police first, then his grandfather, then the family doctor. While waiting for his grandfather to appear, he had called a family friend, Floyd Holliday, to make arrangements to move in temporarily with that family while his mother was recuperating in the hospital. Frost later wrote to Prescott to praise him for his mettle: "Disaster brought out the heroic in you," he said. "You now know you have the courage and nerve for anything you may want or need to be, engineer, inventor or soldier."[42]

To Untermeyer, Frost bared his soul: "I took the wrong way with [Carol]. I tried many ways and every single one of them was wrong. Some thing in me is still asking for the chance to try one more. There's where the greatest pain is located. I am cut off too abruptly in my plans and efforts for his peace of mind." His son, he explained, had failed at farming and failed in his occasional attempts to write poetry. "He was splendid with animals and little children," Frost recalled. "If only the emphasis could have been put on those. He should have lived with horses."[43]

It had been a dismal decade for Robert Frost. The death of Marjorie in 1934 had stunned him, and Elinor's death had nearly undone him. Now he would have to cope with the loss of a beloved son whose sense of failure in life he could not, despite his consistent efforts, undo. In his notebooks, Frost wrote, "Nature is chaos."[44] And now he had to find a way out of the chaos.

18   CORRIDORS OF WOE
1941–1944

*If you are going deeply into poetry, give your whole self to it—go
the whole hog. Too many take it carefully, and fail. If it is to be
your life, make everything else subordinate to it.*

—FROST TO DANIEL SMYTHE, DECEMBER 21, 1940

In March 1941, Frost moved into a newly purchased residence—38
Brewster Street, in Cambridge. This would be his permanent address
in the Boston area from now on. It was a substantial double house on
three floors in what was known as Brewster Village. The apartment he
had been renting before had grown far too small for his many books,
his beloved dog Gillie, and the various houseguests who periodically
came through, including Lesley, Irma, Lillian, and his grandchildren.

That same month, he traveled to Washington, D.C., to give a talk
at the Library of Congress in connection with an exhibition of his
work that had been partly curated by Lesley. In connection with this,
he gave a lecture in the large Coolidge Auditorium entitled "The Role
of a Poet in a Democracy." Democracy was not a goal so much as a
way, a process, he argued: "Had it been nothing but the goal, democracy and I would probably never have met. I'm not far-seeing enough
for goals." He went on to discuss a familiar American symbol, the pyra-
mid with an eye at the apex that adorns the great seal of the United
States, maintaining that "all figures, all figurative things in verse or in
prose, may be taken more than one way." This symbol meant to him

personally that in a democracy the government must put certain restraints upon itself. Only God has perfect vision—hence the all-seeing eye in the apex. Frost noted that he had always admired George Washington because he'd refused to seize absolute power after the conclusion of the Revolutionary War. This talk, in the usual Frostian manner, was disconnected but suggestive. The thinking rarely progressed in a linear fashion, but moved from flash point to flash point.

The talk was well publicized, adding to Frost's reputation as a national sage, and Harvard was eager to keep him after the Emerson fellowship expired. President Conant appointed him as Fellow in American Civilization; the job requirements were, as usual, minimal. Frost was merely expected to act as "roving consultant in History and Literature," and he would receive $3,000 for this responsibility. Conant also hoped that Frost would go around to Harvard's seven residential houses to conduct group discussions on American civilization. Eager to maintain a presence in the academy, he agreed to these generous terms.

Despite his continuing grief over Carol's death, he began to pull together a new volume of poems. As usual, he had many poems in his folder that had been written, or partially written, many years before. Some of these were as good as anything he had yet published, such as "The Subverted Flower," which would go into the new collection. This strange yet wonderful poem was written well before the publication of A Boy's Will, but because of its explicit representation of sexuality, Frost had resisted publishing it until now, after Elinor's death (she was obviously the model for the teenage girl in the poem). Even after it appeared in print, he refused to recite the poem in public. "I'm shy about certain things in my books," he told one interviewer. "I'd rather they'd be read."[1]

Another old poem resurrected for the new volume, A Witness Tree, was "The Quest of the Purple-Fringed," which had been published as "The Quest of the Orchis" in the Independent in 1901—a full four decades earlier! Frost quietly changed the title because he had mistaken the purple gentian—a late bloomer—for the purple orchis, which comes early. The poem was written in Allenstown, New Hampshire, in the summer of 1896, but it does not seem out of place in this late collection; Frost's style had simply not changed so drastically that early and later work could not be readily juxtaposed.

At the center of the new volume was one of his finer poems on a public theme, "The Gift Outright," which he would read in 1960 at John F. Kennedy's inauguration. Though written in 1935, it was held back until December 5, 1941, when Frost read it aloud at William and Mary College. In the *Atlantic Monthly*, he commented that the poem was "as poetic as I ever get." He also claimed (as he so often did for poems) that it was written without hesitation, though a perusal of his notebooks suggests otherwise; various lines from this poem can be found in fragments in earlier notebooks. What Frost probably meant was that various fragments suddenly came together into the shape of this poem during one session of writing. There is clearly a fierce sense of unity here, a rhetorical control that only the most skillful of poets can ever manage:

> *The land was ours before we were the land's.*
> *She was our land more than a hundred years*
> *Before we were her people. She was ours*
> *In Massachusetts, in Virginia,*
> *But we were England's, still colonials,*
> *Possessing what we still were unpossessed by,*
> *Possessed by what we now no more possessed.*
> *Something we were withholding made us weak*
> *Until we found out that it was ourselves*
> *We were withholding from our land of living,*
> *And forthwith found salvation in surrender.*
> *Such as we were we gave ourselves outright*
> *(The deed of gift was many deeds of war)*
> *To the land vaguely realizing westward,*
> *But still unstoried, artless, unenhanced,*
> *Such as she was, such as she would become.*

This poem has largely been ignored by serious critics of Frost, though it remains a favorite of readers. In the current climate, it may

seem horribly chauvinistic, even belligerent, with its apparent celebration of "many deeds of war." The land was, indeed, not "ours," but
belonged to Native Americans in reality and to various European powers on paper. Frost's poem ignores the Native American angle altogether, focusing on the fact that the Old World owned the New and
tracing a weakness to this dependence. There is something peculiar
but marvelous about the notion of finding ourselves, as a nation, in
"surrender" to some dark, complex aspect of ourselves that had been
consciously withheld until this giving up occurred. Frost reads the
national psyche here with considerable freshness and bravery.

The poem is written from the point of view of a poet deeply
confident in his own identity. As usual, it is also more nuanced and
reflective than first meets the eye. The notion of possessing something
"we now no more possessed" is not only cleverly worded; Frost has an
intuitive grasp of what "possession" means, playing delightfully with
the term in its multiple meanings (as in being "possessed" by a vision,
for example). In 1919, Frost remarked that "America isn't American
enough for her authors to be very American yet," making a distinction
between the country as a named place and a lived-in, "possessed"
place, where values are shared, and where community is finely
webbed and wholly integrated. Elsewhere, he said that you have
to "possess a place, and be possessed, to own it," and by "own" he
meant both to take legal and figurative possession and to "own up
to" it.

One can hardly imagine a better brief description of our national
history than Frost's image of "the land vaguely realizing westward."
Both "vaguely" and "realizing" are unexpected, and perfect. The poet
gets the haphazard, unplanned quality of the process in the former
term and underscores the seeming historic inevitability of it in the latter; in Frost's version of social Darwinism, morality is stripped to the
bare essentials: there were millions of strong transplanted Europeans
in the East, and they would eventually need room to expand; they had
greater numbers and better weapons than the native people, so they
overcame them; indeed, they nearly wiped them out altogether! That
they remained "unstoried, artless, unenhanced" is also part of the story,
and Frost does not (as a lesser, merely patriotic poet might have done)

overly praise these conquerors, who even seem more like a virus than a nation.

The poem was published in the spring of 1942, only a few months after the United States had entered the Second World War. It is interesting to note that Frost was no mere jingoist; in fact, a part of him resisted the idea that fighting to save Britain from the Germans was necessarily our duty. To the end, a certain skepticism shaded his comments on the war. "Our seaboard sentimentalists think of nothing but saving England," he had written to his son-in-law Willard Fraser the previous fall. "Some of them would go so far as to sacrifice America to save England. They are the Anglophiles with an English accent." Frost had typically derided self-conscious Anglophiles ever since his days in England. "We are able to fight and we are not afraid to fight," he said. "My only doubt is whether we need to join in England's fight. I should like it better if we had it all to ourselves and if we won we would get the loot, the glory, and the self-realization."[2]

Lest he be regarded as anti-English, he acknowledged that he considered England the greatest world power since Rome. But he believed that President Roosevelt had left the United States inadequately prepared for this war. In a less comprehensible gesture, he would often accuse Britain of starting something that it could not finish, as if Hitler had been challenged to a fight. "Frost was oddly naive about politics," one friend suggested. "He had theories, lots of them, but they were often based on school yard dynamics; he was not a sophisticated political thinker, although he could offer startling insights, and occasionally strike a remarkably prophetic note."[3]

The war also made Frost worry that he might not be able to support himself, and his family, with money from speaking engagements. He envisioned colleges shutting down, or not having the money to hire visiting lecturers. Anxiously he wrote to Earle J. Bernheimer, offering various manuscripts for sale for extraordinary sums, and (much to his relief) Bernheimer often took the bait. Sensing an opportunity, the wealthy collector came to Ripton to make a unique offer. If the poet would regularly send him odd manuscripts, documents, galleys, and so forth, Bernheimer would pay him $150 a month.

Frost accepted the proposal on the spot. This money, in addition to the consultant's fee he was getting every month from Holt, assured him a decent living for the foreseeable future, although "he was never really free from worrying about money, even when he had enough. There was never enough, in his mind. He remained suspicious of the future, and was perpetually anticipating some dire event that would wipe him out financially."[4]

Frost's uncertain state of mind is registered in a poem sent to Louis Untermeyer on January 15, 1942:

> *To prayer I think I go,*
> *I go to prayer—*
> *Along a darkened corridor of woe*
> *And down a stair*
> *In every step of which I am abased.*
> *I wear a halter-rope about the waist.*
> *I bear a candle end put out with haste.*
> *For such as I there is reserved a crypt*
> *That from its stony arches having dripped*
> *Has stony pavement in a slime of mould.*
> *There I will throw me down an unconsoled*
> *And utter loss,*
> *And spread out in the figure of a cross.—*
> *Oh, if religion's not to be my fate*
> *I must be spoken to and told*
> *Before too late!*

A version of this poem existed as early as 1921, another dark time for Frost; he pulled it from his files now, reworked the ending, and sent it to his best friend for a reaction. But the poem was too personal, and Frost never included it in a book. He did not want the public to know this much about the "corridor of woe" his life had become. He did not like the image of himself as "an unconsoled / And utter loss."

He spent the winter of 1942, as usual, in Florida, with Kay. They were still busily involved in finishing Pencil Pines, as Frost called the two prefabricated bungalows erected there. It was an unsettled period for him, and not only because of the war. He was waiting for the publication, in April, of *A Witness Tree*, his first book of poems since 1936. His anxiety was fueled by an article that Carl Sandburg published in the March *Atlantic Monthly*. Responding indirectly to Frost's often quoted remark that he would as soon play tennis without a net as write free verse, Sandberg noted, quite rightly, that this "is almost as though a zebra should say to a leopard, 'I would rather have stripes than spots,' or as though a leopard should inform a zebra, 'I prefer spots to stripes.' "5

A Witness Tree is uneven, although it contains a number of poems that count among Frost's best, including "The Silken Tent," "I Could Give All to Time," "The Most of It," "The Subverted Flower," and "The Gift Outright." As a whole, the book testifies to a range of personal feeling that moves well beyond the more circumscribed emotional world of his previous volume, *A Further Range*. For a poet approaching his seventieth year, this volume represents no small feat. Lyric poets rarely continue to produce work of the highest quality at this age (although, of course, some of the best work here was written much earlier). As William H. Pritchard puts it, "If *North of Boston* reveals the narrative Frost at his best, *A Witness Tree*—so it seems to me—does the same thing for the lyric Frost."6 Having suffered so many deaths of close family members in a brief space of time, and thus "circumstanced with dark and doubt," Frost was nevertheless able to move forward into a clearing, to find a lyric space where being "not unbounded" (as he said in "Beech") was a cause for celebration. Once again, limits proved, for him, affirming.

The book was dedicated to Kay: "To K.M. for her part in it." It contains forty-two poems gathered in five sections, with two prefatory poems that shed light on the title and provide the reader with a point of entry. "Beech" sets the tone for the book as a whole and suggests that the title of the book operates on various symbolic levels:

> *Where my imaginary line*
> *Bends square in woods, an iron spine*
> *And pile of real rocks have been founded.*

> *And off this corner in the wild,*
> *Where these are driven in and piled,*
> *One tree, by being deeply wounded,*
> *Has been impressed as Witness Tree*
> *And made commit to memory*
> *My proof of being not unbounded.*
> *Thus truth's established and borne out,*
> *Though circumstanced with dark and doubt—*
> *Though by a world of doubt surrounded.*

The poem is founded, literally, on the tree that marked the boundaries of the Homer Noble farm, an old sugar maple marred by a spike, situated near a rock cairn that delineates the poet's property. This "imaginary" line is imaginary only in that it is "unseen." It is real enough, just as the poet's inner life is real, marked off from a "world of doubt" that surrounds it. The tree is "wounded," as Frost has been wounded in life; but the wounds are, paradoxically, essential; they are delineating, self-defining. As ever, Frost's nimble mind cannot help playing with words, such as "impress," which moves on both literal and symbolic planes. To amplify the symbol of the "witness tree" even further, Frost added some lines from *The New England Primer* as his second prefatory poem:

> *Zaccheus he*
> *Did climb the tree*
> *Our Lord to see.*

So the tree becomes a point of vantage, and the book as a whole is meant to become a vantage from which the careful reader can survey Frost and his world.

The first section is called "One or Two," and includes fourteen poems. "The Silken Tent" opens this sequence, and its grandeur and ease are such that few lyrics could possibly match it—or comfortably follow it in a sequence. That the section contains such poems as "All Revelation," "Happiness Makes Up in Height for What It Lacks in

Length," "The Most of It," and "The Subverted Flower" is fortunate; otherwise, it would have seemed all downhill from the start. But this section is consistently good, and the poems as a whole meditate on the isolation of the human soul and the need for love, though many of them suggest that "counter-love, original response" is impossible to achieve. "The Subverted Flower," surely the most unsettling of Frost's love poems, offers a dark testament to the torments of lust and the ways that physical desire gets in the way of spiritual union.

Frost moves from couples into the larger world in the next four sections. The second begins, resoundingly, with "The Gift Outright." But Frost is almost always less successful in the public realm, and he fails in most of these poems ("The Gift Outright" excepted) to maintain the level of writing seen in the first section. In fact, the book loses force throughout the last four parts.

Nonetheless, some memorable poems occur later in the volume, including "The Lesson for Today" and "November." The former is a fine narrative poem of ideas, in the Horatian vein of "New Hampshire" and "Build Soil," and it resonates with epigrammatic reflections on science, religion, and death; the latter is a rarely noted yet beautiful poem that laments "The waste of nations warring," although it was written in 1938, when the war still loomed in the middle distance. "It Is Almost the Year Two Thousand" began as a fragment in 1920 that was originally called "Nothing Gold Stays." A part of this separated off, becoming "Nothing Gold Can Stay," one of Frost's finest epigrams; the remaining lines now became a fresh poem:

> To start the world of old
> We had one age of gold
> Not labored out of mines,
> And some say there are signs
> The second such has come,
> The true Millennium,
> The final golden glow
> To end it. And if so
> (And science ought to know)

We well may raise our heads
From weeding garden beds
And annotating books
To watch this end deluxe.

Here Frost seems to anticipate the upcoming fiery end of the war at Hiroshima and Nagasaki, as some critics have suggested.[7] More obviously, the poem can be read in the context of "Nothing Gold Can Stay," where the poet declares, "Nature's first green is gold." That brief lyric turns on the idea of change, of Heraclitean mutability, as "leaf subsides to leaf." Thus the "final" end, witnessed at the millennium by the gardener (who from firsthand experience really knows that "nothing gold can stay"), is "deluxe" only in the sense of devalued, commercial goods: brilliant for a day. That is, nothing deluxe remains deluxe.

The final three sections of the collection amplify themes already raised in the first two, with several further ventures into the realm of political commentary. Repeatedly, Frost makes fun of social engineering as a solution to human woes, arguing that only a higher being can solve such a problem, as Zaccheus learned when he climbed the sycamore "Our Lord to see." Put another way, as in "The Secret Sits," Frost notes:

We dance round in a ring and suppose,
But the Secret sits in the middle and knows.

Lawrance Thompson oversimplifies when he says that the Secret in this poem is God. More plausibly, the Secret is the mystery at the heart of all being. There is "a secret inside things," Frost wrote in his notebook in 1910, and he never lost patience with this secret, or with the human incapacity to know what the point of life might be.[8] A poet has to allow for mystery, has to cultivate it just as he cultivates the silence that underlies, that buoys up and surrounds, language itself.

The last section of *A Witness Tree* plays off "Trespass," which takes up a theme raised in a more jocular way earlier in the volume in "To a Young Wretch," where the poet contemplates the theft of a spruce from his pasture by a young man looking for a Christmas tree. "Trespass" links back to "Beech," the literal "witness tree." Now Frost admits that he "had set no prohibiting sign," and that his "land was hardly fenced." The fence is symbolic, and must be respected by hikers, just as Frost's own boundaries must be respected by readers. The presence of visitors "Busying by my woods and brook / Gave me a strangely restless day," the poet tells us, but he does not regain a sense of his own boundaries until the unwanted trespasser asks for a glass of water, thus acknowledging that Frost, or the poet, is in possession of his own source of nourishment. The trespasser, after all, cannot just presume; he must *ask* for water. It is not his to take, only to accept:

> *Then came his little acknowledgment:*
> *He asked for a drink at the kitchen door,*
> *An errand he may have had to invent,*
> *But it made my property mine once more.*

And so readers knock at the poet's door. They may not have "really" wanted a drink, but in accepting one, they establish a bond with the poet, becoming something less than a trespasser; indeed, these visitors/readers play a part in reaffirming the boundaries that the poet was at pains to stake out.

A *Witness Tree* was largely celebrated by critics across the board. "His writing is clearer, more pointed, simpler, and richer than it ever has been," wrote Adam Margoshes in *Current History*.[9] Wilbert Snow noted that the book contained "half a dozen poems which have a right to stand with the best things he has written."[10] "This is a beautiful book, serene, observing, and passionate," declared Stephen Vincent Benét in the *Saturday Review of Literature*.[11] Reviewers often noted that many of the poems in this collection were rhymed fancies, and that few of them possessed the "bullet-like unity of structure" found in the best dozen or so poems in the book."[12] Yet all agreed that here was a noble book by a poet who had turned himself into an American institution. Frost had done this by managing to raise "perfectly common, seemingly simple, speech to a moving and memorable experience," as W. T. Scott wrote in *Poetry*.[13]

. . .

By mid-June, Holt had sold over ten thousand copies of the new volume, and sales showed no signs of letting up. Frost was joyous: "Really ten thousand in less than two months beats everything," he wrote to his editor. He was also delighted by the prospect of a forthcoming critical book on him by Lawrance Thompson called *Fire and Ice: The Art and Thought of Robert Frost*. This was the first full-length, critical study of his poetry, and Thompson had already shared the manuscript with him. "I have read enough of the book," Frost wrote to Thompson on August 20, 1942, "to see I am going to be proud of it. I take now and then a dip into a chapter gingerly. I don't want to find out too much about myself too suddenly."[14]

Frost even began to soften in his attitude to the war, in part because he had several close friends and relatives who had joined the military: Lawrance Thompson had been commissioned into the U.S. Navy, while Willard Fraser and young Prescott had enlisted. As might be expected, Frost was both elated and terrified by Prescott's enlistment in the Army Signal Corps. He had hoped that his grandson might get a place at West Point, but Prescott had his own plans—which demonstrated a quality of independence that Frost admired. In January 1943, Prescott was sent to Colorado for basic training, but only a few weeks after arriving he came down with a pulmonary problem, a family weakness that seemed to pass from father to son to grandson. Frost immediately wrote to John Bartlett to ask for help with Prescott. "I reminded him in my only letters so far that he had you or the thought of you for moral support not too far off," he said. "There is nothing you can do. But I thought if he was invalided out temporarily and not sent clear home he might find time on his hands and you might help him spend it by asking him for a night's visit at Boulder."[15]

Prescott recovered nicely, but he did visit the Bartletts one weekend, "charming everybody with his easy manner of talking, and a gift for story-telling and humor 'like his grandfather,' " Margaret Bartlett Anderson recalled.[16] The boy's clear affection and admiration for his grandfather was gratifying for the Bartletts to see, since they knew that Frost's relations with Prescott's father had been anguished.

As soon as he learned that Prescott was out of danger, Frost left for his Florida retreat. His interest in the botanical world of that semi-tropical state was, quite naturally, stirred by the acquisition of five acres, and he began to cultivate a grove of fruit trees on this formerly scrubby property. From Florida, Frost wrote to Prescott, "My chief interest in the war comes from your being in it. I don't listen to radio commentators and I hardly look at the papers. The headlines seem to be written by people who don't know anything about war."[17]

Despite this fresh interest, the war seemed far away. Frost had plenty of battles nearer home, and his mind dwelled on them. One of these was the long-standing issue of institutional affiliation. He had no genuine financial need to belong to a college faculty, but he liked working in an academic context. The contact with young people was satisfying, and the attentions paid to him by the faculty and larger community at Amherst, Michigan, and Harvard had sustained him through difficult periods. In playing out the role of public poet at these institutions, he had honed a sense of self and discovered (or created) a persona that felt natural. It was a complex mask: wise, witty, compassionate, ironic, cool, tough. In a sense, it was artfully composed of his own idiosyncratic mix of attributes.

Frost soon began to cast about for a more substantial academic connection than his current arrangement with Harvard. "I have decided to break the ice by setting foot in Amherst before all hearts are completely frozen over against me," he wrote to George Roy Elliott, explaining in the same letter that he had recently run into Alexander Meiklejohn, his old antagonist, and "made up."[18] He renewed contact with several old friends on the Amherst faculty, including George Whicher, Theodore Baird, and Reuben Brower, but this overture came to nothing.

As if Providence had heard his inward call, Frost was visited from out of nowhere by Ray Nash, a lecturer in the art department at Dartmouth, in March 1943. In some ways, Frost had never completely lost touch with Dartmouth. He liked to visit Hanover, where his daughter Irma had recently moved with her husband, John Cone, and their two sons. Despite his abbreviated career as a student at Dartmouth, he had kept a warm place in his heart for the college. "Ray

Nash was convinced that having Frost on the faculty was terribly important for Dartmouth, and Hopkins agreed," one professor recalled. "I think Frost had an affection for the college—especially the students. He was always warm toward them, called them 'my boys.' "[19]

Not long after Nash's visit, Frost went to the University of Indiana to spend three weeks as writer-in-residence. He was following in the footsteps of Bernard DeVoto, who had recently given some lectures there. The subject of DeVoto naturally arose at a faculty dinner party, and Frost made some out-of-school remarks about his old friend, saying that DeVoto had been under the care of a psychiatrist, and that the doctor had warned DeVoto about keeping company with Frost, whose presence was "too strong for DeVoto." This odd, unflattering remark got back to DeVoto, who confronted Frost directly: "Various remarks you made about me in Bloomington have been faithfully reported to me. I find myself not liking one of them."[20] Chapter and verse were spelled out.

Frost wrote to him immediately. The letter begins:

Benny Benny!

The first thing Kay did when she got here was to give me what you in your unconventional Western way would call Hell for talking about you too much in company. (She did not say in public.) And now comes your letter to give me more Hell for the same thing. I feel injured and misunderstood. You bring up an evening at Bloomington when the conversation not unnaturally got round more than once to your lecture there and to your latest book.

He goes on to give more details, portraying himself as DeVoto's defender. The letter ends: "Now let's forget differences and get to writing again."[21] DeVoto did, eventually, relent, but it took more than this cozy letter. Nevertheless, one sees Frost in a fascinating mode here as he attempts to justify himself, no doubt coloring the situation with his own rose-tipped brush. Like many great talkers, he could not resist

embellishing, shaping a story to his own ends, building a scrap of information, a fragment of gossip, into a full anecdote. Very quickly, he
came to believe his own fabrications, which meant that on successive
tellings he was, indeed, telling the "truth."

In May, Frost learned that *A Witness Tree* had been awarded the
Pulitzer Prize. As in the past, Louis Untermeyer had played a key role
in this award. The prize committee consisted of Untermeyer and two
other friends of Frost's: Bliss Perry and Wilbur L. Cross. Everyone
agreed that Frost's volume was the best collection of poems to appear
in 1942, but Perry and Cross felt that it was unseemly to award any
poet the prize four times. They voted, instead, for *Have Come, Am
Here*, a volume of José Garcia Villa. In those days, the committee's
decision was not final; it was merely a recommendation to the trustees
of Columbia University, who controlled the Pulitzer awards. Untermeyer wrote a minority report to the trustees explaining the situation,
and they sided with him. Frost was duly awarded the prize.

"Prizes are a strange thing for me to have come by, who have hated
competition and never wanted to be anybody's rival," Frost wrote to
one friend. "I could never have written a single poem if I had had to
have even in a remote corner of my mind the least thought that it
might beat another poem. Poetry is 'too high for rivalry.' It is supposed
to differ in kind rather than degree."[22] This remark stands in contrast
to earlier comments that Frost had made where he compared poetry to
boxing—remarks that had been much discussed in the press. In fact,
Frost's truest feelings were reasonable and complex; he certainly
understood the obvious, that poems "differ in kind rather than
degree," and he was wise enough to refrain from thinking of himself as
a poet in competition with others when he was actually writing. In
certain public situations, however, he could feel threatened; then he
would lash out, brag, or assume a macho stance. In this regard, he was
much like Hemingway, though the latter carried the art of machismo
to a higher, more absurd, level.

The arrangement with Dartmouth was made final that summer.
Frost would be called the George Ticknor Fellow in the Humanities
and would receive a salary of $2,500 a year, with an expense allowance

of $500 each year as well. He would live in Hanover and be available to students three times a week in the fall term, in early winter (before his usual trip to Florida), and in the late spring again. It was expected that he would give an occasional reading or lecture to the community as a whole, and that he would appear on ceremonial occasions, such as graduation. The contract was renewable each year, for an indefinite period.

"It was a great stroke of luck for Dartmouth," one administrator at the time recalled. "Frost was the only poet most Americans had ever heard of. They read his work, and admired him. He was an institution, and this connection to Dartmouth was good for us. In wartime, especially, it showed that civilization was continuing, and that the arts mattered and were part of a young man's education."[23] It was also good for Frost, who needed a better platform than the fellowship at Harvard was providing. He wanted to be the center of attention, and this simply wasn't possible at Harvard.

Frost took up an office in September in the Baker Library of Dartmouth—a splendid (and relatively recent) structure at the center of the campus. He did not live in Hanover but would come for weekends during the fall term, staying at the Hanover Inn. Each Friday night he would lecture in the small classroom adjacent to his office. He would be available for students at certain times on Saturdays and Sundays. The students were a mix of regular Dartmouth undergraduates and naval trainees in the Dartmouth V-12 program. Since Frost was famous, he attracted large numbers of students, so those who were admitted to the course (which had nondepartmental status) were lucky to get in.

Frost was not teaching a subject; he taught himself—his way of being in the world, the atmosphere of his mind. His conversation ranged widely over current affairs, the war, philosophy, agriculture, and—of course—poetry.[24] His vitality—intellectual as well as physical—struck everyone in the classroom. His face was huge, with shaggy white eyebrows overshading his bright eyes. His hands were rough and large, and he used them expressively when he talked. There were often long gaps of silence, and these were followed by sudden bursts of thought. Frost never spoke quickly, however; his low, rumbling voice lingered over each phrase. There was a good deal of repetition of phrases. Sentence fragments were common—part of a manner he had developed over years of lecturing. His wit was stunning, marked by verbal play, by quirky (often folksy) turns of phrase, by unusual juxtapositions. The range of reference was dazzling, moving from ancient astronomy to medieval Latin to baseball. Frost was the embodiment of Emerson's vision of man thinking.

One friend of long standing who attended every public performance by Frost was Sidney Cox, a member of the English department. Cox became a familiar companion in Hanover, and he and the poet were often seen together circling Occom Pond, a lovely body of water just off the Dartmouth campus. Other friends on the faculty included Stearns Morse, George Wood, Francis Childs, and Hewette Joyce, the last of whom Frost had gotten to know at Bread Loaf. Frost found the company exceptionally congenial, and would often sit in the lobby of the Hanover Inn with colleagues or students. "It was never 'too late' for Frost to hold forth, although 'too early' was another matter," one friend recalled. Frost still liked to sleep late when he could.

In April 1943, Frost had begun work on a short play that he called *Forty-third Chapter of Job, a Masque of Reason*. He intended to follow this with a complementary play to be called *The Whole Bible, a Masque of Mercy*. Through the summer, in Ripton, he continued working on the play, and in October he persuaded Kay Morrison to go with him to New York to talk to a Broadway producer about the possibility of mounting the two short plays, back to back. The producer was not overly excited, and Frost soon realized that his plays were not going to be ideal vehicles for staging. Broadway, then as now, was mainly a venue for commercial plays, and Frost's verse drama would hardly fit that bill.

He called these plays masques, but they were unlike the court plays pioneered in the sixteenth century by playwrights such as John Lyly. Those lush spectacles had been designed to entertain the queen and her courtiers and were highly stylized. Milton, in *Comus*, attempted a more poetic version of the masque, extending the genre into realms more closely identified with dramatic verse. What Frost did was to combine various elements from the traditions of Platonic dialogue, Puritan allegory, and closet drama, drawing on resources already developed (by himself) in earlier attempts at dramatic poetry—as in *North of Boston*.

Critics have largely been unwilling to take seriously either *A Masque of Reason* or *A Masque of Mercy*. George F. Bagby, for example, dismisses the masques in a parenthetical remark: "(I pass over *A Masque of Reason* and *A Masque of Mercy* as inessential parts of Frost's canon.)"[25] Poirier, Pritchard, Oster, and others give the poems barely a nod or ignore them altogether. John F. Lynen makes a significant nod in their direction: "No discussion of Frost's dramatic work would be complete without some consideration of the masques," he writes.[26] "They are poems rich in wit, utterly graceful in the tact with which they treat of the most difficult problems." But even Lynen pauses before the masques only briefly.[27]

Viewed biographically, the poems can be seen as Frost's attempt to grapple with the corridors of woe into which he had been plunged by the deaths of Marjorie, Elinor, and Carol. There was also the constant, unresolvable matter of Kay: he loved her, but she belonged to another. Frost seems to have identified on some level with the character of Job in *A Masque of Reason*, and with good cause. The question of why God would permit human suffering engaged him passionately. This great question, posed by college sophomores in their dormitories each year and then ignored for a lifetime, played on Frost's mind. His own lyrical poems had taken up repeatedly the question of evil, and in the best of them, such as "Design," the question itself had been elegantly framed. With wisdom and immense good humor, he now approached the same philosophical puzzle in dramatic form.

Oddly enough, these meditative dialogues are not very dramatic. In *A Masque of Reason*, Job and his wife (speaking from the afterlife) question God about his motives for afflicting Job. The masque itself purports to be an additional chapter to the existing Book of Job, but unlike the original, Frost's modern postscript is essentially humorous, even puckish, in tone, although there is plenty of serious thinking here. The masque turns on a fierce question put to God by Job himself: "Why did You hurt me so?"

In the original story, God was seen to negotiate with the Devil before Job; here, the Devil is brought in at the end, rather superficially, as if to see whether another perspective on the question might be useful. The question of suffering is unanswerable, as Frost knows; thus, Job and his wife, even the Devil, expect more of God than He is willing to give. For the most part, God evades the questions put to Him, often making frivolous responses. The core of God's response occurs in this reply to Job:

> . . . *the discipline man needed most*
> *Was to learn his submission to unreason;*
> *And that for man's own sake as well as mine.*

Having suffered hugely over the past decade, Frost had been forced to perform his own "submission to unreason." At times, his life had seemed a catalog of misfortunes. To an astonishing extent, however, he seems to have come to terms with this suffering by the mid-1940s.

Job, by contrast, is not satisfied with God's answer, and he forces Him into making a curious confession:

> *I was just showing off to the Devil, Job,*
> *As is set forth in Chapters One and Two.*

Job responds:

> *'Twas human of You. I expected more*
> *Than I could understand and what I get*
> *Is almost less than I can understand.*

A Masque of Reason is an oddly affecting work, somewhat out of character with Frost's other poems, although the bantering irreverence would have been familiar to audiences who had heard him lecture. An arresting aspect of the poem is the skeptical quality of the intelligence at work; Frost's language seems to draw on some deep reservoir of ancient wisdom, and part of that wisdom has to do with the doomed nature of human intelligence itself, which is always searching for "the reason" something happened. Frost, in his modernity, accepts the irrationality of the universe; indeed, he embraces it.

After a lung infection that kept him in Dick's House, the Dartmouth College infirmary, throughout the 1943 Christmas season, Frost returned to Pencil Pines in Florida. Lillian and Prescott had been living there since Prescott was given a medical discharge from the army in July, and now they moved into a cottage owned by a friendly neighbor, Elmer Hjort. Kay Morrison came too, occupying one of the two cottages.

Frost was still recovering from the lung infection in Florida, although he continued to tinker with A Masque of Reason. His spring lecture schedule had begun to fill up, and he felt anxious about what lay before him: a series of readings and talks at the University of Chicago, Rockford College (Illinois), Miami University (Ohio), the University of Cincinnati, Kenyon College, and Harvard. He would also return to Dartmouth for a week in late spring—part of his responsibilities as Ticknor fellow.

It was as if the call to perform healed his body. By spring he was vigorously charging from campus to campus, and he returned to Ripton in late spring in better shape than he had known for some time. One of the problems—a relatively minor one—that arose that summer was a feeling of hostility that seemed to be coming his way from Louis Untermeyer, who had left his Adirondack farm to join the Office of War Information as senior editor of publications. Untermeyer had urged Frost to get involved in war activities, but the old poet resisted. He wanted to remain above the battle, a "separatist," as he put it, a hater of "gang thinking." As he had written in "A Considerable Speck," he rejected the notion of universal brotherhood completely:

> *I have none of the tenderer-than-thou*
> *Collectivistic regimenting love*
> *With which the modern world is being swept.*

By contrast, Untermeyer was a liberal, with a strong interest in socialist ideas (he had, indeed, had significant Marxist sympathies before the war). As the extent of Hitler's campaign against the Jews became known, Untermeyer (who was Jewish) hurled himself more avidly into the war effort and tried, repeatedly, to interest Frost in the cause. He stopped by the Homer Noble farm to see him in July and, for the first time, the atmosphere between them was strained. When, by the second week of August, Untermeyer had not responded to a note Frost had sent him, the poet wrote a lengthy epistle in blank verse to Untermeyer that began:

> *I'd rather there had been no war at all*
> *Than have you cross with me because of it.*
> *I know what's wrong: the war is more or less*
> *About the Jews and as such you believe*
> *I ought to want to take some part in it.*
> *You ought to know—I shouldn't have to tell you—*
> *The army wouldn't have me at the front.*
> *And hero at the rear I will not be.*

In a crucial moment in this casual verse-epistle, Frost maintains that he has four essential connections in his life: "Kay, Lesley, you and Larry." Larry, of course, was Lawrance Thompson, who had grown close in the past few years in his Boswellian role. As if to defend himself against any charge of anti-Semitism, Frost wrote:

> *One of my four you'll notice is a Jew—*
> *No credit claimed for either him or me.*
> *The best part of my friendship for your race*
> *Is that I thought of it as lost in ours,*
> *And the long time it's taken me to see*

It was in part at least a race apart.
And even the part that is a race apart
I sympathize with. Give them back I say
All Palestine. No race without a country
Can be a nation.

Frost argues here that he has always considered Jews a part of the American nation as a whole, hence "lost in ours." But he goes a step further to suggest that he felt sympathy even with those who refused to be assimilated, such as the Zionists. In the end, however, Frost laments, "I'm so sick of all the vexing questions / This war has raised." He wishes for an end to hostilities in general, and a return to normalcy in his friendship with Untermeyer, which had sustained him over so many years.

As might be expected, Untermeyer was moved by the effort Frost had made to see that all fences were suitably mended. "Once more, you accomplish that miraculous thing of saying profound things as though you were not saying anything at all, as though you were musing for the sake of musing—and being amusing," Untermeyer responded.[28] There would never again be major difficulties between them.

Frost traveled from Cambridge to Hanover each weekend to resume his second year as Ticknor fellow. Quite often, he would visit local schools and colleges to lecture or read. "He used often to come to Exeter," recalls Gore Vidal, who met Frost that autumn at the Phillips Exeter Academy in New Hampshire in 1944. "His friend Hyde Cox had gotten a job there, as a schoolmaster. Frost was a frequent visitor to the school. I don't think a year went by without his reading and visiting classes. The boys were trooped into the chapel to listen to the great man read. Cox would introduce him in the most reverential tones. One time, he and Cox and a few students were walking in the nearby woods, and Frost bent down to lick a tree. 'Ah, you can taste the salt. We're close to the sea.' Cox was so impressed that he repeated this anecdote on several occasions."[29]

Cox himself recalls that Frost "was pleased that I had gone into teaching. He had encouraged me along those lines—he had, of course, been a teacher himself for such a long time. He had thought deeply about teaching."[30] Hyde Cox was soon added to the list of close associates that included Kay, Lesley, Untermeyer, and Thompson. Indeed, one sees Frost in old age gathering a close circle of reliable friends—and this was not "boughten friendship"—at his side. This was the real thing.

As the war drew to a close, Frost found himself in a remarkable position: greatly in demand on the lecture circuit, the recipient of four Pulitzers, and quite pleased by the circle he had established as he moved among his various residences. His health, if anything, appeared to have improved. He felt strong. "What he needed more than anything now," recalled one friend, "was the response of an audience, preferrably a young audience."[31] Fortunately, he was in a good position now to satisfy this need. He had made poetry his life, taken "the road less traveled by," and—to his amazement—it had "made all the difference."

19 THE HEIGHT OF THE
ADVENTURE
1945–1947

A good many things I have no heart for anymore, but I still like marked attention that savors of affection.
—FROST TO OTTO MANTHEY-ZORN, APRIL 22, 1947

Frost lingered in Florida throughout the early spring of 1945, savoring the bright weather. He wrote to Sidney Cox describing his "occupations," which included "watering our grove, building a stone wall (nearly forty linear feet), walking two level miles for groceries, and eating papayas. Let's see what else. Kathleen and I went down to Key West to see old friends. It is a cramped little island. We had a talk with John Dewey there. He's eighty-five. We are giving it out that I am practically seventy, and I've been yours in friendship exactly half the time. Have you stopped to realize it? Thirty-five is exactly half of seventy. See!"[1]

In March, *A Masque of Reason* was published to generous reviews. Mark Shorer hailed it as "a kind of ballet in verse" in the *Atlantic Monthly*.[2] *Time* praised the "ruminative philosophic wit whose pentameters are salted with gentle satire and unobtrusive learning."[3] Only here and there a discordant note could be heard, as when Conrad Aiken (a poet who wrote uncomfortably in the long shadows of Frost and Eliot, who had both been his contemporaries at Harvard) chided in The *New Republic*: "Dare one whisper, of a poet to whom one so gratefully owes so much, that a little more affectionate and affective care with his blank verse might have prevented its becoming quite so—and frequently—unrewardingly blank?"[4]

Frost felt, however, that *A Masque of Reason* had not been properly understood, especially by Lawrance Thompson, his friend and biographer, who reviewed it in the *New York Times Book Review*.[5] The masque was meant to embody Frost's stance as an Old Testament Christian, to underline his philosophical dualism of spirit and matter, and to underscore the conflict between justice and mercy (more pronounced in *A Masque of Mercy*) that was central to his thinking. The satire of the masque was directed not at Christianity, as Thompson suggested, but at a kind of rationalism that characterized modern secular thinking.

Peter J. Stanlis recalls, "Frost had spent the summer of 1943 talking with Rabbi Reichert about the Old Testament, with special concern for the Book of Job, on which Reichert was a recognized authority. After Frost wrote *A Masque of Reason*, he read it to Reichert, who waxed enthusiastic about it. A very significant event happened after the book's publication. Larry Thompson reviewed it, showing his total misunderstanding of the essential point of the satire by claiming it was an ironical 'unholy play' which satirized Christianity. This provoked a furious response in Frost, and undoubtedly contributed much to the growing alienation between Frost and Thompson."[6]

In April, Frost celebrated his seventieth birthday in Amherst with close friends, then returned to Hanover for three weeks to finish off his second year as Ticknor fellow. From there, he returned to Ripton, where he spent the summer working quietly on *A Masque of Mercy*, his companion piece to *A Masque of Reason*. The new drama moved closer to allegory than the previous one, parodically so, with Jonah coming back in the character of Jonah (or Jonas) Dove, who discusses the matter of divine justice with a latter-day reincarnation of St. Paul ("the fellow who theologized / Christ almost out of Christianity") and a vaguely artsy couple who run a proletarian bookstore. He is Keeper (full name: His Brother's Keeper) and she, Jesse Bel (Jezebel). At the center of the discussion is the Pauline idea that God allows injustice in the world so that mercy can overcome it—a mode of argument familiar to readers of *Paradise Lost*. The central idea of the masque, embodied in its concluding line, spoken by Keeper, is, "Nothing can make injustice just but mercy."

The drama begins happily enough, in New York City, with the bookstore owner and his wife and a customer chatting. Suddenly, a fugitive appears at the door. "God's after me!" he cries. He introduces himself as Jonas Dove, although Frost and the others refer to him as Jonah. Like Job in *A Masque of Reason*, Jonah is obsessed with the question of divine justice. One hears Frost distinctly in Jonah's lament about

> This modern tendency I find in Him
> To take the punishment out of all failure
> To be strong, careful, thrifty, diligent,
> Anything we once thought we had to be.

Paul's sense of mercy is ultimately more vital than either Keeper's socialist vision of justice (he considers Karl Marx the Messiah) or Jonah's Old Testament version. When Keeper decides to plunge into the cellar of his bookstore to contemplate this insight, the door mysteriously slams shut and he dies of fright (not quite instantly: he lingers for a few remarks, like a dying soprano in an Italian opera). The scenario is cartoonish, even slapstick, and a challenge to readerly patience.

A Masque of Mercy is much less successful than its predecessor. The flippancy of the language, with glancing allusions to contemporary culture (a quip about the *New Yorker* magazine, for example, is oddly out of place), seems ill suited to the material. In attempting to create concrete universals, as Milton did with the characters of Sin and Death in *Paradise Lost*, Frost fails to give credible or particular life to them. Keeper is strangely ignorant for the owner of a bookstore (he thinks that Rockwell Kent wrote *Moby-Dick*), and his wife, too, is unevenly drawn, her rhetoric veering from the profound to the idiotic. Neither Jesse nor Paul reacts to Jonah's death in a way that any reader would find convincing.

One of the peculiar aspects of this masque is the consistent echoing of "Home Burial." "She's had some loss she can't accept from God," says Jonah of Jesse Bel, for example, as if to explain her oddness. But Jesse Bel never really emerges in this closet drama as a figure with a consistent point of view. Even the central characters, Paul, Jonah, and Keeper, are puppets on the mental stage of Frost's interior mind, mouthing sentiments that he apparently felt the need to express at the moment despite their lack of any organic role in the unfolding drama. *A Masque of Mercy* is less interesting as poetry than as evidence of a shift in Frost's thinking as he moved into his eighth decade. His mind was turning more and more to mercy, veering away from a rigid sense of justice; indeed, Jonah dies saying, "I think I may have got God wrong entirely." To which Keeper, wisely, responds: "All of us get each other pretty wrong."

Frost lingered over this play throughout the summer. It must have seemed peculiarly relevant to him as atomic bombs dropped on Hiroshima and Nagasaki in early August, raising profound questions of both justice and mercy. In general, as might be expected, Frost rejoiced that the war was coming to an end; but he understood that the nuclear age was looming. "The new explosive can be bad for us," he wrote to Lesley, "but it can't get rid of the human race for there would always be left, after the bomb, the people who fired it—enough for seed and probably with the same old incentive to sow it."[7] With eerie detachment, he added, "There's a lot of fun in such considerations."

Frost's third year as Ticknor fellow took a slightly different course. There was a new president at Dartmouth now, John Sloan Dickey, and he wanted Frost to spend more time on campus. Frost decided to live in Hanover for several weeks at a time, in fall and spring. "He was not really teaching an academic course," Dickey recalled. "Frost was a presence, and important to us, and we hoped for more of him. He was amenable, too. Very quick to agree to whatever I proposed." Frost offered to grade the students, but Dickey explained that this was unnecessary; he recalled a time when Frost asked everyone to write something for the next class: "He gathered the papers, and then asked the students if anyone felt that what he had written was of permanent value, even to himself. When nobody responded, he said, 'I'll be damned if I'll be a perfunctory reader of perfunctory writing,' then simply threw the whole batch of student work into the wastebasket, unread. It made quite an impression on them."[8]

This sense of theatricality only added to Frost's popularity. The student body swelled with servicemen returning from the war, and many of them wanted to have the experience of encountering Frost. "Frost was popular with us," recalls Philip Booth, a Dartmouth student after the war whose own poetry Frost came to admire. "He was keenly interested in all of us, and wanted to hear about our experiences. He was especially interested in those of us who were married. I suspect he was attracted to young married couples—it may have reminded him of his own early days with Elinor." Frost eagerly sought out Booth and his young wife and would often have dinner with them in their tiny apartment, talking happily until after midnight.[9]

Frost had difficulty balancing his need for contact with people and his desire for solitude; poems, as he often noted, rooted in the latter. One new poem written in 1945 was "One Step Backward Taken." It harks back to Frost's experience of a flood in 1927, when he was traveling by train across Arizona on his way home to Amherst; looking out the window, he saw a bridge washed out with a car balanced on one bank, edging backward carefully each time a slice of earth fell away—an astounding image that Frost puts to good use in the poem:

> Not only sands and gravels
> Were once more on their travels,
> But gulping muddy gallons
> Great boulders off their balance
> Bumped heads together dully
> And started down the gully.
> Whole capes caked off in slices.
> I felt my standpoint shaken
> In the universal crisis.
> But with one step backward taken
> I saved myself from going.
> A world torn loose went by me.

> *Then the rain stopped and the blowing*
> *And the sun came out to dry me.*

The first seven lines comprise a movement of sorts: a vision of the "universal crisis" collapsed into an image of colliding elements of nature. Uncharacteristically, Frost refuses to punctuate the lines normally; the syntax, in effect, mimics the confusion created by the disruption. Like the wary animal in "A Drumlin Woodchuck" who makes its "own strategic retreat," the poet (emulating the driver in the car on the edge of the precipice) withdraws to save himself as a "world torn loose" went by him.

"Directive," one of Frost's most central poems, was also written during this period. Although past the time of life when major poems came regularly, here he recovers temporarily his full powers in a poem that reconsiders his entire poetic project, interrogates it thoroughly—much as Yeats had done in "The Circus Animals' Desertion" (1939), one of his best late poems. "Directive" is both epitaph and poetic credo. As the latter, it offers a "directive" to his imagination, a map of his inner landscape. As in Milton's "Lycidas," the poet confronts one of his major themes: how to survive an overwhelming experience, one that threatens to destroy the imagination itself.[10] Both Milton and Frost take the reader through a harrowing reconstruction of emotional destitution, confronting the dark aspect of sentimentality, which is death to the poet. While Milton looks forward to "fresh woods and pastures new," Frost is able to say (to himself as much as to his reader): "Here are your waters and your watering place. / Drink and be whole again beyond confusion."

At the outset in "Directive," the poet confronts a nearly obliterated landscape, discovering a "house that is no more a house / Upon a farm that is no more a farm" within a "town that is no more a town." Like Virgil beside Dante in the *Inferno*, Frost accompanies us "Back out of all this now too much for us." He returns to a time "made simple by the loss / Of detail." The details, perhaps, would hurt too much if we had to experience them again freshly. We don't know, and don't even want to know, the names of the lost.

The reader should be warned that Frost is a guide "Who only has at heart your getting lost." This is the Christian (or, more specifically, Pauline) paradox: that only the lost can be saved. One must plunge into loss and despair before arriving at a condition of salvation. This line also echoes Thoreau, who writes in *Walden*, "Not till we are lost, in other words, not till we have lost the world, do we begin to find ourselves, and realize where we are and the infinite extent of our relations."

The traveler in the poem is taken on a "serial ordeal," coming upon a deserted village with its "forty cellar holes." This is, as Katherine Kearns has noted, "a deconstructed land that evades the pitfalls of both town and farm even as it repudiates the possibility of an uncorrupted wild space."[11] "Directive" seems to occupy some of the emotional terrain of Eliot's *The Waste Land*—that is, the modern world is seen as a broken place, a ruined landscape where all traditional symbols are drained of content. Indeed, Frost seems to allude directly to Eliot by putting a broken chalice in the poem as the guide claims to have hidden "a broken drinking goblet like the Grail" in the instep arch of an old cedar near the brook that runs by the property.

Perversely, the chalice is "Under a spell so the wrong ones can't find it, / So can't get saved, as Saint Mark says they mustn't." Frost refers here to Mark 4:11–12, where Jesus says, "Unto you it is given to know the mystery of the kingdom of God: but unto them that are without, all these things are done in parables. That seeing they may see, and not perceive; and hearing they may hear, and not understand; lest at any time they should be converted, and their sins should be forgiven them." The uninitiated, those spiritually unprepared for the experience, cannot participate in the revelations offered here. Those who have not received their education by metaphor—their training in parables, so to speak—will be left out.

Not all critics have been impressed by Frost's cleverness here. The poem "hints at ironies that cannot be consequential except to those who have enclosed themselves within the circuit of Frost's own work, and for them the ironies ought to be of a claustrophobic self-reference that is at odds with the pretentiously large rhetorical sweeps and presumptuous ironies in which the poem indulges itself," complains Richard Poirier. But even Poirier cannot deny that parts of this poem represent instances of Frost's "descriptive and visionary genius," especially the "wildly brilliant" opening.[12]

The narrative builds to the point where a brook is found: "Too lofty and original to rage." It is near its source, so icy cold. Frost seems to invite the reader who has followed him into this wild to go back to whatever source has been important for him or her. "Go back to a favorite poet, or a place you almost forgot," Frost once said to an audience before a reading of this poem. So the poet directs the reader to reconnect to some important emotional source (as in the Latin roots of the word religion: *re-ligio*, meaning "to link back").

In the end, the poet encounters a torn landscape but still refuses to give in to despair. He urges himself (as much as the reader whom he serves as guide):

> Make yourself up a cheering song of how
> Someone's road home from work this once was,
> Who may be just ahead of you on foot
> Or creaking with a buggy load of grain.

He adds, memorably: "The height of the adventure is the height / Of country where two village cultures faded / Into each other."

Encountering such a charged scene, Frost nevertheless refuses to succumb to nostalgia, although (as with many great poems) that threat is always present. The exact setting for "Directive" doesn't really matter, but Frost would certainly have had in the back of his mind the farm at Derry and the brook nearby, Hyla Brook, where his children played. There is also an abandoned farm much like the one in "Directive" not far behind the Homer Noble farm. But abandoned farms, even whole villages, are commonplace in northern New England. "As a hiker," recalls Reginald L. Cook, "Frost came across them regularly. It would be a mistake to try to locate this farm anywhere in particular. It is typical, even universal, in its complexion and details."[13]

One geological point of interest in the poem is the appearance of some dramatic ledges. In a memoir by the sculptor Walker Hancock (who did a bust of Frost), one finds this interesting recollection: "Frost had explored some of the woods of Cape Ann with us. One day I showed him 'the Ledges.' These are a wide stretch of granite on my property that had been laid bare long ago by quarrymen who never thereafter carried out their intention to excavate at that location. They are now strangly beautiful—quite remote, surrounded by pines and bordered with little pools. Still visible are marks of the boulders that were pushed across them in the ice age. Frost was especially interested in them, and a short time later these lines appeared in his poem entitled 'Directive' (first published during the winter of 1946):

> The ledges show lines ruled southeast-northwest,
> The chisel work of an enormous Glacier
> That braced his feet against the Arctic Pole."[14]

"Directive" stands somewhat by itself in Frost's work, not quite resembling anything that came before, but lodged firmly in the tradition of what M. H. Abrams has called the Greater Romantic Lyric.[15] In Abrams's outine of the genre, typified by Wordsworth in "Lines Composed a Few Miles Above Tintern Abbey," the poet (as solitary speaker) returns to a place that has been meaningful at some past time. He sinks into deep meditation, having been forced by the circumstances to contemplate lost time, and having had his sense of spirituality quickened by the encounter with nature. The poem moves toward a resolution that rises to levels of ecstasy or determination—a totalizing moment or epiphany of sorts. The reader has the experience of having been taken on a journey that is both physical and spiritual, one colored and given texture by a particular landscape. In attempting such a thing, and succeeding so magnificently at an age when most writers have long since abandoned, or been abandoned by, the muse, Frost was once again proving himself worthy of his reputation.

In late September 1946, Frost lectured at Kenyon College in Ohio. Among those in the audience was the critic Lionel Trilling, who recorded the event in his journals:

At Kenyon: Frost's strange speech—apparently of a kind that he often gives—he makes himself the buffoon—goes into a trance of aged childishness—he is the child who is rebelling against all the serious people who are trying to organize him—take away his will and individuality. It was, however, full of brilliantly shrewd things—impossible to remember them except referring to the pointless discussion of skepticism the evening before, he said: "Skepticism"—is that anything more than we used to mean when we said, "Well, what have we here?"—But also the horror of the old man—fine looking old man—having to dance and clown to escape (also for his supper)—American, American in that deadly intimacy, that throwing away of dignity—"Drop that dignity! Hands up" we say—in order to come into anything like contact and to make anything like a point.[16]

This account is harrowing to read. Trilling cringed at the manner Frost had evolved over many years: the joshing, avuncular, ingratiating manner that won over large audiences but, at least in Trilling's mind, demeaned the great poet and his work.

After the Kenyon visit, Frost stopped by to see Victor and Louise Reichert in Cincinnati. Louise Reichert recalls that "Frost could be a temperamental houseguest, although he was often considerate and kind, too." The rabbi was busy preparing a sermon for the eve of Sukkoth, the Feast of Tabernacles, "when Frost made it clear he wanted to give the sermon that day." He had a strong didactic streak, and the notion of giving an actual sermon was attractive to him. Reichert eagerly made a place in the ceremony for his friend. He had always believed "that Frost had strong connections to Judaism, more so than most Christians."[17] Reichert pointed to the recent masques, which were centered on the Old Testament stories of Job and Jonah. (It should be noted that Frost's God is almost always the fierce Jehovah of the Book of Job and not the more gentle Elohim who visited Adam and Eve in the Garden of Eden.)

Reichert recorded Frost's sermon, and later surprised him (unpleasantly) with a printed version of what he had said. Frost began by saying that he had once valued courage above all other virtues, but he currently favored wisdom over courage. "Now religion always seems to me to come round to something beyond wisdom," he added. "It's a straining toward wisdom that will do well enough in the day's work, you know, living along, fighting battles, going to wars, beating each other, striving with each other, in war or in peace—sufficient wisdom." Frost had taken his cue from the Union Prayer Book, which had been read only minutes earlier by the rabbi: "Look with favor, O Lord, upon us, and may our service ever be acceptable unto Thee." Circling back to this prayer, Frost dwelled on the idea that only God's grace or mercy makes any gift one can give Him acceptable.

Frost had been working on *A Masque of Mercy* throughout the fall, even as he traveled, and his sermonizing in Cincinnati sparked a number of ideas; in particular, the notion of what gifts are acceptable to God became a focus for the concluding speeches of Paul and Keeper. Rather quickly, Frost was able to bring the masque to an end, and in November he sent it to Holt for publication in early winter. At the same time, Frost gathered the poems he had written over the past few years into a volume called *Steeple Bush*, also planned for publication by Holt in 1947.

In many ways, Frost's life had improved after a troubling decade of personal disasters. His living arrangements, which closely involved the Morrisons, were more than satisfactory, and he liked having a range of bases: Ripton, Cambridge, Miami. The Dartmouth appointment had worked out well, and President Dickey intended to renew the Ticknor fellowship as often as Frost would let him. "It was only in our interest to keep him," Dickey said. But family pressures continued to make the poet's life uneasy.

Most of the family pressures now came from Irma, who had separated from John Cone in 1944. Irma's troubled mental state had made her a difficult wife, and in 1946 Cone decided to divorce her. By now, her paranoia had grown to the point where the doctors who saw her predicted she would soon find living on her own difficult if not impossible. Having recently experienced the suicide of Carol, Frost dreaded a similar turn in Irma's life. Her younger son, Harold, was only six, and Frost considered the relations between mother and son unhealthy.

Irma, having essentially been abandoned by her husband, clung to the boy.

She had been living in Hanover, New Hampshire, with Cone but now wanted to leave that town, which was full of bad memories. She turned to her father for help, as she had in the past; as ever, he was willing and able to assist her, but the anxieties were difficult for him to bear. Furthermore, he did not exactly relish her proximity, which was bound to create awkward situations. Nevertheless, Frost and Kay went searching for a house for Irma and Harold near Cambridge.

They located one in nearby Acton, just far enough away from Cambridge so that Irma would not be on her father's doorstep every day. It was a small, two-bedroom cape that Frost could rent inexpensively. By early winter, Irma and her son were settled there, and Frost was able to escape to Florida.

A good deal of time at Pencil Pines was spent making plans for his next birthday, on March 26. The prospect of an upcoming honorary doctorate from the University of California at Berkeley appealed to him, not only because he always enjoyed being honored; it had been over sixty years since Frost left San Francisco with his sister and mother, and he looked forward to revisiting old haunts. The one awkwardness of the trip was that two of Frost's biggest collectors, Earle J. Bernheimer and Louis Mertins, lived in California, and both would be falling over themselves to play host to their favorite poet. Frost expected complications.

In fact, the visit to California was a complete success. Mertins and Bernheimer organized a gala dinner at the Hotel Mark Hopkins in San Francisco, with a hundred guests present, many of them old friends from Bread Loaf, including Wallace Stegner and Edith Mirrielies. The waiters carried in a vast birthday cake with "Stopping by Woods on a Snowy Evening" written in white frosting against a chocolate backdrop.

The night after this party, Mertins drove Frost to Beverly Hills, where Bernheimer lived in a splendid house. Another birthday celebration was held there, with dozens of well-known writers, businessmen, actors, and local worthies in attendence. It was a bit overwhelming for Frost, who grew increasingly exhausted by having to meet and exchange pleasant words with so many strangers. He now began to regret a promise to return to Redlands a few days later, where Mertins had arranged for him to lecture at the local university. But he did so, and lectured to a crammed auditorium for over an hour and a half.

One marvels at Frost's stamina. He was seventy-two, but age seems not to have dampened his appetite for travel or public exposure. He stopped briefly in Ann Arbor on the way home, then spent only a week in Cambridge before returning to Hanover for his spring work as Ticknor fellow. This was followed quickly by a visit to Amherst, where he stayed in the home of the new president, Charles W. Cole, who had been his student at Amherst some years before.

He had always liked Cole immensely, and was relieved that Stanley King was gone. (Unfairly, he always imagined that King had plotted to get rid of him at Amherst.) Once again, he dropped heavy hints to Cole that he was still not averse to the idea of returning someday to the Amherst faculty. Cole, wisely, remained neutral on the subject, although he made it clear that Amherst had always considered Frost a significant member of its extended family.

Back in Cambridge in early May, Frost was startled one afternoon by an unexpected visit from T. S. Eliot, who appeared in the doorway of his house on Brewster Street wearing a mackintosh and carrying a folded umbrella. It had been over a decade since Frost had last seen him, and Eliot had aged significantly, his face chiseled by time, his shoulders slumping. He had come to the States to visit a brother who was ill; to defray expenses, he had accepted an offer to lecture at Harvard. Eliot fondly recalled having met Frost in 1928 at the home of Harold Monro in London; they had also, of course, seen each other briefly at the St. Botolph Club in Boston in 1932 during the time of Eliot's Norton lectures. It amazed Frost that Eliot—surely the most influential and highly regarded cultural figure of the day—would stop by, unannounced, with flattering words. Sitting over a pot of tea, the two exchanged compliments, talking about works-in-progress, musing on their early days in Britain. They also discussed the sad fate of Ezra Pound, who had been arrested after making treasonous wartime broadcasts on Italian radio. Eliot, who seemed modest and friendly, showed no signs of hostility toward Frost, even though he must have known that Frost had often bad-mouthed him in public over the past two decades. Frost, for his part, was thoroughly won over.

Steeple Bush was published in late May, and the reviews appeared throughout the summer. Like most writers, Frost dreaded the reviews; even the good ones made him anxious and unhappy. "They always get it wrong," he once told an interviewer. Intuitively, he understood that critics would be looking for signs of diminishment. Indeed, the signs were there; only a few of the poems in this collection were equal to his best work. The title refers to a plant (also called hardhack) that grew profusely around the farm in Ripton. The volume was dedicated to Frost's six grandchildren: Prescott, John (Jacky), Elinor, Lesley Lee, Robin, and Harold.

The shrewdest review was written by Randall Jarrell, the most gifted poet-critic of his generation of American poets.[18] Jarrell began with a lengthy, admiring account of "Directive," concluding, "There are weak places in the poem, but these are nothing beside so much longing, tenderness, and passive sadness, Frost's understanding that each life is tragic because it wears away into the death that it at last half welcomes—that even its salvation, far back at the cold root of things, is make-believe, drunk from a child's broken and stolen goblet hidden among the ruins of the lost cultures. Much of the strangeness of the poem is far under the surface, or else so much on the surface, in the subtlest of details (how many readers will connect the 'serial ordeal' of the eye pairs with the poem's Grail-parody?), that one slides under it unnoticing. There are no notes in the back about this Grail." The last quip, of course, refers to the footnotes appended to Eliot's Grail poem, *The Waste Land*. Jarrell also noted that "there is nothing else in *Steeple Bush* like 'Directive.' " The one other poem of some importance, in his view, was "The Ingenuities of Debt," which he praised for its "dry mercilessness."

Jarrell's opinion was shared by many readers, although Frost had by now built up such a layer of goodwill among critics that he was generally praised. As Gladys Campbell observed in *Poetry*, "The time is long past for casual contemporary evaluation [of Frost]. . . . Through textbooks and anthologies some of his poems are so well-known to schoolboys that they are amazed to find that Frost is a living poet. He belongs with Tennyson, Wordsworth, Longfellow—all those who are to be read before examinations."[19]

While *Steeple Bush* is not quite equal to its major predecessors, it has its own peculiar radiance and affect. The first section is "Steeple Bush," and contains seven poems, including "Directive," which overpowers the volume as a whole. It would be hard for a poem of this distinction *not* to overpower its neighbors in a slim volume. The other groupings are "Five Nocturnes," "A Spire and a Belfry," "Out and Away," and "Editorials." Overall, the poems play to each other beautifully, amplifying a theme sounded early, in "Something for Hope," where the poet puts the steeple bush before the reader, a "lovely blooming" that has very little to say for itself apart from this beauty. It cannot be eaten, it crowds out other plants, and even the most resolute gardener will have difficulty getting rid of it. Frost suggests that the cycles of nature will naturally shift the local flora in

> A cycle we'll say of a hundred years.
> Thus foresight does it and laissez faire,
> A virtue in which we all may share
> Unless a government interferes.

With the accumulated wisdom of seven decades, Frost urges "Patience and looking away ahead, / And leaving some things to take their course."

The second section seems lighter in tone, but there is gravity here as well. Frost writes about terror (of the dark, of death), about putting false hope in the comfort of distant lights; "The Night Light" is a compressed and memorable lyric (it was actually written in September 1928—while Frost was visiting England):[20]

> She always had to burn a light
> Beside her attic bed at night.
> It gave bad dreams and broken sleep,

> But helped the Lord her soul to keep.
> Good gloom on her was thrown away.
> It is on me by night or day,
> Who have, as I suppose, ahead
> The darkest of it still to dread.

A cluster of poems follows that contains one rarely noted but quite remarkable poem, "The Fear of God," which might be taken as Frost's look backward on his own career:

> If you should rise from Nowhere up to Somewhere,
> From being No one up to being Someone,
> Be sure to keep repeating to yourself
> You owe it to an arbitrary god
> Whose mercy to you rather than to others
> Won't bear too critical examination.

The poem goes on to urge the reader: "Stay unassuming." He regards "the uniform of who you are" as "the curtain of the inmost soul."

The poems here repeatedly insist on humility, and the poet responds to the bleakness of the universe with a rueful shake of the head. This mode of wisdom-giving continues in "Out and Away," the third grouping, which opens with another strong poem, "The Middleness of the Road." The ease of phrasing and the light, running quality of the lines are stunning. The poet begins with an image of finitude that, mysteriously, beckons toward but cannot approach infinity:

> The road at the top of the rise
> Seems to come to an end
> And take off into the skies.

Quickly, the poem becomes a meditation on "near and far," on the present life in the body, and the spiritual realm embodied in the "universal blue" of the sky. The human mind (represented here as Fancy) cannot take satisfaction in the comforts of what lies near, nor can it leap into transcendence. That is, it cannot consort comfortably with "absolute flight and rest." Before a reading of this poem, Frost once said that "you can only go so far, which is what being human means. We're human. We're not immortal. At least not yet."[21]

The final section, gathered under the title "Editorials," is full of the usual resentment against government planners "With the intention blazoned on their banners / Of getting one more chance to change our manners" ("The Planners"). He believes that "States strong enough to do good are few" ("No Holy Wars for Them"). Even doomsayers are chided in "The Broken Drought." These poems, which would have fit nicely in *A Further Range*, represent an extension of the tonalities of that collection.

"The Ingenuities of Debt," that piece of "dry mercilessness" praised by Randall Jarrell, fits in perfectly with the poems in this section, but it was actually written on the Derry farm some five decades earlier. Typically, it lingered in Frost's folder of unfinished poems for many years. The poem was unfinished largely because it turns on his inventing an ancient inscription from a long-destroyed city in the Middle East, and Frost had trouble getting a good enough line to fit here. It obviously took forty years to find it: "TAKE CARE TO SELL YOUR HORSE BEFORE HE DIES / THE ART OF LIFE IS PASSING LOSSES ON." Once again, the mere presence of a poem written so long before its publication argues against applying any traditional notion of poetic development to Frost. As a poet, he was born whole: fingernails, hair, teeth, everything in place. He didn't "grow" but changed, evolving by extension and amplification.

In his collected edition of 1949, Frost appended three poems to *Steeple Bush*, one of them being "Choose Something Like a Star," which first appeared in a selection of his work made by Louis Untermeyer in 1943. This extraordinary poem—another peak of this period—is written in a measured, four-beat cadence; the opening recalls Keats's famous "Bright Star," which Frost alludes to directly in line 18. By inviting comparison with a famous predecessor, Frost takes a certain risk, but the poem can withstand such scrutiny. The poet addresses the star, which he once told an audience at Bread Loaf was meant to represent "something far away, like a star or an ancient poet."[22] Frost once again adopts the mask of wisdom, suggesting to readers that they (as he presumably has) look beyond whatever is around them to something more permanent, even exalted. The poem ends on a note also heard in Emerson's "Self-Reliance":

> *So when at times the mob is swayed*
> *To carry praise or blame too far,*
> *We may choose something like a star*
> *To stay our minds on and be staid.*

The wordplay on "stay" and "staid" is suggestive—one fastens on to a distant object of veneration, risks becoming "staid" (boring, old-fashioned) in order to be "stayed" (rooted, attached). "We may take something like a star, or a poem, or God, to stay our minds on, and be staid," Frost commented.[23] One of the poets he would himself read for this purpose, as he noted, was Catullus—the ancient lyricist of love.

Frost spent a quiet summer in Ripton, waiting for the reviews of *Steeple Bush*. "He was like most poets," Richard Eberhart says, "fretting over the response of critics. The more well known he became, the worse it seemed if someone didn't like him." As it were, most of the reviews were celebratory—even those that found some falling off in this collection. The harshest response came in *Time*, where the anonymous reviewer said, "Frost is the dean of living U.S. poets by virtue of both age and achievement. At 72, the four-time Pulitzer Prize–winner has lost little of his craftsmanship and none of his crackling vigor. But what was once only granitic Yankee individualism in his work has hardened into bitter and often uninspired Tory social commentary. The 43 poems of *Steeple Bush* do nothing to enlarge his greatness and not one of them could begin to displace the best of his *Collected Poems*."[24] Given that the book contains "Directive," one has to wonder about this reviewer.

Frost reacted badly to the response in *Time*, as any sensitive poet would; but there was enough respect, even adulation, available in other publications to make up for this slight. Writing in the *Saturday*

Review, for example, Leonard Bacon extolled "the bewildering beauty" of the book, finding "sharp imagery" and "savage satire" in the poems. "There is no falling off," he declared.[25] In the *Atlantic Monthly*, Donald A. Stauffer suggested that Frost's poems were "not so much simple as elemental." Stauffer was among the earliest critics to recognize the darker aspect of his vision: "Frost is uncompromisingly aware of an agonizing universe, and creates apocalyptic twentieth-century visions no less grim than Hardy, Yeats, Eliot, and Auden."[26] This line of criticism would be amplified in the next decade by Randall Jarrell and Lionel Trilling—both of whom focused on the tragic sides of Frost almost too intensely.

Frost was, by now, well beyond the harm of reviewers, having ripened into an American institution. More remarkably, he was still writing poems of lasting value at an age when most lyric poets are long past the point of meaningful productivity. In this, he stands beside his great contemporaries Yeats and Stevens, who also managed to find a voice and stance in their later years that allowed them to continue writing poems equal to or better than their earlier work.

20

THE GREAT
ENTERPRISE OF LIFE
1948–1953

There is a shadow always on success
Often mistaken for a sense of sin.

—FROST, NOTEBOOK ENTRY, 1950

Irma's condition deteriorated throughout the summer, and by early August it became clear that she was no longer able to look after herself. One day she left her house in Acton and wandered aimlessly around Cambridge, confused and anxious. Toward the end of the afternoon, she called Lillian, who was staying at her father-in-law's house on Brewster Street (Frost was still in Vermont). Sensing trouble, Lillian persuaded her to come to Brewster Street. That same afternoon, she called Frost to explain the situation, and he contacted his friend Dr. Merrill Moore for help. That night, Kay drove him from Ripton to Cambridge.

By now, it had become clear that Irma's husband, John Cone, would take no further responsibility for her, although he could be counted on to look after Harold. Irma was entirely in her father's charge, and he understood the grim task ahead of him. On Moore's advice, he arranged for Irma to be placed in the state mental hospital in Concord, New Hampshire, aware that he could not afford (literally or figuratively) the kind of continuous help his daughter would require at home. Irma resisted, but not vigorously, as she was driven (by her father and Moore) to the hospital. It was a sad day for Frost, who now looked back over the fate of his children with a sense of despair. As he wrote to Untermeyer, "Cast your eye back over my family luck, and perhaps you will wonder if I haven't had pretty near enough. That is for the angels to say. The valkyries and the eumenides."[1]

Frost returned to Ripton in time for the Bread Loaf Writers' Conference, where he was greeted by the news that Louis Untermeyer would not attend this year—a disappointment for Frost, who always found Untermeyer buoyant and supportive company. In his place was Benny DeVoto, whose relations with Frost had been awkward since 1943, when Frost had made those careless remarks about him in Bloomington. There was also tension between Frost and DeVoto over Kay: DeVoto, like Lawrance Thompson, had grown extremely fond of Kay (and may well have been a lover). The DeVotos and the Morrisons were neighbors in Cambridge, and DeVoto was apparently furious with Frost for attempting (as he saw it) to disrupt the marriage between Kay and Ted.

"Kay Morrison was a planet," Louise Reichert recalls, "and these men circled around her, barely avoiding each other—her husband, Frost, Thompson, DeVoto, others. She was beautiful but cold. The coldness was, perversely, attractive to them all. And she obviously had a way of connecting to them. She was witty and bright. The situation must have appealed to her, at least in some way."[2] Reichert also notes that Kay, who was born in Nova Scotia, had "the stiffness of an Episcopal clergyman's daughter." She retained an elegant detachment from those around her, "a certain aloofness." This manner had been acquired during her teenage years in Philadelphia, where she'd attended the fashionable Miss Hill's School. "Kay had a sense of herself as someone from the upper echelons, though she wasn't haughty. It wasn't that. She was just supremely confident."

Her trim build and auburn hair were complemented by well-chosen clothes. According to Wade Van Dore, she possessed an "outward calmness" that "seemed to be hers by birthright." Others found her extremely remote, even icy. The poet Adrienne Rich, for example, described her as full of "repressed anger and bitterness."[3] Louise

Reichert detected "a feeling of resentment there," although she adds, "Kay could be remarkably good company—when she was around those she liked and trusted." Peter J. Stanlis points to her mercurial temperament: "Kay was a Dr. Jekyll and Mr. Hyde personality. I found her either very warm and friendly, and socially charming, or cold and harshly austere, depending upon circumstances—which had nothing personal about them."[4]

"People knew that the way to Frost was through Kay," one friend noted.[5] Hyde Cox, being well attuned to Frost, understood this point, and proposed a party in Kay's honor in the summer of 1951. Frost replied with enthusiasm, "A tribute to Kay would be the ideal thing for our concerted expense. I'm glad you thought of it and glad of the way you express it. No one can praise her too much for me. I have cried her praises myself in such pieces, to be specific, as The Silken Tent, Never Again Would Birds' Song Be the Same, and—if the truth were known—the character of Thyatira in the better Masque [*A Masque of Reason*]."[6] But not everyone was as sensitive to Frost's feelings about Kay—and Frost "was often anxious on the subject."[7]

Another source of tension this summer was Earle J. Bernheimer, the assiduous collector of Frostiana. For some time, Frost had come to depend on regular infusions of capital from the wealthy Californian. Bernheimer had by now assembled a magnificent trove of manuscripts, letters, printed books, and other items. All along, Frost's hope had been that Bernheimer would one day donate everything to a single university library. "I confess to long having entertained the hope that you would deposit your collection some day where it would link our names in public for the years to come," Frost wrote to him.[8] He had in mind Dartmouth, Harvard, Middlebury, or Amherst as appropriate repositories for his work—all institutions to which he felt some personal attachment.

But on his last visit with Bernheimer in Beverly Hills, he had begun to see the depths of his collector's personal problems. Bernheimer's marriage had broken up, and he was caught in expensively rancorous divorce proceedings. In short, he needed money, and had explained quite frankly to Frost that he might have to sell off the collection piecemeal. His most precious possession was *Twilight*, which he had persuaded Frost to let him own until the poet's death, at which point he had promised to give it to an appropriate library. Without being explicit, Bernheimer was telling Frost that he now considered the little book his to sell to the highest bidder. (He had paid $4,000 to Frost in 1940 to "borrow" it until his death, but it was now worth twice that on the open market—a fact that must have rankled Frost.)

Bernheimer resisted selling the Frost collection for a couple of years, but in 1950 his financial situation had deteriorated to a point where he had no choice. Ironically, the market for such collections had also deteriorated, and Bernheimer recouped only about $15,000 for a collection that would have been worth a great deal more in a few years. *Twilight* itself fetched only $3,500—less than Bernheimer had paid for it; nevertheless, the *New York Times* reported that it was "the highest price ever paid for a single work by an American author."[9]

Frost was upset by the whole affair and told Louis Mertins, "Collecting is the lowest form of literary appreciation. Very low." For his part, Bernheimer was furious that Frost had spoken ill of him and his collection at a point when a good word would have enhanced the value of the whole. Recalling the episode twenty-one years later, Bernheimer said, "Frost did me a good deal of harm through a person who was the editor of the *Antiquarian Bookman* just before my collection came up for auction at the Parke-Bernet Galleries in 1950. Frost, of course, was always a consummate and clever sort of scoundrel and didn't mind lying a little to suit his crochety whims."[10]

The Ticknor fellowship at Dartmouth had been in place now for nearly half a decade, but Frost had been longing to return to Amherst for some time. In February a letter came from Charles Cole, the president of Amherst, inviting him to receive an honorary doctor of letters degree at the commencement in June. (His previous honorary degree from Amherst—his very first, awarded in 1918—was an M.A.) Frost accepted with alacrity, and believed an offer to join the Amherst faculty was not far away.

Frost was also to receive another honorary degree that summer, from the fledgling Marlboro College in southern Vermont. Marlboro's first president was Walter Hendricks, whom Frost had met as a student at Amherst just after the First World War. Hendricks, in fact, had had a checkered history with Frost and his family. In an early delusional episode, Irma had accused Hendricks of trying to molest her, and Frost had at first believed his daughter. When it became clear to him that Irma was imagining the situation (from this point on she frequently imagined that men were trying to molest her), Frost had made amends with Hendricks. The friendship between them had been fully restored, and it meant a lot to Hendricks to have Frost as the main speaker at his inauguration.

In late fall, Frost at last (after many anxious months of waiting) received a letter from President Cole saying that Amherst would indeed like to reestablish a connection. Frost was offered a position as Simpson Lecturer in Literature. In exchange for a salary of $3,000 per year (equivalent to the Dartmouth fellowship), he would be expected to spend one month each semester in residence at Amherst. No formal teaching duties were involved, but he would give at least one lecture and one reading a year; he might also attend classes as a guest and meet with students informally. The intention was to continue this association for as long as Frost felt willing and able to maintain it.

Frost wrote to Cole, "Your letter of some time back brightened in the New Year for me by wiping out the last of any lingering estrangement I may have felt (however mistakenly) from Amherst College."[11] He remembered the role played in his life by Alexander Meiklejohn, whom he called "my first Amherst president to whom I owe my existence among you." Meiklejohn, he said, "picked me up out of nowhere and sprang me full fledged a professor among the professors. I saw him long enough for a good old fashioned Scottish tilt at logic with him. His spirit never dies."

Over the next few weeks, Frost proved an able negotiator, managing a five-year contract at $3,500 per year, with an annual retirement allowance of $2,500 per year after that. Frost regretted leaving Dartmouth, but he had no choice now. Dartmouth's president, John Sloan Dickey, recalled: "Frost had a long-standing allegiance to Amherst. It was the first college that had taken him in. I don't think any college before this had ever taken a poet on board—as a poet, to be a poet. Amherst had been remarkably foresighted. We understood perfectly well that Frost had no choice now. He had to go back to Amherst."[12]

That spring, Frost delivered his final lecture as Ticknor fellow in the Great Issues course that was the brainchild of Dickey. "He was at his best that day," Dickey recalled. "He recited Shakespeare from memory—the sonnets. He talked about the difference between science and the arts, favoring (of course) the latter. He mixed some politics into the talk—always provocative, always thoughtful. The boys found him delightful, often very funny." Another member of the audience sensed in Frost "a peculiar combativeness, a defensiveness. He seemed to be challenging the students—laying down the gauntlet. But his timing was perfect. You had the sense of a mind whirling around a subject, coming at it from many angles. It was a singular mind. There was nothing like Frost in performance when it was going well."[13]

The saga of Ezra Pound took an interesting turn in late February 1949. Pound had been at St. Elizabeths Hospital in Washington, D.C., for the past four years—still under indictment for the treasonous broadcasts he had made over Rome Radio in 1941. While imprisoned by the Allied Forces at Pisa, he had begun his *Pisan Cantos*—a harrowing sequence of poems that brought a much-needed focus to his *Cantos*, which for years had meandered (often brilliantly) in pursuit of subjects and themes. Frost still had complicated feelings about Pound, and he was stunned to hear the news that Pound had received the prestigious Bollingen Prize for 1948. The prize committee included T. S. Eliot, Robert Lowell, Karl Shapiro, Allen Tate, W. H. Auden, and Louise Bogan—a virtual *Who's Who* of contemporary poets. For his part, Frost was relieved that nobody had asked him for his opinion on the subject. Privately, to Kay Morrison, he wrote a memo suggesting he would have liked to bring "Ezra out into the open to stand trial like an honest traitor."[14]

Frost's writing career was nearly over, consisting now mostly of Christmas poems printed each year in booklet form and sent to friends, but he still hoped for a new edition of his *Collected Poems*. He had been loyal to Holt many decades—even when much of the adult trade department jumped ship in 1946 to follow William Sloane to a new firm. One officer of the firm who remained steadfastly at Holt was Alfred C. Edwards, whom Frost liked immensely. Direct editorial responsibility for Frost was assumed by Glenn Gosling in 1948. With Edwards and Gosling, Frost planned a new volume, to be called the *Complete Poems of Robert Frost 1949*. This would supercede his *Collected Poems* (1939). The finished edition was beautifully bound in cloth, and included the complete original text of each of Frost's eight volumes, from *A Boy's Will* (1913) to *Steeple Bush* (1947) in chronological order. "An Afterword" containing three recent poems preceded *A Masque of Reason* and *A Masque of Mercy*, which brought the volume to a close. "The Figure a Poem Makes" once again served as an introduction, and there was a full-page photograph of the white-haired Frost by Clara E. Sipprell opposite the title page.

The *Complete Poems* lifted Frost to even higher levels of public recognition. *Time* followed an adulatory review of the book in June with a cover story on October 9, 1950. The anonymous writer said, "Of living U.S. poets, none has lodged poems more surely where they will be hard to get rid of." But this writer also acknowledged that Frost seemed, to many younger writers, a throwback: "Today's bright young men [sic] look to the intricate, mannered, literary methods of T. S. Eliot and W. H. Auden for their models. They grudgingly admire Frost as a kind of 19th Century relic, resent his commanding popularity, and smart under the reproach." Thus far, in the United States alone, Frost's work, the article reported, had sold over 375,000 copies—an astounding figure.

In the magazine's idealized cover portrait of Frost, painted by Boris Chaliapin, Frost offers a slight, wry smile, his white hair adrift. He is standing with a dry stone wall behind him—as if to recall "Mending Wall." There are wintry birches in the back, and a brook runs beside the wall. The poet has an open collar. His face is deeply lined but rugged. One imagines that his hands, which are out of sight, are equally creased and rugged, the hands of a ploughman-poet. The myth of Frost was now gathering tremendous force, yet the poet in his private notebooks acknowledged, "There is a shadow on success."[15]

Myths are hard to maintain. The public face of a man of letters—the "smiling public man" that Yeats wrote about in "Among School Children"—often seems to hide a more fragile self. Frost, perhaps more so than most, was fragile inside. He still suffered often from depression—"a daily gloominess" that he noted in his journals. Close friends were aware of the energy he put into public performances, even dinners and casual meetings. "You could sense the strain, even with the brilliance," one noted. Frost seemed increasingly "to need long hours alone, time to read or think, to walk in the countryside by himself. But it became harder and harder for him to find this kind of solitude. And part of him didn't want it. Part of him said, 'I must go out.' "[16]

It seemed to many that Frost would soon receive the ultimate accolade: the Nobel Prize in Literature. He was told in the winter of 1950 that he was among those nominated by the Swedish committee, but the award failed to come. Perhaps in recompense, the U.S. Senate decided to toast Frost on his seventy-fifth birthday with a resolution to offer him the "felicitations of the Nation which he has served so well." As Robert Penn Warren said, "After the war, the only two American poets on the mountain peak were Eliot and Frost, but Frost was more American. Eliot had a remoteness—he had lived abroad his whole adult life. Frost was rooted in his own landscape, he was America's own voice, and that was recognized. He was hardly a prophet without honor. In fact, the opposite was true. There was no end of honor."[17]

The Bernheimer episode had left a bad taste in Frost's mouth, but he soon gravitated toward Louis and Marguerite Cohn, two booksellers with whom he had been friendly in recent years. The Cohns had supplied Bernheimer with many of his first editions of Frost, and had gotten Frost to sign them. The Cohns, in fact, had bought a significant part of Bernheimer's collection when it went on sale at Parke-Bernet. Despite the evident dispersal of his books and manuscripts, Frost still entertained hopes of having a substantial repository of his work somewhere.

In 1950 Frost met Edward Connery Lathem, a Dartmouth student now in his senior year. Lathem had been collecting first printings of Frost poems in magazines for several years, while still an undergraduate, and showed great interest in the poet and his work. An attractive young man with a keen and sympathetic intelligence, Lathem had been raised in rural New Hampshire. Not long after graduating in 1951, he became director of Special Collections for the Baker Library at Dartmouth and began building up their impressive collection of Frost books and manuscripts. (He eventually became Frost's literary executor.)

From his first years of teaching, at Pinkerton and elsewhere, Frost had fastened on to, even singled out, certain students. John Bartlett was the first of these, and he remained a lifelong friend. But others had followed, especially in the years after Elinor's death, when Frost was lonely. Increasingly, he depended on these young men for friendship: Hyde Cox, Edward Lathem, and others. He also reveled in the company of younger poets, and admired especially Richard Wilbur, Donald Hall, Adrienne Rich, Philip Booth, and William Meredith. In his last years, he enjoyed the company of Peter Davison, a young poet whose father was Edward Davison, the English poet who had nearly become Frost's official biographer.

Davison lived in Cambridge, and he saw Frost regularly. He remembers: "I was often a visitor to his living room and can even recollect the fragrance of it, a little like dusty patchouli. Frost's workroom, which I only once saw, was upstairs, with a Morris chair in it, a writing board across the arms, and a snowdrift of papers which, in the early afternoons, were shoveled and stacked by Kathleen Morrison, the devoted, astringent, and affectionate amanuensis who gave order and grace to his life in these years." Davison recalled many small dinner parties at the homes of Archibald and Ada MacLeish and the Howard Mumford Joneses. These dinners would often be attended by younger poets in Frost's circle. "We all cherished these evenings with him, especially the males: he was less open, perhaps, to the women poets," says Davison.[18] The one exception was Adrienne Rich, who had a deep knowledge of Frost and had been a student of Theodore Morrison's at Harvard. She and Frost got along exceptionally well.

Frost's circle in Cambridge was wide, and included John Holmes, a professor at Tufts, as well as Harvard professor I. A. Richards. The latter was a huge presence in the 1950s, an influential literary critic and theorist who also wrote poetry. He and Frost would meet for dinner or afternoon tea, and the conversation would often continue for many hours. Richards recalled that Frost "had an unusually theoretical mind, and liked to talk about language and meaning. He thought that poets understood more about language than linguists. Poets were the historians of language, he said. He knew vast stretches of English and American poetry by heart, and reached easily for examples in his conversation. I was always startled by his verbatim recall of poets from Shakespeare through Tennyson."[19]

In public, Frost was consistently genial, even charming. In letters to friends and collectors, he maintained a gentle, Olympian tone, even when the subject was grave. In the summer of 1951, for example, a malignant growth on his face required surgery at the Mary Hitchcock Memorial Hospital in Hanover (and would require further surgery a few years later). Frost wrote jocularly to Louis Cohn about "what the sculptors did to me at the Hanover Hospital. General Ridgeway in Asia would call it operation Save Face, and that's all right with me, if it turns out that my face is saved—more or less."[20]

Although Frost wrote very little major poetry in his last decade or so, he had certainly not abandoned the idea of verse composition, and scattered through his later work one finds a number of memorable poems. To a large extent, his sense of self-value depended on the continuing production of verse. In his notebooks, he wrote, "We'll have to have a new book pretty soon again only to show our development hasn't been arrested by prosperity. Kay says so."[21] But it would be a dozen years before *In the Clearing*, his final volume, would appear, in 1962.

One of the best of the later poems is "How Hard It Is to Keep from Being King When It's in You and in the Situation." This amusing parable, which Frost read to the American Academy of Arts and Letters in the spring of 1950, concerns a king and his son who escape life in the palace to pursue a new life "in the guise of men." Richard Poirier finds it "remarkable for the clarity and candor with which Frost

declares what he has been about."[22] The king in the poem becomes
a cook in some other king's kitchen, but his natural wisdom shines
through, and he is allowed to lecture his new boss on governance and
the conduct of life. One "lesson" he presents is also a retrospective key
to Frost's own poetry:

> "The only certain freedom's in departure.
> My son and I have tasted it and know.
> We feel it in the moment we depart
> As fly the atomic smithereens to nothing.
> The problem for the King is just how strict
> The lack of liberty, the squeeze of law
> And discipline should be in school and state
> To insure a jet departure of our going
> Like a pip shot from 'twixt our pinching fingers."

From beginning to end, Frost writes of journeys; departures and
sudden arrivals are frequently the occasion for a poem. The arrival, as
in "Directive," "The Wood-Pile," or "Ghost House" (which antici-
pates "Directive" by several decades), is often in a deserted landscape.
Even "Into My Own," which opens *A Boy's Will* and remains the entry
into Frost's *Complete Poems*, is about a journey that the poet does
not make:

> One of my wishes is that those dark trees,
> So old and firm they scarcely show the breeze,
> Were not, as 'twere, the merest mask of gloom,
> But stretched away unto the edge of doom.

Although Frost presents himself as a "realist," he repeatedly suggests that the landscapes he writes about are interior settings, more
dreamscape than landscape. He feels a pang of regret that the trees
swaying before his eyes are "the merest mask of gloom" and not something hard and real. The power of Frost's poetry derives, in part, from
the aura of powerful sentiment barely held in check. "A poet is a

master of sentiment," he said to himself in his notebooks.[23] "You've got to feel it, the emotion," he said elsewhere, "but you hold back from saying it, keep it in. The power is there."[24]

Frost thought a good deal about the nature of poetry, and his notebooks of 1950–55 are full of jottings such as these:

> Poetry is a process
> Poetry is the renewal of words
> Poetry is the dawning of an idea
> Poetry is that which tends to evaporate from
>   both prose and verse when translated
> Poetry is the liberal arts.

For Frost, poetry was life, or the perpetual effort to relate poetry to life and life to poetry. Poetry not only provided a spiritual life for Frost, it offered a concrete living, as he remarked in 1952: "Poetry has got me indirectly or directly practically all the living I have had."[25] It got him his job at Pinkerton, his Amherst job, the Michigan fellowships, the positions at Dartmouth and Harvard. It also brought him the substantial income (usually between two and three hundred dollars per reading) that came from his countless appearances at colleges and universities. Victor Reichert recalled that "performance was not incidental for Frost. His poems were meant to be embodied, to be 'said,' and he liked to say that they were especially meant for his voice. Reading aloud to audiences was more than just a way to earn a living. It was *making* a living in the profoundest sense."[26]

Frost increasingly spent time with Hyde Cox, who reminded him of Edward Thomas: intellectually gifted, emotionally fragile, unsure of his own course in life. Frost had first been attracted by the young man's frank indecision about a career as he wandered the country doing odd jobs. In the early 1940s, Cox had gone into publishing, taking a job with the firm of Duell, Sloan and Pearce, but life in the city grated on his nerves. Frost urged him to go into teaching, and Cox soon followed this advice by accepting a position at Phillips Exeter Academy. In the late forties, he became a lobster fisherman in Gloucester, Massachusetts, where his house nearby in Manchester overlooked the sea.

Eventually, Cox became an active participant in the cultural life of Gloucester and president of the Cape Ann Historical Association—as well as an ardent friend of Frost's.

Cox acted as intermediary between two important artists who had some interest in working with Frost: Walker Hancock, the sculptor, and Andrew Wyeth, the painter. Hancock, in March 1950, sculpted an impressive head of the poet in Gloucester, a piece that Frost considered the best likeness of him ever done. In 1952, as Frost's eightieth birthday approached, Cox and Wyeth discussed the possibility of having some Wyeth paintings of New England landscapes as illustrations to an expanded edition of *North of Boston* that Frost hoped Holt would publish as part of his birthday celebrations. The book project never came to fruition, largely because Frost had not written enough poetry since the publication of *Steeple Bush* in 1947 to warrant a new edition; but he and Wyeth remained on friendly terms; indeed, their work has a great deal in common—a vivid, if mannered, realism, and a devotion to the natural world, to ordinary people, to simplicity of surface with apparent depths below. Both men acquired huge followings among people who did not ordinarily read poems or look at paintings, yet both also won the respect of academic critics.

When in Amherst, Frost often visited Robert Francis, a poet who lived in a secluded cottage called Fort Juniper, on Market Hill Road. "He would come unannounced," Francis recalled, "but I was happy to see him. I'd admired him for many years, and he knew that. I used to send him poems, and he was very shrewd and generous. He was usually open, kind in his own way, but he could frighten you. There was so much not spoken, held in reserve. And he took offense easily, which meant you had to be careful." The friendship was dampened when Frost discovered a poem called "Apple Peeler" that Francis wrote about a "virtuoso" who could peel an apple in one "unbroken spiral," a maneuver like "a trick sonnet."

"Frost thought I was making fun of his sonnet 'The Silken Tent,' which is written in a single sentence," said Francis. But I explained to him that other poets did it. David Morton, for example, did it often. Frost gave me a wicked smile, a half smile, and said, 'Oh, so he does? I see. I see.' But he didn't see. We never spoke about it again, though. I think he enjoyed having something over me, even if it was nothing."[27]

The two of them—older and younger poet—would drink the dandelion wine that Francis made himself, and take long walks in the surrounding woods. "Frost seemed happier, in a way, in his later years than I remembered him in the thirties. He had had family troubles in those days, and his mood seemed much darker. Now he was the acknowledged king of poetry. Nobody doubted it. He could hardly keep up with the honors—prizes, honorary degrees, invitations to address this or that group. But he was able to relax in his role, to play the role. His brain was still teeming with ideas about poetry, and he never lost his interest in nature. We shared these two interests, poetry and nature. He would stop on our walks to examine a shrub or a strange fern—so alert to everything. 'If you don't know something specifically,' he would say, 'you don't know it.' "

It was in the summer of 1953, after a visit to North Carolina, that Frost wrote "Kitty Hawk," which he regarded as "the most important poem that he wrote in his last decade," and a poem that "had immense personal meaning."[28] Frost later called it "a longish poem in two parts. Part One is a sort of personal story, an adventure of my boyhood. I was down there [in North Carolina] once when I was about nineteen. Alone, just wandering. Then I was invited back there sixty years later. . . . I use my own story of the place to take off into the story of the airplane. I make a figure of speech of it: How I might have taken off from my experience of Kitty Hawk and written an immortal poem, but how, instead, the Wright brothers took off from there to commit an immortality." The second part of this two-part poem "goes into the thought of the on-penetration into matter and our great misgiving," he added, calling this "the philosophical part" of the poem.[29]

At Bread Loaf in 1959, before reading "Kitty Hawk," Frost mused aloud that "the whole, the great enterprise of life, of the world, the great enterprise of our race, is our penetration into matter, deeper and deeper; carrying the spirit deeper into matter."[30]

In Part One, Frost recalls his trip into the Dismal Swamp:

> *When I came here young*
> *Out and down along*
> *Past Elizabeth City*
> *Sixty years ago,*
> *I was, to be sure,*
> *Out of sorts with Fate,*
> *Wandering to and fro*
> *In the earth alone,*
> *You might think too poor-*
> *Spirited to care*
> *Who I was or where*
> *I was being blown*
> *Faster than my tread—*
> *Like the crumpled, better-*
> *Left-unwritten letter*
> *I had read and thrown.*

Frost is utterly in control of the rhyme and meter, an old master of the craft returning to a hot point in memory that still smoldered after so many decades.

The poem meanders, although not randomly, attached to a biographical matrix but swirling into other regions effortlessly. He sees himself here "like a young Alastor," referring to Shelley's hero in "Alastor," who (as Shelley himself said in his introduction to the poem) represents a "young man of uncorrupted feeling and adventurous genius led forth by an imagination inflamed and purified through familiarity with all that is excellent and majestic to the contemplation of the universe." That contemplation begins freshly in Part Two, as Frost with Blakean intensity imagines the penetration of spirit into matter, taking the first flight of the Wrights as a fitting example of one attempt at such:

> *Spirit enters flesh*
> *And for all it's worth*
> *Charges into earth*

> *In birth after birth*
> *Ever fresh and fresh.*

The poem sprawls in the latter half, lacking the autobiographical narrative of the first part; but it remains an important example of the later Frost: canny, sharp, witty, unpredictable.

The honors kept rolling in. In June 1953, for instance, Frost accepted from the University of North Carolina at Chapel Hill his twenty-fifth honorary degree. This honor was especially meaningful, since Frost often visited Chapel Hill to read and lecture, at the invitation of his friend Clifford Lyons, a professor in the English department. Only a couple of months before this honorary degree, he had been awarded a $5,000 prize from the Academy of American Poets. Not long before that, he had toured the West Coast, concluding his tour with a reading at the University of California at Berkeley that drew twenty-five hundred people—one of the largest groups ever to attend a poetry reading in Berkeley. The appeal of Frost seemed to go beyond poetry now; he had turned himself, or been turned, into an American emblem.

Frost's eightieth birthday was celebrated in grand style. The day before, he gave a news conference in New York at the Waldorf-Astoria Hotel, answering questions from two dozen reporters for three hours before a dozen television cameras and under hot lights. That same evening, Holt sponsored a dinner for eighty dignitaries at the hotel, with a guest list including not only poets and critics but senators and jurists. Alfred Edwards, from Holt, spoke movingly of Frost's unique place in American letters.

The next morning, on his actual birthday, Frost traveled to Amherst, where a small black-tie dinner sponsored by Amherst College was held at the Lord Jeffrey Inn. On behalf of everyone there, Hyde Cox presented Frost with a watercolor by Andrew Wyeth called *Winter Sunlight*. Robert Francis, who was at the dinner, recalled "the immense delight of Frost at receiving this gift. He was especially fond of Cox, who spoke so sweetly, unpretentiously." Raymond Holden read a letter from the governor of New Hampshire, and Archibald MacLeish sat next to Frost and spoke with great dignity about Frost's unique place in American literature—even though they had not always seen eye to eye in the past. The playwright and novelist Thornton Wilder sat on his other side. Louis Untermeyer was also there, and spoke affectionately about his longtime friend, quoting some lines from memory. President Cole of Amherst spoke, too, saying how glad the college was to have Frost back in its fold. "Overall, the speeches could have been pro forma, but they weren't," recalled Francis. "It was all quite genuine."

Frost spoke last. As reported in the *Amherst Alumni News*, he responded to the often-quoted line that "poets die young" by saying that they die in many ways: "not just into the grave, but into businessmen, into critics, or into philosophers." He claimed to be unsettled by the fact that so many of his friends at the head table had used the word "great" in talking about him. "People say you're this and you're that and you wonder if you're anything," he said. "All I've wanted to do is to write a few little poems it'd be hard to get rid of. That's all I ask."[31]

21   THE WINTER OWL
1954–1959

*No sweeter music can come to my ears than the clash of arms over
my dead body when I am down.*

—Frost to Lionel Trilling, June 18, 1959

Frost had always been averse to foreign travel, and (except for a few
days in Cuba in 1939) he had remained on American soil ever
since his last, unhappy visit to Europe in 1928. But his stature had
grown so remarkably—he was, indeed, the uncrowned king of poetry
in America—that appeals for him to travel abroad as a representative of American culture presented themselves with increasing fre-
quency. In his final years, he would visit Brazil, England, Israel,
Greece, and Russia, and each trip would attract considerable attention
from the press.

In July 1954, Lesley approached her father about a possible journey
to the World Congress of Writers in São Paulo, Brazil—part of that
city's elaborate quadricentennial festivities. Lesley had by now become
quite an expert on South America, having traveled there frequently as
a lecturer for the U.S. Information Agency, for whom she had recently
worked in Spain. The U.S. was invited to send one poet and one novelist to this conference, which was not the sort of mass event Frost
normally would attend. "I only go when I'm the show," he would often
say. On this occasion, the novelist who had agreed to go was William

Faulkner—the Nobel laureate in 1950. This was somewhat intimidating to Frost, at first, even though Lesley assured her father that Faulkner admired him and would be pleased for him to accept the charge.

Lesley appealed to her father's sense of patriotism, explaining that U.S. relations with South America were at an all-time low; there was every reason to try to mend this situation. The blatantly poor relations between the U.S. and Brazil had, in fact, been exacerbated when the U.S. denied a visa on political grounds to one of Brazil's most celebrated writers, José Lins do Rêgo. Frost's presence as part of the U.S. delegation would send a strong, positive message to the Brazilian people—or so Lesley convinced her father.

Frost had a warm friendship with the former governor of New Hampshire, Sherman Adams (whom Frost had first met when the governor came to hear him read in Boston at the St. Botolph Club), and Adams was now working in the Eisenhower White House as special assistant to the president. Adams, too, encouraged Frost to go to Brazil. With pressure from all sides, he agreed to undertake the excursion, and he was pleased that Lesley would go with him.

The two of them left from Idlewild Airport in New York on August 4, traveling for twenty-four hours to São Paulo. They arrived exhausted, yet a busy round of sightseeing, parties, press conferences, and poetry readings lifted Frost's spirits during his ten days in Brazil. Wherever he went, he was met by enthusiastic crowds. As reported by the *New York Times*, he managed to slip a number of barbed political comments into his lectures. "Decency, honor, and not too much deceit are about the best one can aspire to in international relations," he said on one public occasion. He loudly claimed to oppose "one-worldism"—an idea popular among liberals of the day—and said he believed that each nation should press for distinction. "There cannot be anything interesting between nations unless they are both distinctly nations."[1]

Frost had been fretting about the meeting with Faulkner, but as it transpired they barely encountered each other. Faulkner (whose work Frost disliked intensely) was drunk in his hotel room most of the time.

An outraged Frost wrote home to Kay, "It was as I feared with Faulkner. He has stolen the show by doing nothing for it but to lie up dead drunk like a genius. The consul . . . has been caring for Faulkner day and night, bathing him in the tub and feeding him in bed."[2]

Frost disliked Brazil on the whole—the teeming slums, the monotonous landscape, the urban sprawl—but he worked extremely hard, giving solid performances wherever he went. One of those who saw him in Brazil was Elizabeth Bishop. She had expected to find him a "malicious old bore," she recalled, but was deeply impressed by his presentation, saying that he did "a marvelous job." Bishop found him "amazing for a man eighty years old" and noted that the audience responded warmly; "the Brazilians got every joke," she added, amazed.[3]

Frost was taken by the landscape of Peru, which Lesley had talked him into visiting on the way home. The flight over the Brazilian jungle was thrilling, and he enjoyed seeing the Amazon, crossing the Andes, and viewing Lake Titicaca by air. "You see unbroken wilderness," he said. "You couldn't tell whether it was trees or what it was, or just nothing. And then there'd be a little thing that looked like a loaf of bread—shaped like a loaf of bread—and you could interpret that into a community house where savages lived, and the trodden ground around it marked it and you could see a little thread of path off from it."[4] The Frosts stayed in Lima with the American ambassador, Harold Tittmann, who hosted a large reception in Frost's honor. The best part of the visit to Peru, according to Frost, was an afternoon spent at an Incan site in the nearby mountains.

They returned to the U.S. via Washington, D.C. "I saw [John Foster] Dulles when I came back," Frost told an audience at Bread Loaf the next summer, referring to Eisenhower's secretary of state, "and was supposed to tell him what to do. . . . Well, you know what I told him to do? I told him to be nicer to the cultural relations people in those places. They haven't diplomatic standing. They can't go through red lights."[5]

Frost returned to a busy time. He was now eighty, and—not surprisingly—the honors tap flowed. "We decided to give Frost a second honorary degree in 1955," President Dickey of Dartmouth said.

"An honorary doctor of letters had been awarded by President Hopkins in 1933, and a second degree was unprecedented. We gave him a doctor of laws this time, in part to reinforce the connection between Frost and Dartmouth."[6] Frost responded to Dickey's invitation: "Nothing but great friendship would have put that into your head."[7]

"One of the memorable things about the commencement, in June, was the quilt of doctoral hoods he was given," Dickey recalled. Frost by now had received twenty-six doctorates, and he mentioned to one of his favorite collectors, Howard G. Schmitt of Hamburg, New York, that his closet was bursting with doctoral hoods. "You can't throw them away, and you can't use them," he said. Schmitt had a bright idea, and enlisted his three aunts to make a quilt of them. He presented Frost with this unique item at a reception held at the president's house. "It was like the coat of many colors," Dickey remembered. "Frost was very pleased, and said he was eager to go to sleep that night under such a weight of honor." Frost's attitude toward all the glory heaped on him was "more bemused than anything. He enjoyed it, of course. He seemed genuinely to like public occasions. But he was a solitary man, at heart. The honors, as he knew, were nothing beside the poems. The poems were everything. In that sense, he was the complete poet."[8]

The year 1955 was not without its darker moments. The only son of Kay and Ted Morrison was killed while changing a tire beside a country road, sending Kay into a deep gloom that washed over onto Frost, who found himself in the reverse position of trying to cheer up Kay. There was also the unresolved hurt over Irma's hospitalization. Frost avoided seeing Irma because each visit extracted too much pain, yet her continuing illness was like a hole in a tooth that keeps attracting the tongue. "He was himself struggling with many demons—family problems, unresolved. He thought of the universe as a dark place with intermittent glints of light," one friend mused.[9]

In his later years, Frost maintained a bright exterior in public, but in private moments he confided to friends, or to his journal, a sense of the potential chaos everywhere around him, as when he wrote in his notebook, "Every human being must learn to carry his own craziness and confusion and not bother his friends about it. He will have clarifi-cations but they will be momentary flashes like this: light shapes like poems . . . smoke rings."[10]

The world continued to beckon, distracting Frost from dark thoughts and dangerous solitude. Shortly after his eighty-second birthday, in the late spring of 1956, he was visited in Ripton by Conger Reynolds, a representative of the U.S. Information Agency, who said that he and President Eisenhower hoped Frost would be willing to help in matters of public relations. Frost was flattered to receive this kind of attention and said he would do what he could—although he declined to write the essay about "American life" that Conger suggested. Frost did not easily, or happily, write essays, and this sort of assignment was far from the sort of thing he might be willing to attempt.

The following December, Frost received a letter from Harold E. Howland of the State Department; it informed him that the U.S. Embassy in London was planning an exhibition focused on his life and work (the idea had been suggested by Sherman Adams). The exhibition would occur in the spring—only a few months away—but it was hoped that Frost might visit England at this time. "The Depart-ment of State, recalling your splendid cooperation in visiting Latin America . . . whole-heartedly endorses the Embassy's suggestion," Howland wrote.[11] The government rightly thought that Frost, with his charm and high visibility, and with his long-standing connections to Great Britain, would be a good cultural ambassador at a moment when relations between the two countries were strained over the recent Suez crisis, in which the U.S. had opposed the disastrous Anglo-French invasion of Egypt.

Frost liked playing hard to get, and he played this game with the State Department, asking Sherman Adams, his friend in the Eisen-hower White House, to make sure that he was really needed. "What I need to know is how much I am wanted and at what level," he said. "It would be no small undertaking for me to go abroad."[12] Frost's health was now quite good, but he suffered from a hearing loss that could make public occasions embarrassing for him, and he was (as always) prone to lung problems. "He was strong enough to go," his granddaughter Lesley Lee Francis recalls, "but risk was involved, and discomfort."[13]

Harold Howland later remembered the specific words Frost used to respond to this invitation when he called on the poet in Ripton to urge his going. "I was re-reading recently the life of Voltaire," Frost said. "You will recall that Voltaire, in 1778, left the serenity of his village residence in Ferney, Switzerland, to again appear with the crowds of Paris. It was a strenuous visit and he died on that trip. His age then, as mine now, was 82. Nevertheless, if my country believes I can be of any use in reminding the British people of our own warm affection and strong friendship, why, of course, I'll go. I don't want to be an unguided missile, however; don't spare me. Tell me where you want me to go and when. I'll be ready."[14]

Frost hoped for more from England than merely an exhibition at the U.S. Embassy. Working through Kay, he let it be known that honorary degrees from both Oxford and Cambridge would be welcome. Of American poets, only Longfellow in 1868 and James Russell Lowell in 1873 had received this double honor. Kay contacted I. A. Richards and Jack Sweeney, who was the curator of the Amy Lowell Poetry Collection at Harvard, and they were able to pull enough strings in high places to bring off the desired results. The letters of invitation from Oxford and Cambridge arrived in March, and Frost's feelings are evident in his response to Oxford: "Few things could give me the pleasure of such an honor from the country ('half my own') that published my very first book. That was nearly fifty years ago when I was living and writing not fifty miles down the line from you in Beaconsfield. I shall look at it as a rounding out that we seldom get except in story books and none too often there."[15]

Frost set off for England on May 17, 1957. After an overnight flight of twelve hours, he was met at the airport by Carl Bode, the head of the U.S. Information Agency in London, and by two dozen reporters and photographers. Exhausted, he was ushered into a press room for a brief television interview, then driven to the Connaught Hotel. Among those he planned to connect with were Lawrance Thompson (who followed him from New York by one day), Edward Lathem, now a student at Oxford, and Lesley Lee, who was then working at the U.S. Embassy in Madrid.

The next afternoon Frost addressed an audience of seven hundred at the Senate House of the University of London, reminiscing about his crucial years in England. He recalled that Harold Monro of the Poetry Bookshop had introduced him to Ezra Pound and F. S. Flint (who was in the audience, seated near Helen Thomas). Pound, he said, had sent him a calling card that read "At home—sometimes." Frost referred to Pound's "selfish generosity"—his penchant for helping young poets. But he was not, Frost noted wryly, "beyond helping himself." Frost also recollected the goodwill of Mrs. David Nutt, the English publisher who had "launched him into the world."

Noticing that T. S. Eliot was sitting in the third row, Frost made a witty remark about poets who give up their citizenship. "I can understand how someone of another nationality might wish to become an American," he said, "but I could never see how an American chose to become, for instance—a Canadian."[16] This produced laughter all around, even from Eliot. The long-running rivalry between Eliot and Frost had mellowed considerably over the years, largely because Eliot consistently refused to notice it. "Eliot was peculiarly without interest in this sort of battle," recalled Stephen Spender.[17] "He quite admired Frost, although he considered him so very American, especially in his competitiveness."

Frost next visited Durham, where an honorary degree had been bestowed upon him in absentia in 1952. By May 27, he was back in London, where a dinner in his honor was given at the Athenaeum in Pall Mall. This dinner, hosted by John Lehmann and *London Magazine*, was attended by the poet C. Day-Lewis, who had written the introduction to the Penguin edition of Frost's *Selected Poems*. The next day, Frost dined at the Garrick Club, in the theater district, as the guest of the publisher Rupert Hart-Davis.

The round of luncheons and dinner parties continued, with virtually every day crammed with events. It was all quite exhausting for him. Indeed, a sore throat and fever threatened to turn into pneumonia, so Frost had to lie low for a couple of days in London, canceling a lunch date with Helen Thomas and her son—much to their sadness and regret. He wanted to feel well for the Oxford appearance.

His anticipation of the upcoming trip to Oxford was intense, and he refused to let illness get the better of him. Almost defiantly, he attended a high-table dinner presided over by Sir Maurice Bowra, the warden of Wadham College, the next night. Bowra had asked Edward Lathem, as a friend of the poet's, to coordinate the schedule of events that had been established for this period. "Frost stayed at Wadham throughout his visit," Lathem recalls, noting that Bowra was the poet's official host.[18]

The next morning Lathem took Frost for a long walk around the ancient university. They stopped by at the Bodleian Library to see an account of Longfellow's Oxford visit nearly a century earlier. Then they toured a few of the colleges. At University College, Frost noticed a clematis vine climbing one of the walls and picked from it a large blossom, which he placed in the buttonhole of his lapel. At the college entrance, they encountered a white-marble memorial to Shelley, representing the drowned poet's body lying nude on the shore of Viareggio. "Immediately upon seeing it, Frost winced and turned away," Lathem recalls. They ended the tour at Lathem's college, St. John's, with its elaborate gardens now in full blossom. Frost—always eager to "go botanizing"—identified a number of trees, shrubs, and flowers that are not found in New England.

The honorary-degree ceremony took place at two in the Sheldonian Theater, and the degree citation (read in Latin) was apt: "In truth he has for so long now devoted himself to the arts of the poet and the husbandman that his work has passed into his character, nay, into his features which reflect the genius of the poet, the sturdiness of the farmer, and the peace of old age. . . . Amid the clash of arms and the mounting terror of our new instruments of war, his poetry, with its echoes of Virgilian serenity, has brought, and will continue to bring, unfailing consolation to a suffering world."[19]

While in Oxford, Frost was often in the company of W. H. Auden,

who was the current Professor of Poetry. The day after the degree ceremony, in fact, Auden acted as interlocutor between Frost and a gathering of American Rhodes scholars. At lunch, Frost dined with Lord and
Lady Beveridge and a group of their friends, taking his granddaughter
and Edward Lathem as companions. That same afternoon, he spoke to
a large audience at the Taylorian. It was "jam-packed with people, who
stood all down one side. The balcony was also filled," recalls Lawrance
Thompson in his notes. He goes on: "Frost's preliminary talk worked
variations on the same pet theme: the venture of the spirit into the
material world. 'God's venture into the material—at a great risk—set
us an example.' As he got on to the reading of his poems, he showed
that he was in fine form, and the crowd was with him all the way. . . . I
have never heard him read better than at Oxford."[20]

From Oxford, on June 5, he was driven to Cheltenham to see John
Haines, whom he had not seen since 1928. "This was the emotional
high point of his visit," notes Lesley Lee Francis. "No doubt the subject of Edward Thomas came up. My grandfather was obviously very
moved by this visit. The friendship with Haines meant a good deal to
him. They had never lost touch."[21]

The next day Frost revisited the Dymock region, in Gloucestershire, a trip that rekindled memories of his English sojourn there in
1914–15. At Little Iddens, he eagerly rushed to an old box hedge
beside a square water tank and an old pump at the side door. "This
pump must be the same one I used," he said, trying the handle. He
went inside to inspect the house, which had changed remarkably little
in forty years. He also paid a call at the Old Nailshop, the cottage
owned by Wilfrid Gibson (although it was now called Wayside—a
much less interesting name). It was here that, night after night, he had
exchanged poems and ideas with Gibson, Lascelles Abercrombie,
Rupert Brooke, and John Drinkwater. "We drove by what used to be
The Gallows, the house that my grandparents shared with the Abercrombies," Francis remembers, "but it was in ruins. There was only one
wing left standing, that hidden by shrubs."[22]

The last stop was Oldfields, where Edward Thomas had lived. Frost
started toward the house, but was overcome with emotion. "There is

no need to go inside," he said, turning instead toward the nearby orchard, where he and Thomas had been sitting together when the news broke that the Great War had started.[23] After standing alone in the orchard for ten minutes, he walked silently back to the car, perhaps recalling (as he wrote in "Iris by Night") a time when "One misty evening, one another's guide, / We two were groping down a Malvern side / The last wet fields and dripping hedges home."

Frost returned to London in time for a luncheon at the Savile Club. Stephen Spender was the host, and he invited Frost to reminisce to the group (which included Graham Greene and Isaiah Berlin) about his early days in England. Frost rose, and seemed exhausted at first, his voice barely audible; but soon, as he recalled the war years, his friendship with Edward Thomas, and the encouragement he'd gotten from Harold Monro, Frank Flint, and others, "he grew more animated, and spoke with a peculiar, grainy eloquence, seeming to draw energy from the performance, which grew stronger and stronger."[24] E. M. Forster was among the guests, and some trouble arose between them, as described by Edward Lathem in a letter home (June 1957): "Frost and Forster had been seated side by side, but Mr. Frost because of his deafness had not understood who Forster was when they were introduced. On top of this, the person sitting on the other side of RF and the man across the table monopolized his attention at dinner [sic], and he had not talked to Forster during the meal. Then, when RF got up to talk afterwards, Forster kept giggling to himself, and finally right out loud. Whereupon, Frost turned round and asked him what he was laughing at. Forster, thus rebuked, sat stiff and silent for the rest of the evening. The climax of the infelicity came when, as the guests were departing, RF asked Forster right out who he was or whether he wrote or some such crushing thing, and Forster went off, it was said, quite miffed by the whole affair."[25]

The next major event was a dinner on June 11 at the English Speaking Union. "It was a black-tie event," Lathem recalls. "There was a single, large table. T. S. Eliot, as toastmaster, was seated at one end. Mr. Frost sat at the other end, next to Mrs. Eliot. At the close of the meal Mr. Eliot stood up, champagne glass in hand, obviously intending to propose a toast. Frost could not, at the distance involved, hear what was being said, and when everyone rose, Frost looked questioningly down the table at me, seeking confirmation that it was he who was the subject of the toast. In response I made a gesture above my head, indicating a crown. He understood at once that the toast was in fact to the queen, and he rose. What was particularly interesting, and quite touching really, was how perceptively, as well as sensitively, T. S. Eliot reacted to the situation, realizing Frost's degree of deafness was such that there would be a problem about his hearing the remarks Eliot intended to make next. He simply declared that he was now going on to say some things about the guest of honor, and he thought it would be appropriate for Mr. Frost to come and sit beside him while he did so."

At this point, while Frost was slowly making his way to Eliot's side, Mrs. Eliot asked that Lathem move temporarily into what had been Frost's place. As he did so, she said, speaking softly, "We did not have a chance to chat with one another before dinner. However, I noticed that you talked with my husband, and I do know who you are." She then added, "You are a protégé of Mr. Frost." Lathem demurred, and when told that Frost himself was the source of this identification, replied, "Mr. Frost would have said to you, 'Ed Lathem is one of my boys,' and that's not the same thing as a 'protégé.' " Smiling, Mrs. Eliot conceded, "Yes, that *is* what he said, that you are one of his boys."[26]

Eliot offered a warm toast. "Mr. Frost," he said, "I never heard your name until I came to this country. I heard it first from Ezra Pound, of all people. He told me about you with great enthusiasm. I gathered that you were a protégé of his of whom he expected a good deal. At the same time, I gathered that your work, or what had appeared at that time, was not in Ezra Pound's opinion required reading for *me*. He may have been right, at that time, because I was still in a formative period, and goodness knows what would have happened if you had influenced me at that stage. But, you know, as one gets older, one cares less about movements and tendencies and groups. We all have our own idiom and metric and subject matter, but I have long come to feel that there are only two kinds of poetry—good and bad. And the bad poetry can be very much of one's own type, and the good poetry can be of a very different type." With astounding generosity, Eliot continued, "Mr. Frost is one of the good poets, and I might say, perhaps *the* most eminent, the most distinguished, I must call it, Anglo-American poet now living."

Frost was immensely moved, and he rose to answer Eliot's generous toast. "There's nobody living in either country I'd rather hear that from," he said.[27]

The degree from Cambridge followed on June 13. Lathem, who had previously fixed an appointment to meet with E. M. Forster, and was aware of the unfortunate circumstances at the Savile Club luncheon in London, arranged to have Frost and the poet's granddaughter accompany him to Forster's rooms at King's College on the day before the degree ceremony. Lesley Lee Francis found the novelist "incredibly old and shrivelled, and with an odd way of speaking so that one could hardly understand a word he said." Lathem recalls that while in Forster's study Frost mentioned his admiration of Forster's recently published (1956) biography of Marianne Thornton. In doing so, he pointed to a portrait hanging above Forster's fireplace mantel—the portrait that had in fact been used as a frontispiece illustration for the book—and declared "And there she is!" (He later wryly confided to Lathem, "If I hadn't recognized that picture, he wouldn't have believed I knew the book.") All hurt feelings on Forster's part were now dispelled. The two got along well, and the visit was concluded by Forster's personally taking his visitors to see the college chapel. Edward Lathem wrote in a letter home at the time, "Everything had gone splendidly: they [Forster and Frost] had enjoyed each other and RF had from their pleasant conversation become completely rested after his trying morning. He told me that he was entirely revived and no longer felt tired at all."[28]

On June 15, Frost flew to Dublin, where he was met by the president of University College, Dublin, and by C. P. Curran, with whom he had stayed during his fleeting visit in 1928. After four days of sightseeing and various ceremonial luncheons and dinners, Frost was given his third honorary degree—this one from the National University, with the prime minister of Ireland, Eamon de Valera, presiding. Frost was deemed "a splendid presence, with his shock of white hair, his leathery face and thick hands."[29] Quite sincerely, he expressed admiration for Irish poetry, especially Yeats, to his hosts. The next afternoon, with Lawrance Thompson at his side, Frost flew from Shannon to Idlewild. It had been an event-crammed, rewarding journey, one that had certainly helped strengthen the Anglo-American cultural connection. "In a way, the English journey completed something that had been begun many years earlier," says Lesley Lee Francis, "and it rounded out a particular story. My grandfather thought this was his final journey, his last hurrah. He had put so much into it—one State Department official told me that few younger men could have sustained that schedule."

While staying at the Connaught Hotel in London, Frost ran into another guest, Archibald MacLeish, who had been campaigning for some time now to get Ezra Pound released from St. Elizabeths Hospital. He had recently drafted a letter to U.S. Attorney General Herbert G. Brownell on the subject, and both T. S. Eliot and Ernest Hemingway (who, like Frost, had incurred an early debt to Pound) had agreed to sign it. MacLeish knew that Frost was a friend of Sherman Adams's, and he hoped that the poet might be willing to use this influence on Pound's behalf.

Frost had recently softened on the subject of Pound. Rereading Pound's early essay on his poetry as reprinted in *The Literary Essays of Ezra Pound* (1954), he was moved by the clarity and force of the argument. Pound had clearly been among the earliest advocates of Robert Frost, and his support had made a huge difference at a crucial moment in his career.

Pound had certainly behaved in a foolish and traitorous way by broadcasting on Mussolini's radio waves, but as MacLeish made clear in his letter to Brownell, many Nazis "convicted of the most heinous crimes" had nevertheless been released and rehabilitated. Pound, he said, was "one of the most distinguished American writers of his generation," and he deserved better treatment.[30]

Frost signed the letter, joining MacLeish in Washington on June 19, 1957, for a meeting at the office of Deputy Attorney General William P. Rogers. Rogers explained that Pound had gotten involved with a segregationist poet from Tennessee named John Kasper, and this had caused the Justice Department to hesitate in releasing him. But Frost persisted, meeting again with Rogers on his own in October. "MacLeish got the ball rolling on the Pound case," recalled Robert Penn Warren, "but it was Frost, almost singlehandedly, who pushed it through." Once he had decided what must be done, he was tenacious. And more so than MacLeish, a New Deal Democrat with strong Rooseveltian ties, Frost had clout with the Eisenhower White House.

Eisenhower himself was, as noted in his memoirs, pleased to have support from Frost. On February 27, 1958, the president showed his appreciation by inviting him to the White House for a stag dinner that included the president's brother Milton, his son John, and a few others, such as Sherman Adams. It was Adams who now took up the Pound case in earnest. When by mid-April the release of Pound had not occurred, Frost traveled again to Washington to put further pressure on William Rogers, who agreed to expedite matters. He connected Frost with a well-known lawyer, Thurman Arnold, who successfully brought the case before the District Court.

When the *New York Times* ran a front-page story about Pound's release, it gave most of the credit to Frost, praising his "persistent public and private campaign during the last two years."[31] MacLeish also acknowledged that Frost's influence had been vital to the outcome. "Frost gets a large part of the credit," he wrote to Hemingway. "The old boy despises Ez for personal reasons but once he got started nothing could stop him and I think Rogers finally gave up out of sheer exhaustion."[32] For his part, Pound was peculiarly ungrateful when told about Frost's work on his behalf. "He ain't been in much of a hurry," he said. When he boarded a liner for Genoa, in New York, he reportedly gave the fascist salute.

One of the more frustrating aspects of old age for Frost was the difficulty of writing poems. It became harder and harder to focus, and the last poems—those written from the fifties until his death—were often occasional in nature; they did not have the force and originality of his earlier poems, though the Frostian manner was there. One exception was a fierce and beautiful lyric written around New Year's 1958. "Questioning Faces" contains six lines:

> The winter owl banked just in time to pass
> And save herself from breaking window glass.
> And her wings straining suddenly aspread
> Caught color from the last of evening red
> In a display of underdown and quill
> To glassed-in children at the windowsill.

The poem seems to beckon, obliquely, to Wallace Stevens, who ended "Sunday Morning" with a brilliant image of pigeons sinking "downward to darkness, on extended wings." In many ways, Frost was himself the winter owl, banking repeatedly to avoid smashing into the glass wall of death. Again and again, he rose to triumph—in readings, in lectures, in flights of fancy—in a kind of private war on dissolution.

The poem was based on a memory that predated the Second World War. "Once sitting in the kitchen," he told Daniel Smythe, "in the last of a sunset, a great owl darkened the room. For a minute in the last sunlight, he showed the whole underside—the quills clear. The sight of that bird right close to you is just like a favor, something you did not expect—as if someone were on your side."[33] Again, the note of Emersonian correspondence can be discerned: the owl is spirit embodied, penetrating matter deeper and deeper. And there is risk here, the bravura of the bird-spirit as it spreads its wings, glorying in its sense of self.

The routine of Frost's life was now firmly in place. Summers in Ripton, with appearances at the Bread Loaf Writers' Conference, were followed by a brief residence at Amherst, where he lectured and read his poems in Johnson Chapel; as ever, he stayed in comfort at the Lord Jeffrey Inn, which had become a home away from home. The early winter was passed in Cambridge, while the Christmas holidays were spent with Hyde Cox at Crow Island, his estate by the sea in Manchester. Early in the New Year, he left for Pencil Pines, and Kay would usually join him for a period. In March or early April, he returned to Cambridge, usually paying another call on Amherst. By late May or early June, he was back in Ripton for the summer.

While in Ripton, he would regularly have dinner at the Waybury Inn, in East Middlebury. The innkeepers, Robert Kingsley and Harold Curtiss, became good friends, and would reserve a special table for their favorite guest. "As he grew more and more famous toward the end of the fifties, we would have to put him at a table where visitors wouldn't bother him. They would often just come over and ask for an autograph, but he didn't like to be disturbed during a meal," says Curtiss.[34] "He rarely drank anything more than a sweet daiquiri. That was his drink. Every meal started with one daiquiri."

Frost often came into the inn with Kay and Ted Morrison, or one or another of the visiting faculty at Bread Loaf. "Once, he brought Pearl Buck to dinner," recalls Robert Kingsley. "Another time, he appeared with Stewart Udall, the Arizona congressman." There was no end of poets who came to visit Frost at his cabin in the summer: Theodore Roethke, Robert Lowell, Philip Booth, William Meredith. "He was remarkably kind to younger poets," says Meredith. "He was completely genuine, and warm."[35] Richard Eberhart recalls that "the Frost place was a New England attraction—a poetry attraction. Anyone who had an interest in poetry would want to go there. Frost seemed almost self-destructively open to everyone. He liked company, and there was no end to it."[36]

The poet Galway Kinnell called on Frost unannounced one day at the Homer Noble farm. "It was the New England habit," he says. He was led into the parlor by Kay. Frost came in, and Kinnell explained that he was a poet. Frost said, "Say one of your poems." Kinnell did, and Frost was very complimentary. "I felt as though he had welcomed me into the world of letters," says Kinnell. "It was an important moment for me. I felt somehow legitimized, affirmed."[37]

Harold Curtiss was part owner of Camp Keewaydin on Lake Dunmore, one of the oldest boys' camps in the United States, and he invited Frost to attend the camp's fiftieth-anniversary ceremony during the summer of 1959—not long after he got back from England and Ireland. "Frost was quite happy to come," says Curtiss. "He arrived in a dark suit, a white shirt—on a very hot day. The lake was glittering behind him, and the children were gathered at his feet. He took off his jacket and tie, and read some of his poems and spoke. He was quite imposing. You could just feel his greatness. He walked straight toward one small boy and said, 'Does your dog ever talk to you? Mine talks to me.' From that moment on, he had everyone in his hands."

In October 1958, Frost became the poetry consultant at the Library of Congress, succeeding Randall Jarrell. The position had no specific responsibilities, although Frost was expected to spend various intervals of time, through the period of his appointment at the library. The duties of the job, as Richard Eberhart (a former consultant) says, "included maintaining the poetry collection at the library, inviting poets to read, and being the symbolic figurehead for poetry." Frost hoped for some genuine influence in the political realm, although his access to the White House was lessened by the departure of Sherman Adams (after a minor scandal) in September.

Nevertheless, Frost worked extremely hard, pursuing his role with energy and imagination; he was so successful, in fact, that he was given the title of honorary consultant in the humanities during the Kennedy administration. Frost's achievement during these years was considerable. "He did a lot to bring culture and politics together," Eberhart recalls. "Before him, the White House largely ignored their cultural responsibilities. You could not ignore Frost. He wouldn't let you." This cultural work led to his being awarded a Congressional Gold Medal (passed by Congress and signed by President Eisenhower in 1960 but bestowed, in 1962, by President Kennedy).

One of the high points of these public years was the dinner in New York sponsored by Holt in honor of Frost's eighty-fifth birthday on March 26, 1959. Stanly Burnshaw, an officer of Holt, recalled, "The birthday dinner at the Waldorf-Astoria began in the usual manner—cocktails and drinks—for a hundred fellow-poets, critics, and friends."[38] At the dinner, Frost sat beside Edward Rigg, of Holt, and the featured speaker, Lionel Trilling. W. H. Auden and Stanley Burnshaw were also at the head table, with Louis Untermeyer and other close friends.

Trilling's speech raised many eyebrows, including Frost's. "We have come to think of him as virtually a symbol of America," Trilling said. But "the manifest America of Robert Frost's poems is not the America that has its place in my own mind." Trilling objected to this "manifest America," which was largely rural in character. He spoke of its being "an ideal common to many Americans" who shared "a distaste for the life of the city and for all the city implies of excessive complexity, of uncertainty, of anxiety."

Trilling talked at length about the difference between city and country, confessing his own preference for the former. This could not have pleased Frost, who considered himself an advocate and spokesman for rural life. Then Trilling owned up to a long-standing "resistance to Frost's great canon of work," saying that only recently had this attitude "yielded to admiration." Much to the surprise of many, he went on: "I have to say that my Frost . . . is not the Frost I seem to perceive existing in the minds of so many of his admirers. . . . He is not the Frost who reassures us by his affirmations of old virtues, simplicities, pieties, and ways of feeling: anything but." Instead, he believed that Frost in his best poems represented "the terrible actualities of life." In sum, he said, "I regard Robert Frost as a terrifying poet."[39]

Trilling's remarks created a fuss, but he was merely reiterating a line of criticism popularized by Randall Jarrell a few years before, a viewpoint substantially present in Frost criticism for several decades. "It was a way of talking about his work that didn't so much displease or surprise Frost as unsettle him," recalled Victor Reichert, who was present that evening. "Afterward, when he rose to speak, he was unusually halting. He forgot some lines of his own poems—a rare thing for him. He asked the audience if they really did find him so terrifying."[40] Frost's speech ended the dinner, which was followed by "an odd commotion," says Burnshaw, "as scores of guests gathered in groups. Others stepped close to the poet, several speaking at once. Trilling . . . quickly excused himself and departed for home."[41]

J. Donald Adams, a columnist for the *New York Times Book Review*, was at the dinner, and had been shaking his head in disbelief throughout Trilling's speech. He seemed not to understand that Trilling meant well, and was merely trying to underscore an important aspect of Frost's poetry and to suggest that he was not old-fashioned but a fiercely modern poet who grasped the harsh realities of twentieth-century life. Nothing that Trilling said was untrue. But Adams still regarded Frost as a poet who gave comfort in a comfortless world, and he scolded Trilling in his column, telling him to "come out of the Freudian wood . . . and face the facts of life."[42] Adams, by calling attention to Trilling's speech, turned the incident into a minor scandal.

In the end, Frost was glad to have people talking about him, and was not nearly so upset by Trilling's speech as Adams believed. He had long been familiar with the line taken by Trilling. As always, he wanted everything both ways at once, and this was no exception; he courted the popular audience who found his work comforting and inspiring—the readership represented, in effect, by Adams—and he also courted serious academic critics like Trilling and Jarrell. To be taken seriously as a modernist pleased him, and the work itself demanded this vein of interpretation. From *A Boy's Will* through *Steeple Bush*, his best poems dealt with stark existential questions. Loneliness and the fear of total obliteration are central to his poetry, wherein the wild landscapes and decimated towns of rural New England often become a mirror for the soul's emptiness.

Trilling himself wrote to Frost to express hope that his comments at the birthday party had not distressed him unduly. Frost wrote back: "Not distressed at all. Just a little taken aback or thrown back on myself by being so closely examined so close by. It took me more than a few minutes to change from thoughts of myself to thoughts of the difficulty you had had with me. You made my birthday party a surprise party. I should like nothing better than to do a thing like that myself— to depart from the Rotarian norm in a Rotarian situation. You weren't there to sing 'Happy Birthday, dear Robert,' and I don't mind being made controversial. No sweeter music can come to my ears than the clash of arms over my dead body when I am down."[43]

Ever keen to make an impact on the larger world, Frost had suggested at a press conference just prior to his eighty-fifth birthday party that Senator John F. Kennedy was likely to be the next president. This was widely quoted in the press, and Senator Kennedy himself was impressed enough to write a note to thank Frost for the remark. "I want to send you my own very warmest greetings on [a day] which is for all of your admirers a milestone, but for you is only another day in the life of a young man," wrote Kennedy.[44] Thus began a relationship that would bear fruit, some of it strange, in the next few years.

Frost knew that Yeats, before him, had played an important role in Irish politics, becoming a senator in the Irish Free State, and he vaguely imagined that he, too, might have some public role to play. But Frost was too independent-minded for politics, which requires a temperament given to compromise and consensus. He was, as ever, the "lone striker" of his poem, although he clearly sought—and to a remarkable degree won—a huge public. For now, he would have to content himself with having his official term at the Library of Congress extended for a further three years as "consultant in the humanities"—a position more honorific than real, although Frost was determined, even at his great age, to remain as involved as possible.

22   AGES AND AGES HENCE
1960–1963

Great times to be alive, aren't they?
—FROST TO JOHN F. KENNEDY, JULY 24,1962

The presidential election of 1960 was perilously close, with Kennedy and Nixon dividing the electorate almost evenly. Frost, who had supported Eisenhower with enthusiasm, balked at the prospect of a Nixon presidency, preferring the debonair, highly cultured senator from his own neck of the woods. "The only Puritans left these days are Roman Catholics," he had declared when touting Kennedy at his eighty-fifth birthday dinner, and now as he traveled across the country to read and lecture, he seemed almost to be campaigning for Kennedy.

The intermediary between Kennedy and Frost was Congressman Stewart L. Udall, who had come into contact with Frost during his tenure as poetry consultant at the Library of Congress. They often dined together when Frost was in Washington, and Udall had recently stopped by to see Frost in Ripton. "It was Udall who suggested to Kennedy that Frost read a poem at his inauguration," recalls William Meredith, who had grown increasingly close to Frost in the past year. "It was a novel idea, and one that focused attention on Kennedy as a man of culture, as a man interested in culture."[1] Furthermore, Kennedy had long admired Frost. "He liked poets and poetry, and he knew

Frost's work well. There was, of course, the Harvard and Cambridge connection, too," says Gore Vidal. "During his campaign, he had a set speech that always ended with his thanking those who had come, then he'd quote Frost—from the end of 'Stopping by Woods' about having 'miles to go before I sleep.' That was the coda, always the same quote."[2]

It was at Kennedy's home in Georgetown, in early December of 1960, that Udall raised the possibility of Frost reading at the inaugural ceremony. "Oh, no!" Kennedy had said, when Udall first suggested it to him. "You know Frost always steals any show he is part of." Kennedy was joking, but he may have entertained real misgivings about Frost. In any case, he went along with Udall's proposal, believing that the benefits of associating with a beloved national icon outweighed the minor risks.

Kennedy telephoned Frost in Cambridge to discuss what he might read at the ceremony, gingerly suggesting that he write a poem especially for the occasion. The poet quickly dismissed the president-elect's notion: "Oh, that could never happen," he said. Kennedy followed with another suggestion: How about his reading "The Gift Outright," changing the last line from "such as she would become" to "such as she will become," making it a bit more optimistic and emphatic. "I suppose so," Frost responded, hesitantly. Even a president-elect should not tamper with his work.

"Frost stayed at my house in the few days before the inauguration," recalls Hyde Cox, "and he began to work on a poem specifically for the occasion. He felt he ought to."[3] Frost struggled right up to the night before the ceremony on January 20, 1960. What he had written was called, simply, "Dedication," and he read it to a surprised Stewart Udall when the congressman came to pick him up at the hotel just before the inauguration. "Will it be all right if I make a few prefatory remarks?" Frost asked Udall. Already worried about Frost upstaging Kennedy, Udall asked how long the remarks might take. "Oh, I don't know," Frost said. "You can never tell, can you?" Udall was not amused.

The poem opens:

>Summoning artists to participate
>In the august occasions of the state
>Seems something artists ought to celebrate.
>Today is for my cause a day of days.

Sweeping grandly through the history of Europeans in the New World, beginning with Columbus, Frost prophesied "A golden age of poetry and power / Of which this noonday's the beginning hour." The poem is dreadful, but nobody could expect a poem written to order to meet Frost's usual standards. It was at least appropriate for the occasion.

The newly minted poem was meant by Frost to serve as a preamble to his reading of "The Gift Outright." It had been typed the night before in the hotel office, and the letters were not adequately dark. Frost worried that, in the January sun, he might have difficulty reading, and Udall volunteered to have the poem hastily retyped that morning on a special large-print typewriter with a fresh ribbon.

The ceremony began at ten on a bright, bitterly cold day with snow covering the ground. Richard Cardinal Cushing gave the invocation—thus recognizing the president-elect's Catholicism, an American first. Marion Anderson sang the national anthem, and Lyndon B. Johnson was duly sworn in as vice president. One hour into the ceremony—just ahead of Kennedy's swearing in—Frost was called forward. He ambled slowly to the podium, then fumbled for a while with his manuscript; at last, haltingly, he began to read his "Dedication." But the light struck the page in such a way that he could not see, and he said, "I'm having trouble with this." The new vice president tried to help by shielding the page with his top hat, but Frost brushed him aside with a joke. He then delighted the audience by launching into "The Gift Outright," which he declaimed by heart. He ended magnificently, dragging out the last line: "Such as she was, such as she *would* become, *has* become, and I—and for this occasion let me change that to—what she *will* become."

The crowd began to cheer, drowning out a gaffe: Frost thanked the "president-elect, Mr. John Finley." (John Finley was a classicist at Harvard whom Frost knew slightly.) But the mistake passed unnoticed, and Frost was easily forgiven by those who heard it. He was by now the embodiment of American poetry: an icon caught in the act of being an icon. As the *Washington Post* said the next morning, "Robert Frost in his natural way stole the hearts of the Inaugural crowd."[4] Decades later, Americans who watched the ceremony on television still recall the hoary-haired figure in the black overcoat who put aside the script he could not read to recite from memory in his folksy manner. Poetry and politics had rarely rubbed shoulders so publicly in the history of the republic.

Paying a call on the freshly installed president at the White House before he left Washington for Cambridge, Frost deigned to offer grand-fatherly advice: "Be more Irish than Harvard. Poetry and power is the formula for another Augustan Age. Don't be afraid of power."[5] In a thank-you note to Frost, a week later, Kennedy scrawled in the margins, "Power All the Way." He pointedly, it seems, did not include the other half of Frost's formula ("poetry and power") for the new Augustan Age, perhaps knowing intuitively what W. H. Auden once wrote, that "poetry makes nothing happen" but "survives in the valley of its making."

Frost was lifted high, emotionally, by the national attention that came his way. "After the inaugural poem," a friend recalls, "Frost's fame penetrated to a new level. People on the street suddenly recognized him. He could not go into a restaurant without someone asking for his autograph or wanting to shake his hand."[6] For a man prone to depression, the adrenaline lift of public activity was extremely useful, and Frost was therefore highly responsive to a request that arrived barely eight weeks after the inauguration for him to visit Israel and Greece. The invitation came from Hebrew University, asking Frost to deliver the first lecture in their new program on American culture and civilization. "For Frost, who had always had so much interest in the Old Testament, this was irresistible," noted Victor Reichert. "When somebody suggested he was too old for such a trip, he said he must go *because* he was too old."[7]

Frost hoped that Kay would go with him, but she refused. Lawrance

Thompson, however—always the faithful (if somewhat resentful) amanuensis—agreed to go. This excursion was quite an undertaking for a man of nearly eighty-seven, but "he believed every trip was going to be his last, and he wanted to make sure to get it in," says Lesley Lee Francis. According to Thompson, Frost was now hotly in pursuit of "more fame and more glory," that elusive halo.[8] There was also Frost's genuine wish to see Israel and Greece, the two cultures from which Western civilization had got its "running start / As it were from scratch," as he wrote in "Kitty Hawk."

The itinerary included Israel, Greece, and England, with Frost's eighty-seventh birthday celebration to occur in Cambridge with E. M. Forster—an odd final twist, promoted by Thompson but never quite to Frost's liking. Flying first-class overnight to the Lod airport in Israel, Frost was surrounded by reporters, most of them en route to the opening of the new Sheraton Hotel in Tel Aviv—the first American-owned hotel in that city. Also on the plane was Harry Golden, a writer who in conversation with the poet kept making comparisons between Frost and Carl Sandburg, much to Frost's annoyance. He was especially upset when Golden told him they had similar haircuts. In his biography, Thompson finds this moment of apparent rivalry more telling than, perhaps, it really is; Frost certainly knew by now that his work had overshadowed Sandburg's, and the comparisons launched by Golden must have been simply annoying.

Relations between Frost and Sandburg were actually quite cordial, though Frost was often annoyed by the fact that the press constantly linked them when they had little in common apart from a shock of unruly white hair. Sandburg's fragile, imagistic lyrics and rambling Whitmanesque poems bore no resemblance to Frost's work. It irritated Frost that Sandburg went around the country with his guitar, making a spectacle of himself instead of behaving in a more "dignified" way. More important, Sandburg was a liberal, defined by Frost as "someone who can't take his own side in a quarrel." "We're entirely different in our work," Frost said of Sandburg. "He has a good heart. He says in his poetry, 'The people, yes.' I say, 'The people, yes—and no.' " As ever, Frost was a bundle of contradictions, but never irrational. He had put both agricultural life and the common man at the center of his best poems, celebrating physical work better than any poet before him. His poems were full of men digging, mowing, raking, and piling hay, mending walls, chopping firewood, planting seeds, pruning trees, picking apples, and so forth. Nevertheless, he maintained his anti–New Deal conservatism to the end, believing it was better for one to provide for oneself and one's family than to have the state do it. He hated the notion of the collective, of the masses. And he was always resistant to the concept of trying to legislate morality. "Laws are what make crime," he wrote in one of his last journal entries.[9] In this, he was perhaps less a conservative than a libertarian.

During his ten days in Israel, Frost stayed at the majestic King David Hotel—the former headquarters of the British during the Mandate and the scene of bloody fighting during the War of Independence in 1948. Its amber stone walls were still pocked from gunfire, a vivid reminder of that war. Frost and Thompson were given a tour of the Jordanian Old City the next day, followed by American cameramen from NBC as they entered the ancient walled city through the fabled Dung Gate. Led by an Arab guide, they climbed the narrow, winding pathway of the Via Dolorosa, tracing the Stations of the Cross. Frost was taken inside the Church of the Holy Sepulcher, one of the holiest sites of Christianity, and shown the spot where the True Cross was supposedly planted. The guide asked if he wanted to kiss the spot—the traditional gesture for pilgrims—but Frost claimed (half whimsically) that he was "not good enough for that." To Thompson, Frost expressed his personal disbelief in the literal aspects of Christianity, although he said he preferred these myths to the more secular myths about the origins of humanity that had come down from Darwin.[10]

The centerpiece of the Israeli visit was the lecture at Hebrew University on March 13. Frost announced, humorously, that he was not going to *talk* about American civilization but to *be* it. He quickly moved into a reading of several of his major poems, then opened the floor to questions from the capacity audience. The cameramen from NBC were still following him, and he was bathed in bright light. He explained to the university audience that he had spent much of his life "as a professor, among professors," and he argued that "education elevates trouble to a higher plane." In essence, he gave a brilliant

defense of his own skeptical approach to life, a life "with more questions than answers." The performance—mostly a monologue, with a
few polite interruptions from the audience—lasted for two hours, with
huge applause at the end. As usual, Frost had delivered value for
money.

He spent the rest of the week touring the country and meeting with
local dignitaries, including President Itzhak Ben-Zvi. Although Frost
had previously said that he viewed Israel as an "American colony," he
found the strangeness of the landscape, architecture, customs, and
food more than he had banked on. Making matters worse, he was soon
gripped by a fierce intestinal disorder that meant he had to spend most
of his time in the hotel room. He asked Lawrance Thompson to cancel
the English leg of the journey, and he nearly canceled the Greek portion, too.

After a couple of days in bed, he felt well enough to continue on to
Greece, where he was met by the American ambassador, Ellis O.
Briggs, whose wife took Frost in hand, prescribing a diet of tea and
custard that worked almost miraculously to soothe Frost's digestive
problems. The recovery was so remarkable that Frost felt strong
enough to lecture three times. The Greek audiences were impressed by
his energy, wit, and ample knowledge of ancient Greek culture. By
chance, an old friend and colleague from Amherst, G. Amour Craig,
was visiting Greece with his wife at this time, and they took Frost
to the Acropolis. But extensive sightseeing was out of the question:
Frost had managed to summon the strength for three public performances, and that was all there was left in him. Thompson said in his
notes that Frost seemed "terribly homesick" and wanted to get back to
Cambridge as soon as possible.

He was driven to the airport in the ambassador's limousine and
deposited like a head of state on the runway itself. He and Thompson
stopped only briefly in England on the way home—just long enough
to attend a party honoring him at the U.S. ambassador's residence.
He also had tea with Sir Charles Tennyson, a descendant of the great
Victorian poet, who headed a society, as Frost put it, "created for the
prevention of forgetting Tennyson." The excursion to see E. M. Forster

in Cambridge was canceled because Frost began to experience intestinal problems again, with added dizziness and faintness of breath.

An English doctor was recommended by the U.S. Embassy, and the diagnosis (delivered to Thompson) was unnerving: "I can tighten up his bowels, all right," the doctor said, "but it's his heart that worries me." The beat was irregular and slow. When Thompson conveyed this to Frost, the poet grew panicky. He dictated a wire to Kay: "I AM ORDERED HOME BY EMBASSY DOCTOR, WORN OUT." They flew home two days later, with Frost "unsteady on his feet, pale, shaky—like a very old man."[11]

Frost went home to Cambridge to be nursed by Kay. Showing great resilience, he appeared at Amherst two weeks later for his usual round of talks and readings. "One of the main things about Frost's life in these last years was his robustness," recalls Jack A. W. Hagstrom, who by now had become a doctor. Hagstrom found Frost "astonishingly fit for a man his age, always ready to go on long walks, eager to stay up late. There was never any sign of his wanting to go to bed. He would never say, 'I'm tired, and I need to get some sleep.' "[12] Frost held court in the lobby of the Lord Jeffrey Inn until well past midnight most evenings.

The next big event on Frost's plate was a reading at the State Department in Washington, billed as "An Evening with Robert Frost." It had been planned for some time, and the president and first lady were planning to attend. Once again, Stewart Udall—now secretary of the interior in the Kennedy cabinet—was involved in arranging this event. Gratefully, Frost wrote to him, "By the accident of our falling in friendship with you and Lee [Mrs. Udall], we have been brought out on top of a new pinnacle of view that makes me for one feel dangerously like a monarch of all fifty states I survey."[13]

The reading was held in the State Department auditorium on May 1, with a full house that included numerous members of the U.S. House and Senate, a couple of Supreme Court justices, and various ambassadors from abroad. Douglas Dillon, the secretary of the treasury, introduced Udall, who, in turn, introduced Frost. Much to the poet's disappointment, President Kennedy was prevented from coming by a sudden crisis in Southeast Asia—the very beginnings of U.S. involvement with Vietnam. Frost began the hour with observations on the differences and similarities between science and poetry, one of his favorite topics, then read a selection of his most well known poems. The audience was so taken with him that they called him back on stage for several encores.

The following day, Frost had a chance to do something for Stewart Udall, who had been called onto the carpet for allegedly asking a wealthy oilman to solicit his associates to contribute to a $100-a-plate Democratic fund-raiser. Udall and Frost were planning to have lunch together anyway, but Udall asked the poet to appear next to him at a press conference beforehand. In essence, Frost would appear as a tacit character witness. With some reservations, he agreed to help the man who had done so much for him in the past year: quite literally, he stood beside him, so that photographers could mark the event. Somewhat pointedly, he refused to make any comment on Udall's situation.

Frost remained in Washington for a couple of weeks, giving another lecture as consultant in the humanities to the Library of Congress, and performing other small duties associated with the job. He was, however, glad to get back to Vermont, where his latest, and final, book of poems awaited finishing touches. "He was aware that this would be his swan song to poetry," a friend recalled. "It had already been postponed many times, largely because Frost was unsure about the quality of the poems."[14] For some time now, the working title had been *The Great Misgiving*, a suitably ambiguous phrase. Frost reconsidered at the last moment and chose a more obvious and optimistic title, *In the Clearing*—derived from "A Cabin in the Clearing," the third poem in the book (which had been his Christmas poem for 1951).

Frost worked on the volume right through the new year 1962, finishing the last poem (which he characteristically claimed to have written "right off the reel" in one sitting) on January 12, at Pencil Pines. The poem is fresh and lyrical, addressing a theme familiar to readers of Frost's earlier work:

> *In winter in the woods alone*
> *Against the trees I go.*
> *I mark a maple for my own*
> *And lay the maple low.*
>
> *At four o'clock I shoulder ax,*
> *And in the afterglow*
> *I link a line of shadowy tracks*
> *Across the tinted snow.*
>
> *I see for Nature no defeat*
> *In one tree's overthrow*
> *Or for myself in my retreat*
> *For yet another blow.*

This poem, stylistically, might well have been included in *A Boy's Will*. Frost recapitulates a familiar theme: the poet striking out by himself, moving "Against the trees." There is no merging with nature; the human separation, even exclusion, from nature is Frost's perennial subject. There is a sense of violence, too, as the poet lays the maple low with his ax in an act of defiance, of asserting his will over the natural state of things. But, wisely, Frost sees "no defeat" for nature in this single act of transgression. And, by implication, there is no defeat for the poet himself in death. The last two lines, to my ear, suggest defiance, a point Frost emphasized at a reading of this poem when he said the last line was "a threat to write another book."[15]

As ever, Frost drew on earlier material for several of the poems included in this volume, including "The Draft Horse," written in 1920, about the same time he wrote "The Lockless Door" (which was published in *New Hampshire*). This strange, even cruel, poem opens with a typical Frostian image:

> *With a lantern that wouldn't burn*
> *In too frail a buggy we drove*
> *Behind too heavy a horse*
> *Through a pitch-dark limitless grove.*

As George Monteiro notes, there are echoes here of "Stopping by Woods on a Snowy Evening," although the "little horse" is replaced by a "too-heavy horse."[16] Overall, the effects of the later poem are immeasurably darker, and less subtle, than "Stopping by Woods."

In the second stanza, something astonishing and unexpected happens:

> And a man came out of the trees
> And took our horse by the head
> And reaching back to his ribs
> Deliberately stabbed him dead.
>
> The ponderous beast went down
> With a crack of a broken shaft.
> And the night drew through the trees
> In one long invidious draft.

Read solely on a literal level, these stanzas make no sense. Men do not leap out of the woods and stab a horse to death, at least not in the realm of ordinary reality. I read this as a poem about the failure of vision, with the "too frail" buggy in the first stanza standing in for the poet's craft, which seems to be failing him here. It is depression, accompanied by a lack of imagination, that leaps from nowhere and hobbles the poet at the source of his creative power.

The speaker, part of a "we" who is not identified, seems bewildered by the experience and defensive. He does not want to "ascribe" to hatred any more than seems absolutely necessary. The poem ends:

> We assumed that the man himself
> Or someone he had to obey
> Wanted us to get down
> And walk the rest of the way.

Frost takes for granted a violent, confusing universe where dark agents enforce their wishes in the most unexpectedly harsh fashion. He also takes for granted that his work as a poet has been, and will continue to be, hampered by fierce and unexpected bouts of anxiety and depression—indeed, by a lack of imaginative power.

Many poems in this book fall into the category of light verse, though there is often a darker side to the joke, as in "The Objection to Being Stepped On," a poem about stepping on a rake and being smacked in the "seat of my sense." Frost, as ever, enjoys the doubleness of a concept; a tool may turn unexpectedly into a weapon; indeed, the Latin word *arma* (as Frost knew) could be translated either way. The poem had been Frost's Christmas poem for 1957, and was probably based on the time Elinor, in 1927, stepped on a rake and broke her nose when the handle flew up into her face. Frost's own meditations on this poem before a reading at Bread Loaf certainly reach beyond anything that is actually in the text: "You have to be reminded," he said, "that the Hungarian Revolution that occurred just before my time, that I heard a lot about when I was young, was all fought with farm tools—the poor peasants—pitchforks and flails and anything they could lay hands on. Weapons go to tools and tools go to weapons—it's back and forth."[17]

"Away!" and "A Cabin in the Clearing" count among the better poems in the volume, and they show off Frost in two of his favorite forms: the brief, ironic lyric and the dramatic dialogue in blank verse. The former ends with an aphoristic snippet worthy of one of poetry's great aphorists:

> *And I may return*
> *If dissatisfied*
> *With what I learn*
> *From having died.*

The latter offers a conversation between a garden mist and a wreath of chimney smoke, which are both watching two human beings in their cabin. As Richard Wilbur said, "The 'clearing' of the poem is a little area of human coherence, a bit of the universe become a colony of mind."[18] As ever, Frost leaps to metaphysical considerations from small, familiar images. The world, for him, is a cache of symbols; hardly anything is not useful to the observant eye.

The volume was published on Frost's eighty-eighth birthday, and was an immediate best-seller, eventually reaching sixty thousand copies—a staggering amount for a book of poetry. The reviews were usually respectful; indeed, most of them were written by friends and admirers: Richard Wilbur, Peter Davison, John Ciardi, John Holmes. For most critics, the publication of In the Clearing was another occasion to look back on the whole of Frost and to ponder the shape of the career. Ciardi, for instance, writing in the Saturday Review of Literature, noted "two main stages" in Frost's verse: "the poet of passion and the poet of wit and whimsy."[19] Shrewdly, Ciardi observed that in many of Frost's poems a mix of these two modes occurs, and this can be confusing. It was Frost himself who once wrote: "It takes all sorts of in and outdoor schooling / To get adapted to my kind of fooling."

Many poems in this last volume do not do justice to the man who wrote "Mowing," "Home Burial," "The Road Not Taken," "Birches," "After Apple-Picking," "Design," "The Silken Tent," "The Most of It," and "Directive." But enough glimmers of that poet occur to make one grateful for the book's existence. In a way, one can often learn to read a poet better by focusing on his or her lesser poems, where the dazzle is less intense, and hence the lineaments of the art more visible.

It had been a difficult winter for Frost. On his customary stopover in Georgia at Agnes Scott College, he had felt that some of the questions from the audience were belligerent, and he'd vowed never to return to the college, which had been a regular point on his compass of readings for many years. He arrived in South Miami quite ill, and was soon hospitalized with a case of pneumonia. Throughout February he lay quietly at Pencil Pines, recovering with the aid of two nurses.

Returning to Cambridge in March, he was well enough by his birthday to respond to a letter from President Kennedy urging the poet to accept from him personally the Congressional Gold Medal that had been authorized during the previous administration. Thus Frost traveled again to Washington. The evening of the same day he received the medal, a party for his eighty-eighth birthday was held for him at the Pan American Union building, with two hundred invited guests in attendance. A number of friends gave toasts in his honor, including Chief Justice Earl Warren, Adlai Stevenson, Justice Felix Frankfurter, Mark Van Doren, Al Edwards, and Robert Penn Warren. Robert Penn Warren recalled, "It was one of those rare public events when people from many fields—all of them distinguished—join to celebrate a poet. Frost was recognized as more than a poet. He was a monument. He looked the part, too, with a massive head, his hair unruly and long and snowy. He was the last to speak, and it was late. Everyone had gone on too long. But Frost was sparky. He was ready for his say. He told jokes, and held the floor for over half an hour. He recited a few poems, but mostly he talked. There was granite in his voice, steady and strong. He was as happy as I'd ever seen him."[20]

Frost ended his talk with a tribute to Kay Morrison, whom he called his "devoted secretary" and praised for her "two decades, even more, of friendship." He then recited "Never Again Would Birds' Song Be the Same," which he claimed "was written for her in the first place." He spoke the poem slowly, paused, and with a gesture of the hand toward Kay, repeated the last two lines:

> *Never again would birds' song be the same.*
> *And to do that to birds was why she came.*

He returned to Cambridge, then to Amherst for ten days in residence at the Lord Jeffrey, as usual. He was basking in the success of *In the Clearing* now, with frequent calls from Al Edwards bearing news of strong sales and good reviews. His energy was high, as the Scottish poet Alastair Reid noted at a dinner party in late April in Cambridge. "I went to dinner at the house of Peter Davison," Reid remembers, "and Frost was the centerpiece, the attraction. He clearly expected everyone to listen to him, and they did. He talked excitedly about poetry, about politics—whatever came into his head. The evening wore on, and there was no sign of his stopping. I was told that recently he had given a reading at Sarah Lawrance that lasted for three hours, and nobody dared interrupt him. The level of energy was amazing. Nobody could leave the dinner, not without offending Frost. So we stayed, and stayed."[21]

In early May, he returned to Washington to spend a week as consultant in the humanities—part of the busy public round that now made up his life. One night, while he was dining with the Udalls, an intriguing possibility was set before him. Udall wondered if Frost might go to the Soviet Union if an exchange could be arranged. The poet indicated interest, but said he would have to think it over carefully. He was now a very old man, and his health was uncertain. With some trepidation, he recalled the trip to Israel and Greece, which had put immense strain on his heart. He decided he would go only if a personal invitation from President Kennedy arrived, and he hinted that if he went, he hoped very much to meet the Soviet premier, Nikita Khrushchev.

Frost wrote a long, somewhat unctuous, letter to Kennedy, his enthusiasm for this trip spilling over into the margins. "How grand for you to think of me this way and how like you to take the chance of sending anyone like me over there affinitizing with the Russians," he exclaimed. Frost said he could imagine "the Russian and the American democracies drawing together, theirs easing down from a kind of abstract severity to taking less and less care of the masses: ours creeping up to taking more and more care of the masses as they grow innumerable." He spoke of a "noble rivalry" between the two great superpowers.[22]

The State Department arranged the trip for August, and Frost invited his friend Frederick B. Adams, director of the Pierpont Morgan Library in New York, to accompany him. Stewart Udall was going, too—it was originally his trip; as secretary of the interior, he was heading a delegation to visit hydroelectric plants. A young poet and Russian translator, F. D. Reeve, was also invited along (at the suggestion of William Meredith) to help with the language. Reeve recalls, "The assignment was unusual for all three of us. Frost had traveled to England and Israel in recent years, but he hadn't been abroad much and never under such authority. Adams, as a leading librarian, had dealt with many people of various persuasions, but never with Russians in their own country. And I, though I had been to Russia and I remembered Frost personally in a hazy, boyish way—he had taught our high school English class one day twenty years before—had never been a cicerone, much less aide to such a man."23

One intriguing absence on this trip was Lawrance Thompson. After the Israel-Greece trip, where a good deal of tension between Thompson and Frost had developed, Frost was perhaps not eager to spend much time in close quarters with his biographer once again. He pretended that he had meant nothing by not inviting him, but Thompson knew better. Indeed, this may well have been the fatal straw that turned Thompson against Frost in such a way that he would take it out on the poet in his three-volume biography, where he never lost an opportunity to discover and underline faults in Frost.24

On the plane going over, Frost mused to Reeve, "It's a grand adventure, isn't it? This going to Russia, I mean. Crazy, too. At my age going all the way over there just to show off." Frost was in high spirits, meditating on poetry: "Every poem has its own little tune," he said. "That's the way it comes to me, as a tune. You got to know how to do that, say it so you get the tune, too. Rhyme. You can't do it without that. Most of the time. You got to know how to take care of the rhyme."25

Arriving in Moscow on August 29, Frost was greeted by a delegation that included two American diplomats and five members of the Writers Union, including Yevgeny Yevtushenko, a young star on the poetry scene (his "Babi Yar" had been published to vast acclaim the year before, and "Stalin's Heirs" was soon to appear). The writers who gathered around Frost were sympathetic to the fiercely independent quality of his work, and they appreciated his humanism. "For them," says Reeve, "Frost personified this tradition [of humanism]. Frost's most important accomplishment in Russia was not the political embassy he aspired to but the enactment of freewheeling literary activity which he, by his poetry readings and by his talk, encouraged among the Russians."26

Frost, Adams, and Reeve were driven in long black Zims to the Sovietskaya, a prestigious hotel reserved for foreign guests. (Udall was lodged elsewhere.) On the outside, the hotel was modern looking in the dreary style of 1930s modernism; inside, the lobby was adorned with clunky pillars of marble and leather armchairs. Small clusters of visitors—Arabs, Chinese, French—moved about in self-contained groups. Frost was besieged by requests for interviews, and he readily gave them. As Reeve put it, "the business of being the leading American poet as an official guest in Moscow nearly overwhelmed us."[27]

Frost was occupied during the day with appearances and interviews, and often dined at night with well-known Soviet writers, including the seventy-year-old novelist Konstantin Paustovsky, and Kornei Chukovsky, the eighty-year-old critic and writer of books for children. Chukovsky was a winner of the Lenin Prize and, only a few months before, had received an honorary degree from Oxford University; he told Frost that his collection of Russian folktales had sold over sixty million copies. "Chukovsky's acumen and style, his erudition and unusual knack for the apt gesture, set the tone of the evening," Reeve said.[28]

One evening they went to a café as the guest of Yevtushenko, whose youthful arrogance and energy were a contrast to Frost, who seemed reserved by comparison. Other young poets were there, including Yevgeny Vinokurov and Andrei Voznesensky. The host kept filling everyone's glasses with wine, playing the role of *arbiter bibendi* to the hilt. At one point, the conversation turned to good people versus bad, and Yevtushenko suggested that there were few bad people in the world, but they were well organized. He said they occasionally even provoked good people into "doing good." Frost replied, "Yes, like killing them."

Frost recited "Stopping by Woods on a Snowy Evening" to the whole café—to everyone's obvious pleasure. The group went back to Yevtushenko's apartment for dinner. "Frost was enjoying himself among these vibrant, self-confident poets," said Reeve, "but, I think, he more and more felt that their world was scarcely his."[29]

On September 3, Frost's party traveled to Leningrad, one of the world's most beautiful cities and a virtual museum of Russian imperial history, with palaces and elegant town houses, museums and libraries.

The Leningrad *Pravda* recorded Frost's arrival the following day, and its assessment of his career focused on the proletarian nature of his work:

> Literary critics rightly call Frost a worker poet, a poet of labor. Farmers, hired hands, woodchoppers, workers are the central figures in his verse tales. The poet is very familiar with the people he writes about: for thirty-eight years he worked as a village teacher, a farmer, a newspaper reporter, before he made up his mind to publish his first book of verse.
>
> Frost's poetry is profoundly civic. In many of his works he reflects on the human worth of the simple laborer, on his creative energy and love of freedom. Frost can genuinely be regarded as a spokesman of the dreams of the progressive, democratic segments of contemporary America. The basis of his creative writing is philosophic reflection on the permanent grandeur of the laboring man, the humanistic idea of the harmonious and all-inclusive reconstruction of the world.[30]

Pravda was not entirely wrong. Frost is genuinely a poet of labor, a man whose actual experience on the farm had profoundly affected him; more than any other poet of similar stature, he celebrates work, putting the activity of labor at the center of many of his best poems. Nevertheless, "the harmonious and all-inclusive reconstruction of the world" could not be called a self-conscious aspect of his project.

The highlight of the visit to Leningrad was an encounter with Anna Akhmatova, the greatest Russian poet of the century. They met over lunch at the dacha of Mikhail Alexeyev, a literary critic and director of research at Pushkin House. The dacha, some fifty minutes from Leningrad by car, was an airy and bright country house surrounded by a waist-high wooden fence. Akhmatova arrived shortly after Frost, "in a dark dress, a pale lilac shawl over her shoulders, august and dignified with her white hair and deep eyes."[31] The poets greeted each other deferentially, and the conversation at lunch ranged widely over favorite writers, from Greek and Latin to American and

English. Akhmatova proved an erudite, formidable conversationalist, and Frost was impressed. Despite obvious differences, these poets had something in common: both came of age just before the First World War broke out and both were known for clear, distinct imagery and traditional subjects. Both had suffered much, achieved much, and been granted huge amounts of respect in their own countries. (Akhmatova, in particular, had been attacked for her refusal to write poems that seemed appropriately political, and it was only during the recent cultural thaw that she had been rehabilitated.) For both poets, the effort to bring ordinary speech into the realm of poetic expression had been central to their poetic enterprise.

Reeve thought that Frost "seemed to feel out of things" when several Russians began to sing the praises of Akhmatova. He tried to rescue the situation by praising Frost, and made remarks meant to draw attention his way. But the old poet turned on him, furious: "No more of that, none of that, you cut that out," he snapped. When Reeve tried to explain what he meant, Frost hushed him, saying, "Cut it out."

Frost declined to recite any poems, but encouraged Akhmatova to do so, and she offered two poems in Russian; her nobility and passion communicated itself, even though Frost did not understand what she was saying. He thanked her sincerely. "It's very musical," he said. "You can hear the music in it. It's very good."

That night, Frost gave a public reading at Pushkin House, on Vasily Island just across from the Winter Palace. The auditorium was crowded, and the audience responded warmly to Frost, even to his characteristic joking. He recited (often from memory) many of his classic poems, including "Two Tramps in Mud Time," "Birches," and "Mending Wall." The poems were then read in translation by young Russian poets, although sometimes the translations and originals did not exactly coincide. No one seemed to care. The applause was thunderous.

Back in Moscow a day later, Frost eagerly awaited an invitation to meet with Premier Khrushchev. It looked, at first, as though only Stewart Udall would meet the premier, and this upset Frost terribly. When he learned that Udall had, in fact, already departed for Georgia, where Khrushchev was staying at his dacha, Frost was outraged, considering this a form of desertion. He had been wanting to confront the Soviet leader, to show his mettle in the face of immense power. Meeting Khrushchev had come to seem a test of some kind, and he wanted it to happen. When the invitation finally came, he was both thrilled and nervous.

Shortly before the trip began, Frost experienced severe stomach cramps, but a suggestion that the trip be canceled was dealt with sternly by Frost: "No, this is what I came for." He flew on September 7, as planned, to the Crimea. At the airport in Sochi, he and his group were greeted by an official delegation and driven in a limousine to Georgia, an hour away, where the premier's dacha was located on a lush hilltop. First, however, they stopped to rest and eat at the guest house of the Ministry of Health.

Frost was by now feeling worse, and a local doctor was called in. She examined Frost and said he was neither very well nor very sick. He was suffering from a case of nervous indigestion, she suggested. If the situation worsened, he must return at once to Moscow for further treatment. Frost, of course, refused to entertain this idea. He would meet Khrushchev at whatever cost to himself.

Frost's Soviet hosts soon informed the poet that the premier was sending his own physician to look after him, and that he would come himself to see Frost as soon as possible. Soon a slim, middle-aged doctor appeared in a tan nankeen jacket. He examined Frost with self-conscious gravity. The patient had developed a fever, and seemed agitated and weak; his stomach rumbled. The doctor quizzed Reeve about the poet's past medical history, his recent travel, and the background to his present condition. A bland diet and rest were recommended.

Outside the room, palm trees swayed in the warm winds. Before long, Khrushchev himself appeared at the guest house and spoke in the hall with the doctor. Frost was informed of the premier's arrival, and immediately rose to put on socks and shoes. Reeve could see that Frost was terribly anxious, but still eager for this encounter. He had definite things he wanted to say.

Khrushchev came into the bedroom in a dapper olive-tan suit, which he wore over a beige Ukrainian blouse—rather different from the image he had projected on his visit to America some years before. He seemed, to Reeve, full of vigor and courtesy. He said he was honored to meet Frost, and warned him to follow the doctor's orders carefully. Frost expressed pleasure that the premier had made this effort to see him, and joked that doctors could not be trusted. He boasted that he would live to be a hundred, which would make him half the age of his country at its bicentennial. The conversation ranged widely, from art to poetry and the relation of the artist to society. Frost said that Khrushchev had obviously done a good deal to support poetry: he was very impressed with what he had seen of Russian poets. He also brought greetings from President Kennedy.

Khrushchev apparently suspected that Frost was holding back, that he had something in particular to say to him, so he asked the poet directly if this was the case. Frost acknowledged that he did. For years, he had thought about the conflict between the superpowers, and now was his chance to put a significant oar in the water. He "made it clear that he assumed the Soviet system was here to stay," says Reeve, "that, like it or not, socialism was inevitable," and he told Khrushchev that he admired the way he used power with courage and audacity.[32] In this he was quite sincere: Frost always admired people who could summon and utilize authority well.

Turning to the role of the poet, Frost suggested that a poet could help a government foster character: "A great nation makes great poetry, and great poetry makes a nation."[33] Circling around this theme, he spoke warmly of the "noble rivalry" between the United States and the Soviet Union, and pressed for "candid understanding" between the superpowers. He also argued for the benefits of cultural exchanges.

Then he moved to the core of his burden: the Berlin situation. With stunning audacity, he proposed reuniting East and West Berlin, a suggestion that provoked Khrushchev into defending the current arrangement. He was genuinely worried, the premier said, about the threat posed by West Germany, and he regretted the fact that NATO had allowed it to become remilitarized. He added that NATO was not a real threat, given Soviet military power: within thirty minutes,

Soviet missiles could blast all of Europe to smithereens. He told Frost that Kennedy himself had wanted to sign a pact with him, but that he couldn't because of political conditions in the United States.

Frost returned to the issue of Berlin, saying that this unstable arrangement could provoke a world war. Perhaps to flatter the premier, he said that the next hundred years belonged to the United States and the Soviet Union together. At this point, Khrushchev noted that "the Warsaw Pact countries were forging ahead economically and that they would soon overtake the Common Market," at which point Frost returned to his earlier theme of "horse-trading, of recognizing the present limits of political power and the continual drawing closer of the capitalist and the planned economies, of what he called the democracy straining upward toward socialism and the socialist democracy humanizing downward from the severity of its ideal."[34]

At a crucial turn, Frost declared, "God wants us to contend." He added, "You have only progress in conflict." Khrushchev responded by saying that the Warsaw Pact nations were young and vital, but that the United States and Western Europe were based on a system thousands of years old; indeed, they were saddled with a "defunct economic system." "This reminded him," said Reeve, "of an anecdote reported in Gorky's memoirs of Tolstoy, where Tolstoy told about being too old and too weak and too infirm to do it but still having the desire."[35] Frost laughed, and said perhaps he and the premier were too old to "do it," but that the United States was still too young to have to worry in that regard.

Frost reminded Khrushchev that both the United States and the Soviet Union had a common European ancestry, with certain cultural values that were shared; by contrast, he said that Africa showed an "absence of culture," while China was "impossibly foreign." Khrushchev remained passive, patient, even indulgent. He and Frost soon agreed that there should be no name-calling, no propaganda or blackguarding between their two countries.

After ninety minutes had passed, Khrushchev asked if Frost was not getting tired. Frost said no, and that he was delighted to have such a frank exchange. In fact, he felt quite well now. Khrushchev, in turn,

434 | ROBERT FROST

said it was a pleasure to meet such an eminent poet; he asked that Frost convey his greetings to President Kennedy when he returned home and pass on the substance of their conversation. They stood together, shook hands, and the premier left, followed by his aides.

Frost immediately slumped back onto the bed, putting his feet up. "Well, we did it, didn't we?" he said to Reeve, obviously pleased by the meeting. "He's a great man," he added. "He knows what power is and isn't afraid to take hold of it. He's a great man, all right."[36] Reeve reminded Frost that he had wanted to give the premier a copy of *In the Clearing*, and Frost hastily inscribed a copy and gave it to Reeve to take to Khrushchev before he departed. "I took it downstairs and handed it to Khrushchev, who was sitting beside the drive in a green, open Chaika convertible," Reeve recalls. "His secretary and doctor were in the back. The escort was a short way off. For a moment it seemed improbable, there in that lush, azure world, that the dramatic meeting which we all had been at had actually occurred."[37]

It had been a spectacular meeting. The most powerful figure in the Soviet Union had met with an American cultural icon, and they had freely talked about matters of huge cultural import. They had exchanged witticisms and barbs, had praised each other for their vitality, and had acknowledged the responsibility of government in the maintainance of cultural traditions. They had, as Reeve put it, "decried the horrors of war and insisted on the necessity of using force to maintain control, to preserve pride, to assert tradition."[38]

On Sunday, September 9, Frost and his companions flew home on a Pan American jet. The seventeen-hour flight exhausted him further, and when he arrived at Idlewild Airport he was in no condition to be interviewed; but a cluster of reporters surrounded him, and he made some off-the-cuff remarks about his meeting with Khrushchev that he would soon come to regret. "Khrushchev said we were too liberal to fight," he remarked. "I suppose he thought we'd stand there for the next hundred years saying, 'on the one hand—but on the other hand.'" When asked if he had any message to deliver to President Kennedy, Frost acknowledged that he did. "I don't 'plan' to see him. I wait for the President," he said.[39]

As it was, Kennedy never called or even sent a note to thank Frost for his efforts, and Frost was deeply hurt. Even worse, letters arrived questioning Frost about the remark that Americans were "too liberal to fight." He was accused of aiding and abetting those, like the John Birch Society, who actually sought to make matters worse between the Soviet Union and the United States.

Reeve was philosophical about Frost's remarks: "Plunged into a press conference at Idlewild, just off the plane and tired after two weeks on the road and a seventeen-hour trip home, Frost may appear to have put his foot in it, so to speak, in quoting Khrushchev as he did. But he had expressed many times before this press conference both his own attitude toward liberalism and the attitude he understood Khrushchev to be taking. He believed that the world today is dominated not so much by ideals and 'isms' as by actual power balance. He urged that his country be ready ultimately to risk its own defense and be willing always to make every gesture of magnanimity. Political power, cultural excellence, and moral integrity were, for him, inseparable. Those 'liberals' who lacked his strength of conviction seemed to him, as he put it, sapheads. He didn't admire them. He deeply admired Khrushchev, a card-carrying member of the Communist Party—'he's our enemy and he's a great man'—for the drive and purposefulness of his vision of power."[40]

Old age had finally caught up with Frost, who now stumbled from crisis to crisis. Most frightening, a prostate condition that had plagued him for some years became suddenly worse after he got back from Russia, and his doctor in Cambridge explained that surgery loomed in the not-too-distant future. In the meanwhile, he refused to lie low. First, he visited Dartmouth, where he gave a major address, then traveled to Amherst for his usual fall stint, staying at the Lord Jeffrey for ten days. The current president of Amherst, Calvin H. Plimpton, announced that a recent gift of $3.5 million would be used to construct a major new building at the center of the campus: the Robert Frost Library. The long, often affectionate, and mutually productive relationship between Frost and Amherst would be fittingly marked. Frost was profoundly moved by this gesture.

On October 20, Frost headed to Washington, D.C., where he

addressed the first National Poetry Festival three days later at the Library of Congress. This was a particularly tense week in Washington as the Cuban missile crisis was under way, posing a very real threat of nuclear war. Only President Kennedy's firm, clear-eyed handling of the situation averted disaster, and Frost was duly impressed by the president's resolve. While giving his talk at the Library of Congress, he interrupted himself to return to the remark he had made at Idlewild: "I've joked about liberals a great deal," he said, "and there's been something going around. I wonder how many of you've heard it: that I was told in Russia that Americans were too liberal to fight, or something like that. Nothing like that did I hear. What I heard was, rather, a pleasantry from the greatest ruler in the world, you know, the almighty, and in his genial way he just said, 'As Tolstoy said to Gorki'—or vice versa, I've forgotten which; it was a very literary conversation—'As Tolstoy said to Gorki, "There's such a thing as a nation getting so soft it couldn't—wouldn't fight."' See, that's all. He was just saying there was such a thing, and he might be suggesting that we better look out. See, that's all, it was a pleasantry. It wasn't a defiant thing, nothing was defiant."[41] The old tongue still flickered back to this broken mental tooth. He wanted to put something right that he had got a little wrong by speaking too offhandedly.

Frost went on to Ohio, where he spoke at Kenyon College, then to Michigan to receive an honorary degree from the University of Detroit and to give a reading. His host was Peter Stanlis, who recalls that "Frost was very nervous before the reading, which was held in a huge auditorium. Over ten thousand people were there—the largest audience Frost had ever read to—and they cheered the poet. There was great enthusiasm for this reading. He was in wonderful form."[42]

Frost continued on to Chicago for a celebration of the fiftieth anniversary of *Poetry*, a magazine that had been so influential in making his name known to the reading public so many decades before. On November 27, he was back in Hanover, to speak at Dartmouth's newly built Hopkins Center on the subject of "extravagance." He referred to the extravagance of the building—an elegant glass-and-steel structure with tall windows overlooking the green—and went on to talk about the "extravagant universe."[43] "And the most extravagant thing in it, as far as we know, is man—the most wasteful, spending thing in it—in all this luxuriance." He added that poetry itself was "a sort of extravagance, in many ways. It's something that people wonder about. What's the need of it? And the answer is, no need—not particularly." He went on to read his poem "Away!" In that autumnal poem, he says:

> *I leave behind*
> *Good friends in town.*
> *Let them get well-wined*
> *And go lie down.*
>
> *Don't think I leave*
> *For the outer dark*
> *Like Adam and Eve*
> *Put out of the Park.*

In other words, he was not going to the land of the dead as an exile. Rather, he was going home.

> *Forget the myth.*
> *There is no one I*
> *Am put out with*
> *Or put out by.*
>
> *Unless I'm wrong*
> *I but obey*
> *The urge of a song:*
> *"I'm—bound—away!"*
>
> *And I may return*
> *If dissatisfied*
> *With what I learn*
> *From having died.*

Frost had by now acquired a benevolent, almost welcoming attitude toward death, keeping a little in reserve: the threat to "return" if he found himself "dissatisfied." But he did not want to end his Dartmouth talk on that note. He concluded with "The Night Light," a little poem that had appeared in *Steeple Bush* as one of the five "nocturnes."

> She always had to burn a light
> Beside her attic bed at night.
> It gave bad dreams and troubled sleep,
> But helped the Lord her soul to keep.
> Good gloom on her was thrown away.
> It is on me by night or day.
> Who have, as I suppose, ahead
> The darkest of it still to dread.

"Suppose I end on that dark note," he told the overflow student audience in Spaulding Auditorium, adding emphatically: "Goodnight, goodnight to all of you." He walked off the stage to a standing ovation.

Returning to Cambridge, he gave a reading at the Ford Hall Forum, in Boston, on December 2, 1962. This was another regular stop on his yearly compass of readings. As usual, he put every ounce of himself into the performance, but the prostate problem had become severe, and Frost now faced the long-awaited operation. After the reading he felt weak and dizzy and was short of breath; he had to be helped to his car. He may have sensed as he left the Forum that Sunday night that he had just given his last public reading.

He entered Peter Bent Brigham Hospital the next day. An examination showed that his prostate was abnormally large and his bladder was infected. A diagnosis of chronic cystitis was put forward, although the doctors were worried about the condition of his heart as well—the beat was irregular and weak. Soon a bladder stoppage occurred, and tests showed that colon bacilli had collected there; this complication required immediate surgery.

The procedure took place on December 10, and revealed even worse problems. The prostate was malignant, and the disease had spread to the bladder. But the operation was successful, the cancerous tissue apparently removed. Frost spent two weeks in recovery, but on December 23, a pulmonary embolism nearly killed him.

He recovered, but he was obviously in bad shape. On top of everything, his heart had been damaged. "With all these countless friends in the hospital and without, I find myself better than a little less than bad," he commented to one friend, showing that he still had his wits about him. He was cheered when, during the first week of the new year, Yale awarded him the Bollingen Prize for poetry. The award gave him, he declared, "one new reason to live."

But another embolism struck him on January 7, and he barely managed to continue living. Through all of this, Kay Morrison and her daughter, Anne Morrison Gentry, attended Frost on a daily basis, controlling the flow of visitors, who included his daughter Lesley, Edward Lathem, Hyde Cox, Franklin Reeve, Stewart Udall, Al Edwards, and John Sloan Dickey. When he was not greeting visitors, he worked on a poem that he planned as a sequel to his Christmas poem of 1962, which he had called "The Prophets Really Prophesy as Mystics/The Commentators Merely by Statistics." In the new poem, a king summons prophets to his court to interpret his dreams, but he discovers they are all "false mystics" and orders them to be taken away and "executed, every one." Then, suddenly, a wastrel wanders in:

> The king said "Who are you? I thought I had you all wiped out. False
>   prophets."
> He answered "I was not a member of the guild."

The poem is fragmentary, but it remains interesting as an example of what was on Frost's mind now, as the last hour approached. He was dwelling on the subject of legitimacy, thinking about how one tells a "false mystic" from a true one. He was questioning his own voice, and arguing that a true prophet dreams "the only dream there is to dream," a dream of reality. Anything less than the truth would have seemed too weak for a man faced with his own finitude.

Louis Untermeyer spent an hour with Frost on January 22, talking about the Russian trip, about poetry and politics, and about their long friendship. It had recently been announced, much to Frost's chagrin, that John Steinbeck had won the Nobel Prize in Literature. Frost realized now that this, the ultimate accolade, would be denied him.

For the next week, he received visitors and vaguely worked on his final poem about the king and the prophets. On January 27, Ezra Pound's daughter, Princess Mary de Rachewiltz, stopped by to thank him for his efforts on behalf of her father. "You are a dear and so is Ezra," Frost said. "I've never got over those days we had together." He added, thoughtfully: "Politics make too much difference to both of us. Love is all. Romantic love—as in stories and poems. I tremble with it. I'd like to see Ezra again."[44]

When she was gone, Frost dictated a response to Roy Elliott and his wife, Alma, who had written a note wishing his speedy recovery. Frost's note ended: "If only I get well . . . I'll go deeper into life with you than I ever have before."[45] Frost had known Elliott since 1919, when he published "The Neighborliness of Robert Frost"—an early and important article that Frost regarded as crucial to his personal myth-making. Later, they were colleagues and friends at Amherst. As ever, Frost was incredibly loyal to old friends, who by now were legion.

He died the next day, near midnight, losing consciousness soon after another blood clot reached his lungs. "I feel as though I were in my last hours," he had said to Jack Sweeney and his wife that same afternoon, and his predication was correct. A great and long life had come, quietly, to an end. America had lost a poet of astounding grace and wisdom, one who had lodged dozens of poems in places where they could certainly not be gotten rid of easily, or at all.

CONCLUSION

In the first stanza of "Revelation," an early poem, Frost writes:

> *We make ourselves a place apart*
> *Behind light words that tease and flout,*
> *But oh, the agitated heart*
> *Till someone really find us out.*

As Theodore Morrison, the husband of Kay, mused in an appreciative essay that appeared four years after the poet's death, "Frost wanted to be found out—by the right people in the right way."[1] One might say that Frost's life was a complicated game of deception and revelation, of creating masks and winking through the eyeholes in them. His poems, even his life, often seem an elaborate construction, remarkably interdependent.

The poetry itself is marked by an unbelievable, even visionary, clarity. As he asked bluntly in "Riders," "What is this talked-of mystery of birth / But being mounted bareback on the earth?" Frost was indeed a roughrider, a man with roots in the American Wild West—a boy from San Francisco whose own father, William Prescott Frost, was lured by fantasy, by the "easy gold at the hand of fay or elf" offered by the prospect of riches and glory on the frontier. But tragedy came early, and by the age of eleven Frost had lost a father, and lost a way of life.

The recklessness of his father, however, remained an essential part of his nature. He saw himself as an individualist out to conquer the world, a gambler who risked everything in trying to make a life of poetry. "All or nothing," he once told an interviewer, "that is how I wanted it, how I have lived." His poems are full of outsiders, wanderers on the fringe of town at the edge of night, characters who plunge into the woods alone. William Frost's sense of adventure, his wildness, his skepticism, and his heroic self-conception remained a highly visible part of his son's character.

Against that worldly figure rose Isabelle Moodie, his Swedenborgian mother, an otherworldly creature who left her son an opposing model of selfhood. "He lived, more than anyone I ever knew, in the spirit," recalled Rabbi Victor Reichert. "The outside was bluff, the inside was deep and true. He was always in search of God—or some quality that could be identified with that word." That hunger for the absolute is evident from first to last. In "Kitty Hawk," for instance, one of his last important statements in poetry, he writes:

> But God's own descent
> Into flesh was meant
> As a demonstration
> That the supreme merit
> Lay in risking spirit
> In substantiation.

Frost wanted to go "deeper and deeper into matter," risking spirit in substantiation. His poems might be considered a lifelong homage to the things of this world, those facts which are "the sweetest dream that nature knows." As he writes in "In Hardwood Groves," "However it is in some other world / I know that this is the way in ours." Earth, for him, was the "right place for love," and he kept his eye fixed firmly here, allowing himself occasional flights only because he understood, even liked, the oppositional tug of gravity. Like the mythical hero Antaeus, he derived his strength from attachment to the ground.

In the tradition of Emerson, his most significant literary ancestor, Frost read nature as a symbol of the spirit, but he read nature more closely than did Emerson, for whom nature was more of an abstraction than a daily reality. Frost was an obsessive student of his physical habitat, and he went "botanizing" with a vengeance, learning the names of things wherever he lived or traveled. Like many close readers of nature, he could not avoid generalizing from observation; as he wrote in "The Onset," "I know that winter death has never tried / The earth but it has failed." He understood the opposite, too, that "leaf subsides to leaf," as he said in "Nothing Gold Can Stay." The cycles of nature are cycles of destruction and regeneration, but destruction is real as well as painful, and it must be accounted for.

Frost's skepticism was rooted in a belief in God that varied in its conventionality. As he wrote to Louis Untermeyer early in their friendship, "I discovered that do or say my damnedest I can't be other than orthodox in politics, love, and religion: I can't escape salvation."[2] But Frost was a skeptic as well, using his skepticism as a way of protecting his religious faith. It is easy to look at "For Once, Then, Something" or "Design" and imagine that Frost scorned religious faith; but even those poems are cannily made to keep the "wrong" people from understanding exactly what he thought and felt about some important things (as he suggests in "Directive"). Doubt is an integral part of genuine faith, and Frost explored the theology of doubt with astounding honesty and passion. But his many doubts never added up to a denial of basic things of the spirit, since spirit was a vital part of his dualism, along with matter.

Frost had a rich, complex intellectual life, and was fascinated by Darwin, Bergson, William James, and many others; as might be expected, the reading and thinking he did affected the shape of his poems. As Robert Faggen says, "The figure a Frost poem makes, as he says, 'from delight to wisdom,' is often one from enthusiasm and desire for insight to skepticism and uncertainty, compromise that steps back from assertion or statement to point toward something, perhaps chilling, beyond our passion."[3] "My poems," Frost wrote to a friend in 1927, "are all set to trip the reader head foremost into the boundless. Ever since infancy I have had the habit of leaving my blocks carts chairs and such like ordinaries where people would be pretty sure to fall forward over them in the dark. Forward, you understand, and in the dark."[4] He referred to this as his "innate mischievousness."

Almost uniquely among the modern poets, Frost was interested in science, and he knew a great deal about physics, astronomy, botany, and geology. "Science is nothing but practical experience carried to a greater extent," he wrote in his notebooks. "It pushes knowledge from miles to light years. It teaches us on the job what is possible in material strength, speed and finish, what is sufficient to do and think."[5] In effect, his engagement with science kept him from falling into sentimental attitudes toward religion or the human heart, making it possible for him to write poems such as "The Most of It," "Acquainted with the Night," and "Desert Places." In the latter, he talks of those places "so much nearer home" where he can scare himself with his "own desert places." Indeed, those deserts were there, in his life and mind, and every poem was an attempt to rescue some clarity, to find oases of language in deserts of thought and feeling.

His own physiological makeup was such that he never felt quite free of a tendency toward depression, although I hesitate to say that he suffered from bipolar disorder: one cannot, retrospectively, make such a diagnosis. The manic talker, the robust public performer, and the witty conversationalist were surely the flip side of his persistent, ingrained melancholy. And as Ed Ingebretsen has shown, Frost turned his incipient melancholy into abiding interests in the Gothic and the darker sources of religious vision.[6]

Needless to say, the serious mental illness that plagued Frost's sister, Jeanie, as well as Carol and Irma, represented the outer edge of his own instability. He might well have gone that way were it not for the spirit of independence, resilience, and combativeness that were part of his artist's will to power. "But this inflexible ambition trains us best," he as a boy of twenty wrote to William Hayes Ward in 1894. Even then, he knew himself well, and he never lost that ambition. "I expect to do something to the present state of literature in America," he said to John Bartlett in 1913, and he did.

Frost has been condemned by earlier biographers as selfish and egotistical, a poor father and an inattentive husband. Yet the evidence suggests that he was faithful to Elinor throughout their long marriage; each book was written, as he said, "for love of her." Hardly a poem was not composed with her in mind as the ideal reader. After her death, he found Kay Morrison, who stood in as muse, closest reader, and best friend—roles that Elinor had fulfilled "willingly, with grace and patience, for over four decades," as her granddaughter Lesley Lee Francis notes. It is also clear from Elinor's letters that she regarded her husband with deep affection and respect.

The situation of the family was such that Frost was very much at home each day, in daily contact with his children. This was certainly true at Derry, when the children were young. He took them for long walks in the woods and (together with Elinor) taught them to read and write. His playfulness and inventiveness—as reflected in Lesley's childhood notebooks—were vital to their imaginative development. One can hardly imagine a father more accessible to his children. As one sees, he encouraged them throughout their lives with loving consistency, engaging them emotionally and advising them with care and thoughtfulness. It may well be, in fact, that he remained in a parental role too firmly, and well past the point where he should have let go—at least financially.

One of his very last letters, written shortly before his death, was to his daughter Lesley. The tone was typically supportive, encouraging, grateful, and frank: "You're something of a Lesley de Lion yourself," he wrote, responding to a quip of hers. "I am not hard to touch but I'd rather be taken for brave than anything else. A little hard and stern in judgement, perhaps, but always touched by the heroic. You have passed muster. So has Prescott. You have both found a way to make shift. You can't know how much I have counted on you in family matters. It is not time yet to defer a little to others in my future affairs but I have deferred not a little in my thoughts to the strength in you and

Prescott and Lee and very, very affectionately to K Morrison and Anne Morrison Gentry, who are with me taking this dictation in the hospital, and to Al Edwards in all his powerful friendship. . . . I am too emotional for my state. Life has been a long trial yet I mean to see more of it. We all liked your poems. It must add to your confidence that you have found a way with the young."[7]

The view of Frost as monster and misanthrope that has been lodged in the minds of readers by previous biographers is hugely distorted. While hardly a saint, Frost was a passionate, headstrong man who believed deeply in his own vision. Like any human being, he was not without jealousy; indeed, he could be irritable and difficult, even mean-spirited, when it came to his poetic rivals. But to a remarkable degree, he succeeded in uniting his vocation and his avocation, and in making a place for himself in the world of letters, "a place apart."

Above all, Frost was a lover of paradox. So it should offer no surprise that while he was a "lone striker," the opposite is also true of him, that he sought public recognition and institutional support with indefatigable energy. A recent critic, Mark Richardson, cautions against reading Emersonian self-reliance into every aspect of Frost. "Potent American individualism notwithstanding," he writes, "Frost sought and achieved a kind of 'social approval' unprecedented for an American poet." Richardson locates a tension in Frost between "formity" and conformity"—a dichotomy elsewhere characterized as "originality" versus "governance."[8] His point is well taken. Frost was not just an individualist, hell-bent on noncomformity. He believed in a proper blend of rule and energy, of social conformity (law, order, form) and individual freedom (wildness, a willingness to break forms, standing apart).

The contradictions of his life and work remain stunning. He was a loner who liked company; a poet of isolation who sought a mass audience; a rebel who sought to fit in. Although a family man to the core, he frequently felt alienated from his wife and children and withdrew into reveries. While preferring to stay at home, he traveled more than any poet of his generation to give lectures and readings, even though he remained terrified of public speaking to the end. He was a democrat who hated Franklin Roosevelt, a poet of labor who could not support the New Deal. He believed passionately in war as a rational and justifiable response to certain international crises, yet he could not stir in himself much interest in the Second World War. He was an ardent Eisenhower supporter who campaigned for John Kennedy with enthusiasm in 1960—and who publicly identified himself with Kennedy by reading at his inauguration. He was a fierce anticommunist who embraced Nikita Khrushchev personally, calling him "a great man." As Katherine Kearns has said, Frost's "near-phobic distaste for systems . . . exceeds even the most potent American individualism."[9] In a sense, Frost made himself a representative American by amplifying his individuality, by finding a voice for Everyman in the persona of the Lone Striker. By making himself eccentric, he found the center.

Frost's portrait of the stoic, independent-minded men and women who worked the harsh, unyielding soil north of Boston in the early part of this century reminds us that, like William Faulkner, his contemporary and peer, he understood that universality is often the product of intense local habitation. He knew that a literary artist must inhabit a specific place and learn the speech of that place and time. "Locality gives art," he wrote in an early notebook, and he sought locality in his life and art.

With vast curiosity about the natural world, he was well suited to the task of bringing this region to life with unusual specificity. Few poets, before or after, have so consistently or specifically evoked a particular place. His poetic universe is dense with flora and fauna that he had observed firsthand. "He walked in the woods every day that he could," recalled Reginald L. Cook, who often walked with him in the later years. "It had been a lifelong habit, this walking. Like Wordsworth, he walked and looked, he listened. He knew the birdcalls, the names of the flowers, their patterns of blooming. The life cycles of trees were always of close interest to him. Mushroom, mold, or fungus—everything caught his eye. He understood the rhythms of farm life, having farmed and lived around farming for most of his adult life. Right to the end, he kept a garden. The physical world was metaphorical, of course, a source of metaphors and images for his poetry, but it was real, too. He could keep the figurative and literal in balance. That was his genius."[10]

It is thrilling to watch his mind as it culls an image from daily life, transmogrifies what it finds, gives it the grandeur and elevation of permanence in art. The dark recesses of his life, the chaos, disappointment, and confusion he experienced, only tempered the steel of his character. The final image of Robert Frost is one of resolution and independence, of a man whose purpose in life was to find meaning in language, "risking spirit / In substantiation," as he wrote in "Kitty Hawk." This was, indeed, the great enterprise of his existence, nobly carried forward over many decades.

Any biographer of Robert Frost must tremble slightly when coming across his note to Sidney Cox in 1932: "To be too subjective with what an artist has managed to make objective is to come on him presumptuously and render ungraceful what he in pain of his life had faith he had made graceful."[1] Indeed, one of the commonest mistakes made by biographers involves reading the life too closely into the work. This mistake has often been made in the numerous biographies and memoirs of the poet that exist to date. The reader must, in fact, wonder why another biography of Frost is necessary. A brief look at the extant biographical writing on this subject will, I think, suggest that Frost has generally not been well served by his biographers.

As I see it, there have been three waves of Frost biography, with the most recent (by Jeffrey Meyers in 1996) serving as a throwback to the second phase. The first wave began with a little book still worth reading: *Robert Frost: A Study in Sensibility and Good Sense* (1927) by Gorham B. Munson. The biographer races through the life and work straightforwardly, seeing Frost as a classical humanist, a man of enduring "good sense," a phrase he repeats frequently. This goodness of sense is said to hark back to the ancient Greeks and Goethe. Munson writes:

What [Frost] trusts is his own experience (having good sense he knows that there is nothing else to trust) and his own experience happens in Frost's case to be mediatory in character. Being intelligent, being deeply emotional, being obliged to make terms with practical life, the man of good sense casts up a rough balance of these three aspects of his life and travels, so far as he is permitted so to do, in the center of the highway.[2]

Munson argues that Frost's "comprehensive answer" to the questions of existence is "the natural . . . vision of life." He concludes that this "man of good sense and fine sensibility has succeeded in writing, and for that he will be treasured in what we hope, against many odds at present, will be the long and noble course of American literature."[3]

While Munson may have been the first biographer, he was working from a view of Frost already in play. For some years Frost had been regarded by journalists and critics as a worldly-wise but genial philosopher of common sense and ordinary experience. This view was in fact promoted by Frost, who was a remarkably good publicist for himself. Frost also possessed immense personal charm, which made him a natural for the lecture circuit. Beginning in 1915, when he returned to the United States from England, the road show continued until his death in 1963. Audiences were treated to the slow-talking, witty, wisecracking, rueful, commonsensical, quasi-philosophical man of letters—a carefully composed mask no less artful than those constructed by Oscar Wilde or Mark Twain before him.

This platform Frost is the poet Elizabeth Shepley Sergeant wrote about in 1927, in an endearing profile: "Even when [Frost] consents to sit on a platform he has a vanishing and peripatetic look, and the doctrine he enunciates in his dry, sly, halting way is very different from the glib aestheticism his students might expect of a poet. Perfectionist and polisher of words though he is, he proclaims words to be 'less than nothing unless they amount to deeds, as in ultimatums and battle cries.' "[4] Like so many of Frost's early biographers, Sergeant mistook the mask for the man.

In 1935, Robert Newdick of Ohio State University wrote to Frost to suggest a reordering of certain poems in his collected edition. This initial contact led to correspondence and various meetings, and Newdick (on his own) began to collect material for a biography of Frost. As it were, Newdick only managed to write about a hundred pages of his book before dying, unexpectedly, in 1939. What might have been an excellent full-length study of Frost's life and work was brought to an untimely halt. The surviving manuscript, with a good deal of additional material gathered by Newdick, was published in 1976 as *Newdick's Season of Frost: An Interrupted Biography of Robert Frost*, edited by William A. Sutton. It remains a valuable resource for biographers.

The image of Frost as farmer-poet offering homespun wisdom from the lecture platform prevailed through the mid-sixties. This view was given minor expression in Sidney Cox's book-length portrait, *A Swinger of Birches* (1961), a posthumously published memoir by a man who knew Frost for over forty years. It found its fullest expression in Elizabeth Shepley Sergeant's *Robert Frost: The Trial by Existence* (1960). She attempts a broad portrait of "one of the most beloved poets and sages of our midtwentieth century," but she was not a sophisticated critic, and her readings of the poems are often embarrassing; her interpretation of the life was not much better. Frost, she tells us, owns "the stability and optimism of the Victorian age." She writes somewhat breathlessly about his struggle to overcome personal odds in order to achieve "a positive view of life," and she virtually never tires of celebrating "this great, witty, complex, and endearing personality so loved by the American people."[5] For all its obvious flaws, *The Trial by Existence* is rich in quotations from Frost, who spoke freely to Sergeant on many subjects, and for this alone it retains considerable value.

The Sergeant book was followed quickly by a minor biography in the sentimental groove by Jean Gould called *Robert Frost: The Aim Was Song* (1964).[6] The subtitle says it all: Gould writes, she says, as "a devoted Frost reader." She claims that her book is full of direct quotations from Frost, although she met him only briefly and by her own admission "did not take notes except in a few instances."[7] The book moves inexorably toward the nonconclusion that "Robert Frost was a songster till the end—and a lover of life."[8] Her readings of the poems are, as might be expected, naive—indeed, the poems are taken as exact transcriptions of actual events. Would that she had known of Frost's warning to Sidney Cox.

The great corrective to the Cox-Sergeant-Gould picture of the lovable sage was Lawrance Thompson. A Princeton professor, Thompson had written the first full-length critical book on Frost, called *Fire and Ice: The Art and Thought of Robert Frost* (1942). Frost liked it, and he asked Thompson to write his official biography. (Thompson, it should be noted, at first demurred, suggesting Bernard DeVoto or Louis Untermeyer as more likely candidates.) He did sign on, though one wonders if he would have done so had he known the work would consume the rest of his life—on many levels.

A major problem arose when Thompson took against his subject in a rather chilling way (the turn came in about 1945). Thompson's dislike of his subject vitiates his book, as Donald G. Sheehy has suggested in a comprehensive article on the subject.[9] Thompson's three volumes (the last volume was co-written by R. H. Winnick, a friend and former graduate student) run to almost a thousand pages, piling detail upon detail, often uncritically. The word "monster" appears not only in Thompson's actual text (where it does, several times); it was also the predominant word used by reviewers to describe Frost after reading Thompson. Reviewing the final volume in the *New York Times Book Review* (January 16, 1977), for example, David Bromwich found himself repulsed by the figure conjured in those pages, saying that "a more hateful human being cannot have lived." Howard Moss, a poet and the longtime poetry editor of the *New Yorker*, likewise decided that Frost must be "a mean-spirited megalomaniac." Countless readers and reviewers echoed these sentiments.

Was Frost, as Thompson suggests, really such a selfish, egomaniacal, dour, cruel, and angry man? Certainly the evidence of many who knew the poet well runs counter to this claim. And there is in the poems themselves a deep core of natural sympathy for human beings that would seem to oppose this assessment.

Part of the difficulty in trying to assess Thompson's work lies with a general naïveté that exists when it comes to thinking about literary biography. Few genres have been less theorized, and this has led to much confusion about the nature of biographical work. An assumption is often made that biographies are true or false in the way scientific data is true or false. I would rather emphasize that biographies have a lot in common with novels. This does not mean that they are "made up" or "not true." Rather, the word "fiction" derives from the Latin *fictio*, which means shaping, and the job of the fiction maker is in certain respects similar to the work of the biographer. He or she must assemble, must *discover*, a "story" in the countless random facts that make up an individual life. A lot depends on the story or mythos developed by the biographer.

In Thompson's case, the biography was driven by a mythos that distorted, rather than clarified, the material at hand. His story about Frost (only slightly caricatured) runs something like this: An innocent and idealistic youngster was brought up by an occasionally cruel father and an overprotective, insufferable mother. Largely because of his mother's pampering, he came to believe that things would go his way in life, but they rarely did, and therefore he became angry and resentful. His high school sweetheart, for example, did not simply fall head-over-heels when he snapped his fingers, and this led to near-suicidal behavior on his part. Later, his children did not listen to him when he told them what to do, and he turned vengeful. He failed at a long succession of tasks: getting through college, making a go of farming, getting his poems published. All of these failures, Thompson implies, "caused him to become self-protectively arrogant." He eventually began to confuse himself with the God of the Old Testament, and would strike out viciously at those who got in his way.

As Frost developed, says Thompson, the "imagined forms of retaliation kept changing, even as the actual forms of humiliation changed." An example follows:

> In Salem, when he became the best pitcher on his grammar
> school team, he dreamed he would some day achieve renown as
> a hero in the major league of his choice—and even a baseball

could serve as a lethal weapon if carefully aimed at the head of an enemy batter. Later, in high school, where his baseball dreams were spoiled, he achieved excellence as a scholar, and thus found a successful way of scornfully triumphing over those who were better than he at baseball. As soon as he began publishing poems in the high school literary magazine, he began to dream that some day his reputation as a literary hero would provide him with another way of triumphing over his enemies.[10]

A quick glance at Thompson's index should alert the careful reader to his presuppositions. Under the poet's name one finds these damning subheads: "Anti-intellectual," "Baffler-Teaser-Deceiver," "Brute," "Charlatan," "Cowardice," "Enemies," "Hate," "Insanity," "Murderer," "Pretender." With these categories firmly in place, Thompson is able to sift through the data and create a figure shockingly in contrast to the genial farmer-poet described by Munson, Sergeant, Gould, and scores of magazine profilers.

On the other hand, one has to admire the detail accumulated by Thompson, in the biography itself and in the two thousand pages of typed notes he left behind. These notes inevitably form a kind of (slippery) base upon which all future biographers must rest, since Thompson had unique access to his subject. Indeed, Thompson was probably too close to Frost to write about him with any degree of objectivity. His personal dislike of the man, perhaps aggravated by a clandestine affair with Kay Morrison, made the possibility of writing a well-balanced biography remote. Thompson's private attitude to Frost is vividly on display in a letter to Kay written in 1945: "I admire you deeply for the long-suffering patience with which you've accepted [Frost's] self-indulgence when it comes to asking more of your time and strength and life than he has a right to ask. . . . You've done a superb job under the most exasperating conditions, and I respect all your decisions and actions in the difficult task of walking a tightrope during all these emotional hurricanes and thunderstorms of his."[11] The wonder is that Thompson was able to write as well as he sometimes did about Frost. (I should emphasize here that Thompson's work, despite its serious flaws, remains groundbreaking and indispensable: the starting point for any serious biographical scholarship on this subject.)

A third wave of Frost criticism began with the reaction against Thompson that inevitably set in. William H. Pritchard's *Robert Frost: A Literary Life Reconsidered* (1984) represents an important corrective. Pritchard's book is not, strictly speaking, a biography but a reading of the poems in the light of Frost's personal experience. He dwells on the teasing aspects of the verse, reading the poetry back into the life rather than the other way around. "I am concerned to identify and describe Frost's play of mind as it reveals itself in an art which is notable for the amount of felt 'life' it contains," writes Pritchard, "and in a life which is notably artful, constantly shaped by the extravagant designs of his imagination."[12] It remains my favorite book on Frost.

Four years after Pritchard's book, *Into My Own: The English Years of Robert Frost* (1988), by John Evangelist Walsh, was published. Walsh concentrates exclusively on Frost's three years in England (1912–15), a period of huge importance for understanding his development as a poet. Like Pritchard, Walsh takes Thompson to task for his mean-spirited work, suggesting that "only after successive loss, disappointment, and tragedy had taken their toll of an essentially brave and generous heart did Frost's view of life, his attitude toward people and events, start to unravel."[13] The English years are given their full due here, in a well-researched book worthy of its subject.

A further corrective to Thompson came with Stanley Burnshaw's *Robert Frost Himself* (1986), a memoir of the poet by his former editor at Henry Holt (who had known Frost personally since 1929). While oddly shaped and often rambling, Burnshaw takes us back to the Frost of Sergeant and Gould without sentimentalizing his subject. He ends with a quotation from a review of Frost's *Selected Letters* by Randall Jarrell that is worth citing:

> In the end he talked as naturally as he breathed: for as long as you got to listen you were sharing Frost's life. What came to you in that deep grainy voice—a voice that made other voices sound thin or abstract—was half a natural physiological process and

half a work of art; it was as if Frost dreamed aloud and the dream were a poem. Was what he said right or wrong? It seemed irrelevant. In the same way, whether Frost himself was good or bad seemed irrelevant—he was *there*, and you accepted him.[14]

The tone of this quotation fairly mirrors the attitude of Burnshaw toward his subject.

Lesley Lee Francis, the poet's granddaughter, published another memoir, *The Frost Family's Adventure in Poetry*, in 1994. Her book marks a further step in rewriting Thompson. Drawing on a cache of family papers, Francis portrays Frost as an attentive, loving father who taught by example and precept what it meant to "live by poetry," cultivating, as Francis says, a "trusting, childlike view of life" and encouraging "a freshness of response to the world." She concludes that "academic scholars . . . often lost sight of a life that was no less poetic than the poems it produced, poems addressed to all kinds, and [that] reach out to challenge us, to 'rumple our brains fondly,' as he would tell his students."[15] The subtitle of her book, *Sheer Morning Gladness at the Brim*, directs us to a man with a view of life radically in contrast to the dour figure portrayed in Thompson's book.

The most recent biography of the poet, *Robert Frost*, by Jeffrey Meyers (1996), represents a throwback to Thompson. It contains little in the way of original research, although Meyers churned up a lot of dust by presenting the relationship between Frost and Kay Morrison in a melodramatic fashion. The intimate nature of this relationship had already been suggested by Pritchard and explored in depth in an impressively balanced and detailed article by Donald G. Sheehy that appeared in 1990.[16] Meyers does not mention the Sheehy article, nor the passage in Pritchard where he writes about Frost's proposal of marriage to Kay Morrison. He relies heavily on an interview with Kathleen Morrison's daughter, Anne, who seems not unbiased in her views—to put it mildly.

Meyers sensationalizes Frost's various life crises unduly, as Helen Vendler has noted: "Many of his pages read like newspaper précis of the plots of soap operas."[17] This aside, the book is also plagued by misinformation. For example, Meyers has Frost being expelled from Dartmouth instead of choosing to leave—a blatant mistake, based on one interview with a man who was simply wrong. The documentary record at Dartmouth does not support Meyers's claim, nor does Frost's own account of his withdrawal, which he repeated many times with no inconsistencies. As Vendler says, "a scrupulous biographer would have recognized, in support of Frost's version, that he also left Harvard (in good standing) without finishing." Similarly, Meyers's treatment of Lesley Frost, the poet's daughter, is "horrendously distorted," according to her daughter.[18]

The most inept part of Meyers's biography, however, occurs when he reads the poems biographically. Two brief examples will serve to make the point. In a self-proclaimed "new reading" of "Design," Meyers rehashes (without acknowledgment) the famous readings of this poem by Randall Jarrell and Lionel Trilling, then adds his original touch: "In 'Design,' the normally black spider and blue heal-all . . . are both wickedly white—a play on Elinor's maiden name."[19] Thus Elinor absurdly (and irrelevantly) becomes the witch who cobbles together the unholy elements of white spider, white moth, and white heal-all!

Even more shocking is his reading of "The Silken Tent," a poem which opens:

> She is as in a field a silken tent
> At midday when a sunny summer breeze
> Has dried the dew and all its ropes relent,
> So that in guys it gently sways at ease.

Meyers swoops on the last line, noting that the breeze "has dried the dew on [the tent's] ropes so that it sways in 'guys' (a triple pun on ropes, mockery and men)."[20] In other words, Kay Morrison (whom he regards as the undisputed subject of the poem) was swaying "in guys"— as if Frost would resort to such a bizarre colloquialism here. Vendler comments, "The illiteracy of such 'readings' points to how greatly Meyers misunderstands the directions for reading encoded in a poem, the extent to which semantic possibility is controlled by context."[21]

Frost himself cautioned against finding in his poems irrelevant ambiguities, with connotations spreading like ink on blotting paper. Metaphors and symbols provide a way of delimiting (as well as opening out) meaning; thus, the poet controls the reading of a poem, sharply defining its boundaries. No one understood this better than Frost. "The direction of the piece combs the word into the single one of its meanings intended like a hair," he once said. "Some would have it that the words are cowlicks that won't be combed straight in a direction."[22] Similarly, in "Education by Poetry," he warned that "unless you are at home in the metaphor, unless you have had your proper poetical education in the metaphor, you are not safe anywhere. Because you are not at ease with figurative values: you don't know the metaphor in its strength and its weakness. You don't know how far you may expect to ride it and when it may break down with you."[23]

My hope, of course, is that my own biography sets the record straight here and there, putting in place a fresh mythos, one that combs the facts in a certain direction but does not preclude a future biographer (and there will be many) from combing the same material differently. In my readings of the poems, I have tried hard not to "render ungraceful what [Frost] in pain of his life had faith he had made graceful."

NOTES AND SOURCES

All quotations from Frost's published poetry will be found in *The Poetry of Robert Frost: Collected Poems, Complete and Unabridged*, ed. Edward Connery Lathem (New York: Henry Holt and Co., 1976).

1 ONCE BY THE PACIFIC

[1] This quotation, like many that follow, is from a tape in the Amherst College Library (ACL). Other tapes are from the Dartmouth College Library (DCL) and the Middlebury College Library (MCL). I am grateful to Joseph Matazzoni for supplying me with transcripts of most of the significant tapes of Robert Frost.

[2] Interview with Robert Penn Warren, July 7, 1988.

[3] Quoted by Robert Newdick in *Newdick's Season of Frost: An Interrupted Biography of Robert Frost*, edited by William A. Sutton (Albany: State University of New York Press, 1976), 13.

[4] *Selected Letters, Robert Frost*, edited by Lawrance Thompson (New York: Holt, Rinehart, and Winston, 1964), 5. Hereafter *SL*.

[5] *SL*, 8.

[6] Newdick, 14.

[7] Louis Mertins, *Robert Frost: Life and Talks-Walking* (Norman: University of Oklahoma Press, 1965), 23.

[8] *SL*, 530.

[9] Interview with Victor Reichert, July 9, 1984.

[10] Letter to Jay Parini, February 5, 1998.

[11] Interview with Victor Reichert.

[12] *SL*, 226.

[13] *SL*, 595.

[14] Newdick, 15.

[15] *The Letters of Robert Frost to Louis Untermeyer* (New York: Holt, Rinehart and Winston, 1963), 483. Hereafter cited as Untermeyer.

[16] Interview with Richard Eberhart, April 20, 1976. I interviewed Eberhart many times on the subject of Frost, beginning in 1975.

[17] Reginald L. Cook notes, MCL.

[18] *SL*, 88.

[19] *SL*, 271.

[20] Letter to Jay Parini, February 5, 1998.

2 HOME IS WHERE THEY HAVE TO TAKE YOU IN

[1] Quoted by Gardner Jackson in "I Will Teach Only When I Have Something to Tell," *Boston Sunday Globe* (November 1924), 3.

[2] Houghton Library, Harvard University.

[3] Elizabeth Shepley Sergeant, *Robert Frost: The Trial by Existence* (New York: Holt, Rinehart and Winston, 1960), 19.

[4] Tape in ACL.

[5] Interview with Richard Eberhart.

[6] Interview with Reginald L. Cook.

[7] See Richard A. Proctor, *Our Place Among Infinities* (New York, 1876), 37–38. Proctor writes: "We may believe, with all confidence, that could we but understand the whole of what we find around us, the wisdom with which each part has been designed would be manifest; so clearly understand all as to be able to recognize the purpose of this or that arrangement, the wisdom of this or that provision. Nor, if any results revealed by scientific research appear to us to accord ill with our conceptions of the economy of nature, should we be troubled, on the one hand, as respects our faith in God's benevolence, or doubt, on the other, the manifest teachings of science. In a word, our faith must not be hampered by scientific doubts, our science must not be hampered by religious scruples."

[8] Elinor White Frost to Mrs. Edna Davis Romig, February 4, 1935. Courtesy of Frederick B. Adams, Jr.

[9] Reginald L. Cook interview.

[10] Sergeant, 23.

[11] *High School Bulletin* (October 1891), 5–6.

[12] Quoted in Edward Connery Lathem and Lawrance Thompson, *Robert Frost and the Lawrence, Massachusetts, "High School Bulletin": The Beginning of a Literary Career* (New York: The Grolier Club, 1966), 16.

[13] *High School Bulletin*, May 1892, 4.

[14] Frost retold this story countless times, to friends and interviewers.

[15] *Lawrence Daily American* (July 1, 1892), 1.

[16] Mertins, 47.

[17] Edward Connery Lathem, "Freshman Days," *Dartmouth Alumni Magazine* (March 1959), 17–20.

[18] This copy of the *Independent* is still in the Dartmouth College Library.

[19] Frost to Harold Goddard Rugg, October 15, 1914. DCL.

[20] *Robert Frost: Collected Poems, Prose, and Plays*, ed. Richard Poirier and Mark Richardson (New York: Library of America, 1995), 807. Hereafter *CPPP*.

3 MASKS OF GLOOM

[1] Sergeant, 34.

[2] Belle Frost alludes to Rob's reaction in a letter written the following September.

[3] SL, 332.

[4] Sergeant, 34.

[5] SL, 19.

[6] SL, 20.

[7] SL, 24.

[8] Sergeant, 40.

[9] Peter J. Stanlis to Jay Parini, February 5, 1998.

[10] Louis Mertins, *Robert Frost: Life and Talks-Walking*, 197.

[11] The pronoun was "She" in the original manuscript, then changed to "He" when published in the *Independent* in 1897.

[12] Elinor's copy—the only one in existence—is in the Barrett Collection at the University of Virginia Library (hereafter UVL).

[13] From the epigraph to Moore's "A Ballad: The Lake of the Dismal Swamp," in *Poetical Works*, ed. A. D. Godley (Oxford: Oxford University Press, 1924), 99.

[14] Cook notebooks, MCL.

[15] Bread Loaf tape, August 1956. ACL.

[16] Susan P. Holmes, "Robert Frost in Lawrence—a Remembrance of 60 Years," *Lawrence Eagle-Tribune* (May 9, 1963), 16.

4 TRIALS BY EXISTENCE

[1] Tape at DCL.

[2] Tape at ACL.

[3] Daniel Wilson, *Science, Community, and the Transformation of American Philosophy, 1860–1930* (Chicago: University of Chicago Press, 1990), 96.

[4] William James, *Psychology: Briefer Course* (New York: Henry Holt, 1892), 179–80.

[5] Robert Faggen, *Robert Frost and the Challenge of Darwin* (Ann Arbor: University of Michigan Press, 1997), 33.

[6] Notebooks in DCL.

[7] James, 459.

[8] William James, *The Will to Believe and Other Essays in Popular Philosophy* (New York: Longmans, Green, 1897), 29.

[9] See *SL*, 531, where Frost refers to Santayana's notions of "true illusion and false illusion" as "poppycock."

[10] Interview with Victor Reichert.

[11] *SL*, 30.

[12] *CPPP*, 877.

[13] *CPPP*, 736.

[14] Gorham B. Munson, *Robert Frost: A Study in Sensibility and Good Sense* (New York: George H. Doran, 1927), 127. These remarks come from a talk that Frost gave at Wesleyan University in December 1927.

[15] Interview with Lesley Lee Francis, August 19, 1997.

[16] Interview with Victor Reichert.

[17] Rose C. Feld, "Robert Frost Relieves His Mind," *New York Times Book Review* (October 21, 1923), 2.

[18] William R. Evans. *Robert Frost and Sidney Cox: Forty Years of Friendship* (Hanover: University Press of New England, 1981), 76.

[19] Tape of talk given at Bread Loaf, August 1958. MCL.

5 A FARM IN DERRY

[1] Mertins, 58.

[2] Frost talk at Bread Loaf, 1954. MCL.

[3] *CPPP*, 506.

[4] Evans, 56.

[5] *SL*, 80.

[6] Reginald L. Cook, *Robert Frost: A Living Voice* (Amherst: University of Massachusetts Press, 1974), 123.

[7] William H. Pritchard, *Frost: A Literary Life Reconsidered* (New York: Oxford University Press, 1984), 28.

[8] Richard Poirier, *Robert Frost: The Work of Knowing* (New York: Oxford University Press, 1977), *passim*.

[9] Katherine Kearns, *Robert Frost and a Poetics of Appetite* (New York: Cambridge University Press, 1994), 112.

[10] *Derry News*, March 28, 1902.

[11] Lecture at Amherst, 1959. Tape at ACL.

[12] Interview with Lesley Lee Francis.

[13] Lesley Lee Francis, *The Frost Family's Adventure in Poetry: Sheer Morning Gladness at the Brim* (Columbia: University of Missouri Press, 1994), 17.

[14] Interview with Robert Penn Warren.

[15] Francis, 27. She is quoting from her mother's journal.

[16] *SL*, 171.

[17] Charles Darwin, *The Voyage of the Beagle* (New York: Anchor Books, 1962), 29.

[18] Faggen, 280.

[19] Interview with Hyde Cox, September 13, 1996.

[20] Mertins, 197.

[21] See Peter J. Stanis, "Robert Frost: The Conversationalist as Poet, 1895–1915." *Modern Age* (Fall 1997), 323–34.

[22] Mertins, 197–98.

[23] Francis, 19.

[24] Thompson, *Robert Frost: The Early Years*, 308.

[25] Interview with Lesley Lee Francis on September 19, 1996.

[26] A cache of letters from Lillian Frost to various friends was passed on to me by Lesley Lee Francis.

[27] Talk at Bread Loaf, 1957. Tape at ACL.

[28] Mertins, 187.

6 THE ACHE OF MEMORY—PINKERTON AND PLYMOUTH

[1] Wolcott to Merriam, January 29, 1906. DCL.

[2] *The Catalogue of Pinkerton Academy* (Derry, NH, 1906), 7.

[3] There is a cache of papers by former students at the Dartmouth College Library, with Frost's marginal comments and corrections.

4 Margaret Bartlett Anderson, *Robert Frost and John Bartlett: The Record of a Friendship* (New York: Holt, Rinehart and Winston, 1963), 9.

5 *SL*, 41–42.

6 Mertins, 72.

7 Cited by Thompson, *The Early Years*, 572.

8 This poem was sent to Susan Hayes Ward at Christmas and it appears, for the first time, in *CPPP*, 519.

9 Interview with Thomas Vance, September 1978.

10 From Frost's Introduction to the posthumous work by Sidney Cox, *A Swinger of Birches: A Portrait of Robert Frost* (New York: New York University Press, 1957), viii.

11 *SL*, 72.

12 Cook, *Robert Frost: A Living Voice*, 124.

13 Conrad Aiken, *Ushant* (New York, 1952), 157.

14 Faggen, 40.

15 William James, *Pragmatism: A New Name for Some Old Ways of Thinking—Popular Lectures on Philosophy* (New York: Longmans, Green, 1907), 63.

16 MS Huntington Library. Quoted by Thompson in *The Early Years*, 582.

17 Reginald L. Cook interview.

18 Lesley Frost to David Tatham, May 24, 1969, quoted by the recipient of the letter in David Tatham, *A Poet Recognized* (Syracuse, NY: Syracuse University Press, 1970), 23.

19 Elinor Frost to Mrs. John Lynch, October 25, 1912. DCL.

20 Ibid.

7   A PLACE APART

1 *Times* (London), December 20, 1910, 4.

2 Elinor Frost to Mrs. John Lynch, October 25, 1912. DCL.

3 Ibid.

4 *SL*, 63.

5 Elinor Frost to Mrs. John Lynch, October 25, 1912. DCL.

6 Pritchard, 16.

7 Robert Francis, *Robert Frost: A Time to Talk—Conversations and Indiscretions* (Amherst: University of Massachusetts Press, 1972), 16.

8 Lesley Lee Francis, 46–47.

9 John Evangelist Walsh, *Into My Own: The English Years of Robert Frost* (New York: Grove Press, 1988), 77.

10 Ford Madox Ford, *Return to Yesterday* (London: Gollancz, 1931), 419.

[11] See F. S. Flint, "Contemporary French Poetry," *Poetry Review* (October 1912), 355–414.

[12] Frost to F. S. Flint, January 21, 1913. University of Texas Library. Hereafter UTL.

[13] Thompson, *The Early Years*, 411.

[14] D. D. Paige, ed., *The Letters of Ezra Pound* (London: Faber, 1960), 16.

[15] SL, 78.

[16] *Poetry* (May 13, 1913), 72–74.

[17] SL, 90.

[18] Anonymous review in the *Academy* (September 20, 1913), 360.

[19] Frost to F. S. Flint, June 19, 1913. UTL.

8 IN A YELLOW WOOD

[1] F. S. Flint to Robert Frost, undated. UTL.

[2] SL, 79.

[3] SL, 110–14.

[4] SL, 140.

[5] SL, 107–08.

[6] I am grateful to Karen L. Kilcup for pointing this out to me. See her book *Frost's Feminine Voice: Engendering the Self-Made Man* (Ann Arbor: University of Michigan Press, 1998).

[7] Lesley Frost, *New Hampshire's Child: The Derry Journals of Lesley Frost*, with notes and index by Lawrance Thompson and Arnold Grade (Albany: State University of New York Press, 1969), 5–6.

[8] Quoted in Elizabeth Shepley Sergeant, *Fire Under the Andes: A Group of North American Portraits* (Port Washington, NY: Kennikat Press, 1966), 200. (All other quotations from Sergeant are from *The Trial by Existence*.)

[9] Quoted in Cleanth Brooks and Robert Penn Warren, *Understanding Poetry* (New York: Holt, Rinehart and Winston, 1976), 471.

[10] Thompson, *The Early Years*, 432.

[11] *Interviews with Robert Frost*, ed. Edward Connery Lathem (New York: Holt, Rinehart and Winston, 1966), 112.

[12] As in *Blum's Farmer's and Planter's Almanac*, 1850 edition (Winston-Salem, North Carolina), 13.

[13] Lawrance Thompson and R. H. Winnick, *Robert Frost: The Later Years, 1938–1963* (New York: Holt, Rinehart and Winston, 1976), 316.

[14] Poirier, 104.

[15] Marion Montgomery, "Robert Frost and His Use of Barriers: Man vs. Nature Toward God." *South Atlantic Quarterly* (Summer 1958), 349.

[16] Notes of Charles Foster, DCL.

[17] Reuben A. Brower, *The Poetry of Robert Frost: Constellations of Intention* (New York: Oxford University Press, 1963), 24.

[18] Walsh, 144.

[19] SL, 98.

[20] SL, 92.

[21] SL, 96.

[22] Letter to Gertrude McQuesten, undated. Boston University Library.

[23] Mertins, 117.

[24] Frost to F. S. Flint, May 18, 1914. UTL.

[25] Mertins, 132.

[26] Helen Thomas, with Myfanwy Thomas, *Under Storm's Wing* (Manchester: Carcanet Press, 1988), 229.

[27] Eleanor Farjeon, *Edward Thomas: The Last Four Years* (Oxford: Oxford University Press, 1958), 88.

[28] Lascelles Abercrombie, "A New Voice," *Nation* (June 13, 1914), 423.

[29] Interview with Victor Reichert.

[30] Richard Aldington in the *Egoist* (July 1, 1914), 248.

[31] Letter from Frost to John Haines, April 2, 1915. DCL.

[32] Frost to Grace Conkling, June 28, 1921. UVL.

[33] Thomas, 228.

[34] The three reviews by Edward Thomas appeared in the *Daily News* (quoted here from Farjeon, 77–78), in the *New Weekly* (August 8, 1914), and in the *English Review* (August, 1914), 22.

[35] SL, 140.

[36] Edward Thomas to Frost, December 15, 1914. DCL.

[37] Sergeant, 87.

[38] Frost to John Haines, April 2, 1915. DCL.

[39] R. Newdick, "Robert Frost and the Dramatic," *New England Quarterly* (June 1937), 67.

[40] Edward Connery Lathem, *Robert Frost: His American Send-Off* (Lunenburg, Vermont: Stinehour Press, 1963), 15.

[41] SL, 138.

[42] SL, 151.

[43] Robert Graves, "The Truest Poet," *Sunday Times* (February 3, 1963), 11.

[44] SL, 147.

[45] SL, 152.

[46] SL, 103.

[47] Frost to John Haines, January 5, 1915. DCL.

9 HOME AGAIN

[1] Amy Lowell, "North of Boston," *New Republic* (February 20, 1915), 81.

[2] Sylvester Baxter, "Talk of the Town," *Boston Herald* (March 9, 1915), 9.

[3] Lascelles Abercrombie to Louis Untermeyer, February 20, 1915. Bodleian Library, Oxford University.

[4] Untermeyer, 4–5.

[5] Louis Untermeyer, "Robert Frost's 'North of Boston,'" *Chicago Evening Post* (April 23, 1915), 11.

[6] William Stanley Braithwaite, "Robert Frost: New American Poet: His Opinions and Practice—an Important Analysis of the Art of the Modern Bard," *Boston Evening Transcript* (May 8, 1915), 4.

[7] SL, 180.

[8] Frost Collection. DCL.

[9] Frost to George H. Browne, June 1, 1915. DCL.

[10] Frost at Bread Loaf Writers' Conference, 1957. Cook notes, MCL.

[11] John F. Lynen, *The Pastoral Art of Robert Frost* (New Haven: Yale University Press, 1960), 35.

[12] Jessie B. Rittenhouse, "North of Boston," *New York Times Book Review*, (May 16, 1915), 189.

[13] *New York Times Book Review* (August 8, 1915), 28.

[14] William Dean Howells, "Editor's Easy Chair," *Harper's* (September 1915), 635.

[15] Frost to Browne, October 27, 1915. DCL.

[16] SL, 192.

[17] Reprinted in Lathem, *Interviews*, 9–15.

[18] Untermeyer, 27.

[19] Reprinted in Lathem, *Interviews*, 18–21.

[20] Frost to John Bartlett, August 8, 1915. DCL.

[21] SL, 209.

10 A PERSON OF GOOD ASPIRATIONS

[1] SL, 184–85.

[2] SL, 216.

[3] SL, 217.

[4] SL, 225.

[5] Pritchard, 89.

[6] Untermeyer, 104.

[7] See Andrew J. Angyal, "Robert Frost's Poetry Before 1913: A Checklist," (*Yearbook of American Bibliographical and Textual Studies*, 1977), 101, 104.

[8] Quotations from the Amherst College catalog, 1918.

[9] Untermeyer, 47.

[10] Untermeyer, 63.

[11] Sergeant, 199.

[12] Frost notebook, 1917. DCL.

[13] Thompson, *The Years of Triumph*, 100.

[14] Henry A. Ladd, "Memories of Robert Frost," *Touchstone* (February 1939), 13.

[15] Frost to G. F. Whicher, June 22, 1918. ACL.

[16] Sergeant, 213.

[17] *SL*, 226.

[18] E. A. Richards, "A Reality Among Ghosts," *Touchstone* (February 1939), 18.

[19] *SL*, 242.

[20] *SL*, 250.

[21] *SL*, 483.

[22] Interview with Victor Reichert.

11 LIVING IN VERMONT

[1] Frost to Sidney Cox, July 17, 1920. DCL.

[2] Frost to John Haines, October 20, 1920. DCL.

[3] See Thompson, *The Years of Triumph*, 136–50.

[4] Raymond Holden, "Reminiscences of Robert Frost," typescript in Dartmouth College Library. This is quoted by Jeffrey S. Cramer, *Robert Frost Among His Poems: A Literary Companion to the Poet's Own Biographical Contexts and Associations* (Jefferson, NC: McFarland, 1996), 83. This book has been especially useful to me in my research, often pointing me in specific directions with regard to the biographical contexts of particular poems.

[5] Pritchard, 171.

[6] Joseph Brodsky, Seamus Heaney, and Derek Walcott, *Homage to Robert Frost* (New York: Farrar, Straus and Giroux, 1996), 62.

[7] *SL*, 245.

[8] Thompson, *The Years of Triumph*, 127.

[9] Frost's remarks as recorded by John T. Bartlett, "Notes from Conversations with Robert Frost," June 27, 1932–April 8, 1934. UVL.

[10] See G. R. Elliott, "The Neighborliness of Robert Frost," *Nation* (December 6, 1919).

[11] DCL.

[12] Brodsky, Heaney, and Walcott, 87.

[13] *SL*, 259.

[14] Arthur Hazard Dakin, *Paul Elmer More* (Princeton: Princeton University Press, 1960), 192.

[15] *SL*, 257.

[16] *SL*, 261.

[17] *SL*, 273.

[18] *SL*, 269.

[19] As told to Peter J. Stanlis. Letter to Jay Parini, February 15, 1998.

[20] Mertins, 81–82.

[21] Kearns, 63.

[22] Lowell, 107.

[23] Mertins, 81–82.

12 THE MIND SKATING CIRCLES

[1] Frost to John Haines, September 20, 1922. DCL.

[2] "Did Vermont Have No Candidate?" Editorial, *New York Times* (June 9, 1922), 14.

[3] Quoted by Thompson, *The Years of Triumph*, 211.

[4] Interview with Robert Penn Warren.

[5] Frost to George F. Whicher, December 1922. ACL.

[6] *SL*, 286.

[7] Frost to Haines, September 20, 1922. DCL.

[8] Interview with Philip Booth, November 3, 1996.

[9] Frost to A. B. White, December 14, 1922. DCL.

[10] Reprinted in Lathem, *Interviews*, 40–42.

[11] Untermeyer, 156.

[12] For a useful study of Frost and religion, see Dorothy Judd Hall, *Robert Frost: Contours of Belief* (Athens, OH: Ohio University Press, 1984).

[13] *SL*, 293.

[14] Interview with John Sloan Dickey.

[15] Untermeyer, 166.

[16] Interview with Thomas Vance.

[17] From the journals of Wilfred Davison, transcribed by Reginald L. Cook. MCL.

[18] *SL*, 296.

[19] *SL*, 482.

[20] Brodsky, Heaney, and Walcott, 81.

[21] James M. Cox, "Robert Frost and the End of the New England Line," in *Frost: Centennial Essays* (Jackson: University of Mississippi Press, 1974), 556.

[22] Untermeyer, 167.

[23] *Recognition of Robert Frost*, ed. Richard Thornton (New York: Holt, 1937), 169–170.

[24] SL, 303.

[25] In fact, Frost was fifty-one, there being some confusion over his birth date.

[26] SL, 310.

[27] CPPP, 712. Originally published in the *Christian Science Monitor* (May 16, 1925).

[28] SL, 312.

[29] SL, 315.

13 TAKEN AND TOSSED

[1] Quoted by Peter J. Stanlis in a letter to Jay Parini, February 15, 1998.

[2] Frost to John T. Bartlett, December 11, 1925. UVL.

[3] " 'To Otto as of Old': The Letters of Robert Frost and Otto Manthey-Zorn, Part 1," ed. Donald G. Sheehy, *New England Quarterly* (September 1994), 372.

[4] SL, 325.

[5] SL, 323.

[6] Irving Babbitt, *The New Laokoön* (Boston: Houghton Mifflin, 1910), 3.

[7] George F. Bagby, *Frost and the Book of Nature* (Knoxville: University of Tennessee Press, 1993), 59.

[8] S. T. Coleridge, *Biographia Literaria*, ed. George Watson (London: J. M. Dent, 1956), 173–74.

[9] M. H. Abrams, *The Mirror and the Lamp: Romantic Theory and the Critical Tradition* (New York: Oxford University Press, 1953), 283.

[10] John Hurd, Jr., "Poets and Writers Flock to Bowdoin for the Round Table of Literature," *Boston Globe* (May 10, 1925), 18.

[11] Cook, *Robert Frost: A Living Voice*, 125.

[12] SL, 328.

[13] Elinor Frost to Edith Fobes, July 20, 1926. DCL.

[14] SL, 333.

[15] Albert J. Robbins, *An Interlude with Robert Frost: Being a Brief Correspondence with the Poet and Recollections* (Bloomington: The Private Press of Frederic Brewer, 1982), 5.

[16] Faggen, 291.

[17] Pritchard, 188.

[18] Brower, 189.

[19] Thompson, *The Years of Triumph*, 85.

[20] Interview with Jack W. C. Hagstrom, November 4, 1997.

[21] Charles W. Cole, *Massachusetts Review* (Winter 1963), 239.

[22] Elinor Frost to Edith Fobes, February 22, 1927. DCL.

[23] Interview with Victor Reichert.

[24] Peter J. Stanlis mentioned this in a letter to Jay Parini, February 15, 1998.

[25] Harold H. Watts, "Robert Frost and the Interrupted Dialogue," *American Literature* (March 1950), 71.

[26] Welford Dunaway Taylor, *Robert Frost and J. J. Lankes: Riders on Pegasus* (Hanover, NH: Dartmouth College Library, 1996), 1.

[27] Gorham B. Munson, "Robert Frost," *Saturday Review of Literature* (March 28, 1925), 625.

[28] SL, 346.

[29] Interview with Peter J. Stanlis, May 30, 1997.

[30] Interview with Reginald L. Cook.

14 ORIGINAL RESPONSE

[1] Cook notes. MCL.

[2] Interview with Peter J. Stanlis.

[3] Frost to John W. Haines, August 28, 1928. DCL.

[4] Letters of Frost and Manthey-Zorn, edited by Sheehy, 378.

[5] John W. Haines, "Home Places. II. England," in Thornton's *Recognition of Robert Frost*, 96.

[6] Mertins, 177.

[7] Wilbur Snow, "The Robert Frost I Knew," *Texas Quarterly* (Fall 1968), 21.

[8] Frost to Theodore Morrison, October 11, 1928. DCL.

[9] SL, 351.

[10] Frost to John Haines, October 11, 1928. DLC.

[11] Frost to John Haines, November 2, 1928. DCL.

[12] Interview with Lesley Lee Francis, June 29, 1997.

[13] Untermeyer, 192.

[14] Thompson, *The Years of Triumph*, 366.

[15] Wade Van Dore, *Robert Frost and Wade Van Dore: The Life of the Hired*

Man, revised and edited by Thomas H. Wetmore (Dayton, OH: Wright State University Press, 1986), 4.

[16] I am grateful to Robert Hill for pointing out to me the ambiguity of this line.

[17] Randall Jarrell, *Poetry and the Age* (New York: Knopf, 1953), 49–50.

[18] J. J. Lankes to Edee Bartlett Lankes, July 13, 1929. DCL (copy); original in the private collection of Mr. Junius B. Lankes.

[19] Ibid.

[20] *SL*, 649.

[21] Letter to Jay Parini, February 19, 1998.

[22] Quoted in Thomas Mann, *Freud, Goethe, Wagner* (New York: Knopf, 1937), 53.

[23] Unsigned review of *West-Running Brook*, "Robert Frost's Poems and the Outlook on Life," *Springfield Union-Republican* (December 30, 1928), 7E.

[24] Granville Hicks, "The World of Robert Frost," *New Republic* (December 3, 1930), 77–78.

[25] Genevieve Taggard, "Robert Frost, Poet," *New York Herald Tribune Books* (November 30, 1930), 9.

15 BUILDING SOIL

[1] Untermeyer, 199.

[2] Ibid, 211–12.

[3] *The Selected Letters of Marianne Moore*, general editor: Bonnie Costello (New York: Knopf, 1997), 300.

[4] Ibid, 207–08.

[5] *SL*, 376.

[6] *SL*, 378.

[7] Cook, *Robert Frost: A Living Voice*, 110.

[8] It is interesting that Elinor abhorred the New Deal even more so than Frost, and was highly vocal about her feelings.

[9] Cook notes. MCL.

[10] Ibid.

[11] Elinor Frost to Edith H. Fobes, September 1, 1931. DCL.

[12] Elinor Frost to Edith H. Fobes, February 2, 1932. DCL.

[13] *SL*, 384.

[14] *SL*, 384–85.

[15] W. H. Auden, *The Dyer's Hand* (London: Faber & Faber, 1963), 342.

[16] Letters between Frost and Manthey-Zorn, edited by Sheehy, 386.

[17] *SL*, 394–95.

[18] He said this to Robert Penn Warren, who printed the remark in his textbook *Understanding Poetry*, which he co-edited with Cleanth Brooks (1939).

[19] Stanley Burnshaw, *Robert Frost Himself* (New York: George Braziller, 1986), 53.

[20] *SL*, 462.

[21] Malcolm Cowley, "The Case Against Mr. Frost," *New Republic* (September 11, 1944), 312–13. Reprinted in Cox, *Robert Frost: A Collection of Critical Essays*, 36–45.

[22] Frost in 1958 recording. ACL.

[23] Untermeyer, 241.

[24] *SL*, 409.

16 HIS OWN STRATEGIC RETREAT

[1] Untermeyer, 250.

[2] Notes to John Bartlett. UVL.

[3] Frost to Wallace Stevens, July 28, 1935. DCL.

[4] *Letters of Wallace Stevens,* selected and edited by Holly Stevens (London: Faber & Faber, 1966), 278.

[5] Frost notebooks, 1935. DCL.

[6] Letters between Frost and Otto Manthey-Zorn, edited by Sheehy, 397.

[7] Elinor Frost to Natalie Davison, February 8, 1935. DCL.

[8] Donald W. Craig, "Frost Delivers Lectures on Poetry," *Amherst Record* (May 29, 1935), 2.

[9] Anderson, 187.

[10] Interview with Robert Penn Warren.

[11] *I'll Take My Stand: The South and the Agrarian Tradition*, by Twelve Southerners (New York: Harper & Row, 1962), 29.

[12] Ibid., 10.

[13] Frost notebooks, 1935. DCL.

[14] Interview with Victor Reichert.

[15] *SL*, 425.

[16] Cook notes. MCL.

[17] Frost to Sidney Cox, March 29, 1936. DCL.

[18] Interview with Hyde Cox, September 3, 1996.

[19] Lawrance Thompson misdates the initial meeting between Frost and Morrison. It is corrected in Morrison's own hand in the margins of her copy of *Robert Frost: The Years of Triumph*. I am grateful to Edward C. Lathem for pointing this out to me.

[20] Interview with Louise Reichert, August 24, 1996.

21 Kathleen Morrison, *Robert Frost: A Pictorial Chronicle* (New York: Holt, Rinehart and Winston, 1974), 14.

22 Lawrence C. Dame, "1000 Hear Poet Give Views on Life in Harvard Lecture," *Boston Herald* (March 19, 1936).

23 Hyde Cox interview.

24 Robert Lowell, *Interviews and Memoirs*, ed. Jeffrey Meyers (Ann Arbor: University of Michigan Press, 1988), 64.

25 Quoted by Paul Mariani, *Lost Puritan: A Life of Robert Lowell* (New York: Norton, 1994), 152.

26 Peter Davison, *The Fading Smile: Poets in Boston, from Robert Frost to Robert Lowell to Sylvia Plath, 1955–1960* (New York: Knopf, 1994), 274.

27 Newton Arvin, "A Minor Strain," *Partisan Review* (June 1936), 27–28.

28 Horace Gregory, *New Republic* (June 24, 1936), 214; R. P. Blackmur, "The Instincts of a Bard," *Nation* (June 24, 1936); Rolfe Humphries, "A Further Shrinking," *New Masses* (August 11, 1936), 41–42.

29 Linda W. Wagner, ed., *Robert Frost: The Critical Reception* (New York: Burt Franklin, 1977), 137.

30 Elinor Frost to Edith Fobes, August 1936. DCL.

31 Elinor Frost to Richard Thornton, September 13, 1936. DCL.

32 *SL*, 421–32.

33 Frost to Theodore Morrison, October 2, 1937. DCL.

34 *SL*, 453–54.

35 Bernard De Voto, "The Critics and Robert Frost," *Saturday Review* (January 1, 1938), 3–4.

36 Helen Muir, *Frost in Florida: A Memoir* (Miami: Valiant Press, 1995), 26. Muir is quoting the *Stetson Reporter*.

17 DEPTHS BELOW DEPTHS

1 Frost notebooks, 1935. DCL.

2 Frost to Carol Frost, April 15, 1938. UVL.

3 *SL*, 470.

4 Interview with Hyde Cox.

5 Thompson, *The Years of Triumph*, 507.

6 Untermeyer, 308.

7 *SL*, 471.

8 Thompson, *The Years of Triumph*, 511.

9 Donald G. Sheehy, "(Re)Figuring Love: Robert Frost in Crisis, 1938–1942," *New England Quarterly* (June 1990), 179–231.

[10] Interview with Lesley Lee Francis, April 6, 1997.

[11] Interview with Louise Reichert.

[12] Letter to Jay Parini, February 18, 1998.

[13] Thompson and Winnick, *Robert Frost: The Later Years*, 13.

[14] Notes of Charles Foster, DCL.

[15] Wallace Stegner, *The Uneasy Chair: A Biography of Bernard De Voto* (New York: Doubleday, 1974), 206.

[16] Thompson and Winnick, *The Later Years*, 10.

[17] Interview with Wallace Stegner, July 5, 1980.

[18] Pritchard, 233.

[19] Interview with Allen Ginsberg, April 5, 1997.

[20] Merrill Moore to Grenville Clark, July 21, 1938. DCL.

[21] Foster notes, DCL.

[22] Cramer, 124.

[23] Poirier, xiv–xv.

[24] Lathem, *Interviews with Robert Frost*, 119.

[25] Frost notebook, undated. DCL.

[26] Interview with Robert Francis, June 20, 1978.

[27] Frost notebook, 1935. DCL.

[28] Quoted in *Robert Frost: A Descriptive Catalogue of Books and Manuscripts in the Clifton Waller Barrett Library, University of Virginia*, compiled by Joan St. C. Crane (Charlottesville: University Press of Virginia), 250.

[29] Pritchard, 237.

[30] T. J. Wilson to Robert Frost, January 28, 1939. Holt archives, Princeton University Library.

[31] *Family Letters of Robert and Elinor Frost*, edited by Arnold Grade (Albany: State University of New York, 1972), 207. Hereafter *Family Letters*.

[32] Ibid., 209.

[33] Thompson and Winnick, *The Later Years*, 42.

[34] Frost to James B. Conant, no date. DCL.

[35] Interview with Louise Reichert.

[36] Interview with Joseph K. Smith, August 16, 1995.

[37] In an unpublished letter of December 13, 1939, which is in the Louis Untermeyer Papers at the Library of Congress, Frost likened his condition to that which the French called *acedie*—a state of existential anxiety.

[38] *SL*, 487.

[39] Cox interview.

[40] Thompson and Winnick, *The Later Years*, 61.

[41] Frost took the deed of property from J. Joseph Williams and Mary M.

Williams in October 1940, according to Deed Book 2099, p. 471, in the Public Records Office of Dade County, Florida.

[42] *Family Letters*, 218.

[43] *SL*, 491.

[44] Frost notebooks, 1939–41. DCL.

18 CORRIDORS OF WOE

[1] Interview with Richard Poirier in *Writers at Work: The Paris Review Interviews, Second Series* (New York: Viking Press, 1963), 26.

[2] *SL*, 494.

[3] Interview with Reginald L. Cook.

[4] Interview with Victor Reichert.

[5] Carl Sandburg, "Those Who Make Poems," *Atlantic Monthly* (March 1942), 344–46.

[6] Pritchard, 239.

[7] Thompson and Winnick, *The Later Years*, 95.

[8] Frost notebook, 1910. DCL.

[9] Adam Margoshes, "Robert Frost, Semi-Poet," *Current History* (June 1942), 302–03.

[10] Wilbert Snow, "Robert Frost, Dean of American Poetry," *New York Herald Tribune Books* (May 10, 1942), 5.

[11] Stephen Vincent Benét, "Frost at Sixty-Seven," *Saturday Review of Literature* (April 25, 1942), 7.

[12] Snow review, 5.

[13] W. T. Scott, "Frost's Seventh Book," *Poetry* (June 1942), 146–49.

[14] *SL*, 503.

[15] Anderson, 202.

[16] Anderson, 202.

[17] *Family Letters*, 241.

[18] *SL*, 506.

[19] Interview with Thomas Vance.

[20] Winnick and Thompson, *The Later Years*, 107.

[21] *SL*, 509.

[22] Frost to George F. Whicher, April 2, 1943. ACL.

[23] Interview with Orton Hicks, April 1976.

[24] This description of Frost's teaching at Dartmouth comes from notes taken in 1976 in conversation with retired Dartmouth professor Alexander Laing.

[25] George F. Bagby, *Robert Frost and the Book of Nature* (Knoxville: University of Tennessee Press, 1993), 178.

[26] Lynen, 136.

[27] See Peter J. Stanlis, "Robert Frost's Masques and the Classic American Tradition" in *Frost Centennial Essays* (Jackson: University Press of Mississippi, 1974), 441–68.

[28] Louis Untermeyer to Frost, August 31, 1944. DCL.

[29] Interview with Gore Vidal, September 2, 1994.

[30] Interview with Hyde Cox.

[31] Interview with Victor Reichert.

19 THE HEIGHT OF THE ADVENTURE

[1] Frost to Sidney Cox, March 7, 1945. DCL.

[2] Mark Shorer, "A Masque of Reason," *Atlantic Monthly* (March 1945), 133, 195.

[3] "New England Questions," *Time* (May 7, 1945), 100.

[4] Conrad Aiken, "Whole Meaning to Doodle," *New Republic* (April 16, 1945), 514.

[5] Lawrance Thompson, "Robert Frost Rediscovers Job," *New York Times Book Review* (March 25, 1945), 3.

[6] Letter to Jay Parini, February 18, 1998.

[7] Quoted in Thompson and Winnick, *The Later Years*, 133.

[8] Interview with John Sloan Dickey.

[9] Interview with Philip Booth, October 19, 1996.

[10] George W. Nitchie, *Human Values in the Poetry of Robert Frost* (Durham, NC: Duke University Press, 1960), 146–49.

[11] Kearns, 205.

[12] Poirier, 100.

[13] Interview with Reginald L. Cook.

[14] Walter Hancock, *A Sculptor's Fortunes* (Gloucester: Cape Ann Historical Association, 1997), 200–01.

[15] See M. H. Abrams, *Natural Supernaturalism* (London: Oxford University Press, 1971), 453–54.

[16] Quoted in *Partisan Review: The Fiftieth Anniversary Edition*, edited by William Phillips (New York: Stein and Day, 1985), 26. I am grateful to George Monteiro for bringing this quotation to my attention.

[17] Interview with Louise Reichert.

[18] Randall Jarrell, "Tenderness and Passive Sadness," *New York Times Book Review* (June 1, 1947), 4.

[19] Gladys Campbell, "A World Torn Loose Went by Me," *Poetry* (December 1947), 145.

[20] Frost included a draft of this poem in a letter to John W. Haines of September 23, 1928—as Louis Mertins notes, 178, quoting a letter from Haines to this effect. Thus Thompson and Winnick are way off base when they date the poem to the mid-forties; see *The Later Years*, 411.

[21] Bread Loaf Writers' Conference reading, 1959. Tape in ACL.

[22] Cook, *Robert Frost: A Living Voice*, 183.

[23] Robert Frost, "Remarks on the Occasion of the Tagore Centenary," *Poetry* (November 1961), 118.

[24] *Time* (June 16, 1947), 102.

[25] Leonard Bacon, *Saturday Review of Literature* (May 31, 1947), 15.

[26] Donald A. Stauffer, "The New Lyrics of Robert Frost," *Atlantic Monthly* (October 1947), 115.

20 THE GREAT ENTERPRISE OF LIFE

[1] Untermeyer, 346.

[2] Interview with Louise Reichert.

[3] Jeffrey Meyers, *Robert Frost: A Biography* (Boston: Houghton Mifflin, 1996), 243.

[4] Letter to Jay Parini, February 18, 1998.

[5] Interview with Louise Reichert.

[6] Frost to Hyde Cox, June 12, 1951. DCL.

[7] Interview with Louise Reichert.

[8] *SL*, 527.

[9] Arthur Dempsey, "About Books," *New York Times Book Review* (December 24, 1950), 12.

[10] Earle J. Bernheimer to John S. Van Kohn, March 28, 1971. DCL.

[11] Frost to Charles Cole, undated [1947]. ACL.

[12] Interview with John Sloan Dickey.

[13] Interview with Harold Bond, October 1977.

[14] Thompson and Winnick, *The Later Years*, 176.

[15] Frost notebook, 1950. DCL.

[16] Interview with Reginald L. Cook.

[17] Interview with Robert Penn Warren.

[18] Davison, 15.

[19] Interview with I. A. Richards, November 12, 1977. (I met with Richards at the home of Richard Eberhart in Hanover, New Hampshire.)

[20] *SL*, 549.

[21] Frost notebooks, 1950–55. DCL.

[22] Poirier, 82.

[23] Frost notebooks, 1950–55. DCL.

[24] Cook notes. MCL.

[25] *SL*, 551.

[26] Interview with Victor Reichert.

[27] Interview with Robert Francis.

[28] Interview with Reginald L. Cook.

[29] John Ciardi, "Robert Frost: Master Conversationalist at Work," *Saturday Review* (March 21, 1959).

[30] Reginald L. Cook, *Robert Frost: A Living Voice*, 131.

[31] "Amherst Honors Robert Frost," *Amherst Alumni News* (April 1954), 3.

21 THE WINTER OWL

[1] "Robert Frost, 80, Gives a Recipe for Diplomats," *New York Times* (August 10, 1954), 5.

[2] Frost to Kathleen Morrison, August 1954. DCL.

[3] Elizabeth Bishop, *One Art: Letters*, ed. Robert Giroux (New York, 1994), 276, 365, 370.

[4] Cook, *Robert Frost: A Living Voice*, 103:

[5] Cook, 104.

[6] Interview with John Sloan Dickey.

[7] Frost to John Sloan Dickey, February 1955. DCL.

[8] Interview with John Sloan Dickey.

[9] Interview with Reginald L. Cook.

[10] Frost notebooks, 1949. DCL.

[11] *SL*, 560–61.

[12] Frost to Sherman Adams, January 4, 1957. DCL.

[13] Interview with Lesley Lee Francis.

[14] Harold Howland note. DCL.

[15] *SL*, 564–65.

[16] Thompson and Winnick, *Frost: The Later Years*, 224.

[17] Interview with Stephen Spender, April 12, 1994.

[18] Interview with Edward C. Lathem.

[19] *An Oxford Keepsake: Robert Frost D. Litt (Oxon) 1957*, privately printed for Mr. and Mrs. Edward Connery Lathem. DCL.

[20] Notes of Lawrance Thompson (copy). DCL.

[21] Interview with Lesley Lee Francis, October 19, 1997.

[22] Interview with Lesley Lee Francis.

[23] Accounts of this vary. Lesley Lee Francis says they did not stop. Thompson and others say they did.

[24] Interview with Stephen Spender. I am also grateful to Sir Isaiah Berlin for his account of this meeting.

[25] Quoted in a letter to Jay Parini, March 9, 1998.

[26] Interview with Edward Connery Lathem.

[27] Tape in DCL.

[28] Quoted in letter to Jay Parini, March 9, 1998.

[29] Lawrance Thompson notes. DCL.

[30] Quoted by Harry M. Meacham, *The Caged Panther: Ezra Pound at St. Elizabeth's* (New York: Twayne, 1967), 118–19.

[31] Anthony Lewis, "Court Drops Charge Against Ezra Pound," *New York Times* (April 19, 1958), 1, 23.

[32] Quoted by Scott Donaldson, *Archibald MacLeish: An American Life* (Boston: Houghton Mifflin, 1992), 447.

[33] Smythe, 57.

[34] Interview with Robert Kingsley and Harold Curtiss, October 20, 1997.

[35] Interview with William Meredith, August 18, 1997.

[36] Interview with Richard Eberhart.

[37] Interview with Galway Kinnell, October 11, 1997.

[38] Burnshaw, 103–08.

[39] Trilling's speech is quoted by Burnshaw, 103–05.

[40] Interview with Victor Reichert.

[41] Burnshaw, 105.

[42] *New York Times Book Review* (April 12, 1959), 8.

[43] SL, 583.

[44] SL, 581.

22 AGES AND AGES HENCE

[1] Interview with William Meredith.

[2] Interview with Gore Vidal.

[3] Interview with Hyde Cox.

[4] "Frost's Poem Wins Hearts at Inaugural," *Washington Post* (January 21, 1961), 8.

⁵ Thompson and Winnick, *The Later Years*, 283.

⁶ Interview with Harold Curtiss.

⁷ Interview with Victor Reichert.

⁸ Thompson notes. DCL.

⁹ Frost notebooks, 1955. DCL.

¹⁰ Thompson notes. DCL.

¹¹ Thompson notes. DCL.

¹² Interview with Jack A. W. Hagstrom.

¹³ *SL*, 585.

¹⁴ Interview with Reginald L. Cook.

¹⁵ Reginald L. Cook, *Robert Frost: A Living Voice*, 192.

¹⁶ Monteiro, 52.

¹⁷ Reginald L. Cook, *Robert Frost: A Living Voice*, 132–33.

¹⁸ Richard Wilbur, "Poems That Soar and Sing and Charm," *New York Herald Tribune* (March 25, 1962), 3.

¹⁹ John Ciardi, "Robert Frost: American Bard," *Saturday Review of Literature* (March 24, 1962), 16.

²⁰ Interview with Robert Penn Warren.

²¹ Interview with Alastair Reid, November 5, 1997.

²² *SL*, 589.

²³ F. D. Reeve, *Robert Frost in Russia* (Boston: Atlantic–Little, Brown, 1964), 3–4.

²⁴ See Afterword: Frost and His Biographers.

²⁵ Reeve, 14.

²⁶ Reeve, 20.

²⁷ Reeve, 26.

²⁸ Reeve, 50–51.

²⁹ Reeve, 63.

³⁰ Reeve, 69–70.

³¹ Reeve, 81.

³² Reeve, 111.

³³ Reeve, 112.

³⁴ Reeve, 113–14.

³⁵ Reeve, 114–15.

³⁶ Reeve, 116.

³⁷ Reeve, 117.

³⁸ Reeve, 119.

³⁹ Lathem, *Interviews*, 291.

⁴⁰ Reeve, 120.

⁴¹ Frost's speech is reprinted in *National Poetry Festival, Held in the Library*

of Congress, October 22–24, 1962 (Library of Congress, Washington, 1964), 228–59. Also quoted by Thompson and Winnick, 328.

[42] Peter J. Stanlis interview.

[43] This talk was published as "Robert Frost on 'Extravagance,' " in the *Dartmouth Alumni Magazine* (March 1963), 21–24.

[44] Recorded by Anne Morrison Gentry. Quoted by Thompson and Winnick, 343.

[45] SL, 596.

CONCLUSION

[1] Theodore Morrison, "The Agitated Heart," *Atlantic Monthly* (July 1967), 72.

[2] SL, 221.

[3] Faggen, 9.

[4] SL, 344.

[5] Frost notebooks. DCL.

[6] See Ed Ingebretsen, *Robert Frost's Star in a Stone Boat: A Grammar of Belief* (San Francisco: Catholic Scholars Press, 1994).

[7] SL, 595–96.

[8] Richardson, 5.

[9] Kearns, 26.

[10] Interview with Reginald L. Cook.

AFTERWORD: FROST AND HIS BIOGRAPHERS

[1] SL, 386.

[2] Munson, 112–13.

[3] Munson, 115.

[4] Elizabeth Shepley Sergeant, "Good Greek out of New England," in Thornton, 149.

[5] Sergeant, *Robert Frost,* 432–33.

[6] Jean Gould, *Robert Frost: The Aim Was Song* (New York: Dodd, Mead & Company, 1964).

[7] Gould, ix.

[8] Gould, 295.

[9] Donald G. Sheehy, "The Poet as Neurotic: The Official Biography of Robert Frost," *American Literature* (October 1986), 393–409.

[10] Thompson, *The Years of Triumph,* xiv–xv.

[11] Lawrance Thompson to Kathleen Morrison, September 2, 1945. DCL.

[12] Pritchard, xvii–xviii.

[13] Walsh, 9.

[14] Burnshaw, 304.

[15] Lesley Lee Francis, 2.

[16] Donald G. Sheehy, "(Re)Figuring Love: Robert Frost in Crisis, 1938–1942," *New England Quarterly* (June 1990), 179–231.

[17] Helen Vendler, "Dark and Deep," *London Review of Books* (July 4, 1996), 3.

[18] Interview with Lesley Lee Francis.

[19] Meyers, 217.

[20] Meyers, 265.

[21] Vendler, 5.

[22] Frost notebook, undated. DCL. Included in *Prose Jottings of Robert Frost: Selections from His Notebooks*, eds. Edward Connery Lathem and Hyde Cox (Lunenburg, VT: Northeast Kingdom Publishers, 1982), 7.

[23] CPPP, 721–22.

SELECTED BIBLIOGRAPHY

I. WORKS BY FROST

The Letters of Robert Frost to Louis Untermeyer. Ed. Louis Untermeyer. New York: Holt, Rinehart and Winston, 1963.

Prose Jottings of Robert Frost. Ed. Edward Connery Lathem and Hyde Cox. Lunenburg, VT: Northeast Kingdom Publishers, 1982.

Robert Frost: Collected Poems, Prose, and Plays. Ed. Richard Poirier and Mark Richardson. New York: Library of America, 1995.

Selected Letters of Robert Frost. Ed. Lawrance Thompson. New York: Holt, Rinehart and Winston, 1964.

II. INTERVIEWS WITH FROST

Cook, Reginald L. *Robert Frost: A Living Voice.* Amherst: University of Massachusetts Press, 1974.

Francis, Robert. *Frost: A Time to Talk—Conversations and Indiscretions.* Amherst: University of Massachusetts Press, 1972.

Lathem, Edward Connery, ed. *Interviews with Robert Frost.* New York: Holt, Rinehart and Winston, 1966.

Mertins, Louis. *Robert Frost: Life and Talks-Walking.* Norman: University of Oklahoma Press, 1965.

Smythe, Daniel. *Robert Frost Speaks.* New York: Twayne Publishers, 1966.

III. BIOGRAPHIES AND MEMOIRS

Anderson, Margaret Bartlett. *Robert Frost and John Bartlett: The Record of a Friendship*. New York: Holt, Rinehart and Winston, 1963.

Burnshaw, Stanley. *Robert Frost Himself*. New York: G. Braziller, 1986.

Cox, Sidney. *A Swinger of Birches: A Portrait of Robert Frost*. Introduction by Robert Frost. New York: New York University Press, 1957.

Francis, Lesley Lee. *The Frost Family's Adventure in Poetry: Sheer Morning Gladness at the Brim*. Columbia: University of Missouri Press, 1994.

Gould, Jean. *Robert Frost: The Aim Was Song*. New York: Dodd, Mead and Company, 1964.

Meyers, Jeffrey. *Robert Frost: A Biography*. Boston: Houghton Mifflin, 1996.

Muir, Helen. *Frost in Florida: A Memoir*. Miami: Valiant Press, 1995.

Munson, Gorham B. *Robert Frost: A Study in Sensibility and Good Sense*. New York: George H. Doran, 1927.

Newdick, Robert. *Newdick's Season of Frost: An Interrupted Biography of Robert Frost*. Ed. William A. Sutton. Albany: State University of New York Press, 1976.

Pritchard, William, H. *Robert Frost: A Literary Life Reconsidered*. New York: Oxford University Press, 1984.

Reeve, F. D. *Robert Frost in Russia*. Boston: Little, Brown, 1964.

Sergeant, Elizabeth Shepley. *Robert Frost: The Trial by Existence*. New York: Holt, Rinehart and Winston, 1960.

Thompson, Lawrance. *Robert Frost: The Early Years, 1874–1915*. New York: Holt, Rinehart and Winston, 1966.

———. *Robert Frost: The Years of Triumph, 1915–1938*. Holt, Rinehart and Winston, 1970.

Thompson, Lawrance, and R. H. Winnick. *Robert Frost: The Later Years, 1938–1963*. New York: Holt, Rinehart and Winston, 1976.

Walsh, John Evangelist. *Into My Own: The English Years of Robert Frost*. New York: Grove Press, 1988.

IV. CRITICISM

Bagby, George. *Robert Frost and the Book of Nature*. Knoxville: University of Tennessee Press, 1993.

Brodsky, Joseph, Seamus Heaney, and Derek Walcott. *Homage to Robert Frost*. New York: Farrar, Straus and Giroux, 1996.

Brower, Reuben. *The Poetry of Robert Frost: Constellations of Intention*. New York: Holt, Rinehart and Winston, 1965.

Cook, Reginald L. *The Dimensions of Robert Frost*. New York: Rinehart, 1958.

Cox, James M., ed. *Robert Frost: A Collection of Critical Essays.* Englewood Cliffs: Prentice-Hall, 1962.

Cramer, Jeffrey S. *Robert Frost Among His Poems: A Literary Companion to the Poet's Own Biographical Contexts and Associations.* Jefferson, NC: McFarland, 1996.

Faggen, Robert. *Robert Frost and the Challenge of Darwin.* Ann Arbor: University of Michigan Press, 1997.

Frost: Centennial Essays. Compiled by the Committee on the Frost Centennial of the University of Southern Mississippi. Jackson: University of Mississippi Press, 1974–78.

Gerber, Philip L., ed. *Critical Essays on Robert Frost.* Boston: G. K. Hall, 1982.

Kearns, Katherine. *Robert Frost and a Poetics of Appetite.* Cambridge: Cambridge University Press, 1994.

Kemp, John C. *Robert Frost and New England: The Poet as Regionalist.* Princeton: Princeton University Press, 1979.

Lentricchia, Frank. *Robert Frost: Modern Poetics and the Landscapes of Self.* Durham: Duke University Press, 1975.

Lynen, John F. *The Pastoral Art of Robert Frost.* New Haven: Yale University Press, 1964.

Monteiro, George. *Robert Frost and the New England Renaissance.* Lexington: University Press of Kentucky, 1988.

Nitchie, George W. *Human Values in the Poetry of Robert Frost.* Durham: Duke University Press, 1960.

Oster, Judith. *Toward Robert Frost: The Reader and the Poet.* Athens: University of Georgia Press, 1991.

Poirier, Richard. *Robert Frost: The Work of Knowing.* New York: Oxford University Press, 1984.

Richardson, Mark. *The Ordeal of Robert Frost.* Urbana: University of Illinois Press, 1997.

Sheehy, Donald G. "The Poet as Neurotic: The Official Biography of Robert Frost." *American Literature*, October, 1986, 393–409.

———. "(Re) Figuring Love: Robert Frost in Crisis, 1938–1942." *New England Quarterly*, June, 1990, 179–231.

Thompson, Lawrance. *Fire and Ice: The Art and Thought of Robert Frost.* New York: Russell & Russell, 1942.

Thornton, Richard. *Recognition of Robert Frost: Twenty-fifth Anniversary.* New York: Henry Holt, 1937.

INDEX